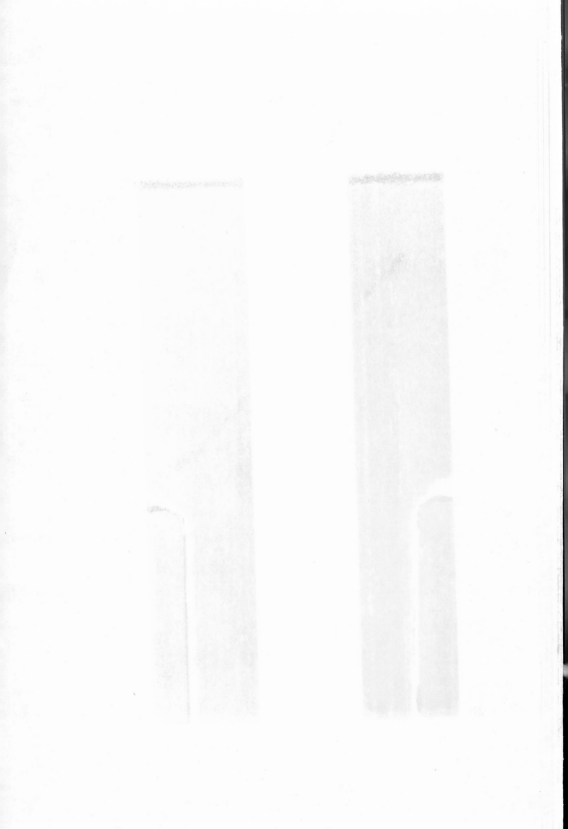

RED SUNSET

RED SUNSET

THE FAILURE OF SOVIET POLITICS

Philip G. Roeder

PRINCETON UNIVERSITY PRESS   PRINCETON, NEW JERSEY

Library of Congress Cataloging-in-Publication Data
Roeder, Philip G.
Red sunset : the failure of Soviet politics / Philip G. Roeder.
p. cm.
Includes bibliographical references and index.
ISBN 0-691-03306-4 (alk. paper)—
ISBN 0-691-01942-8 (pbk. : alk. paper)
1. Soviet Union—Politics and government. 2. Soviet Union—
Constitutional history. 3. Authoritarianism—Soviet Union. I. Title.
JN6511.R44 1993
321.9'2'0947—dc20 93-4047 CIP

Contents

Figures

Tables

Preface

AT THE END of the twentieth century two developments profoundly influenced the research of social scientists: one was a change in the real world that we study; the other was a change in the methods we use to study it. The world was altered by the collapse of Leninism in the Soviet Union and the half-dozen or so states on which it imposed its rule. Our methods were affected by the emergence of a new concern with institutions as an omnipresent aspect of human existence that patterns our expectations and behavior. This study brings together these two developments in an examination of the failure of Soviet political institutions.

This book confronts what is destined to be one of the great puzzles left to future analysts by the twentieth century—why did Soviet Bolshevism fail? It is addressed to an audience that comes to this question from very different backgrounds and interests. The specialist in Soviet or Russian affairs should gain a new perspective on familiar events. I make no pretense that this manuscript unearths some previously unknown document or event that offers a key to Soviet affairs; instead, I offer a fresh perspective for making sense of events that have largely been known to us. Comparativists with little interest in the fine details of Soviet politics should find a case study that illuminates a theoretical approach that could as easily be applied to many of their own areas of interest. I hope this project will encourage others to take seriously the dynamics of authoritarian institutions—whether in the former Soviet Union, its successor states, or elsewhere.

This work is a product of my long fascination with the dynamics of policymaking in the Soviet Union that began in graduate school. Yet, the final shape of this project is the result of my association with remarkable colleagues in La Jolla at the University of California, San Diego. The heady environment of tough, but supportive dialogue has enabled me to sharpen analysis and reach to larger theoretical issues. In particular, Susan Shirk has contributed enormously to the ideas in this book, through our long conversations about Leninist polities and our collaboration in the classroom. Her own recently published book on *The Political Logic of Economic Reform in China* complements the present volume. My discussions with Tun-jen Cheng, Alan Houston, Victor Magagna, Samuel Popkin, and Matthew Shugart have broadened the horizons of this project. Incisive conversations with Mathew McCubbins have sharpened the logic in this book as well as my wits. Good colleagues are among the most prized possessions of a political scientist, and in La Jolla I have been particularly blessed.

Research for this book was assisted by unusually able graduate students, including David Auerswald, Barton Fischer, Christopher Nevitt, and Michael Tierney. These four and my graduate students in seminar have been more than assistants; they have been invaluable colleagues as they challenged me to tighten logic and draw out the implications of my work. Mike, in particular, has read this manuscript more times than any human should endure and has seldom let me off the hook when I have become intellectually sloppy. These research assistants were supported in part by grants from the Committee on Research at UCSD and from the University of California's Institute on Global Conflict and Cooperation. For all this invaluable support I am, indeed, grateful.

Many colleagues in La Jolla and around the country have kindly shared their time and expertise to comment on drafts of this manuscript. Insightful comments by George Breslauer and Barbara Geddes on early papers were critical in helping define this project. Comments by Richard H. Phillips and William Zimmerman on a chapter I contributed to the volume *Beyond the Soviet Threat*, edited by Bill, helped me write the chapter on military planning for this book. For comments on the penultimate draft of this book I can only begin to thank Richard Anderson, Nathaniel Beck, Mark Beissinger, George Breslauer, Peter Cowhey, Paul Drake, David Laitin, Arend Lijphart, Victor Magagna, Mathew McCubbins, Ellen Mickiewicz, James Clay Moltz, Jack Snyder, and John Willerton. It is a testimony to the community of ideas among political scientists that these fine scholars have been so giving of their time and expertise. I thank them all.

La Jolla, California

RED SUNSET

CHAPTER ONE

Why Did Soviet Bolshevism Fail?

ON 25 DECEMBER 1991 Mikhail Gorbachev stepped down as president of the Soviet Union, workers lowered the red flag of Soviet power over the Kremlin for the last time, and the Soviet state for all intents and purposes ceased to exist. This followed by only four months Mr. Gorbachev's announcement that he had stepped down as general secretary of the Communist party of the Soviet Union, disbanded the Party's leading organs, ended its guiding role within the Soviet state, and, thus, brought to a close nearly three-quarters of a century of Communist party rule. The collapse of the Soviet system of interdependent party and state stands in stark contrast to the seeming durability and immutability of Communist rule in earlier decades. Among nondemocratic regimes, the Soviet Union had been one of the most stable. It had survived civil war and international conflagration, it had survived the difficult transfer of power between administrations seven times, and yet, at the end of seven decades it suffered a severe crisis of power.

The Soviet Communists or Bolsheviks had come to power in 1917 as a vanguard to remake society. Seeing change as central to social life, they cast their own movement as a prime engine of historic transformation. Yet, by the time the last leader stepped down, the Party could no longer easily adapt to social change, let alone engineer it. By this time even its leader indicted the Party for having created and presided over an era of stagnation. After seven decades the Soviet Union's stagnation was at the heart of its crisis and failure.

This book argues that the seemingly paradoxical elements of a regime with a transformational mission that led to stagnation, a Party that engineered social change but could not adapt to a changed society, and stability that gave way to collapse are all tied to one another. These contradictions are rooted in the design of Soviet politics. They inhere in the fundamental institutional structure of the Bolsheviks' vanguard regime— what I call the constitution of Bolshevism. This structure had the perverse consequence of giving the Soviet political system vast resources to transform society, but of limiting the polity's ability to transform itself. The one-party regime ultimately fell owing to its inability to respond to immense social changes that had taken place in Soviet society—ironically, social changes that the Party itself had set in motion.

THE SOVIET CRISIS OF REFORM

After the death of Joseph Stalin in 1953 the cardinal problem for the Soviet polity became reform. The polity did not lack powers to transform society; rather it needed the capacity to transform itself—to change its own policy priorities and to adapt to a changing social environment.

The social transformations in the first quarter-century of Communist party rule had been enormous. Multiple revolutions touched all aspects of human existence, including government and law, industry and agriculture, science and culture, family life and social welfare, foreign policy and military affairs. In politics it established a monopoly of power in the Communist party. In economics it began the forced-draft industrialization of a peasant society through the regimentation of production in a command economy. In social relations the Party created new statuses and privileges and harnessed families and nations, culture and science behind its transformational objectives.[1]

The record of the Communist regime is equally remarkable for its difficulty in moving beyond those early objectives. Two closely tied problems plagued it—policy innovation and institutional adaptation. The Soviet Union continued to make progress toward its original objectives, but found it extraordinarily difficult to innovate in either the means used to pursue these objectives or the objectives themselves. Consider just three examples drawn from disparate policy sectors: While industrial production continued to rise after 1945 and placed the Soviet Union among the world's leaders in heavy industrial output, the Soviet economy seemed to become quaintly antique, lagging in sectors, such as plastics or services, that should have become important in subsequent stages of development.[2] While in theoretical mathematics and physics the Soviet Union remained at the forefront, in new fields like cybernetics and computer applications it lagged far behind. While in classical ballet the Bolshoi and Kirov theaters set standards of excellence for the world, in modern dance Soviet troupes were nearly absent. In each of these disparate fields (and many others) a common pattern emerged—the Soviet regime performed well against the standards it had set for itself in its first quarter-century of power, but it was far less adept at policy innovation, far less successful when the task required adjusting means or objectives.

At the root of this inability to innovate was the fact Soviet policymaking institutions found it increasingly difficult to adapt to their changing social environment. The Soviet polity changed the configuration of social forces in society, but it was unable to incorporate its newly created forces. For example, among the most impressive accomplishments of the early social transformations was creation of a new intelligentsia. The number of individuals in the labor force with higher education grew from 136,000 in 1913 to 12 million in 1980; their proportion in the labor force jumped from 1.2 to 10.7 percent.[3] Yet, the political system continued to exclude most intelligentsia from political power and policymaking. Its institutions did not adapt to the growth of these social forces with a commensurate expansion of political participation.

The problems of policy innovation and institutional adaptation are two dimensions of the Soviet crisis of reform. Reform, to paraphrase Albert O. Hirschman, refers to changes in which the power of hitherto privileged groups is curbed and the political power, economic position, or social status of underprivileged groups is correspondingly improved.[4] The inability to reform *itself* was at the heart of the Soviet polity's stagnation.

The problem of reform was not that Soviet leaders refused to change the priorities, practices, or even institutions established in the first quarter-century of Communist rule, but that their efforts to do so were more often than not defeated. Particularly after 1953, the history of the Soviet Union was not a record of *immobilisme*, but a story of persistent and failed attempts at reform beginning with Malenkov's new course and culminating in Gorbachev's new thinking. The political system seemed to actively combat reformers and their plans. Reformers like Georgii Malenkov and Aleksei Kosygin were defeated by more conservative members of the leadership. Measures introduced by reformers who partially succeeded (Nikita Khrushchev, for example) were later reversed by their successors. Thus, in virtually all fields, fundamental priorities, practices, and institutions survived attempts to reform them, despite the immense costs this began to exact. In cultural affairs repeated thaws were followed by new intellectual regimentation. In economics periodic decentralization gave way to recentralization. In politics expansions of popular involvement in the policy process were short-lived. In each case even though a reforming leader successfully won adoption of his reform, sabotage of its implementation led to a policy outcome different from the declared intent of the reform. In most cases reforms were subsequently abandoned and the pre-reform state of affairs virtually restored. Thus, in 1985 assessments of the problems of Soviet society sounded much like those of the three previous decades: culture remained regimented, the economy overcentralized, and politics exclusionary. After 1985, when Gorbachev pressed still harder for change, the confrontation with resistance brought collapse rather than reform of the Soviet Union.

This study examines the sources of these obstacles to reform during the last thirty-eight years of Soviet power—from the death of Stalin in

1953 to the collapse of 1991. It offers an explanation for this recurring pattern of reform and defeat and for the larger problem of stagnation and collapse.

THE ARGUMENT IN BRIEF

In explaining the stagnation and collapse of the Soviet Union, I argue for the central causal effect of political institutions. Specifically, a primary obstacle to reform, particularly during the last thirty-eight years of Communist party rule, was the constitution of Bolshevism. This established a stable political equilibrium among empowered political actors, but the institutionalization of this political system made it increasingly difficult to either innovate or adapt. During the last four decades of the Soviet Union this equilibrium encouraged periodic attempts at reform, but defeated change, and with almost gyroscopic stability righted itself after these disturbances.

A constitution, in the sense this term is used here, is not necessarily a formal document, but it is always a polity's most fundamental rules (whether written or not) defining political roles and relationships. A constitution, as Aristotle defined the term, is "the arrangement which states adopt for the distribution of offices of power and for the determination of sovereignty."[5] It creates roles that exercise the policymaking powers of a political community and defines relationships such as decision rules and accountability.

These fundamental rules shape the political process. The subsequent analysis of the constitution of Bolshevism begins with a static relationship in which the constitution shapes coalition processes and through these influences policy outcomes. The heuristic device that links constitutions to reform is a simple two-step relationship:

Constitution	$\longrightarrow$	Process	$\longrightarrow$	Policy
Roles		*Coalitions*		*Substance*
Relationships				*Attributes*

A constitution as rules governing roles and relationships empowers political actors and guides their interaction. This shapes the coalition-building strategies of political actors. Because coalitions bring together actors with specific policy preferences, these constitutions tend to favor some policy outcomes over others.[6] Coalition-building processes shape both the substantive content of policy and such attributes of policy as coherence and stability. In particular, these coalitions influence the likelihood that innovations will change the distribution of policy benefits and costs.[7]

Constitutions also shape the path of subsequent political development.

Thus, the analysis in the following chapters also treats constitutions dynamically. The strategic choices of actors may change the rules defining roles (such as citizenship) and relationships (such as accountability), which in turn can transform the coalition processes and policy outcomes of a polity. These choices are, of course, constrained by the existing rules of a constitution, which make some strategic choices more likely than others. Thus, the design of a constitution constrains its own developmental trajectory.[8]

In subsequent chapters I argue that the constitution of Bolshevism was founded on a conscious plan to eliminate the accountability of those exercising the polity's policymaking powers to the larger populace. A policy of forced departicipation deprived the vast majority of the adult population of access to the means for autonomous political action. Yet, contrary to their intentions, the Bolsheviks' early decisions led willy nilly to a constitutional order in which policymakers built their power on bureaucratic constituencies. These early decisions created a constitutional order of bureaucratic reciprocal accountability in which policymakers needed the sustaining support of their bureaucratic constituencies, but bureaucrats in turn needed continuing confidence of their patrons to remain in office.

This constitutional structure shaped both the game of politics and the course of subsequent constitutional development. The political game revolved around the formation and change of coalitions between two tiers composed of political leaders and bureaucrats. The development of the constitutional order from 1953 to 1985 institutionalized this reciprocal accountability between tiers in the relationship between Politburo and Central Committee. The political game led to shifting balances of power within the leadership and between leaders and bureaucrats. Specifically, it led to a cycle of alternating collective and directive leadership. The development of the constitutional order from 1953 to 1985, however, institutionalized balancing within the collective leadership and limited this cycling. Institutionalization of reciprocal accountability and balanced leadership increased the stability of the polity, but it also had a most perverse effect—it limited the polity's ability to innovate in policy and to adapt its institutions to social change. The institutionalization of the constitution of Bolshevism brought policy dysfunction and institutional stagnation.

In arguing that institutions played a central role in Soviet politics, this book develops the thesis that the constitution of Bolshevism provides a key to the seeming paradoxes of both a transformational movement that led to stagnation and a stable polity that collapsed. The constitution's ability to survive reform attempts gave it stability; yet this came at the expense of these institutions' ability to adapt to social change. As a consequence of this inability to change piecemeal, the need for reform continued to mount. The stability brought by the constitution of Bolshevism was a short-term asset that masked a dysfunctional flaw—a flaw that over the long term brought wholesale collapse.

THE NEW INSTITUTIONALISM OF AUTHORITARIANISM

The analysis in this study is part of the movement in political science that has been called the new institutionalism or the positive theory of institutions. This intellectual development is concerned with the emergence of institutions such as the constitution of Bolshevism from the choices of self-interested political actors and the consequences of institutions for political choice.[9] At its simplest and most abstract, the new institutionalism movement asserts the utility of the concept of institutions for organizing social analysis.

Institutions are rules that prescribe behavioral roles and relationships among these roles.[10] They are powerful in shaping choices and the consequences of choices; that is, as causal factors institutions are both constraints on the choices of political actors and selection mechanisms that pick winners and losers. First, institutions are rules devised by humans that constrain their social interaction. These rules may be formal or informal, but actors recognize them as constraints on their actions by the costs and benefits they affix to alternative courses of action. By empowering specific political actors, by shaping the choices available to political actors, and by attaching benefits or liabilities to strategies, constitutions shape political behavior. Second, institutions are selection mechanisms. Failure to navigate successfully among these roles and relationships may lead to failure that "selects out" some actors.

Thus, the new institutionalism seeks the source of the regularities of human behavior in the rules that constrain individual choices. In predicting the policy stance of actors, for example, the emphasis is on the constraints of rule-defined responsibilities and limitations of a role.[11] The new institutionalism sees these rules as a fundamental source of the patterning in human action, and so it approaches the analysis of social interaction by seeking to identify its institutions.

This study proceeds from a specific understanding of the nature of institutions: They ultimately rest on reinforcing mutual expectations. I begin with a simple illustration: the rules of the road and the institution of marriage are powerful influences in shaping the behavior of millions of individuals. These institutions are defined by the belief of each actor about what is expected of him or her and what he or she expects others to do. As any Southern Californian can attest, these expectations do constrain behavior (there is a rule of the road, for example), but their relationship to formal legislative enactments is problematic. The strength of an institution depends on the extent to which these expectations converge; institutions are weak when expectations diverge. Institutionalization is the process by which these expectations become mutually reinforcing.[12]

Institutions are seldom static. Individual choices that challenge the prevailing rule may mount and change the expectations that define the institutions. Thus, for example, the rules of the road (much like the rules of marriage) in Southern California have changed under the assault of individual choices; freeway speed limits in cities (rush hour aside) have crept up from 55 to 70 or more miles per hour. The new rule is defined by new expectations, not the more static legislation, but as the orderly movement of traffic attests, the new expectations constrain individual choices as effectively as earlier expectations.

As this implies, the new institutionalism differs from the earlier political science tradition of constitutional engineering; it does not narrow its analysis to formal-legal rules, but it looks for the actual rules in use.[13] The new institutionalism has learned much from the constitutional engineers. It recognizes the power of formal rules to coordinate expectations. Yet, perhaps having learned something from the behavioral interlude in political science as well, the new institutionalism looks for actual rules in practice and recognizes that the always-problematic relationship of formal to actual rules depends on expectations about the behavior of others.

Abstractions and Assumptions

Perhaps the most controversial elements of the new institutionalism, and the social choice tradition of which it is a part, are its assumptions. Like much of the work that inspires it, this book begins from a premise of rationality and an abstract definition of the behavior to be examined.

As an abstraction, the rationality assumption does not literally describe real human decisionmaking. This fact has generated much criticism. One response to this criticism has been to develop rational choice analysis that does not require a behavioral assumption of rationality; one can understand structural constraints solely as selection mechanisms.[14] Actors need neither to understand the rules of the game nor to select the best option under those constraints, but those who choose imprudently will likely fail and be selected out. Indeed, some actors considered in this study did not survive in the political game to a natural death. Yet, this study does not shrink from the premise as a useful devise for thinking about the modal behavior of politicians. The rationality assumption does least violence to reality when applied to elites such as those atop the Soviet political system. As other studies have shown, rationality is a realistic approximation of human behavior in political games when the stakes are high for actors and when they have opportunities to learn through trial and error.[15] The actors with whom this analysis deals are remarkably astute individuals in a high stakes game with the opportunity and motivation to acquire information about the structural constraints and the options relevant to their choices. They had served long apprenticeships and reached the top by their ability to make strategic choices of means in the crucible of Soviet politics.

This study also begins by limiting its analysis to that realm of behavior in which actors seek control over state policy. Rigorous analysis—whether new institutionalist or not—requires such abstract definitions of the behavior to be analyzed. In the present study, I analyze those roles (and the concept of role should be understood as defining an abstract realm of behavior) in which political actors seek at minimum to influence specific policy outcomes and at maximum to control the policy process that issues a stream of policy outcomes. This realm of behavior includes such activities as politicians seeking office and incumbents seeking to retain office. As these illustrations underscore, one aspect of the behavior analyzed here is the pursuit of political survival. David Mayhew's seminal analysis of this behavior among U.S. congressmen posits an "electoral connection": "United States congressmen are interested in getting reelected—indeed, in their role here as abstractions, interested in nothing else." In defending his assumption, he argues that the electoral goal "has to be the proximate goal of everyone, the goal that must be achieved over and over if other ends are to be entertained."[16] Barry Ames has found the survival postulate accurately predicts the behavior of leaders in Latin America.[17] Yet, survival is only one aspect of seeking control over policymaking, which also includes such acts as legislators' attempts to contain executive power and electors' attempts to control their legislators. This motivational postulate is not intended to be understood as a realistic description of humans, who are delightfully much richer and more complex than any abstraction, but this simplification permits us to develop the type of parsimonious cognitive map necessary for thinking about a more complex reality.[18]

This second assumption is important because it seeks to identify a distinctly political realm of behavior. This sets the following analysis apart from a branch of the new institutionalism (neo-institutionalist political economy) that explains political outcomes on the basis of economic motivations.[19] One very powerful expression of this neo-institutionalist political economy is the theory of the revenue-seeking state. Margaret Levi builds her theory on the hypothesis that "rulers are predatory in that they try to extract as much revenue as they can from the population."[20] The predatory state, as a rational economic actor, thus becomes centrally concerned with such matters as minimizing its transaction costs. Yet, in politics, revenue, only a means to controlling policy, is frequently sacrificed for larger purposes. When survival requires reducing revenues, survival wins out. When survival requires increasing transaction costs (for example, through one of those Rube Goldberg-like institutions so common in politics) survival wins out. Neo-institutional political economy expands our knowledge of one subsidiary concern of states, but within that abstract realm we call politics, it runs the risk of elevating a means to an ends. The following analysis examines roles in which incumbents rationally pursue control over the policy of the polity.

Authoritarian Institutions

While the immediate question posed by this book concerns the stagnation and collapse of Soviet political institutions, the larger issue it raises concerns the fragility of authoritarianism. The Soviet Union was one of the twentieth century's most enduring authoritarian polities, and yet in the last decade of the century it fell like a house of cards. Other modern authoritarian polities have been far less stable; many fell with the reign of a single strongman. Because the Soviet Union was one of the most fully developed and most enduring authoritarian polities, the failure of its political institutions naturally invites the question whether authoritarian institutions are inherently short-lived.

To answer the specific question about the Soviet Union and to use this to suggest insights into the larger issue of the fragility of authoritarianism require an understanding of authoritarian political institutions. Yet, authoritarianism poses a particular challenge to the new institutionalism. It places a premium on analysis of informal and unwritten rules hidden by formal, but less significant window dressing. Institutional analysis of democracies has often stopped at analyzing the formal rules that structure the incentives and constrain the strategic choices of political actors. Students of democracy have developed sophisticated analyses of the consequences of electoral laws for the strategic choices of political party leaders, of presidentialism and parliamentarism for the behavior of executives and legislators, and of legislative rules for policy outcomes.[21] Yet formal rules are often not the rules in use under authoritarianism.

The new institutionalism confronts a particular challenge when it studies the Soviet polity. Indeed, until recently the concept of institutions as constraints on the power and behavior of leaders has been largely absent from the analysis of Soviet politics. A prevailing view has been that the rough and tumble of power struggles among leaders not only destroyed embryonic institutions but also prevented new ones from emerging. For example, George Kennan records how Bolshevik leaders destroyed all rules governing relations among themselves. In early political struggles they even managed to destroy the limited ethical code that had served them during their days of plotting revolution and might have served as the seed of a code of mutual relations among governing Bolsheviks.[22] Kennan reflects a tradition of research that begins from the premise that Soviet politics was largely devoid of institutions. In particular, analysts in this tradition argued that there was no established, recognized center of decisionmaking, and consequently there could be no accountability.[23] In the last few decades, however, Western recognition of the real power of institutions in Soviet politics has grown. T. H. Rigby describes the rise of Khrushchev in terms of "the rules of the Soviet political game" and his strategy of making the "structures and written and unwritten rules of the system" work to his advantage.[24] Thane Gustafson and Dawn Mann write of the "unwritten conventions on promotion and representation that have come to limit a general secretary's choices in applying the cadres weapon."[25] Graeme Gill has even argued that many formal rules of the Communist party were real constraints on the behavior of Soviet politicians.[26] Yet, institutions have mostly been seen as peripheral in this polity lacking a constitutional basis.

In the next chapters I argue that we should begin to understand authoritarianism, and Soviet authoritarianism in particular, by looking to its constitutional foundations. In identifying the rules in use, the new institutionalism demands that we take authoritarian political institutions seriously. In recent years the prevailing approach to authoritarian politics has tended to focus on state-society relations and has devoted far less attention to the dynamics within the state. Juan J. Linz's unparalleled survey of the literature on authoritarian regimes, for example, distinguishes democracy from authoritarianism on the basis of the polity's relationship to society. He then distinguishes among alternative authoritarian regimes in a similar way—by the extent to which they permit political pluralism in society and mobilize the population.[27] As important as these issues are, it tells us little about the dynamics within the polity itself. For example, this state-society focus does not tell us to whom authoritarian policymakers are accountable, except to tell us that it is not the populace at large, nor does it permit us to explore the important ways in which authoritarian polities vary with different restrictive groups holding policymakers accountable.

The application to authoritarian polities of a new institutionalism that originated in the study of democracies should not diminish our sense of the differences between these two political forms. The use of concepts common to both does not mean that they are simply alike; rather, it suggests that their political dynamics can be contrasted by common conceptual categories and can sometimes be positioned along dimensions, perhaps at polar opposite ends of some dimensions, common to both.

ALTERNATIVE EXPLANATIONS

In explaining the stagnation and collapse of the Soviet Union by the independent causal effect of political institutions, my analysis stands in tension with a number of explanations that have sought the causes of stagnation and collapse elsewhere—particularly, in Soviet political culture and learning or in Soviet social structure and modernization.

The different explanations that Sovietologists have offered for the stagnation and collapse of the Soviet Union mirror two major divides in political science.[28] First, the subjectivist-objectivist rift runs throughout political science: subjectivist analyses stress the values and cognitions infusing politics, and objectivist analyses stress material and institutional constraints on political action. In focusing on the ideas that structure meanings and motivate action, subjectivists assert that analyses must begin with the problem of understanding the perceptions, ideas, or norms that lie behind events. Subjectivists typically find the sources of the Soviet collapse in political culture or ideology. Alternatively, in analyzing how individuals rationally pursue status, power, or wealth under different conditions, objectivists emphasize "external" constraints on action rather than "internal" understandings.[29] Objectivists may find the sources of Soviet collapse in the command economy or political institutions.

Second, the state-society rift separates society-centered analysis, which stresses the dependence of the political realm on society, from state-centered analysis, which stresses the autonomy of politics.[30] Society-centered analysis explains political outcomes by changes in variables outside the polity, including class structures, factors of production, or social movements. Although society-centered analysis may include the polity as an actor by "bringing the state back in," it treats the state as dependent variable, as a simple cash register that totals up social pressures, or as a neutral referee that officiates among contending social forces. Society-centered analyses are likely to find the sources of collapse of the Soviet system in either the spontaneous development of society or the imperatives of economic development. Alternatively, state-centered analysis stresses the autonomy of the political sphere and the independent causal force of politics. State-centered analyses contend that to understand poli-

tics research must engage it directly.[31] State-centered analyses of the Soviet collapse find its sources in the dynamics of the political process and
Soviet political institutions.

In arguing for the independent causal power of political institutions,
my objectivist state-centered analysis does not deny the contribution of
the causes identified by alternative approaches. It does, however, assert
the primacy of political institutions in explaining how these other factors
came together in the stagnation and collapse of the Soviet polity. These
other approaches offer explanations that are incomplete without politics,
in which politics is a necessary, essential, but missing part of their explanations. The state-centered approach properly privileges political institutions to explain the way in which these disparate factors came together to
bring down the Soviet Union.

Political Culture, Ideology, and Learning

The Soviet Union was built on a distinctive political culture and Marxist-
Leninist ideology. In explaining the stagnation and collapse of the Soviet
system, subjectivists privilege these factors. Stephen F. Cohen, for example, finds the explanation for stagnation in a conservative political culture. He argues that "the main obstacle to reform in the Soviet Union is
not one or another generation, institution, elite, group, or leader, but the
profound conservatism that seems to dominate almost all of them, from
the family to the Politburo, from local authorities to the state
nachalstvo."[32] Similarly, ideological explanations find the roots of resistance to reform in Marxist-Leninist belief. Carl J. Friedrich and Zbigniew
K. Brzezinski, for example, have described the Soviet Union's totalitarian
leaders as individuals inspired by their ideologies, as true believers who
"believe passionately in *their* truth" and "fanatics when it comes to maintaining their ideas." Marxist-Leninists come to power with the ambition
to remake society in the image of these ideas—"to attempt to force history
to fit their conception of it."[33]

In this view, conservatism and ideological despotism naturally resist
reform. Communists may develop more sophisticated and pragmatic variants of Marxism-Leninism, but they cannot abandon the Communist
project. Reform fails because all Communist leaders, even those who are
pragmatic and flexible, remain prisoners of the ideology.[34] When ideology and reality do not correspond, ideologues turn not to policy innovation or institutional adaptation but to violence in order to force reality to
conform to ideological expectation.[35]

The engine for reform, therefore, must be a shift in political culture or
ideology. Carl A. Linden, for example, claims one must explore the "dark

region of political psychology" to find the "moral-political shifts in out-
look [that] presage ultimate changes in the external world of politics."[36]
To explain the Gorbachev reforms Gail W. Lapidus examines the broad
shift in values from party-mindedness to universal moral concerns, from
collectivism to individualism, from dogmatism to tolerance, and from
utopianism to pragmatism.[37] Daniel Chirot summarizes the sources of the
collapse of Communism more simply as the collapse of its moral bases:
"utter moral rot."[38]

The most ambitious theoretical undertaking to explain this shift in cognitions and values is offered by learning theory. George W. Breslauer
argues that one cannot explain ideological and political change over decades of Soviet rule without including the factor of collective learning—
"a process whereby groups reevaluate policies, strategies, or even goals,
in response to experience."[39] In particular, without a theory of collective
learning one cannot explain what Breslauer sees as the growing radicalization of Soviet economic reform programs over time.

Analysis that begins with political culture, ideology, and learning
draws our attention to vitally important aspects of Soviet political life;
yet, privileging the subjective has led to unsatisfactory explanation. First,
in actual empirical applications subjectivists often offer little more than
description, although masked by an illusion of explanation. For instance,
the subjectivist observes the empirical evidence that only conservative
policies are put forward or adopted. Conservatism becomes both the description of this phenomenon and its explanation; the evidence for dependent and independent variables is the same. Similarly, learning is both
the description of the phenomenon of changed discourse and policy as
well as the explanation for these changes; in empirical analyses of learning the evidence for cause and effect is the same. In short, culture, ideology, and learning theory often offer simple definitions or descriptions
masquerading as explanation.

Second, subjectivists frequently give us little analytic purchase in
circumstances characterized by diverse opinions and nonmajoritarian decision processes. Soviet political debates, particularly the early debates
over Soviet power and economic policy, were characterized by a wide
spectrum of options. In each period since then, different leaders have
learned diverging lessons from previous experience. For example, as
Breslauer himself notes, by the early 1960s, many had learned the need
for decentralization and marketization, while others had learned the need
for greater centralization through optimal planning and computeriza-
tion.[40] Many lessons of marketization that prevailed in the 1980s had
actually been learned in the 1920s. Subjectivist analyses beg the question
why the lessons of marketization prevailed in the 1980s, but not in the
1960s? This becomes still more problematic because we cannot answer

this question by simple measures of the "weight" of each view within the leadership. In each debate, the victorious view did not represent a shared lesson learned collectively; rather the victors usually held a minority view that artificially made itself the majority through manipulating political institutions. Moreover, once in power, by shaping the terms of debate and anathematizing some lessons, this determined what lessons could be learned. One needs to examine political institutions to find the tools to think about which lessons can be learned and which are likely to prevail.

Third, a particular problem with the learning approach is that it cannot explain the narrowing of discourse and alternatives that was a prominent feature of Soviet politics from 1917 to 1985. As I stress in later chapters, rather than a steady radicalization of reforms, the alternatives discussed in Soviet politics began to narrow, and the policy outcomes became less venturesome. No debate over economic policy from 1953 to 1985, for example, addressed the range of options put forward in the 1920s. No policy adopted between 1953 and 1985 in this period represented as radical a deviation from past practice as the zigzag from the mobilizational War Communism (1919) to the more market-oriented New Economic Policy (1921) and then back to the mobilizational First Five-Year Plan (1928) and collectivization of agriculture. In addition, to describe the Brezhnev era as a flowering of debate and greater experimentation than earlier periods, as Breslauer's learning theory appears to do, runs flat in the face of the real narrowing of options and reforms after Khrushchev's removal that earned the Brezhnev era the epithet "cult of stagnation." Rather than moving up a learning curve, from 1917 to 1985 the public debates seemed to suffer from collective "dumbing down." The sudden burst of debate after 1985 in which analysts had at first to rediscover lessons such as the New Economic Policy learned six decades earlier was a far more abrupt shift in the direction of discourse and policy than can be explained by more linear and glacial processes like learning. The causes of the dumbing down before 1985 and the radical explosion after 1985 lie within the polity and its institutions.

Social Change and Generations

Soviet politics was clearly constrained by the society the Bolsheviks inherited from the tsarist regime and by the changes they engineered after 1917. Yet, by privileging these social constraints, society-centered analyses see political outcomes not as a reflection of state policies and choices, but as results of causes beyond the control of the state. In explaining the stagnation and collapse of the Soviet Union, these have tended to focus on the processes of social modernization. Autocracy that stifled reform was the result of a preindustrial society or very late industrialization; political change came with social modernization. Decades ago Isaac Deutscher predicted that modernization of the Stalinist autocracy would naturally lead to a more pluralistic society and to both liberalization and democratization of politics.[41] Moshe Lewin and Geoffrey Hosking have both stressed the independent causal effect of urbanization and the professionalization of society, which in Hosking's words, have led to a situation "for more than two decades that society and politics were out of phase with one another."[42] As a result of this imbalance, in Lewin's analysis, the causal link leading from state to society that may have existed earlier was then reversed; the spontaneous developments in society changed the political order.[43]

The most ambitious theoretical undertaking to explain the causal mechanisms behind the social sources of Soviet change has been generational analysis. Resistance to change in the Soviet system is ultimately explained by the attributes, life experiences, and preferences of Soviet generations. Lewin stresses the educational and occupational attributes of the populace and uses the "vocational x-ray" of each generation to explain the changing relationship of society to polity. Between the first and third industrial generations, a Soviet society dominated by workers with limited education gave way to a society with large numbers of service and information professionals possessing advanced education. This change in society affected politics as the younger generation rejected the views and methods of their predecessors.[44]

The life experiences of each generation—and so their world views and values—shifted dramatically with the tumultuous history of the Soviet Union. The continued hold on power by the generation that began their rapid ascent under Stalin—the so-called "Class of '38"—permitted them to fend off reform. This generation, as Robert V. Daniels argues, "resisted or sabotaged innovation and clung to sterile bureaucratic methods and ideological formulas in the face of the new problems and potential of a modern society."[45] The post-Brezhnev generation, according to Timothy J. Colton, is less attached to Stalinist institutions because it did not participate in their creation. It is more assertive because it has not been cowed by Stalinist terror and more enthusiastic about reform because it was not "traumatized by Khrushchev's boisterous reforms." This generation lifted into power individuals "more critical of Soviet failings than their predecessors and with more of the itch for improvement so readily apparent in Gorbachev."[46]

By treating the state as a dependent variable, cash register, or referee, society-centered analyses run the risk of diverting our attention from the power of the Soviet polity to shape society and, in particular, to select winners and losers within society and each generation. At each point, the

polity enjoyed great discretion to promote individuals who did not represent the prevailing attributes, life experiences, or views of a generation. At
times of great tension between society and the Soviet polity the political
system forced society to adjust rather than vice versa. For example, in the
so-called scissors crisis of the mid-1920s, the polity forced society to
abandon the New Economic Policy for the First Five-Year Plan and
forced collectivization.

Generational analysis has led to unsatisfactory explanations of Soviet
political change, owing to its weak deductive foundations. Because we
have a most imperfect understanding of the relationship between life experiences and political attitudes, generational analysis leads to dubious
explanations. Generational explanations can often predict diametrically
opposite consequences that within the logic of the theory are equally
plausible.[47]

Consider for the sake of illustration Colton's elegant deductions from
the life experiences of Soviet generations and the contrary deductions that
could be put forward: Contrary to his explanation, the younger generation might be as conservative as the Western yuppies to whom they have
been compared. Their materialism, individualism, and uncertainty about
their own life opportunities might give them heightened incentive to carve
out a personal niche within the system. They could be more attached to
existing institutions than their elders because they have known no alternatives and take these institutions as the givens of social existence. The
older generation, having lived in the previous institutional order and
knowing the alternatives considered at the time of the creation of Stalinist
institutions, understands that these institutions are mere human artifacts
that they themselves helped mold. The materialistic, ambitious yuppies
may be more conservative than their experimental predecessors. This alternative hypothesis is as plausible as Colton's. The fact that it is counter-
factual begs the question: why did it not turn out this way? But the deductive logic of generational analysis cannot tell us this.

The weaknesses in its deductive logic are further illustrated by compar-
ing Colton's with Seweryn Bialer's conclusions about the impact of the
Khrushchev reforms on the post-Brezhnev generation. Colton sees these
as traumatizing, but inconsequential for the post-Brezhnev generation
that escaped the trauma. Bialer sees the Khrushchev reform in just the
opposite light—liberating and powerfully important in the formation of
the Brezhnev generation: "One of its crucial formative political experiences—if not the most crucial one—took place during the protracted fer-
ment and shock of Khrushchev's anti-Stalin campaign, a campaign that
frankly admitted the monstrosities no one hitherto had dared to name, a
campaign that questioned authority and established truths and thereby
stimulated critical thought."[48] The theoretical apparatus of generation

analysis does not provide us the logical tools to say one or the other deduction is consistent with the premises of the analysis.

Perhaps most important, generational explanations must confront the uncomfortable fact that empirical studies have shown Soviet generations not to be so neatly divided as their analysis suggests. Studies of elite attitudes have found a division between conservatives and reformers *within* each Soviet generation. Robert Conquest, Alexander Dallin, Carl Linden, and Thomas H. Rigby, among others, have documented the existence of such divisions in the generation that ruled after Stalin's death.[49] Mark R. Beissinger and George W. Breslauer find the post-Stalin generation divided as well.[50] Moreover, this division united partisan groups *across* generations rather than dividing along generational lines. Beissinger and Breslauer find surprisingly similar proportions of conservatives and reformers in different generations of elites. For example, on the eve of Gorbachev's administration the publicly articulated positions of Communist party bureaucrats suggested little systematic difference in their attitudes toward change between the generation that began their careers under Stalin and the younger generation. Breslauer's study of articles and speeches by twenty-four Russian Republic provincial (*obkom* and *kraikom*) first secretaries reveals only "marginally greater demandingness and impatience in the post-Stalin generation."[51] Generational analysis begs the question why reformist elements in the next generation should be any more likely to prevail than in past generations. The answer is locked up with politics and political institutions.

Privileging Politics

Learning and generational theories contribute important pieces to the solution of a large puzzle. Yet, they place in the background what should be foremost in any explanation of the failure of the Soviet Union. They tend to treat Soviet politics as derivative of pressures from outside politics—be they from either culture or society. I argue that political institutions explain why the Soviet system could not reform and why it finally collapsed. Analyses that focus on learning or generations beg the question how, in the presence of diverging lessons and heterogeneous generations, one point of view or one part of a generation came to shape policy. Because they do not develop a model of political institutions, the emphases on ideas and generations ultimately rest on a dubious democratic metaphor. They get close to positing a majoritarian process in which prevailing attitudes, or the shifting weight of attitudes within a generation, are translated automatically into policy orientations. This analysis explains changes by the growing number of reformers within the Soviet elite, intelligentsia, and population as though this head count answers the question whether reform will prevail. Indeed, Cohen concludes that his analysis should lead us to exactly this reinterpretation of the system of Communist party rule: "the importance of this deep-rooted conservatism . . . compels us to rethink the whole relationship between a party-state and society in the Soviet Union."[52] Yet this democratic metaphor is most inappropriate when political leaders, enjoying considerable autonomy from social control, can run roughshod over public opinion. If the Soviet experience should tell us anything, it is the importance of understanding how a small vanguard minority can use politics to shape political culture, control learning, transform society, and pick winners and losers from each generation.

State-centered analysis challenges us, to paraphrase Eric A. Nordlinger, not only to bring the state back in, but also to take it seriously. It challenges us to identify the motivations of politicians, which can be distinct from those of major social actors outside politics. It challenges us to identify political institutions that have independent power to shape political outcomes. This does not exclude the importance of the subjective or of society; instead, state-centered analysis places politics at the center of our inquiry.

THE PLAN OF THE BOOK

In this introduction I have promised to explain the stagnation and collapse of the Soviet Union by its constitutional structure. As the reader no doubt suspects, I have set out three daunting tasks that constitute the agenda of this book. First, I seek to demonstrate the central role of the Soviet Union's constitutional order in its decline and fall. Second, I want to lay the foundations for a new institutionalism of authoritarianism—at least to the extent that it will provide the conceptual categories to accomplish the first task. Third, I hope to show the utility of politics-centered institutionalism and hopefully to contribute to saving a part of the new institutionalism in comparative politics from my good friends who seek to submerge more of it in political economy.

This book is divided into four parts. The first part, chapters 1 and 2, surveys broad analytic issues; chapter 2 presents a generalized abstract model of the authoritarian constitution. The second part examines the constitution of Bolshevism and its development toward institutional stagnation and policy dysfunction: that is, more specifically, the decisions that established the constitutive rules of the Soviet polity (chapter 3), the political dynamics that institutionalized reciprocal accountability (chapter 4) and balanced leadership (chapter 5), and how these developments gave rise to institutional stagnation and policy dysfunction (chapter 6). The third part presents three sets of case studies of reform and its defeat, of Soviet stagnation and collapse. These case studies include domestic policy and procedural reforms (chapter 7), attempts to reform military planning (chapter 8), and the broad experiment with constitutional reform from 1987 to 1991 and its failure (chapter 9). The concluding fourth part draws together these lessons with some speculation about future research in the analysis of authoritarianism and the successor republics of the Soviet Union.

CHAPTER TWO

The Authoritarian Constitution

THE NEW INSTITUTIONALISM challenges the ways in which we usually analyze authoritarian politics. It asks us to find the rules that pattern and constrain political choices. It directs us to identify the political institutions that shape political processes and the path of political development. Yet, authoritarianism in turn challenges the new institutionalism by asking it to reach beyond the formal democratic institutions and processes that have hitherto been its focus. Authoritarian polities often hide their rules from public view and mask them by layers of myths intended to deceive. When it does not deceive with facades of democracy, authoritarianism often presents an equally deceptive picture of simply arbitrary rule without constraints, without rules, without institutions.

The analysis of authoritarianism developed in this book proceeds from a model that is a parsimonious abstraction.[1] This structural model is, more specifically, an institutional model of politics. It identifies a relationship linking the constitutional structure of the authoritarian state to its "normal" political processes and to the path of its political development. The analysis begins from the view that the constitutive rules of most polities emerge from bargains among empowered political actors, yet these rules take on a life of their own to constrain the actors' subsequent choices. These rules may continue to constrain choices even when the empowered political actors or their interests change. They may constrain behavior even when the rules no longer yield the results for which they were created or when those results are no longer significant or desired. They may even have interaction effects quite independent of individual rules and so define games that differ greatly from those intended by their authors. Because the constitutive rules are important in all these ways, the rules themselves often become the objects of politics. In short, constitutive rules are products of games of strategy, but in turn they create games of both *normal politics* in which political actors use existing rules to advance their causes and *constitutional politics* in which actors seek to advance their causes by changing the rules themselves.[2]

This chapter begins by presenting conceptual categories according to which the new institutionalism can "read" a constitution. These categories provide the foundations for some comparisons of the structural foundations of the authoritarian polity with those of democracies and for distinguishing types of authoritarian structures. The second and third parts address the consequences of these authoritarian structures for normal politics and constitutional dynamics.

POLICYMAKERS AND ACCOUNTABILITY

A constitution is a set of fundamental rules, formal and informal, according to which a state is constituted and governed. This accords with a common definition that is both ancient and modern. According to Cicero, the term constitution refers to "the total composition, the shape or form of the state."[3] According to S. E. Finer, a constitution is a set of "rules which govern the allocation of functions, powers, and duties among the various governmental agencies and their officers, and define the relationship between them and the public."[4] A constitution is distinguished from other political institutions by its fundamental nature.

A common definition of democratic and authoritarian constitutions focuses on the state-society relationship. Juan Linz defines democracy as a polity in which the whole citizenry must validate the leaders, in peaceful procedures, at regular intervals. In a democracy—at least as an ideal-type—no adults may be denied their place in the selectorate, and no effective policymaking office can be excluded from the requirement of validation. Authoritarianism is the alternative—a polity in which only a part of society must validate the polity.[5] Yet, by focusing on state-society relations alone, the definition of authoritarianism as a regime in which leaders are accountable to only a part of society fails to address three issues central to the constitutional structure of any polity: the structure of policymaking power, the identity of the groups to which policymakers are actually accountable, and the nature of the relationship between these selectors and policymakers.

In the discussion below, I use the term "constitution" to refer to the rules that address these issues—rules that allocate policymaking powers and establish relationships of accountability. In short, a constitution includes rules that provide answers to three fundamental questions about any polity: Where does the state's policymaking power effectively reside? To whom are the holders of this power ultimately accountable? What control do the policymakers exercise over the composition of the group to whom they are accountable? Permit me now to examine each of these issues more fully.

Policymakers

Perhaps the oldest and most enduring distinction among constitutions concerns whether policymaking is assigned to a single individual, a small committee, or a large assembly. On this basis Aristotle distinguished rule by one as kingship or tyranny, rule by the few as aristocracy or oligarchy, and rule by the many as polity or democracy. Aristotle was also the first to note that these different types of policymaking have distinct dynamics.[6] The importance of the structure of policymaking is underscored in the recurring distinction in modern social science between processes of individual and group decisionmaking and, within the latter, between small group and large group processes.[7]

The structure of the policymaking power divides authoritarian regimes according to whether they are characterized by *directive* (one-person) or *collective* (multiperson) rule. The former assigns policymaking to a single leader such as a president or a general secretary; the latter, to a committee such as a junta, revolutionary command council, or politburo. Well after Aristotle's time, this remains a powerful empirical distinction: For example, examining the varieties of Communist regimes in Eastern Europe before 1989, Ellen Comisso finds very different political dynamics under directive (or "patrimonial") rule and collective (or "collegial") rule.[8] For the new institutionalism this is one of the most fundamental distinctions among situations involving choice. The differences between individual choice and collective choice are basic. The movement from the former to the latter introduces a legion of complexities associated with games, including collective action problems, voting paradoxes, and the design of strategies.

The importance of this distinction is illustrated by the Soviet polity, which was characterized by alternating periods of collective and directive rule. Joseph Stalin's dictatorship following the removal of the Right Opposition from the Politburo in 1929 became the quintessence of one-person rule. Yet, upon his death in 1953 he left behind a triumvirate of Georgii Malenkov, Lavrentii Beria, and Viacheslav Molotov, sharing the former dictator's power collectively among themselves and with other leaders. Subsequent periods of collective leadership followed the limited directorship of Nikita Khrushchev and Leonid Brezhnev. As I explore in subsequent chapters, with each change, the dynamics of Soviet politics and policymaking shifted.

Selectors and Accountability

Where policymakers are accountable to others, the body that holds the power to select and remove policymakers constitutes the *selectorate*. A distinction that emerged with representative government concerns the distribution of this right to participate in the policymaking power of the state indirectly through the suffrage. Montesquieu altered Aristotle's categories by distinguishing democracy, aristocracy, and monarchy according to the extent to which this sovereign power of the suffrage is possessed by the people as a whole, only a part, or a single person.[9] This distinction remains a powerful analytic tool in modern social science; Robert Dahl, for example, labels this continuum "inclusiveness."[10]

In all political systems the selectorate is only a part of the *participant* population that can seek to influence the political process without threat of retributive sanctions. In democracies this distinction is often overlooked because the participant population that is *unenfranchised* (that is, not also part of the selectorate) is proportionately small, including resident aliens, felons, the institutionalized, and minors. In authoritarian polities, however, this distinction is significant because the selectorate that holds policymakers accountable may be only a small part of the entire participant population (even where the latter is itself only a part of the adult population).

The new institutionalism stresses that accountability arises in the context of a delegation relationship. Delegation is akin to, but differs from, the exchange relationship that has been more widely analyzed in political economy. In exchange political actors swap resources or rights to their control; the transfer of rights is often definitive, giving the new possessor full right to exercise or even alienate the rights. Delegation, however, is a relationship in which parties assign these rights to another only conditionally. To represent the delegation relationship, the new institutionalism employs the principal-agent model. Principal-agent relations are widespread, existing between stockholder and manager, manager and foreman, client and lawyer, artist and agent, and so forth. In this relationship the principal delegates some rights to the agent, and the agent must exercise these rights in ways that affect the welfare of the principal. This delegation raises problems of accountability: The principal seeks to ensure that the agent exercises these rights for the principal's benefit.[11] The principal enforces this accountability ultimately by mechanisms for rescinding the transfer of rights. To illustrate, in a democracy, as Terry Moe notes, "citizens are principals, politicians are their agents."[12] During their terms politicians are granted "enormously valuable property rights by virtue of their occupation of official positions." Yet, unlike the exchange of property rights, in delegation "politicians cannot sell their rights to the exercise of authority, and they can be dispossessed at the next election."[13] Indeed, in politics, the most important reward may simply be continuation of the delegation relationship, while the most important punishment may be withdrawal of this opportunity to exercise delegated rights.[14]

According to the definition introduced earlier in this chapter, the authoritarian polity differs from the democratic because authoritarian policymakers are not accountable to the adult population at large. Yet, except for the rare extreme of true despotism, authoritarian policymakers are nonetheless accountable to selectorates and the nature of the selectors distinguishes alternative forms of authoritarianism. Indeed, by the nature of these selectors, we can identify three ideal-types of authoritarian polities: (1) leadership is despotic and so not accountable to others' control; (2) leaders are accountable to a restrictive group of social interests; and (3) leaders are accountable to a selectorate drawn from the governing apparatus itself. The first ideal-type is approximated by the rare cases in which a hereditary monarch or modern autocrat cannot be removed by either conspiracy or coup. The second includes traditional kingship elected by landed aristocrats, presidents elected by a narrow social oligarchy, or caudillos empowered by local caciques. The third, a pattern as old as antiquity, survives in the selection of the Pope by the Vatican's college of cardinals or until recently in the mechanisms for selecting the Dalai Lama.[15] With the growth of modern bureaucracy, this third form of authoritarianism is increasingly found in the accountability of leaders to the heads of chief bureaucracies, and not surprisingly, with the early growth of the coercive mechanisms of the modern state, among the earliest and simplest forms of this bureaucratic authoritarianism has been the regime in which military bureaucracies select policymakers and hold them accountable.[16] In the Soviet Union, for example, accountability was structured by the decision to exclude most of the adult population from politics. Considering themselves a vanguard, the Bolsheviks sought freedom to define the interests of the working masses. In April 1924 Stalin explained the vanguard role of the Party in lectures to the Sverdlov University, "The Party cannot be a real party if it limits itself to registering what the masses of the working class feel and think. . . . The Party must stand at the head of the working class; it must see further than the working class; it must lead the proletariat and not follow in the tail of the spontaneous movement."[17] Yet the leadership that emerged within the Party discovered that to sustain itself in power it needed to maintain the support of key bureaucrats, including the Party apparatus, the military and police, and the state economic administration. With time, as subsequent chapters explore, the leaders became accountable to these.

Authoritarianism presents a particular analytic challenge to the new institutionalism because its regimes, particularly those led by strongmen, often obscure the lines of accountability. Because the threats that enforce accountability are never exercised continuously, it is often difficult to identify the lines of accountability when they do not accord with formal rules. This may be particularly obscure when the threat of accountability is seldom invoked because the acumen of leaders has led them to anticipate the reactions of selectors. It is also difficult to identify because authoritarian regimes are often of such short duration that the replacement of the leader does not become an issue. Yet, even in many authoritarian polities with seemingly all powerful leaders, some selectorate shapes the political process. Although Egyptian public life has been dominated by a series of strongmen, including Muhammad Naguib, Gamal Abdul Nasser, Anwar es-Sadat, and Husni Mubarak, each leader rose to power with the support of the military. Each president was selected from the ranks of senior military officers, and each at first had to secure high-level military support to establish his rule. While virtually all important policy decisions were made by the president and his staff, the power of the president rested ultimately on his support in the military.[18] Amos Perlmutter describes the structure of praetorianism in Egypt and other Middle Eastern military regimes as involving "the perfect domination of the military over the executive, as the Revolutionary Command Council [RCC] is established as the instrument for controlling the executive." The chair of the RCC serves as executive, sometimes assuming the posts of president or prime minister; "the major source of support is the general headquarters of the army."[19]

Hierarchy and Reciprocity

The challenge of analyzing authoritarianism calls for a distinction that the new institutionalism has not encountered in democracies: Delegation relationships may be either *hierarchical* or *reciprocal*. In polities with a well-established principle of sovereignty the most important political relationship is hierarchical. A hierarchical relationship involves unilateral delegation in which the right of all agents is conditional but the ultimate principal's right is definitive. Thus, for example, in a democracy (at least in the ideal-type of popular sovereignty) while citizens may deprive legislators of their powers to legislate by either removing them individually or eliminating their posts, legislators cannot in turn deprive citizens individually or collectively of their rights. Of course, legislators do sometimes attempt this, and where they succeed democracy breaks down and is replaced by a form of authoritarianism.[20]

Hierarchical accountability can be found in authoritarian polities, such as the autocratic rule of a hereditary monarch or elective kingship chosen by independent selectors such as medieval Poland's Diet of landed aristocrats.[21] Yet, authoritarian constitutions often establish reciprocal accountability. Under reciprocal accountability neither party is sovereign; that is, both sets of rights are contingent upon the sustaining delegation from the other. Reciprocal accountability is found where selectors such as bureaucrats can be appointed and removed by the very leaders whom they appoint and remove.[22] In traditional court politics and modern bureaucratic authoritarianism the leader may remain vulnerable to subsequent removal by the courtiers or bureaucrats that elevated the leader, but the leader in turn seeks to remove selectors and cultivate new ones so as to consolidate a hold on office. In military regimes, the leader selected by the junta or revolutionary command council consolidates leadership by appointing loyal officers to general headquarters.[23] In the well-balanced ideal-type of reciprocal accountability, each policymaker becomes both principal and agent of selectors and vice versa; each is accountable to the other.

In both hierarchical and reciprocal accountability, a role may be simultaneously a principal and an agent, but with an important difference: In a hierarchy a principal such as a politician is the agent of some *higher* principal that is not also its agent; in a reciprocal relationship this principal is the agent of its *own* agent.[24] Reciprocity, as the term is used here, is a relationship of mutual delegation and accountability.

With the spread of authoritarian regimes ultimately dependent on the sustaining support of governmental bureaucracies, reciprocal accountability is now found widely; indeed, it may be a hallmark of modern authoritarianism. In Egypt, for example, after selection by the military the president acquires enormous powers to subsequently shape the selectorate through removal and promotion. Nasser used his close friendship with the commander-in-chief, who was appointed in June 1953 at Nasser's insistence, to ensure that his allies among the Free Officers dominated the Revolutionary Command Council. Sadat understood that power rested in the military, and, after winning its approval to succeed Nasser, he worked to remove from military posts those who had opposed him or, as in the case of General Muhammad Ahmed Sadek, had supported him but might oppose him in the future.[25] Similarly, in Brazil following the election of General Castello Branco to the presidency on 11 April 1964, officers who had opposed the April coup were purged.[26] Castello Branco then turned against members of the original coup coalition who opposed him for the presidency; these opponents were excluded from centers of power and then the military, while supporters of the president were favored for military promotion. As these examples point out, unlike the ideal type, reciprocal accountability in practice may be manifest nonsynchronously with the exercise of personnel control shifting between leaders and selectors.

To label many authoritarian regimes reciprocal, while labeling democracies hierarchic, runs counter to a familiar terminology—at the risk of some confusion. Nonetheless, the difference once again highlights the distinct focus of the new institutionalism. A common use of these labels describes the relationship *between* the political system and society, not *within* the polity. Thus, in discussions of the relative autonomy of the state or distinctions between strong states and weak states, the relationship of a modern authoritarian regime to society is undoubtedly hierarchical. The new institutionalism, in asking us not only to bring the state back in, but also to take it seriously, asks us to examine the structure of power *within* the polity. Sovereignty—whether the popular sovereignty of democracy or the sovereignty of a divine right monarch—defines a hierarchical relationship; conversely, reciprocity in the relationship between policymakers and citizens is anathema to democratic control and to kings who rule by the mandate of God.

A Model

Bringing together these three structural distinctions, as figure 2.1 depicts, the authoritarian constitution defines a two-tier polity. In the first tier, policymaking power may be directive or collective. This first tier is usually accountable to a selectorate in the second tier. The selectors drawn from either nongovernmental interests or the governing apparatus itself may be only a small part of the participant population. Where this selectorate is in turn accountable to the policymakers there is reciprocal accountability between tiers. (As the dotted line suggests, the relationship to unenfranchised bureaucrats is simply hierarchical.)

This abstract model is intended to draw our analysis to specific structural variables within an authoritarian polity. Of course, no regime fits perfectly into these ideal-type distinctions. Moreover, within a single constitution these attributes may not be fixed over time. The structure of

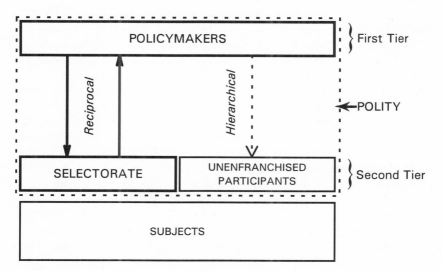

Figure 2.1. Accountability in an Authoritarian Polity

policymaking may vacillate between collective leadership and the directorship of a single leader. Accountability may not be continuous; it may be only intermittent or sporadic. Reciprocal accountability may not be simultaneous; instead, it may be nonsynchronous with alternating periods of accountability of leaders to selectors and selectors to leaders. Over time an authoritarian regime may vacillate between the poles of reciprocal accountability and hierarchical despotism.

This abstract model also draws our attention to important political dynamics of authoritarianism. The constitution of authoritarianism structures normal authoritarian politics. It also nests normal politics within a game of constitutional issues, which I examine in the next two sections.

THE AUTHORITARIAN POLITICAL GAME

The two-tier structure of authoritarianism shapes the conflict and coalition processes at the center of politics. Within the first tier policymakers struggle for power, while in the second tier interests, bureaucratic or social, compete for policy favors. Where there is reciprocal accountability, first-tier policymakers must seek supporters in the selectorate, while second-tier selectors must seek first-tier patrons to remain in the game. The political game revolves around the formation and change of coalitions within and across these two tiers.

This structural model draws attention to three important dynamics in authoritarian polities. First, in the structure of authoritarianism there is the potential for a political cycle of alternating directive and collective leadership. At the creation of a new regime or following a succession, authoritarian leaders who fear creating autocratic power that could be turned against them often rely on collective leadership to check one another. Yet, these collectivities often are characterized by two institutional ambiguities: the relationship of the collectivity's chair to its other members, and the relationship of the collectivity such as Politburo or junta to other decisionmaking centers such as the state cabinet.[27] These ambiguities can set the stage for one member to displace his colleagues in the collectivity and consolidate directive rule.

The rise of one leader from within a collective leadership to dominate the junta, revolutionary command council, or politburo is a common story. For example, in Chile General Augusto Pinochet came to power as one member of a junta, but he successfully placed himself above the other members and gradually transferred many of the junta's prerogatives to his presidency. Revisions of the regulations governing military promotions and retirements permitted the general to purge disloyal officers within the army—the predominant service in the armed forces—and replace them with his followers. After his appointment as president of the junta and supreme chief of the nation (June 1974), the general called junta meetings less frequently and set aside agreements for a rotating presidency. After his elevation to president of the Republic six months later, Pinochet relied more heavily upon his appointed cabinet for routine decisions, while relegating the junta to "the margins of the policy process."[28] He increasingly made all cabinet, judicial, and ambassadorial appointments, despite the provisions of Decree Law 527 for junta involvement; thus, the bureaucracy became accountable to him personally. After that he used the Direccion Nacional de Inteligencia to eliminate opponents throughout the military. When General Gustavo Leigh pressed for limits to Pinochet's power and a return to democratic rule, the air force general was removed from the junta. I should add that Pinochet never successfully transformed reciprocal accountability into hierarchical despotism, and, thus, pressure from the junta forced him to face a national referendum that brought back democracy.

Even the strongest autocrat must leave office, if only upon death, and few have been able to bequeath autocratic powers to a single heir. Following the removal or death of the leader, a new collective leadership is likely to follow. This is a pattern often repeated following the death of communist leaders. Yet, if the institutional ambiguities of collective leadership were not remedied, this only set the stage for a new attempt to consolidate directive leadership.[29]

A second dynamic of authoritarian polities is the potential for a cycle (closely tied to the first) in which the balance of power shifts between tiers. Policymakers attempt to strengthen their hand by reducing their dependence upon the selectorate and increasing their control over it; selectors similarly seek to reduce their dependence on but increase their control over policymakers.[30] Reciprocal accountability, particularly when accountability is exercised nonsynchronously, creates the incentives and occasions for leaders to attempt to limit the opportunities of the selectorate to remove them, and vice versa. As a leader consolidates power within the first tier, opportunities to shape the membership of the second tier through removal and selection grow. Alternatively, the selectorate exercises greatest control over the first tier at the moment of succession, at which time the selectorate may seek to strengthen collective leadership, leadership accountability to the selectorate, and selectorate autonomy.

A third dynamic of authoritarian polities highlighted by this structural model is the link between the policy process and building and maintaining coalitions within tiers and across them. In normal politics policy is often the glue that binds coalitions. The policy process and its outcomes reflect (1) the configuration of power in the first tier, (2) the structure of the suffrage within the second tier, and (3) the balance of power between tiers. First, the policy process and policy outcomes change with the balance of power among first-tier leaders: Collective leadership makes it necessary to balance the policy preferences of first-tier actors, while directive rule permits one leader to impose personal preferences on colleagues.

Second, policy outcomes reflect the structure of the franchise in the second tier. Political leaders use policy as a way to build coalitions with the body enfranchised to select them. For example, Barry Ames argues that Latin American executives seeking "bases of support that will sustain them in office" use "public policy, especially public expenditures, as a weapon for survival." In states where the probability of military coup is higher, "direct budgetary rewards are a logical response to the military threat." Where bureaucrats, local interests, or a social class constitute the critical support group, budgetary allocations reflect their respective power during times of political crisis for a chief executive.[31] In a close comparison of Argentina and Chile, Karen L. Remmer finds that, because suffrage regulations permitted a higher percentage of Argentinean adult males to vote during the first half of this century, "authorities had more incentive to search for lower- and middle-class support in Argentina than in Chile, and the needs and interests of the less privileged accordingly received greater attention."[32] The policies that hold the coalitions of leaders and selectors together reflect the composition of the selectorate that contains potential coalition partners.

Third, policy outcomes reflect the balance of power between tiers. Where accountability between leaders and selectors is reciprocal, the policy preferences of selectors will be constrained by their need to maintain the continuous support of leaders: Not only do leaders provide policy payoffs to constituents, but in turn these constituents must also be sensitive to the policy needs and priorities of leaders. Reciprocity compounds the mutual expectations that Carl J. Friedrich has called anticipated reactions.[33] This mutual influence is illustrated by the policy dynamics of the Brazilian military regime. Thomas E. Skidmore observes that "the essence of organization within any military officer corps is hierarchy and discipline. Yet this structure allows room for an intricate process of participatory decisionmaking. The higher levels retain the final word, but they cannot diverge too far from the views of their junior officers." Hardliners among Brazil's junior officers helped shape the policies of their leaders: "At every turn the president has been dependent for his very power on the active support of the officer corps, which in turn has been dominated by the hard-liners."[34] Yet the hardliners were restrained in opposing their superiors by military discipline and the institutional expectation of military unity. In the context of the two political cycles of vacillation between collective and directive leadership and shifting balance of power between first and second tiers, this reciprocating anticipated reactions may lead the balance of influence over policy to shift between first and second tiers. The policy preferences of the second tier should receive greater consideration from a collective leadership, but the policy preferences of leaders should receive greater consideration from interests as a single leader consolidates directive rule.

Among the important implications of this model of normal authoritarian politics is what it predicts about the chances of policy reform under different forms of authoritarianism. Under stable bureaucratic reciprocal accountability reform may be extraordinarily difficult. This is paradoxical because many such regimes fashion themselves vanguards of change— be it toward socialism in the Soviet Union or Chicago-school capitalism in Latin America—and use their power initially to transform politics, economics, and societies. Yet, once the policy priorities of the restricted selectorate become the new status quo, these authoritarian polities find it difficult to subsequently reform their initial objectives and means. The pressures for policy change emanating from a static selectorate are likely to be more limited than are the pressures from a more open and changing selectorate. Under a stable restrictive selectorate policy reform may only come with changes in the preferences of existing selectors. Yet, this is particularly unlikely where the selectors sit by virtue of their positions in bureaucracies performing assigned static functions. In these circumstances the greatest hope for reform, in a most perverse twist, may be the rise of a despot insulated from the constraints of the selectorate and its bureaucratic missions.

AUTHORITARIAN CONSTITUTIONAL DYNAMICS

Normal authoritarian politics are nested in a constitutional game that governs the shape of the selectorate and its relationship to the policymakers. Constitutions constrain human choice in the game of normal politics, yet they themselves are products of games and strategic choices. The nesting of these games is manifest in their mutual influence. Because outcomes in the constitutional game influence outcomes in the principal game, players may enter the constitutional game in order to influence the outcome in the principal arena.[35] And vice versa, because outcomes in the principal arena change the stakes in the constitutional game, players make strategic moves in the principal arena so as to influence constitutional outcomes. Two constitutional issues are central to the survival of bureaucratic reciprocal accountability: the composition of the selectorate and its relationship to the policymakers. The constitutional development that makes such changes less likely is the process of institutionalization. Let me address each of these three constitutional developments in turn.

Oligarchs' Dilemma

The most important constitutional issue facing authoritarian regimes concerns the distribution of the franchise. Political actors may seek advantage in normal politics by expanding the franchise. Short of this, they may mobilize unenfranchised participants into the political process. For example, many modern military regimes in Latin America create what Fernando Henrique Cardoso calls a "counterbalancing system" between selectors and participants: the selectorate is the armed forces, but in routine policymaking the most important participants are the technicians of the bureaucracy.[36] Latin American political leaders use the unenfranchised bureaucrats to attempt to limit the influence of the military. In Chile, for example, while Pinochet strengthened his hand against the junta by relying on the civilian bureaucrats, his fellow junta member Air Force General Gustavo Leigh responded with a proposal to expand the selectorate by a return to democracy.[37]

The history of exclusive polities is filled with examples of policymakers expanding the political arena in order to change outcomes in the principal political games. For example, in the early American Republic, Jeffersonian "Republicans fought more strenuously for suffrage reform in the north than they did in the south, partly because they were endeavoring to increase their strength in a territory where Federalism for many years was as much a 'natural' phenomenon as Republicanism was in the south." "In self-defense, some Federalists shortsightedly opposed suffrage reform."[38] In Germany, after careful consideration of the likely voting habits of common folk, Otto von Bismarck and his conservative allies in 1867 advocated universal manhood suffrage, while liberals urged property qualifications for the suffrage.[39] In Brazil after 1964, the military regime was torn almost from the beginning between hardliners and moderates. The former sought to postpone elections, while the latter were inclined to expand the political process by including popularly elected civilian politicians. Alfred Stepan argues that, if left unchecked, a consequence of these diverging positions would be "growing pressure for an authoritarian nationalist coup at one end of the ideological spectrum and, at the other, for an extrication coup aimed at holding elections and returning power to civilians."[40] Redemocratization in the 1980s, in fact, came as General Ernesto Geisel sought to stop the erosion of the position of the general-president and his staff and reached out for allies in civil society so as to counterbalance the rising power of the security community within the military regime.[41]

The intersection of primary and constitutional games also raises the issue of constricting the franchise. Where it requires a consensus within the selectorate to exclude some of its own members, this is probably more difficult to engineer than expansion. Nonetheless, the restrictions on Black voters in the American South after Reconstruction and the exclusion of voters by Latin American militaries are evidence that limitations can constitute a powerful strategic move. Constriction of the franchise is easier where access to the constitutional game is more exclusive than membership in the selectorate. That is, participation in the primary game does not necessarily confer access to the constitutional game. For example, the military in a number of Latin American republics has played a gatekeeper role determining who would have access to the political process. In Peru the military sometimes limited membership in the selectorate to itself: In the 1975 Peruvian presidential succession the effective election of Morales Bermudez entailed "initial pronouncements by key army commanders, followed by separate declarations by the navy, air force, and police in support of the pronouncements" all published in the press—a form of balloting by op-ed.[42] At other times the Peruvian military delegated the choice to the adult population in open elections. Nonetheless, the military determined whether the electoral process would remain open or closed; the military monopolized the most important choices in the constitutional game governing suffrage.

Changing the franchise frequently changes the policy agenda and the allocation of policy benefits.[43] In the Third World where the rural majority has been mobilized into politics there has been a significant shift in policy. Samuel P. Huntington notes that with "ruralizing elections" in Ceylon (1956), Turkey (1950), Burma (1960), Senegal (1951), Jamaica (1944), and Lesotho (1965) policies of major parties shifted to accommodate the priorities of the new voters. These included shifts in resource allocations to rural roads and farm subsidies and changes in cultural policies such as language and religion favored by the new rural voters.[44]

In authoritarian politics, players may actually enter the constitutional game so as to change the preferences that must be taken into consideration in the principal game. For example, political elites with agendas likely to be opposed by significant parts of the population have sought to narrow the selectorate and participants. Labeling this strategy "political exclusion," Guillermo A. O'Donnell explains that in bureaucratic authoritarianism "such exclusion means consistent governmental refusal to meet the political demands made by the leaders of this sector."[45] In Argentina technocrats sought to exclude much of the population from participation so that they could pursue their modernization program. Thomas E. Skidmore explains the success of Brazil's economic stabilization policies after 1965 by the ability of the military regime to ignore public opposition: "the principal constraint removed by the authoritarian system was popular pressure. Popular mobilization, whether through elections, strikes, or street demonstrations, was sharply curtailed, sometimes by heavy-handed repression." Thus, the Brazilian regime had much greater freedom to shift the financial burden of public policy onto workers and the rural masses; this produced a real decline in their living standards, even as "other sectors such as the officer corps and foreign investors, who were well placed to pressure the government, have gained."[46] Robert Bates argues that with the effective exclusion of rural populations from African politics "governments remove proposals for comprehensive reforms from the political agenda and forbid organized efforts to alter the collective fate of the disadvantaged."[47] This exclusion from politics permits African governments to pursue policies that favor industry at the expense of agriculture, urban populations at the expense of their country cousins, and large farmers at the expense of small peasants.

Authoritarianism may be unusually fragile because this constitutional game governing suffrage is a prisoners' dilemma among oligarchs. Each oligarch is tempted to expand the political game by including one's own allies or partisans.[48] For oligarchs losing in the primary game, selective expansion of the selectorate may lead to better outcomes—as long as others do not also succeed at including their own partisans or allies. For each oligarch the worst outcome would result if others mobilized their partisans while the oligarch did not. More desirable than this, but certainly less desirable than the original exclusive polity would be the outcome in which each side had expanded the polity with its own partisans; with no change in outcome in the primary game, oligarchs would have sacrificed their exclusive rights. Owing to the constant temptation for oligarchs to defect, the oligarchs' dilemma contains a threat of authoritarian collapse.[49] This fragility is illustrated by the frequency of defections within exclusive elites during ruralizing elections in Third World polities with competitive party systems: In ruralizing elections, according to Huntington, typically the leader of the party reaching out to the countryside was "a former member of the modernizing elite who, in effect, broke from the elite and espoused more popular and traditional appeals."[50]

The oligarchs' dilemma can powerfully shape subsequent constitutional development. Anticipating this fragility, players may seek rules to prevent defection by their fellow oligarchs. For example, to reduce the value of allies outside the participant population, the leadership may strengthen rules limiting access by the subject population to the means of participation. Similarly, to create early warning signals that deter defection, rules may require leaders to submit all their public speeches and publications to prior censorship by the collective. Failure to develop such rules to reinforce the oligarchy can lead to the breakdown of authoritarianism.

Transforming Accountability

A second constitutional issue that can transform authoritarianism concerns accountability between policymakers and selectors. Actors in each tier often seek to establish greater influence over the other tier and to limit their own accountability. The interplay of these pressures may establish or reinforce reciprocal accountability, but these pressures may also transform either hierarchy or reciprocity into the other. This change does not threaten authoritarianism, but it can convert one form of authoritarianism such as bureaucratic authoritarianism into another such as despotism.

The structure of accountability shapes the strategies of actors. In hierarchies principals may seek to design rules that ensure their interests will be promoted by their agents, that payoffs are made only for desired outcomes, and that the delegation relationship continues only as long as the principal's interests are served. Agents may seek rules that increase their discretion in choosing means to achieve the payoff, decrease the chances they will be deprived of payoff for undesired outcomes that are not consequences of their actions, and give them greater security of tenure as agents.[51] In reciprocity these strategies of principals and agents become compounded.

This interplay of strategies in reciprocal accountability is illustrated by the attempts of leaders and bureaucrats to increase the accountability of the other tier and to limit their own accountability. First, actors in each tier can attempt to increase the obstacles to collective action within the other tier and thereby increase the other tier's dependence and diminish its ability to enforce control. For example, leaders may expand the membership of the selectorate not only to include more of their own loyalists, but also to make it more difficult for the selectorate to act together against the first tier. The selectorate in turn can seek to strengthen its own position by rules that reinforce collective leadership in the first tier against the onslaught of a consolidating leader. Second, each side can seek to reduce the personnel control of the other. Leaders may seek security of tenure by the invention of such offices as president-for-life. Selectors who are bureaucrats may seek regulations that guarantee nonpolitical criteria for retention and promotion.

In the interplay of these strategies, the competing pressures from first and second tiers may force compromises that institutionalize reciprocal accountability. Yet, these pressures need not be evenly balanced, and they can lead to a breakdown of reciprocal accountability by transforming it into hierarchy. This transformation does not in itself undermine authoritarianism, but it leads to different authoritarian structures.

Institutionalization

The constitutive rules of an authoritarian regime come to resist significant change as a consequence of the process of institutionalization. Constitutions like other institutions rest on the stable coordination of mutual expectations. Actors act according to rules when each expects others will act according to the rules as well. As Thomas C. Schelling describes such games, "it is a behavior situation in which each player's best choice of action depends on the action he expects the other to take, which he knows depends, in turn, on the other's expectation of his own."[52] In these circumstances constitutions govern behavior the more mutual expectations reinforce one another. The rules of constitutions become stronger as they establish focal points of converging mutual expectations that constrain the strategic choices of political actors who must consider how others will act.

Schelling argues that the focal points for these converging expectations are characterized by prominence or conspicuousness that makes the focal point stand out from alternatives.[53] This focal point may be provided by a formal document, custom rooted in explicit agreements reached sometime in the past, or some shared principles of appropriateness; yet constitutions need not correspond to explicit codes. The constitutive rules of Soviet politics from 1953 to 1986 constrained the strategic choices of political actors, but they bore only tenuous relationship to the Stalin Constitution of 1936 or the Brezhnev Constitution of 1977.

The coordination of mutual expectations becomes a critical issue because the rules of new authoritarian polities are frequently at first characterized by indeterminacy concerning the relationships among players. For example, in the early Soviet polity the formal positions of leaders did not provide them with guaranteed powers. Vladimir Lenin's relationship to other members of the leadership was in no way defined by his position as chairman of the Council of People's Commissars. The power of the general secretary, from which Joseph Stalin rose to despotism, was not foreseen by those who created the post. The division of powers among the leading organs of Communist party and state was ambiguous, leading to considerable overlap of responsibilities. In particular, the relationship of the Party's bureaucracy to the Politburo remained equivocal.[54]

As Samuel P. Huntington stresses, the stability of a political order depends on its institutionalization. The indeterminacy in young authoritarian polities must be reduced by the coordination of mutual expectations about the rules of the game. Institutionalization is the process by which mutual expectations concerning behavioral roles and relationships deepen and become reinforcing.[55] Drawing on Huntington's discussion, we can say that institutionalization is promoted when mutual expectations become more complex and involve more political actors; these expectations become internally coherent and reinforcing among individuals, insofar as these expectations are consistent with expectations in other realms of behavior.[56] Huntington treats these dimensions as covarying, yet, as I discuss in the following chapters, they need not be.

By reducing the indeterminacy of power in an authoritarian regime, institutionalization reduces the vacillation between collective and directive leadership, the shifting power between first and second tiers, and the cycles of policy that accompany these. Institutionalization promotes the stability of a constitutional structure. The more consensus on the rules, the more coherence within the rules, the more consistency between the rules of politics and the rules of other realms of behavior, the greater the stability of the rules of politics. Among the important implications of this is what it predicts about the dangers of institutionalization for the reform of authoritarianism. In particular, institutionalization may lead to stagnation in authoritarianism. Exclusive selectorates, particularly those based on bureaucracies assigned static tasks, are less adaptable. Exclusive polities sometimes seek to adapt to social changes by conscious choice to expand the oligarchy or to change its composition; in this way it can incorporate new social forces or expertise. Yet, in a well-institutionalized authoritarian regime, each such expansion is a difficult political decision. Unlike democracies, which extend the franchise to all adults, the cooptation of new social forces is not automatic; authoritarian polities may not institutionalize routine reform through automatic changes in the selectorate that reflects social change. If institutionalization means making an authoritarian polity stable, it may also be the most important threat to the long-term survival of such regimes. I explore this theme more fully in later chapters.

NOT A THEORY, BUT A MODEL

This chapter has presented an abstract model of authoritarian polities that serves as a basis for subsequent analysis. This structural model identifies the major roles and relationships within these polities. It draws our attention to the structure of policymaking power and the accountability of those holding this power. On this basis it highlights the major dynamics within the nested games of normal politics and constitutional politics.

This abstraction is a model rather than a theory—the necessary step prior to the development of specific theories and the deduction of hypotheses. Models identify what is central, what is peripheral, and some likely relationship among the elements that are important. Unlike the hypotheses of theories that might be derived from it, a model is never directly tested. The measure of a model is not its truth or falsity, for as abstractions models are by definition untrue; these little white lies about reality provide us cognitive maps to think about complexity.[57] The measure of a model is its utility—whether it gives us some analytic purchase on the many problems that are well understood, previously unanswered, and hitherto unseen.

There are a number of ways in which to explore the utility of a model such as this. The long-term objective is to derive specific theories and test these against a broad range of cases. Yet a more practical strategy in an early exploratory stage such as this is to use the model for a richer, close analysis of a single case. This strategy permits the analyst to challenge and expand the conceptual tools of the model as it moves into new realms, to assess whether the model does give us new explanatory power in a range of new issues. Moreover, because political scientists are most commonly engaged in the analysis of single cases (or comparison of cases analyzed seriatim), this strategy permits the analyst to assess the utility of the model for those tasks that political scientists undertake most often. What follows is a case study of one of the twentieth century's most important authoritarian failures—the collapse of the constitution of Bolshevism.

_____ CHAPTER THREE _____

Creating the
Constitution of Bolshevism,
1917–1953

THE CONSTITUTION of Bolshevism was rooted in a search for a political order that would permit the new Soviet regime to engineer a thorough-going revolution in social existence. "Give us an organization of revolutionaries," Lenin had proclaimed, "and we will overturn Russia!" The organization of revolutionaries was to guide the transition from capitalism to communism—not only in the revolutionary seizure of power, but also in the subsequent remaking of society. After Lenin's party took power in 1917 this conception of a vanguard party guided the Bolsheviks as they created political institutions.

These decisions resulted in a very different outcome—an authoritarian constitution based on reciprocal accountability between politicians and bureaucrats. The full implication of these early choices was not immediately apparent; it only became clear in the subsequent play of politics. Yet, the decisions that constituted the Soviet regime set the most fundamental rules of normal politics for decades to follow. For the political actors empowered by these rules, they also created opportunities to be exploited and threats to be guarded against. Thus, these early choices set the agenda for subsequent institutional development.

This chapter examines these choices that defined the constitutive rules of the Soviet polity—the constitution of Bolshevism. I emphasize the structuring aspects of those rules and the consequences of the structuring rules for politics. This chapter is divided into three parts. The first examines the choices that established key formal and informal rules in the first four years of Soviet power. The second part surveys the rules' implications that unfolded in the next three decades and set the major issues on the agenda of constitutional politics. The third compares this picture of Soviet politics with three major analytic approaches previously suggested by western Sovietologists. In this chapter I argue that the model of the authoritarian constitution in the previous chapter permits us to bring together these other, more specific approaches in an inclusive synthesis.

THE BOLSHEVIKS' CONSTITUTIVE
CHOICES, 1917–1921

The Bolsheviks' self-styled role as vanguard of the working class informed their choices as they crafted the constitution of their new political order. The political concomitant of their transformational mission was a four-part institution-building strategy that emphasized departicipation, delegation, control, and discipline. To play a vanguard role the Party concentrated policymaking power within itself and excluded most of the adult population from participation in the policy process. Yet, its ambitious program of transformation also required an elaborate administrative structure and delegation of significant parts of the Party's transformational mission to bureaucracies outside the Party's core of professional revolutionaries. This delegation worked at cross purposes to departicipation and threatened the vanguard role of the party: While departicipation concentrated policymaking within the leading organs of the Communist party, delegation shared this prerogative with other organs. To maintain its vanguard status, particularly as the demands of governance grew, the Party tightened discipline among its members and developed elaborate controls over the bureaucracy. Thus, the constitution of Bolshevism was shaped by this attempt to balance departicipation and delegation and to constrain delegation by discipline and control.

Departicipation

The vanguard role of the Party, as Lenin argued, meant that the Communist party must not become dependent on the working classes' spontaneous impulses and instead must bring to the proletariat true class consciousness and direct its political activity.[1] This became the basis for an exclusionary polity that eliminated from society almost all associational ties that could serve as bases for collective action independent of the Communist party.

This forced departicipation was accomplished through four policies—liquidation, intimidation, reeducation, and demobilization of significant parts of the previously participant population. Liquidation meant physical removal from the political system—particularly through forced emigration, incarceration, or simply murder. This liquidation sought to remove the old order's participant stratum from the new Leninist society. The victims of the Bolshevik secret police or *Cheka* were disproportionately activists and those who by their socioeconomic status were identifiable as potential participants—officials of the old regime and representatives of the former nobility, bourgeoisie, landowners, and clergy.[2] Intimidation deterred from political action those members of the old order's participant population who were not liquidated.[3] A major instrument of intimidation was police terror directed at the population with the education, skills, psychological orientations, and organizational ties that might incline them to participate. Reeducation of the socially mobilized population sought to force departicipation by manipulating the subjective bases of individual political efficacy and group consciousness.[4] For this the Bolsheviks adapted instruments of agitation and propaganda originally developed in the struggle to seize power. Demobilization meant removing the organizational bases for unofficial political action by eliminating independent organizations.[5] Through these four policies the Bolsheviks leveled political society; they left few if any bases for independent political action outside the new political institutions.

In less than a half decade between November 1917 and early 1922, the Bolsheviks forced underground almost all opposition political activity. Within one year of the Bolshevik seizure of power the few non-Communist political organizations that managed to subsist just outside the lengthening shadow of illegality were impotent.[6] Starting with the ban of the Constitutional Democratic party (Kadets) and arrest of its leaders on 11 December 1917 the Bolsheviks began to decapitate and dismember other parties. By the end of that month the Bolsheviks began to arrest leaders of the Right Socialist Revolutionary party (Right SRs) and the Russian Social Democratic Labor party (Mensheviks). By 15 March 1918 they had excluded other parties from the cabinet and then proceeded to remove them from the legislative bodies. In May 1921 Lenin announced the beginning of the final assault: "We shall keep the Mensheviks and SRs (whether they are now open or disguised as 'nonpartisans') in prison."[7]

To enforce departicipation the regime established a monopoly over the resources necessary to mobilize sustained, large-scale political action. Beginning with the press decree of 9 November 1917 the Bolsheviks suppressed all hostile newspapers and began to harass those of legal parties. In the summer of 1918 liberal and socialist newspapers were closed. By the end of 1922 the government had established a monopoly over the distribution of paper and presses and had created a state publishing house (*Gosizdat'*) that began to take over all provincial publishing monopolies.[8] The Party also resolved to control all associational life. Its March 1919 Congress proclaimed: "The Communist party sets itself the task of winning the decisive influence and entire leadership in all organizations of the working people: in the trade unions, the cooperatives, agricultural communes, etc."[9] In short, departicipation, depriving most of the adult population of independent access to the resources needed for sustained collective political action, gave the Party a monopoly over these.

Delegation

The complex tasks of engineering economic, social, and cultural transformation confronted the Party with a dilemma: If the Party assumed all the tasks of governance, including the daily administration of social affairs, it could dilute its vanguard status. Its core of professional revolutionaries might lose their vision and élan as they confronted mundane specialized tasks. Vladimir I. Lenin had seen this problem as early as 1902. In the tract *What Is To Be Done?* he argued that in the revolutionary struggle prior to the seizure of power the Party would maintain its leading revolutionary role only by giving dominant weight in its membership to professional revolutionaries. To reach out to the larger proletariat the Party must surround itself with "the most diverse organizations of all kinds, ranks, and hues," but this movement led by the Party would remain outside its formal organization.[10] Once in power this precedent served as a model for the Party to maintain its vanguard status while governing: The Party would maintain its separate organization in which professional revolutionaries would dominate; dependent, but separate agencies such as the state and public organizations would enable the Party to carry out the many specialized tasks of social transformation.

In 1917 the effective policymaking center for the Party between meetings of its Congress had been the Central Committee, the group that reached the decision to seize power in the name of the proletariat on 7 November 1917. With the success of this October Revolution, the Central Committee had to decide what new organizational structures it would create to carry out the tasks of governance and social transformation.

The structure of the state emerged in a series of decrees and was made formal in the first Soviet Constitution of 10 July 1918. Despite criticisms of bourgeois parliamentary institutions and the announced intention to establish Soviet political institutions on a different model, the Bolsheviks responded to the tasks of governance by creating a state structure that resembled parliamentary democracies. As figure 3.1 shows, the All-Russian Congress of Soviets (legislature), composed of delegations from provincial legislatures (soviets), would exercise supreme authority, but the congress would delegate its powers between sessions to its Central Executive Committee (*VTsIK*). The latter would in turn delegate daily decision-making to the cabinet or Council of Peoples' Commissars (*Sovnarkom*).[11]

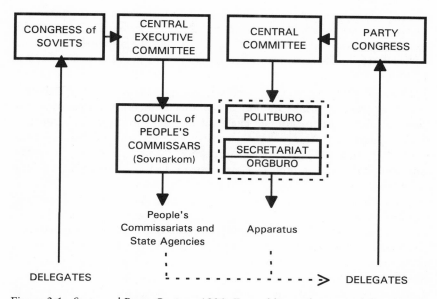

Figure 3.1. State and Party Organs, 1920. Formal lines of accountability among organs are indicated by solid lines, and the reciprocal accountability that resulted from bureaucratic domination of Party Congress delegations is indicated by broken lines.

The new tasks of governance also required a more complex Party structure. Prior to March 1919, Communist delegates from local Party organizations assembled periodically in a Congress that made major decisions, delegating responsibility for running the Party between Congresses to its Central Committee. At its 1919 Congress the Party added three agencies for policymaking and executive-administrative tasks—the Politburo, Secretariat, and Orgburo. The Politburo would make policy between Central Committee plenary sessions; the Orgburo and Secretariat would carry out administrative responsibilities.[12]

The Central Committee initially assigned responsibility for implementing the Party's transformational program to the state cabinet or Sovnarkom. With Lenin serving as its chairman (loosely, "premier"), Sovnarkom, reaching its decisions after debate and majority vote of its members, became the effective decisionmaking body for state policy. Sovnarkom enjoyed considerable autonomy in its daily operation, including independence in the appointment of its own members. People's commissars (ministers) established direct authority over former ministries of the

former regime and transformed these into instruments that could implement Bolshevik policies.[13]

The Central Committee delegated to the Orgburo and Secretariat administrative responsibilities for running the Party as an increasingly complex organization. The Orgburo was to direct all the organizational work
of the Party. The Secretariat was responsible for central direction of local
party organizations, including training and assigning cadres to local organs and overseeing registration of all personnel there.[14] The Secretariat
quickly developed a bureaucracy or *apparat* to exercise control over subordinate Party organizations. The staff of the Moscow Secretariat, performing administrative tasks, grew between 1919 and 1921 from 30 to
602; by August 1922 "responsible workers" numbered 325 in the central
and regional bureaus and an estimated 15,000 in provincial and local
organizations.[15]

From their creation the Politburo, Orgburo, and Secretariat operated
in close coordination through their leading personnel. With Lenin's
growing incapacitation, this coordination fell to Joseph Stalin as the leading figure in Orgburo and the only Orgburo member also sitting in the
Politburo. At the 1921 Party Congress the appointment of staunch Stalin
supporters to two of the three secretary posts ensured the close cooperation of Orgburo and Secretariat. Stalin's appointment on 4 April 1922 to
the newly created post of general secretary made him the only person to
sit simultaneously on Orgburo, Secretariat, and Politburo.

Control

Delegation of decisionmaking to nonparty agencies permitted the Party
to assume the tasks of governance and still maintain its vanguard status.
Yet, delegation also created threats to this status by attenuating Party
control over policy. The Party leadership worried that the agents to which
it delegated implementation did not all share the Central Committee's
preferences or priorities. Lenin highlighted this problem in April 1918
when he told the Central Committee, "the 'administrative' elements provide a host of saboteurs and bribe-takers" and bureaucracy houses
"many waverers and 'weak' characters who are unable to withstand the
'temptation' of profiteering, bribery, personal gain obtained by spoiling
the whole apparatus, upon the proper working of which the victory over
famine and unemployment depends."[16] The answer was tighter *kontrol'*,
which translated as accountability and monitoring.

The key to control was the accountability of bureaucratic personnel to
the Central Committee through its powers of appointment and removal.[17]

The Central Committee's instruments for personnel control over both the state bureaucracy and Party apparat were the Orgburo and Secretariat. To control the state bureaucracy, between April 1920 and February 1921 these central party organs reportedly made 1,715 appointments to Sovnarkom positions in Moscow.[18] The 1923 Party Congress approved General Secretary Stalin's plan to expand this involvement in personnel selection in state economic agencies by "studying each worker bone by bone."[19] Thus, in October 1923 the Orgburo introduced the first *nomenklatura* lists of state positions (initially some 5,000 posts) requiring appointment or approval by the Central Committee's organs.[20]

To control lower levels of the Party apparatus the Secretariat exercised broad powers to assign personnel, to recommend victors in elections, and to confirm or invalidate the results of elections. The thoroughness of this control is revealed in its own report that the Secretariat had engaged in "detailed and attentive accounting of the Party's commanding personnel; reassignment of Party forces to strengthen the most important provincial organizations; selection of organizers for Party work, review of the directors of regional, provincial, and county Party organizations and some secretaries of cells; [and] replacement of workers who did not measure up to the standards set forth by the Party Congress."[21] Thus, at the provincial level in 1922 it reported removing or transferring thirty-seven *guberniia* (province) secretaries and making recommendations in forty-two elections. To lower levels of the Party in the same year it made approximately 5,000 assignments of "responsible officials" and at least as many assignments of other personnel.[22]

From the start the Central Committee confronted two problems that students of bureaucracy have argued are central to the delegation relationship. First, the problem of *hidden information* "derives from unobservability of the information, beliefs, and values on which the decisions of others are based." Second, the problem of *hidden action* "arises from the unobservability of actual behavior" of others.[23] These typically call for colonization and oversight.

One response to the problem of the uncertain beliefs and values of bureaucrats (hidden information) was colonization. By populating the bureaucracy with Communists subject to Party discipline, the leadership would increase the prospects that the bureaucracy faithfully executed the Party program. Amos Perlmutter and William LeoGrande have proposed the term "dual-role elite" to describe the resulting pattern of Party members in key bureaucratic posts. Noting that "virtually every official of consequence within nonparty institutions is a party member," they argue that these dual-role elites are "the principal mechanism through which the party maintains its structural position as system integrator and arbiter."[24] Colonization sought to deprive state organs and public organizations of their independence from the Party. For example, in legislative organs Party discipline and overwhelming majorities meant sessions were seldom the occasions for spirited debate or losing votes for cabinet initiatives. Between the Fourth Congress of Soviets (March 1918) and the Seventh (December 1919) the Bolshevik majority grew from 65 to 97 percent.[25] As in most parliamentary systems, such majorities and tight discipline ensured that decisions of the Party's leading organs would be ratified by the government.

Yet, when it came to controlling the state bureaucracies, the small size of the Communist party, the need for expertise in government, and the absence of this expertise from the Party's membership meant that the Party could not simply colonize the whole state; the bureaucracies had to coopt non-Communists into critical positions. A survey conducted in August 1918 in nine commissariats showed that 20 percent of Soviet officials had previously been officials in the prerevolutionary government.[26] This proportion was apparently even higher among senior officials with critical expertise: In a survey of eight commissariats 68.3 percent of senior officials had been officials in the prerevolutionary government.[27] Communists held only a minority of these posts: 18 percent of all officials in the first set of commissariats and 8 percent of senior officials in the second.[28] Moreover, in the 1920s, as the tasks of governance continued to demand expertise, the Party coopted more officials from the old order into the bureaucracy. A survey of government personnel in 1929 showed that among 10,828 national (all-union) executives fully 48.1 percent were holdovers from the tsarist regime, and, in addition, only 28.6 percent were Party members.[29]

The limitations of colonization made even more pressing the need to create mechanisms of oversight. Central Committee control was reinforced by two means of oversight that Mathew McCubbins and Thomas Schwartz have called "police patrols" and "fire alarms."[30] First, the Party created control and monitoring agencies to act as police patrols undertaking active, direct surveillance. The Party leadership defined kontrol' as a problem of monitoring, verifying fulfillment, inspecting, and auditing. It bracketed the bureaucratic elite with an elaborate, redundant supervisory mechanism made up of interdependent systems of party, state, and people's control. Party control through the apparatus enforced party discipline, managed personnel assignments, and monitored fulfillment of Party policy to guarantee Party guidance within all agencies. State control through Sovnarkom's ministerial bureaucracy maintained both an intradepartmental chain of command within each agency and specialized "external" monitoring bodies such as the police and public prosecutor (Procuracy). Popular control mobilized citizen volunteers in the task of inspection. Initially, "external" state control was primarily the responsibility of the People's Commissariat of State Control—a ministry inherited from the tsarist regime; popular control was the province of workers' inspectorates that sprang up under trade unions. With the creation in 1920 of the People's Commissariat of Workers' and Peasants' Inspection (*Rabkrin*) state and popular control were increasingly coordinated and then subordinated to Party direction.[31]

Second, in a form of "fire alarm" oversight, the Party permitted individuals who charged an agency with violation of Party policy to seek remedies from the Central Committee. To ensure its leadership the Central Committee gave to losing minorities in the Sovnarkom the right to appeal its decision to the Central Committee. This appeal became so common that in 1922 Lenin suggested limits to its use: "We cannot formally abrogate the right to appeal to the CC, because our party is the sole government party. What we must nip in the bud is any attempt to appeal over trifles."[32] Yet this right of appeal was a guarantee of the ultimate authority of the Central Committee over the state bureaucracy.

Discipline

The tasks of governance confronted the Party with new threats to its unity of action. With the establishment of its leading role within agencies, the Party faced growing diversity of purposes within its own membership and within the Central Committee itself. Already in 1921, Nikolai Bukharin observed,

> The party as it existed earlier when there was a single psychology and a single ideology has split into a variety of separate columns representing different outlooks. Military workers, trade union workers, and party workers proper have organized together among themselves. . . . This specialization has split our party, which was earlier psychologically united in a single whole, into a series of groupings with different psychological tendencies.[33]

The problem of growing diversity in the Party was compounded by the decision to coopt leading bureaucrats into the Party. The pressures of limited expertise even led the Party to coopt into its own membership many senior bureaucrats who had been employees of the tsarist government. Among the 10,828 national government executives surveyed in 1929, holdovers from the tsarist government represented 41.6 percent of the Party members in the survey.[34]

The Bolsheviks' response to this growing diversity of purpose was stronger Party discipline. The ultimate sanction enforcing this discipline was the control of the Central Committee's majority over Party membership. The 1921 Party Congress (March) adopted the Resolution "On Party Unity" that in Point 7 prescribed:

> In order to ensure strict discipline within the Party and in all Soviet work and to secure the maximum unanimity in removing all fractionalism, the Congress authorizes the Central Committee, in cases of breach of discipline or of a revival or toleration of fractionalism, to apply all Party penalties, including expulsion, and in regard to members of the Central Committee to reduce them to the state of alternative [nonvoting] members and even, as an extreme measure, to expel them from the Party.[35]

This unity was enforced through rules to silence dissenting minorities, prohibit factions, and centralize authority over local organizations

First, rules establishing strict majoritarianism in Party affairs silenced minorities. The first post-Revolution party rules adopted in December 1919 prescribed that "the strictest Party discipline is the primary duty of all Party members and all Party organizations."[36] After a decision was reached, debate must end and dissenters must both remain silent and carry out the majority's will.

A second response to strengthen unity of action was a rule proscribing organized factions within the Party. The first three years of Soviet power saw the emergence of opposition groups within the Party as various constituencies objected to leadership decisions. The Left Communists in 1918, the Military Opposition in 1919, and the Workers' Opposition and Democratic Centralists in 1920 debated Party policies in local organizations and Party Congresses and sought representation in the Party's leading organs by offering candidates supporting their platforms. Factions that could appeal to the Party membership for support threatened to create within the Party the multiparty system that the Bolsheviks sought to extinguish outside it. Even more threatening was the temptation of these factions to appeal outside the Party membership for support. The resolution on party unity proscribed such groups:

> The congress orders the immediate dissolution, without exception, of all groups that have formed on the basis of some platform or other and instructs all organizations to be very strict in ensuring that no fractional manifestations of any sort are tolerated. Failure to comply with this resolution of the congress will lead to unconditional and immediate expulsion from the party.[37]

Third, the center ensured unity of action by centralizing control over local party organizations. The Party rules adopted in December 1919 reaffirmed the principle of "democratic centralism": decisions reached at the center were strictly binding on all lower-level organizations of the

Party. The rules permitted open discussion by Party members in lower organizations only up to the point the Party's central organs had rendered a decision. Then "the decisions of the party center must be implemented quickly and precisely" (Rule 50).[38] The center could enforce this through its tight control over all party personnel decisions and all expenditures: According to the rules, the center "distributes the forces and funds of the party" (Rule 24) and must confirm the election of all leading organs of lower levels of the Party (Rule 18). The penalty for violations of central directives included dissolution of lower party organizations (Rule 51). Thus, in 1920 the Central Committee in Moscow dismissed the Ukrainian Central Committee elected at the Ukrainian Party Congress, and in 1921 it dismissed the party committee in Samara province; in both instances it picked the successors.[39]

In short, these early choices shaped the processes of politics and political change. In these decisions, the Bolsheviks established several directives: (1) the means of collective political action would be a monopoly of the Communist party; (2) the Party's leading organs would delegate to a complex bureaucracy implementation of significant parts of the Party's transformational mission; (3) the Central Committee would maintain control over these agents through strict accountability of personnel in the bureaucracy; and (4) within the Party unity of action would be maintained through strict discipline. In these rules were the answers to the most fundamental constitutional questions: Who would be the effective policymakers? Who would select the effective decisionmakers? Who would select the selectors? In these rules were the foundations for an authoritarian constitution based on reciprocal accountability between policymakers and bureaucrats.

THE UNFOLDING CONSTITUTIONAL
CONSEQUENCES, 1921–1953

These early choices not only set the rules of normal politics, but they also set the trajectory of the constitution's subsequent development. Yet, the consequences of these early choices were not all immediately apparent; they emerged in the subsequent play of politics. In addition, the consequences were not always what the designers of these rules had intended. Their full import became clear only with the succession struggle that began in 1921 as Lenin was increasingly incapacitated by a series of strokes. The interplay of succession politics and the rules of Soviet politics revealed three structural features of the constitution of Bolshevism: a shifting policy center, reciprocal accountability between these policy centers and bureaucrats, and a leadership consolidation cycle. Because these structural features afforded unequal strategic advantages to some players and contained threats for others, they set the agenda for subsequent constitutional development.

The Shifting Policy Center

The locus of policymaking under the constitution of Bolshevism was not fixed but vacillated among a set of organs with the changing configuration of power in the leadership. As is common in authoritarian constitutions, the constitution of Bolshevism was founded on the principle of collective leadership and created a body for joint decisionmaking—called the Politburo rather than junta—in which leaders could be balanced to represent constituencies in the selectorate. Yet, the policymaking prerogatives of this body could be threatened by the changing configuration of power in the first tier. On the one hand, with consolidation of directive leadership a single member of the collectivity had strong incentive to seek to transcend the constraints of the collectivity by transferring at least some decisionmaking to other forums, particularly the executive agencies of the state. On the other hand, with extreme conflict among leaders, the collective body could become paralyzed, forcing it to defer decisions to the selectorate itself.

Lenin demonstrated that a strong leader could transcend many limits of collective leadership. Lenin was a master of selecting the forum—be it Sovnarkom, Politburo, Central Committee, or Congress—that would give him a favorable response to his initiatives. Most important, he presided over a division of policymaking responsibilities between the state cabinet (Sovnarkom) and the Party's Politburo, in which he served as the critical coordinating figure. During Lenin's active tenure as premier, Sovnarkom remained a vital policymaking center that guided the Soviet state bureaucracy. Yet, with Lenin's growing incapacitation after 1921 and the beginning of the succession struggle, policymaking shifted to the Politburo and Central Committee. This shift was largely attributable to divisions within the Party leadership, the growing importance of new Central Committee constituencies, and the fact that some of these leaders and constituencies found Sovnarkom an unacceptable forum for policymaking. Sovnarkom had become paralyzed.

With Lenin's growing incapacitation, Party leaders began to position themselves for a succession. For some of these leaders Sovnarkom was a less advantageous playing field than the Central Committee, and so their partisans forced stalemates within Sovnarkom by exploiting the rule that permitted losing minorities to appeal their case to the Central Committee where they expected a more favorable outcome. During Lenin's long absences the number of such appeals jumped. It had become difficult to contain the succession struggle within Sovnarkom because leading players in the succession had built their power bases in bureaucracies outside Sovnarkom and were pursuing a strategy of pitting their bureaucratic constituencies against Sovnarkom. Most important, while Trotsky's power base was in Sovnarkom's bureaucracies, Stalin's was in the Party apparatus. Beginning at the 1922 Party Congress Trotsky, criticizing the growth of Party apparatus control over state officials in the provinces, brought a latent institutional conflict to the fore. He continued the attack the following year and in an open letter to party meetings charged it was time "to 'renew the party apparatus' [and] 'replace the mummified bureaucrats by fresh elements.' "[40] Stalin counterattacked at the January 1924 All-Russian Party Conference, where he rallied a majority at the conference by jumping to the defense of his allies in the apparatus, indicting Trotsky for attempting to place "the Party apparatus in opposition to the Party," and proclaiming that the Party is "unthinkable without the apparatus."[41]

Growth of powerful agencies outside the central bureaucracies of Sovnarkom—particularly growth of the party apparatus and provincial governments—was shifting the balance among constituencies in the Central Committee. As figure 3.2 shows, between 1922 and 1923 among full (voting) members of the Central Committee, the balance of power between members drawn from the state bureaucracy and those from the Party apparatus began to shift; similarly, the balance between members drawn from the central organs in Moscow and those from the regional or local organs shifted. From 1923 to 1927, about half the members were from the Party bureaucracy and about half from outside Moscow.[42]

Yet, these new constituencies could not be easily incorporated into Sovnarkom: Enlargement of Sovnarkom to incorporate these constituencies would have come at the expense of the specialized tasks of guiding the state bureaucracy. In addition, Sovnarkom did not represent a level playing field for the interests outside the central state bureaucracy. Any future delegation of policymaking by the Central Committee was likely to be to a body in which these constituencies could be represented alongside the Sovnarkom leadership.

In short, appeals from Sovnarkom to the Central Committee were encouraged because Sovnarkom contained neither the interests represented in the succession struggle nor the balance of constituencies in the Committee. Sovnarkom could serve as an effective policymaking body only as long as it could faithfully reflect the interests caught up in the succession struggle. As soon as major constituencies in the Central Committee were excluded from Sovnarkom, it became paralyzed by appeals.

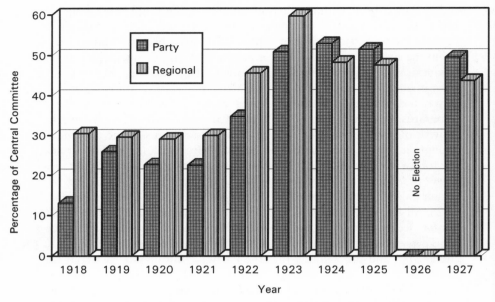

Figure 3.2. Composition of Central Committee, 1918–1927: Proportion Holding Office in Party Apparatus and Regions outside Moscow

The Politburo, alternatively, had more balanced representation of the Party, state, and public-organization bureaucracies. In 1923, for example, only three of the seven Politburo members—the premier, head of economic administration, and defense minister—had their primary office in the central state organs, while the general secretary and head of the Comintern sat in the central party apparatus, the chairman of the trade unions was in a public organization and Moscow's mayor headed local government.[43] The Politburo was an organ where leaders of chief Central Committee constituencies could meet. It is not surprising that with the shift from more directive to collective leadership policymaking shifted from Sovnarkom to Politburo.

Yet, as the leadership conflict grew, this paralyzed even the Politburo itself. The most controversial issues were transferred from the Politburo to the Central Committee—once again to secure factional advantage in the Central Committee that was not represented in the Politburo's composition. Particularly with the rapid growth of the contingent of local party secretaries in the Central Committee, Stalin found it advantageous to rally his constituency in the larger body. As Graeme Gill observes, "In institutional terms this cast the CC in the role of arbiter between the contending sides of a split Politburo, thereby reinforcing the principle of the accountability of the latter to the former."[44]

The temporal sequence from 1921 to 1924 progressed from a strong leader (Lenin) eclipsing the power of the Politburo, to stable collective leadership giving the Politburo greater authority, and then to intense conflict leading to its paralysis and dependence on the Central Committee. This sequence was reversed with the rise of Joseph Stalin: With the moderation of conflict, policymaking shifted back to the Politburo, but as Stalin sought to place himself above the constraints of the collectivity policymaking once again shifted away from the Politburo and was dispersed among several leading organs. In a somewhat paradoxical fashion, while stable collective leadership seemed to be associated with greater concentration of policymaking in a single organ, directive leadership was associated with dispersal of decisionmaking among organs. The key was, of course, that the latter pattern permitted the directive leader to choose his forum, play one decisionmaking body against another, and serve as the key coordinator.

Stalin revealed the extent to which the rules of the constitution of Bolshevism permitted a single leader at the peak of consolidation to set himself above not only the Politburo but also the Central Committee. In his last decade Stalin increasingly bypassed both Politburo and Central Committee, and at the peak of his power Stalin did not rely on any single body but played one against another.[45] During the Second World War Stalin brought his primary advisers together in the State Defense Council. After the war, by a decree of 5 September 1945, many of its responsibilities devolved upon Sovnarkom, and with the March 1946 reorganization of this cabinet as the Council of Ministers, much of this responsibility was concentrated in its inner working body—the Presidium of the Council of Ministers. By the end of Stalin's rule institutional arrangements began to resemble those under Lenin: The state cabinet, from which some Party leaders (notably Andrei Zhdanov and Nikita Khrushchev) were excluded, was the focus for many important policy discussions.[46]

At the peak of Stalin's directive rule, the Politburo itself was seldom convened as a whole. According to Nikita Khrushchev, Stalin arbitrarily excluded some members from its meetings: For example, Stalin personally forbade Kliment Ye. Voroshilov from attending for several years: "When the Politburo was in session and Comrade Voroshilov heard about it, he telephoned each time and asked whether he would be allowed to attend." Many decisions were taken by specialized subsets of the Politburo—the famous "quintets" and "sextets"— that kept their deliberations from each other. Stalin introduced plans at the 1952 Party Congress that would have further displaced the Politburo, by substituting an enlarged Presidium and creating a shadowy, handpicked inner working body—the Bureau of the Presidium of the Central Committee.[47]

Thus, the early choices of the Bolsheviks created a constitutional structure that led to a shifting locus of policymaking. The concentration of policymaking in a single organ under stable collective leadership permitted the leaders of key bureaucratic constituencies to exercise their will as a collectivity and to constrain each other. The dispersal of policymaking among organs under directive leadership expanded the premier leader's discretion in selecting the forum in which to discuss policy. By fragmenting the collective leadership, this latter pattern limited the constraints on the premier leader.

Growth of Reciprocal Accountability

The Bolsheviks' early choices set the stage for the emergence of reciprocal accountability between politicians and bureaucrats. The policy of colonizing key bureaucratic positions outside the Party and coopting the leading cadres of those agencies into the Central Committee resulted in the leaders of key bureaucratic agencies selecting the leading organs of Party and state. Yet, the leaders sitting in the Sovnarkom, Politburo, and Secretariat-Orgburo also served as the heads of specific bureaucracies, and each enjoyed considerable discretion to shape at least part of the bureaucratic selectorate to which they were accountable. Reciprocal accountability meant that the leadership and key bureaucrats depended upon one another for their tenure of office.

Cooptation of bureaucrats into the Central Committee became institutionalized in what Robert V. Daniels has called "job slot representation." Rules—whether informal or just never publicized remains unclear—dating back to the 1920s guaranteed Central Committee seats to the holders of specific bureaucratic offices.[48] With remarkable predictability the bureaucratic post normally brought this status so that a change of incumbent brought a change of representative in the Central Committee.

As is true in parliamentary systems, Party leaders assumed key bureaucratic posts. Thus, for example, Leon Trotsky from 1918 to 1925 led the military first as People's Commissar of Military Affairs and then as chairman of the military council. With the growth of bureaucratic constituencies within the Central Committee this link between Party leadership and bureaucrats became reciprocal as Party members came to build their power on these bureaucratic constituencies, for example, as Trotsky did within the military. Bureaucrats desired to have their chiefs sit in the leadership and expected the leader to impress the urgency of their needs upon other leaders.[49] The institutionalization of leadership accountability to the Central Committee in the 1920s led to *reciprocal* accountability as individual leaders exercised control over separate bureaucracies to bring their loyalists into the bureaucracies and selectorate.

The most important manifestation of this particular form of reciprocal accountability took place within the Party apparatus in what Daniels has called the "circular flow of power":[50] The general secretary used the powers of the Secretariat to secure election of republic and regional secretaries who would support him. In turn these Party secretaries used their control within their respective organizations to ensure election to the all-union Congress of delegates loyal to the general secretary, often simply securing their own election. In the Congress and Central Committee Stalin rallied the secretaries as not only their chief but also the spokesperson for their policy priorities.[51]

Daniels's focus on the Party apparatus misses an important parallel process: At the same time other members of the Politburo engaged in similar strategies to bring their own supporters to the Congress and Central Committee. For example, even as Stalin used the Party apparatus to pack the 1925 Party Congress (December), Zinoviev used his control in Leningrad to hand-pick a delegation that gave him solid support against Stalin. Mikhail Lashevich used his position as deputy commissar of war to organize a faction within the army (and among military delegates to the Party organs) in support of the Zinovievites.[52] All were attempting to shape the selectorate to which they were accountable. The circular flow of power is not only a relationship between the general secretary and Party apparatus but also a strategic move by all leaders locked in a relationship of reciprocal accountability with a bureaucracy.

Opportunities for all Politburo members to bring their loyalists into the selectorate grew apace with rapid expansion of the Central Committee's membership. Membership jumped from nineteen voting members in 1920 to seventy-one in 1927. This growth offered members of the leadership opportunities to expand their followings within the Central Committee. Expansion meant the composition of the Central Committee could change even without a purge of sitting members. In each of the three elections from 1924 (Thirteenth Congress) to 1927 (Fifteenth Congress), no more than one-fifth of the Central Committee members failed to win reelection. Yet the expansion of membership meant that in each election between one-quarter and two-fifths of the elected members were new to the Central Committee. In the Central Committee elected in 1927, members who had served since 1922 constituted only 20.6 percent.[53]

The subsequent play of politics revealed not only the structure of reciprocal accountability between politicians and bureaucrats but also the extent to which the balance of power between tiers within this structure depended at any moment on the configuration of power in the first tier.

Intense conflict in the first tier expanded the power of the Central Committee as the court of appeal from a paralyzed Politburo. Directive leadership revealed how much within a relationship of reciprocal accountability the first tier could turn the tables on the selectorate. The Central Committee declined after Stalin's victory over his opponents at the end of the 1920s. From 1931 to the end of Stalin's rule, a new Central Committee was elected only three times in twenty-three years—in 1934, 1939, and 1952. Meetings became infrequent; apparently in the last sixteen years of Stalin's rule only six were called.[54] The accountability that some party secretaries apparently attempted to exercise over Stalin in 1934 was turned against them in the Great Purge that killed 98 of the Central Committee's 139 voting and candidate members.[55] Yet, this vacillation in the balance of power between tiers did not change the underlying structural feature of reciprocal accountability, and, as I examine in the next chapters, after the return to collective leadership the Central Committee once again became the court of appeal for a divided leadership.

Cycling of Leadership

The opportunities and strategic advantages created by the rules of the constitution of Bolshevism were not evenly distributed; they gave the general secretary a distinct advantage in coalition building. As a consequence of reciprocal accountability, leaders built coalitions among constituencies in the Central Committee by both policy appeals to the bureaucrats and placement of loyalists in key bureaucratic posts.[56] The special place of the Party apparatus as the Central Committee's watchdog over all bureaucracies gave whoever consolidated control within the apparatus advantages in building a coalition of constituencies. These advantages gave the general secretary the means to consolidate directive rule. Yet, the critical element in any coalition underpinning directive rule was the general secretary, and with his death or removal the coalition crumbled. Thus, the history of subsequent Soviet political development was not a linear consolidation of autocracy, but a cycle of alternating directive and collective leadership with the rise and fall of individual general secretaries.

The general secretary could use the Secretariat's control over membership to shape the Party. For example, during the Lenin Enrollment of 1924, Stalin, Zinoviev, and Kamenev sought to bring in members of working-class origins to counterbalance Trotsky's following among students and government officials. An expanding membership was invaluable in this strategy. At the same time expulsions were particularly frequent in party cells in government offices and institutions of higher education. Stalin repeated this ploy against subsequent contenders for power; he expelled their supporters or simply swamped them with new Party members.[57]

A unique opportunity to manipulate the selectorate itself came with the practice of holding so-called enlarged Central Committee plenary sessions. Although joint meetings with the Central Control Commission had been called as early as August 1921, the first formal joint Central Committee-Central Control Commission Plenum was held in 1923. The Party rules gave these enlarged plenary sessions special powers on issues of Party discipline and unity. To manufacture the super majority of two-thirds needed to expel a member of the Central Committee itself, Stalin convened joint meetings with the Central Control Commission, which he dominated. By swamping Stalin's opponents in the Central Committee with Central Control Commission loyalists, joint plena became opportunities for Stalin to shape the Central Committee itself.

Once it had established its majority within a party organ, a coalition could use the rules of majoritarianism to its advantage. For example, in this way the Party apparatus exaggerated its representation in higher bodies. Particularly after 1923, the practice of sending to the Congress a bloc of delegates, which represented the majority rather than a mixed delegation in proportion to the various constituencies in a provincial organization, made it possible to exclude opponents of the general secretary entirely. Similarly, congresses elected an official slate of Central Committee members who supported the general secretary. Prior to 1921 Congress delegates cast votes on individual representatives to the Central Committee, with each delegate casting votes for as many candidates as there were seats on the Central Committee. At the 1921 Party Congress and then routinely beginning with the 1923 Congress, the delegates voted up or down for a bloc of candidates on the single official slate.[58]

Majorities, whether artificially created or not, could use the Party rules on discipline to silence minorities and foreclose debate even before Party bodies had discussed an issue. The import of this strict discipline was illustrated at the 1925 Party Congress in December; the Stalinist majority used this rule to force acquiescence from Lenin's widow Nadezhda Krupskaia who had spoken on behalf of the rights of the Congress's beleaguered minority. Mikhail Kalinin spoke for the majority when he argued that "the idea that truth remains the truth is admirable in a philosophical club, but in the Party the decisions of the Congress are obligatory even upon those who doubt the correctness of the decision."[59] In the Politburo itself between 1923 and 1925 the majority against Trotsky used its power to monopolize the agenda and reach decisions in rump sessions without the minority present.[60]

To prevent the minority within its own membership from appealing outside for a more favorable hearing the Politburo adopted rules that required all its members after 1925 to clear their speeches and publications with the body. To this end the body blocked publication of Zinoviev's article, "The Philosophies of the Epoch," until objectionable parts were removed.[61] This effectively strengthened the Politburo as an institution against the Central Committee—as long as there was a working majority in it. Similarly, to prevent minorities from appealing over the heads of the Central Committee, amendments to the party rules adopted in December 1927 gave the committee a veto over the right to call for an open discussion by the membership at large.[62]

Attempts to reach beyond the Party to build constituencies outside brought swift punishment. The attempt by Mikhail Lashevich to build a constituency within the military brought particularly harsh condemnation from the Joint Plenum of the Central Committee and Central Control Commission in July 1926, dismissal as deputy commissar of war, and expulsion from the Central Committee. The efforts of the United Opposition to pressure the Party by organizing support outside the Party and staging mass demonstrations brought harsh retribution, including arrest of many of their followers, expulsion of their supporters from local Party cells, and in the last months of 1927, the removal of their leaders from the Party organs and expulsion from the Party itself.[63]

The consolidation cycle revealed the advantage enjoyed by a general secretary in building a coalition that bound several constituencies. The personnel powers that came to a general secretary after consolidation within the apparatus could then be used against other bureaucracies. Thus, Stalin won appointment of his allies Mikhail Frunze (1924) and Kliment Voroshilov (1925) as People's commissar of war, who then purged Trotsky supporters from the armed forces—particularly from among political commissars in armed units.[64] Through promotion of Nikolai Ezhov to the party post supervising the police, Stalin in the early 1930s extended his control over the police apparatus and then capped this in 1936 by appointing Ezhov as People's commissar of internal affairs (NKVD).[65]

Through this consolidation of multiple bureaucratic power bases, the directive leader could achieve an apex leadership role, rising above each constituency and so depending on no single constituency. A concomitant of this increased independence from individual constituencies was the growth of Stalin's private secretariat under the direction of Aleksandr N. Poskrebyshev. This body permitted the leader to coordinate all bureaucracies and depend on no one.[66] A consequence of this independence was the leader's ability to turn one bureaucracy against another; for example, Stalin used the police (NKVD) to purge the Party apparatus. Khrushchev recounts his own consternation as Moscow city secretary,

I remember the following state of affairs at the Moscow party conference of 1937. All candidates nominated for membership on the Moscow city and regional committees had to be screened and "sanctioned" by the NKVD. Neither the Central Committee nor the party at large could promote its own members. The NKVD had the last word in assessing the activities of any party member and in deciding whether or not he could be elected to top party posts.[67]

The consolidation of Stalin's directive rule revealed the vulnerability of other leaders and all constituencies under such a distribution of power. The consolidation of this extended power base in the Central Committee permitted the leader to turn on other leaders to remove them and even to turn on the Central Committee and its bureaucratic constituencies.

The death of the general secretary in 1953 led to the disintegration of this extended multibureaucracy coalition and rapid dispersal of power. These developments revealed that the fundamental structure of the constitution of Bolshevism was not hierarchical; instead, it permitted a vacillating balance of power between tiers and within the first tier. Thus, the position of the general secretary's extended, multibureaucracy coalition within the selectorate depended on the continued existence of the general secretary to hold it together. Even the special position of the apparatus vis-à-vis other bureaucracies required the general secretary.[68] Once he was removed, the coalition and apparatus faced enormous collective action problems. Individual leaders of separate bureaucracies that had comprised this coalition such as the police or economic administration vied for precedence after the former leader's death. Without a designated heir—that is, a second secretary who could assume the powers of the former leader—even the Party apparatus would find it difficult to act in concert in the contest of bureaucracies. Indeed, this potentially most powerful bureaucratic constituency was paralyzed by its lack of leadership at the moment when the most important choices about the future constitutional rules were being made. In short, the death of the general secretary revealed a cycle in politics that affected not only the consolidation of power within the first tier and the balance between tiers, but also the relative influence of constituencies in the second.

The Constitutional Agenda

The unequal strategic opportunities and threats revealed in the play of politics from 1921 to 1953 set the agenda for subsequent constitutional development. An important opportunity to change the rules of politics came with the death of Joseph Stalin and the dispersal of power among the constituents of his extended coalition. The opportunity to sit at the bargaining table of constitutional politics was limited to the narrow elite of first and second tiers. The concerns expressed by those empowered in this bargain reflected perspectives shaped by their roles. The impetus to change the rules often came from those who sought rules to remedy what they saw as the deficiencies in the rules that unfolded before 1953—especially, changes to expand their influence in normal politics and erect obstacles to the consolidation of power by others that might again leave them so vulnerable.

These issues were shaped by the structure of the authoritarian constitution that emerged before 1953. For example, within the first tier, some leaders sought to lengthen their tenure by creating obstacles to any attempt by a future general secretary to dislodge them. Some leaders sought to level the playing field in the first tier by resisting appointment of a new general secretary altogether or at least by limiting the personnel powers of the apparatus in other bureaucracies. Many leaders were torn between rules that reinforced a collectivism to serve their survival interests against another consolidating leader and rules that served their own ambition to consolidate greater policymaking authority.

Similarly, in relations between tiers the agenda of rule making after 1953 was shaped by the constitutional structure that had emerged in the first three and a half decades of Soviet power. Some leaders sought rules that ensured their control over bureaucrats, while many second-tier bureaucrats sought to attenuate their accountability to the first tier by rules guaranteeing greater security of tenure and professional criteria for promotion and retention. Actors in both tiers faced a difficult tension between their desire to enforce the collective accountability of the other tier and their desire to ensure the unity of their own constituency across tiers.

Within the second tier many bureaucrats sought rules to change the balance among constituencies. In particular, bureaucrats wanted to establish limits on the intrusion of the apparatus in the state bureaucracy and on the use of terror by the police against them. Some attempted to weaken other bureaucracies or place obstacles in the path of coalition building—for example, by dispersing the resources of other bureaucracies, such as dividing the police among separate organizations.

These issues illustrate the ways in which the two-tier structure of the authoritarian constitution that emerged before 1953 would shape the agenda of constitutional politics in succeeding years. By empowering the players who sat at the bargaining table and structuring their concerns, the constitution shaped the path of its own subsequent development.

ALTERNATIVE MODELS: A SYNTHESIS

In this chapter I have argued that the constitutional decisions of early Soviet power set rules that structured normal and constitutional politics. As a result of these decisions Soviet politics took on the two-tier authoritarian structure in which first-tier policymakers struggled for power while second-tier bureaucrats engaged in a contest for scarce resources. Reciprocal accountability between the two tiers made them mutually dependent. First-tier policymakers had to seek supporters in the selectorate, while second-tier selectors sought first-tier patrons. Leaders and selectors enjoyed secure tenure of office as long as they could maintain sustaining majorities in both tiers. Politics revolved around the formation and change of coalitions within and across these two tiers. The constitution of Bolshevism included within its rules the potential for recurring changes—vacillation between collective and directive leadership within the first tier and a shifting balance of power between tiers. This not only defined normal politics, but it also shaped the trajectory for subsequent development in the rules of politics.

This model of Soviet politics, it should be noted, permits a synthesis of a number of approaches that western Sovietologists have followed to define Soviet politics. These previous efforts have resulted in three models that stress different attributes of the Soviet system: The totalitarian model stresses autocratic control; the conflict school, leadership competition; and the political interests model, bureaucratic influence. Each model draws out the consequences of an element that is an enduring characteristic of Soviet politics—hierarchic control, leadership conflict, or bureaucratic influence. Yet, from the vantage point of the analysis presented in this chapter and chapter 2, these are only parts of a more complete model of the Soviet political process: That is, each treats one of several interdependent variables in isolation and treats what should be a central explanatory variable as a constant. Moreover, all bypass the central issue of reciprocal accountability. The model developed in this book shows how these elements interact in an authoritarian constitutional structure.

The totalitarian model, by stressing the element of control over Soviet society by the leader, describes an autocratic polity at the peak of the consolidation cycle. According to Carl J. Friedrich and Zbigniew K. Brzezinski, the instruments of the autocrat include a single party with an official ideology, using terroristic police control to establish a monopoly over the means of communication, the means of armed coercion, and the economy.[69] The leader dominates the Party and, through the Party, all society. He eliminates independent political actors so that, as Brzezinski and Samuel P. Huntington argue, political initiatives do not "bubble up" from below, but "trickle down" from the Party Secretariat. The decision phase of policymaking is the "brief and unitary" approval of initiatives by the leadership. During the execution phase, totalitarianism provides no opportunity for amendment or sabotage by bureaucrats implementing a policy; faithful execution of the decision under the close scrutiny of the Party apparatus is the norm.[70]

The conflict school and political interests model amend the totalitarian model by drawing out the consequences of conflict within the Soviet leadership and among bureaucratic interests under collective leadership. The conflict model argues that power is normally oligarchic, dispersed among members of the Politburo and the Secretariat who represent real political and organizational interests. An underlying structural reality is the indeterminacy of power so that, to quote Carl A. Linden, "the logic of Soviet politics inclines the leader to seek absolute power over the leading group, but the same logic also impels them to strive to inhibit or prevent the leader from acquiring it."[71] Thus, among these leaders conflict is a continuous fact of political life. The political interests model introduces the element of influence by interests outside the leadership. It criticizes the totalitarian model for assuming that the Party leadership is autonomous of political forces pressing particularistic issues and interests. It criticizes the conflict school for its tendency "to treat such groups as mere objects of manipulation by the top leaders and factions, and to discount the possibility of autonomous action by them."[72] This model asserts that interests become part of the leadership conflict and press their separate agendas on politicians.

These models are powerful tools for analysis of the independent effects of control, conflict, and influence, yet they suffer a common limitation: Each focuses on just one of three interdependent elements of Soviet politics and treats it as a constant rather than a variable. The totalitarian model of Soviet politics describes the consequences of hierarchical control, but it does not provide tools to analyze the political process when no single leader has established autocratic leadership, when there is no unity of views among leaders, or when the leaders must rely on the Central Committee to help resolve disputes within the leadership. The conflict model, by positing continuous conflict, transforms what should be its most powerful explanatory variable into a constant; it does not provide analytic tools to examine the consequences of changes in intensity of conflict—such as differences between periods of collective and directive leadership. The conflict model also provides few tools to analyze the impact on the political process of what it acknowledges to be the natural consequences of this conflict—interest group pressure. The political interests approach analyzes this pressure but recognizes that the influence of polit-

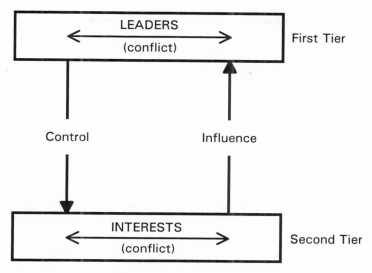

Figure 3.3. Synthesis of Three Models of Soviet Politics

ical interests is not the key to the Soviet political process and cannot be understood in isolation from the elements of control and conflict. None-theless, the political interests approach provides no conceptual tools to analyze the interdependence of interest group pressure and the larger po-litical process.

By bringing together these three elements we have a picture of a two-tier process that resembles a constitution of authoritarianism. As figure 3.3 shows, within the first tier leaders compete for power. Within the second, interests compete for policy outcomes. The two tiers are bound together by the hierarchical control of leaders over interests and the influ-ence of interests over leaders' decisions. Missing from this model, how-ever, is the element of reciprocal accountability. This relationship be-tween leaders and selectorate makes the relationship between tiers one of not only influence and control but also coalition building.

CHAPTER FOUR

Reciprocal Accountability, 1953–1986

STALIN'S DEATH and each leadership crisis that followed called for choices that shaped the rules of politics for succeeding years. One outcome of these choices was growing institutionalization of reciprocal accountability between leadership and bureaucratic selectors focused on the relationship between the Politburo and the Central Committee. A second outcome, which I explore in chapter 5, was the institutionalization of balanced or collective leadership. These were central developments in the constitution of Bolshevism from 1953 to 1986.

The institutionalization of reciprocal accountability resulted from rules that increasingly guaranteed Central Committee control over Politburo membership, leadership control over their respective bureaucratic constituencies, and bureaucratic cooptation into the Central Committee. Figure 4.1 presents a schematic representation of the "mature" relationship of reciprocal accountability that had developed by the end of the Brezhnev administration. The Politburo was accountable to the Central Committee, but the Politburo exercised control over the composition of the Central Committee at two essential selection points: First, appointments to the offices that brought cooptation into the Central Committee were approved by the Politburo. Second, the list of candidates for the Central Committee presented to the Party Congress also required the prior approval of the Politburo. This led to two interdependent relationships in Soviet politics: In the selectoral politics of support (indicated by the solid lines in figure 4.1), leading bureaucrats were appointed by the Politburo, but as a consequence of the cooptation of bureaucrats into the Central Committee through job-slot representation bureaucrats became the selectors on whom the Politburo members depended for their tenure of office. In the bureaucratic politics of information (indicated by broken lines in the figure), the Politburo and bureaucracy—which included ministries, state committees, departments of the Party apparatus, and republic and local authorities—exchanged information and options emanating from bureaucrats and authoritative decisions emanating from the Politburo.

Reciprocal accountability shaped coalition politics. It created the distinctive two-tier structure of authoritarianism. In each tier the actors per-

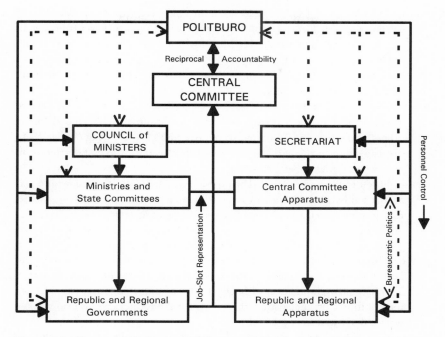

Figure 4.1. Bureaucratic Reciprocal Accountability in Soviet Politics

formed dual roles: First-tier actors were politicians and governors. Second-tier actors were selectors and bureaucrats. Leaders *qua* politicians
had to win or maintain office; leaders *qua* governors had to make policy.
Bureaucrats served as the executors of leaders' policies; in addition, however, many, but not all, bureaucrats *qua* selectors were the constituents
whose support a leader had to gain in order to win or maintain office.
Politburo decisionmakers in the first tier were engaged in a power struggle. Bureaucratized interests in the second tier were engaged in a contest
for scarce resources. Leaders needed supporters in the Politburo and Central Committee to promote their careers and maintain their positions;
bureaucrats needed patrons in the Central Committee or Politburo to
maintain their posts and fulfill their missions. Politics centered on a coalition process within and across these two tiers.

The thirty-three years examined in this chapter sweep across the administrations associated with six Soviet leaders—Georgii Malenkov,
Nikita Khrushchev, Leonid Brezhnev, Yurii Andropov, Konstantin
Chernenko, and Mikhail Gorbachev. For heuristic purposes, these can be
analyzed as five periods (in later chapters some of these are further
subdivided):

March 1953 to June 1957: The post-Stalin collective leadership was led by
a triumvirate of Georgii Malenkov (premier), Lavrentii Beria (minister of
internal affairs), and Viacheslav Molotov (minister of foreign affairs). Following the removal of Beria in July 1953, Nikita Khrushchev (a party secretary) was added to the triumvirate, from where he began to rise to predominance over other members of the collectivity.

June 1957 to October 1964: Nikita Khrushchev exercised directive leadership
after he defeated an attempt by the Anti-Party Group, which included among
others Malenkov and Molotov, to remove him. Yet, growing challenges to
his leadership in the early 1960s ended in a second, successful attempt to
remove him in October 1964.

October 1964 to December 1969: The post-Khrushchev collective leadership was
at first led by a triumvirate of Leonid Brezhnev (general secretary), Aleksei
Kosygin (premier), and Nikolai Podgornyi (Party secretary), with Aleksandr
Shelepin (chair of the Party-State Control Committee) and Mikhail Suslov
(Party secretary) playing active roles in the succession conflict.

July 1970 to November 1982: Brezhnev exercised limited directive leadership, but
he remained constrained by the leaders with whom he came to office.
Through slow elimination of Shelepin (1975) and Podgornyi (1977) from
the Politburo, Brezhnev strengthened his hand but then saw his grip weaken
with old age and failing health.

November 1982 to December 1986: The post-Brezhnev collective leadership remained in turmoil as three general secretaries followed in rapid succession—
Yurii Andropov (November 1982), Konstantin Chernenko (February 1984),
and Mikhail Gorbachev (March 1985).

As figure 4.2 shows, throughout this period the formal structure of leading Party and state organs remained largely unchanged from the 1920s:
The legislature formally elected a corporate chief of state (Presidium of
the Supreme Soviet) and the government (Council of Ministers). The
Party Central Committee was formally elected by congresses that were
convened only about once every five years; the Central Committee in turn
elected the Politburo and Secretariat.

The purpose of the analysis in this chapter is not to offer a rich description of Soviet politics in these years, but rather to identify in a more rigorous manner the influence of Soviet constitutional structure on political
processes. This chapter is divided into three parts. The first examines developments in reciprocal accountability from 1953 to 1986. The second
analyzes the dynamics of coalition building and the consolidation shaped
by this. The third briefly discusses how the politics of accountability in-
tersected the bureaucratic politics of information. The conclusion compares the approach in this chapter with previous analyses of accountability in the Soviet polity.

STATE   PARTY

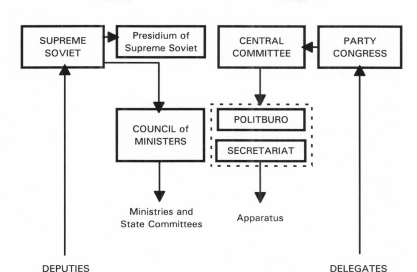

Figure 4.2. Party and State Organs, 1953–1988

DEVELOPMENTS IN RECIPROCAL
ACCOUNTABILITY

Upon Stalin's death accountability was not initially well institutionalized in specific organs. After the first succession-consolidation cycle expectations about the rules of the game were neither strong nor always reinforcing; formal bodies did not at first offer a resolution to leadership crises. Yet, between 1953 and 1986 reciprocal accountability was institutionalized in the relationship of Politburo to Central Committee. This resulted from three developments over the three decades: The locus of policymaking came to be concentrated in the Politburo. The accountability of the Politburo to the Central Committee was confirmed. The role of other agencies outside the Central Committee in leadership selection declined.

One development in this institutionalization of reciprocal accountability was the reduction of fluctuations in the locus of policymaking and its focusing in the Politburo. After Stalin's death the Politburo did not enjoy a premier decisionmaking role. The post-Stalinist triumvirate of Georgii Malenkov, Lavrentii Beria, and Viacheslav Molotov initially sought to preserve the role of the Presidium of the Council of Ministers (CM Presidium) as a second center of policymaking. The triumvirate held key posts in the CM Presidium as well as the Party's Politburo and retained some of Stalin's prerogative to choose the arena in which policy would be discussed. Malenkov, in particular, found advantages in this arena: The Council of Ministers, packed with his loyalists, placed partisans of the Party secretaries at a disadvantage. When Malenkov was forced to relinquish one of his posts less than ten days after Stalin's death, he sacrificed his seat on the Party Secretariat, apparently in the belief the chairmanship of the Council of Ministers (premier) would be an important basis of power in the post-Stalinist polity and the post would give him leading roles in the two most important policymaking centers.[1]

Yet, in the next weeks the Politburo displaced the CM Presidium as the effective policymaking center, much as it had displaced Sovnarkom in the post-Leninist succession. As before, the triumph of the Politburo was linked to the succession struggle—specifically, to the growing conflict among members of the CM Presidium and the involvement of Party secretaries (notably Nikita Khrushchev this time) as strategic allies of the parties to this conflict.[2] This process of displacement was hurried along by the decision to remove Beria from the leadership. (This poignantly illustrates the ways in which Malenkov was able to play on his leading role in both CM Presidium and Politburo to strategic advantage.) After weeks of conspiring, Malenkov called a meeting of the CM Presidium for 14 July 1953 to confront Beria. Knowing that he needed the support of Khrushchev and other Politburo members who did not sit on the CM Presidium in order to succeed, he also invited all Politburo members to attend. With all assembled in the Kremlin, following the script of the conspirators Malenkov opened the meeting as a Politburo session rather than CM Presidium and confronted Beria with the fait accompli of a majority to remove him.[3] After this confrontation the rising role of Khrushchev, still excluded from the CM Presidium, shifted policymaking to the Politburo as the meeting place for all leaders whose views had to be counted.

A second development in the institutionalization of reciprocal accountability was the confirmation of Politburo accountability to Central Committee. Upon Stalin's death expectations about the lines of accountability between leadership and Central Committee were initially less clearly focused. Key assignments on 7 March 1953 were ratified not by the Central Committee, but by a joint meeting that also spoke in the name of the Presidium of the Supreme Soviet and Council of Ministers. The full membership of these bodies was not even assembled. Apparently, although the resolutions of the meeting were published the next day as joint decisions of all three bodies, at most twenty people were present.[4]

Just as in the early 1920s, expectations concerning Politburo account-ability to the Central Committee grew as a result of succession conflict, and they were reinforced with each new leadership crisis. The Central Committee role as arbiter between factions of the top leaders grew with each subsequent leadership crisis in the Khrushchev era. In 1953 Central Committee plena approved Malenkov's removal from his secretarial post (14 March), Beria's removal from all posts (July), and Khrushchev's ele-vation to first secretary (3–7 September). By the time Khrushchev sought to remove Malenkov from the premiership (chairmanship of the Council of Ministers) in February 1955, the protocol of first calling a Central Committee Plenum was well established. In the 1957 Anti-Party Group crisis Khrushchev forced the leadership to call an enlarged meeting of the Central Committee, which overturned the original Politburo majority that sought to oust him.[5]

The accountability of Politburo to Central Committee was reinforced in the next leadership successions—particularly, as the Central Commit-tee demonstrated its power to resolve disputes concerning the removal of Politburo members. In 1964, the second attempt to remove Khrushchev involved the voting members of the Central Committee even more. While in 1957 the anti-Khrushchev conspirators sought to exclude the general membership of the Central Committee from their early planning, in 1964 Khrushchev's opponents brought the members into the process from the beginning. Preparations for the coup involved building a majority in the Central Committee and then calling a plenum. In the half-year prior to the plenum, members of the Central Committee were privately polled by Leonid Brezhnev and Nikolai Podgornyi on their support for a coup. Gennadii Voronov, one Politburo member who supported the coup, re-ports that "all this was being prepared for a year. The threads lead to Zavidov, where Brezhnev usually went hunting. Against each name on the list of the CC Brezhnev placed 'pluses' (for those ready to support him in the struggle against Khrushchev) and 'minuses.' Each person was per-suaded individually."[6] With these preparations a Politburo meeting was called for late in the day of 12 October to be followed by a Central Com-mittee Plenum two days later. The elaborate planning permitted the Polit-buro majority with a solid Central Committee majority to press the issue through the plenum without discussion.[7]

The rapid successions during the 1980s confirmed this accountability. The Politburo assembled within hours of Brezhnev's death on 10 Novem-ber 1982 and held almost continuous meetings the following day to choose Yurii Andropov in time for the 12 November Central Commit-tee Plenum. The Politburo assembled once again after Yurii Andropov's death on 9 February 1984, and after three days of what some observers describe as "round-the-clock" battle it recommended Konstantin Chernenko to the Central Committee Plenum on 13 February. One year later the Politburo assembled at 10:30 p.m. on 10 March 1985—just three hours after Chernenko's death—and the following day the Central Committee Plenum ratified the choice of Mikhail Gorbachev within twenty-three hours of the death.[8]

The actual role of the Central Committee in each succession depended on the unity or division within the leadership. When the Politburo could present a united front in these leadership crises, Central Committee approval of Politburo personnel decisions appears to have been a formality. Against a unified Politburo the Central Committee had serious problems of collective action. For example, in 1982 provincial Party secretaries in the Central Committee apparently sought to oppose the Politburo's choice of Andropov to succeed Brezhnev as general secretary. According to Zhores Medvedev, "When the obkom [provincial] secretaries arrived in Moscow for the Plenum on 11 November, they tried to work out a joint stand. But they had too little time to form any real opposition to Andropov, since the Plenum was held the next day. The speed with which the succession was arranged and the decision that Chernenko should be the person to propose Andropov meant that the election took place without any discussion."[9]

Divisions in the Politburo, however, increased selector influence. When the Politburo was deeply divided, the Central Committee could be decisive. In March 1985, division in the Politburo and a strong Central Committee constituency appear to have been decisive in the election of Mikhail Gorbachev. Viktor Grishin offered a strong conservative alternative to the candidacy of Gorbachev. Egor Ligachev, a Politburo member and Party secretary, relates the events in the Politburo and Central Committee: "Those were anxious days. . . . Totally different decisions could have been made. There was a real danger of that. . . . Thanks to the firm position taken by Politburo members Comrades Chebrikov, Solomentsev, and Gromyko and a large group of provincial Party first secretaries, the March Central Committee plenum adopted the only correct decision."[10] Boris Yeltsin, then a regional party secretary and Central Committee member, credits the Central Committee, rather than the Politburo, with the decisive voice and provides more details on the role of the provincial first secretaries mentioned by Ligachev:

> In fact, on that occasion it was the Plenum of the Central Committee that decided who was to be general secretary. Practically all the participants in that [March] plenum, including many senior, experienced first secretaries, considered that the Grishin platform was unacceptable. . . .

A large number of first secretaries agreed that of all the Politburo members, the man to be promoted to the post of general secretary had to be Gorbachev. . . . We decided to put our weight behind him. We conferred with several Politburo members . . . [including] Ligachev. Our position coincided with his, because he was as afraid of Grishin as we were. Once it had become clear that this was the majority view, we decided that if any other candidate was put forward—Grishin, Romanov, or anyone else—we would oppose him *en bloc*. And defeat him.

Evidently the discussions within the Politburo itself followed along these lines. Those Politburo members who attended that session were aware of our firm intentions, and Gromyko, too, supported our point of view.[11]

Yeltsin claims that the majority in the Central Committee not only tipped the balance in the Politburo but also forced Grishin, who saw the writing on the wall, to withdraw his candidacy.

Ligachev's later memoirs confirm the broad outlines of Yeltsin's account. On 10 March 1985 the Politburo was deadlocked at its first meeting to pick Chernenko's successor. Before the next day's meeting Ligachev and other Politburo members met with provincial party secretaries arriving in Moscow for the Central Committee meeting. The strong support for Gorbachev expressed by these secretaries was reportedly critical to the decisions of several Politburo members, including Andrei Gromyko, to support Gorbachev. At the 11 March Politburo meeting even Grishin was brought around to vote for the nomination of Gorbachev. Ligachev credits the provincial first secretaries with giving Gorbachev "his 1985 landslide victory" as general secretary.[12]

The accountability of the Politburo to the Central Committee constrained the game of electoral politics within the Politburo. Aware of the ability of a minority within the Politburo to appeal to the Central Committee, conspirators had to anticipate the reaction of the larger forum. A majority certain of Central Committee approval—such as the anti-Khrushchevian coalition in 1964—might seek this approval to provide closure to a leadership change and foreclose appeals by the defeated. Alternatively, a Politburo majority uncertain of such approval might seek to postpone meetings with the Central Committee until it could present a common front. For example, the anti-Khrushchev majority in 1957 apparently at first rejected Khrushchev's appeal to call a Central Committee plenum immediately and declared that "it was imperative for the [Politburo] to take a formal vote first."[13] The Politburo majority was forced to face the Central Committee when more than 100 Central Committee members arrived in the Kremlin to demand a plenary session. According to Giuseppe Boffa, the Committee members "who were waiting to be let into the [Politburo] meeting declared that it was they who were responsible for the running of the Party and that they could not be excluded from decisions. . . . In the face of this unequivocal show of strength the [Anti-Party Group] had to resign themselves to a discussion before all the Party representatives after having tried to postpone it further."[14] Anticipating the power of the Central Committee, conspirators in the Politburo may have been deterred from acts against one of their members if they did not expect confirmation in the Central Committee.

A third element in the institutionalization of accountability between Politburo and Central Committee was a reduced role in the selection process for pressure outside the Central Committee by the instruments of armed coercion. During the 1950s the military and police played critical roles in the succession process. In the post-Stalinist settlement, Beria's control of the police apparatus may have been essential to enforcing the initial personnel decisions made by Stalin's heirs. With this support the ten-member body that Stalin had dubbed the Bureau of the Presidium of the Central Committee in effect displaced the recently enlarged Presidium [Politburo] of the Central Committee by removing fourteen of the latter body's twenty-four surviving members. Three months later the armed forces were instrumental in enforcing the decision of the Politburo to remove Beria. Khrushchev recounts the concerns of Politburo members that votes alone would not settle the leadership issue: "His Chekists [police] would be sitting in the next room during the session, and Beria could easily order them to arrest us all and hold us in isolation. We would have been quite helpless because there was a sizable armed guard in the Kremlin. Therefore, we decided to enlist the help of the military."[15] Not only did Marshal Georgii Zhukov and General Konstantin Moskalenko arrest Beria in the middle of the Kremlin meeting, but their troops also neutralized the police within the Kremlin by surrounding the city with armed units. Four years later, in Khrushchev's victory over the Anti-Party Group, his alliance with Marshal Zhukov made it possible to fly in Central Committee members from all over the Soviet Union on short notice and force convocation of the Central Committee.

In subsequent successions, the armed forces played a less active role. In 1964, according to the best available evidence, defense minister Rodion Malinovskii was not informed of the conspiracy until two days before the coup, but he agreed to acquiesce in the assault on his commander-in-chief. At the Central Committee Plenum he declared the full support of the armed forces for the Politburo's decision.[16] Yet, his forces played no overt role in the coup, and no units of the armed forces were called to the Kremlin during the fateful Politburo and Central Committee sessions. The KGB chair Vladimir Semichastnyi, however, was prominent by apparently involving himself in the conspiracy from the very beginning in the spring of 1964. According to Semichastnyi, the plotters "were well aware that it would be impossible to start anything without the KGB."[17] Semichastnyi's police forces may have been essential in neutralizing the armed forces. He claims to have warned the KGB commanders of special departments within the Moscow military district: "In the next few days, if as much as one armed soldier on a motorcycle leaves his barracks, whether with a machine gun or anything else, . . . it will cost you your head."[18]

After the 1960s the armed forces and police were used less frequently as instruments of coercion to resolve the selection of leadership. The further institutionalization of the accountability of Politburo to Central Committee limited, but did not eliminate, the role of the military and the police in the selectorate beyond their formal roles in the Politburo and Central Committee.[19] These remained important institutional bases for Politburo members such as Yurii Andropov and Dmitri Ustinov, much as alternative bureaucracies were bases for other Politburo members, but they were apparently not used to coerce Politburo or Central Committee choices. Three and a half decades earlier armed influence could be critical, but by the 1980s these "votes" outside the Central Committee had declined in importance.

COALITION POLITICS

Reciprocal accountability between politicians and selectors meant that leaders in the first tier had to build or maintain support among bureaucrats; selectors in the second tier needed to maintain the continuing confidence of politicians. These came together in coalitions formed, maintained, and changed by Politburo members. Leaders emerged through concurrent consensus in both tiers, that is, selection of and removal of members of the Politburo required the consent of both the Politburo and the Central Committee. As a result, an aspirant or incumbent leader had to build and maintain support in both. Coalition building consequently entailed two processes: Alliance and division in the first tier as members of the Politburo struggled to consolidate leadership; coalitions between the two tiers formed by leaders with key selectors. For the most part coalitions were not formed horizontally by second-tier actors, but horizontally within the first tier and vertically across tiers at the initiation of first-tier actors.[20] Four aspects of this coalition process are addressed below: sources of the "selectoral motivation" of first-tier actors; second-tier constraints on the pursuit of support in the selectorate; dynamics of competitive coalition building among leaders; and dynamics of consolidation by the general secretary.

The "Selectoral" Motivation

The constitution of Bolshevism made it imperative that Politburo members give special attention to the problem of building and maintaining a coalition that would sustain them in office. The structural design of Soviet institutions, particularly the indeterminacy of power in the first tier, dictated this behavior.[21] The weak institutionalization of power in the Soviet polity forced leaders to attend to both their political survival and expansion of control over the political process. It had to be, to use David Mayhew's terminology, the "proximate goal" of Soviet politicians, without which other goals could not be pursued.

This "selectoral motivation" shaped the coalition formation process. Leaders often acted as though they had subordinated their policy preferences to the task of building coalitions.[22] Stalin's publicly articulated policy positions in the 1920s, for example, moved from moderate defense of the New Economic Policy to a leftist demand for forced industrialization as the requirements of coalition building changed. Khrushchev's public stands shifted from a conservative defense of the priority of heavy industry and military expenditures to a reformist call for savings in the military budget and greater attention to consumer goods production; his coalition was also changing.[23] Alliances formed among leaders were often made for reasons of power. For example, the coalition that came to be known as the Anti-Party Group that formed to remove Khrushchev in 1957 brought together both ends of the reformist-conservative spectrum against Khrushchev in the center, united not by their policy preferences, but by their concerns over Khrushchev's inordinate power.[24]

Holding together a coalition depended on both the power and authority of the leaders.[25] The *power* of a leader consisted to a large extent of others' expectations: compliance with the leader would bring rewards, and noncompliance would bring sanctions. His *authority* consisted primarily of others' expectations that the leader competently fulfill the responsibilities of his position. A significant part of both power and authority was the expectation of first- and second-tier actors who believed the leader's behavior would help them retain their positions and fulfill the responsibilities of their roles. Concern with power and authority meant leaders had to build coalitions with both enfranchised and unenfranchised bureaucrats in the second tier. On the one hand, to remain in office leaders *qua* politicians had to build coalitions that would win them sustaining, concurrent consent within both tiers of the selectorate. On the other hand, to be effective, leaders *qua* governors had to build support even within the unenfranchised participant population—that is, within bureaucracies outside the selectorate. Even though it could not remove him, the unenfranchised bureaucracy could defeat a leader's policies and so erode not only his authority but also his power.

Second-tier Constraints

Leaders' efforts to build coalitions with the second tier were constrained by the configuration of bureaucracies there. That is, leaders were constrained to focus on constituencies that were organized bureaucratically and on bureaucracies that were more prominent in the selectorate.

The constitution of Bolshevism shaped the interests that were available in the second tier as coalition partners. Forced departicipation of society outside the Party excluded from the politics of coalition-building many interests such as independent religious communities that fell outside the formal bureaucratic structure. At the same time, the ban on factionalism inside the Party limited opportunities for interests that fell across bureaucratic lines to organize independently. For example, minorities that simultaneously lost in several bureaucracies found it difficult to come together to articulate their demands. Powerful interests tended to develop within existing organizations.[26]

The importance of organization is illustrated by the debate in the 1960s whether to turn to dirigibles as an economical means of heavy air transport, particularly in remote corners of the Soviet Union.[27] The "dirigible enthusiasts" were scattered among a number of institutions, including the Academy of Sciences, city and local planning agencies, state committees, and ministries. These were at a serious disadvantage because the professional journals and scientific conferences on air transport were controlled by the Ministry of Aviation Production (MAP), which opposed the idea and thus denied enthusiasts the opportunity to present their case before a professional audience. Recognizing their disadvantage in confronting the unified bureaucracy of MAP, the dirigible enthusiasts recommended establishment of a state committee for dirigible building. Seeing the threat this would pose to its monopoly in the field of aviation, MAP outmaneuvered the dirigible enthusiasts and blocked formation of this committee. Both recognized that hierarchically organized interests are more likely to receive attention from the first tier than interests outside the bureaucracy or scattered across bureaucracies.

First-tier efforts to build coalitions were also constrained by the distribution of power in the second-tier. By virtue of their organization, their strategic place in the selectorate, and the resources they controlled, the primary bureaucracies of Soviet society after Stalin's death included the party apparatus, state economic administration, military, and police.[28] Coalitions with these "pillars" of Soviet society defined the major actors in the first tier. Thus, it was important to occupy, place in the hands of clients, or cultivate alliances with incumbents in the following posts: (1) the all-union secretaries and department heads who controlled the Communist party apparatus; (2) the chairman of the Council of Ministers and members of the Council of Ministers Presidium who controlled the state economic machinery; (3) the minister of defense who commanded the armed forces; and (4) the head(s) of the separate or unified police organizations.

With the institutionalization of Politburo accountability to the Central Committee increasingly the balance of votes among these groups mattered. Ellen Jones argues that "Soviet Party and governmental institutions are premised on the existence of conflicting organizational interests." Both in theory and practice, she argues, "committee procedures are deliberately designed to routinize and systematize the interaction of organizational representatives."[29] Thus, in 1956, all 133 voting members were office holders in the major bureaucracies—except perhaps the editors of the Cominform journal and of *Voprosy istorii*. In the next six Central Committees elected from 1961 to 1986, officeholders in these bureaucracies averaged 94 percent of the voting membership.[30] Yet, not all bureaucratic constituencies were represented equally in the selectorate. As Robert V. Daniels observes, "systematic analysis of the composition of the Central Committee shows that ever since the late 1920s membership has been accorded almost exclusively on the basis of the tenure of high bureaucratic office in the party apparatus, the government, and the military, with small numbers allocated to the top people in the trade unions, diplomacy, and cultural and scientific work."[31] This allocation of positions in the Central Committee constrained the coalition-building efforts of leaders by making some constituencies more valuable than others.

Competitive Coalitions

The efforts of individual Politburo leaders to build coalitions were competitive. In this process each leader faced three imperatives. The imperative of *exclusion* led each first-tier actor to seek to exclude other first-tier actors from the institutions on which he built his coalition. The natural extension of this was to purge from these organizations followers of these other leaders as well. The imperative of *differentiation* led first-tier actors to build different institutional bases. This followed quite naturally from the first imperative that meant they could not easily build secure competing bases within the same institutions. The imperative of *aggregation* led first-tier actors to seek to expand their power bases by building alliances and extending control beyond the initial ("core") constituencies of their coalitions.

These imperatives are illustrated by the three successions since 1953—post-Stalin (beginning in 1953), post-Khrushchev (beginning in 1964), and post-Brezhnev (beginning in 1982). In the post-Stalin succession leaders sitting atop the state ministerial bureaucracy (Malenkov), Party apparatus (Khrushchev), police (Beria), military (Lazar Kaganovich), and foreign ministry (Molotov) built separate institutional bases (differentiation), struggled to exclude others from these (exclusion), but then sought to expand their bases (aggregation). Malenkov cultivated a loyal following within the state administrative agencies. Although he initially attempted to control both Party and state, Malenkov was forced to choose. His choice of the latter was influenced by pressures from Khrushchev to exclude him from the Secretariat and Malenkov's concern that abandoning the state machinery might leave it to Beria, who at that moment would have been a still greater threat. Beria's efforts focused on the newly united ministries of Internal Affairs and State Security (MVD and MGB). Beria, selecting loyal followers to head the police apparatus in each republic, from there sought to expand his support in the republics. He used his police to oversee purges in the party and state bureaucracies of the Ukraine and the Caucasus republics and sought to cement alliances with still other republic leaders by promises of greater autonomy and reduced pressures for russification. Khrushchev moved rapidly to control the Party apparatus—particularly after his elevation to first secretary in September 1953. Between the summer of 1953 and the end of 1954, Khrushchev replaced the first secretaries in at least six of the fourteen union-republic party organizations with his own associates. In 1954 Khrushchev began to pack lower levels of the apparatus after enlarging the county (*raion*) secretariats from three to four or five secretaries. His apparatus presided over an exchange of party membership cards that permitted him to purge the membership of opponents.[32]

A decade later the post-Khrushchev succession brought another round of competitive efforts to consolidate leadership in different bureaucracies. The imperatives of exclusion and differentiation led to a confrontation among first-tier actors with alternative institutional bases in the state bureaucracy and Party apparatus. Leonid Brezhnev had succeeded Khrushchev as general secretary, but initially shared control of the Party apparatus with Nikolai Podgornyi, who sat as the "second secretary" in the Secretariat. With his associate atop the department responsible for local party organizations, Podgornyi was in a strategic position to build a following in the Party apparatus. Brezhnev moved quickly to exclude

Podgornyi from the Secretariat and to purge Central Committee departments of his followers. Podgornyi was transferred to the more honorific post of chief of state (chairman of the Presidium of the Supreme Soviet). Shelepin used his post as head of the Party-State Control Committee, responsible for party discipline and bureaucratic monitoring, to challenge the supremacy of the Party apparatus. Shelepin extended his coalition by alliances with complementary organizations in the areas of mobilization and control, using his long-time associates in the Komsomol (Sergei Pavlov), the militia or MOOP (Vadim Tikunov), and the KGB (Vladimir Semichastnyi). Shelepin apparently encouraged rumors that his rapid rise would soon culminate in his ascendancy over his peers in the collective leadership.[33]

A decade and a half later, in the post-Brezhnev succession Andropov came to office with his strongest client network in the police and his most important ally—Dmitri Ustinov—in the Ministry of Defense. His brief tenure as Party secretary for six months before Brezhnev's death had given him only a limited clientele in the Party apparatus, although he found a number of secretaries willing to ally with him in his campaign to break stagnation. Andropov began to move to exclude the supporters of Brezhnev and his chosen heir—Konstantin Chernenko. Chernenko's strongest network of support was also in the Party apparatus, but among Brezhnev appointees who were scared that Andropov or Gorbachev would remove them. Andropov and Chernenko struggled for control of the apparatus and cohabited it with yet another leading contender—Mikhail Gorbachev. While Andropov was general secretary Gorbachev held the vital post in the Secretariat charged with overseeing personnel and organizational matters. According to Marc Zlotnik's calculations, in this competition for control of the apparatus through appointments and exclusion, by late 1983 and early 1984 more new appointees to key regional and all-union posts were linked to Gorbachev than to any other leader.[34]

Consolidation of Leadership

The inequality of constituencies and the imperatives of aggregation and exclusion could result in directive leadership. *Consolidation* was a process by which a politician established power and authority in various policy realms. Consolidation was measured by the extent to which a politician could direct policy in an issue realm and the number of realms in which the same politician directed. The inequality of constituencies and the unequal strategic advantages in exclusion and aggregation made consolidation by the general secretary the most likely source of directive rule.

TACTICS OF CONSOLIDATION

Consolidation required both establishing firm control within and expanding beyond a base bureaucracy. A useful heuristic device illustrating this is presented in figure 4.3. Leaders developed not only horizontal ties to one another but also vertical ties to key bureaucratic constituencies. Thus, in 1954 Khrushchev allied with Molotov and key conservative constituencies to oppose Malenkov and his more reform-minded coalition (both indicated by solid lines in figure 4.3.)

Within their respective bases, as the senior officers of their bureaucracies, members of the Politburo exercised hierarchic personnel control. That is, subject to the constraints of collective approval, each enjoyed an advantage in shaping the personnel of their respective bureaucracies. For example, upon assuming office the chairman of the Council of Ministers brought to commanding positions a team with which he could work. Although his choices had to be confirmed by the collective leadership in the Politburo, he selected the candidates. Between March 1953 and December 1987 each of the six chairmen brought in a new team to the CM Presidium. The rate of appointments was six times higher in the first twelve months of their respective administrations than in other years: It averaged 5.3 appointments in the first twelve months of the six chairmen, compared with only 0.9 per year for the other years.[35] Similarly, a new minister of defense brought new senior military personnel. A change of minister—and after 1957 this usually came only with the minister's death—brought rapid turnover among the commanders-in-chief of the major services and the military districts. Indeed, the average turnover rate in the first year of a new minister (35 percent) was nearly double the average for years two through nine.[36]

To expand their policy leadership beyond their initial base a general secretary and other leaders in competition with him turned to three tactics: (1) *aggrandizement*, accumulating posts that conferred leadership within policy realms; (2) *clientelism*, appointing loyalists to commanding posts so as to gain indirect control through these dependent appointees; and (3) *alliances*, cultivating loyalty among incumbents.[37] In these tactics, consolidation depended on a combination of power and authority. That is, leadership depended not only on the expectation of others that a leader possessed and would use sanctions and rewards but also on the expectation that the leader would enable them to fulfill their responsibilities successfully.

Through aggrandizement a leader could gain direct control over key bureaucracies. Stalin's tenure set the precedent that for the head of the Party (first or general secretary) the two most important posts to add were head of the state ministerial bureaucracies (chairman of the Council of Ministers) and commander-in-chief (chairman of the Higher Military

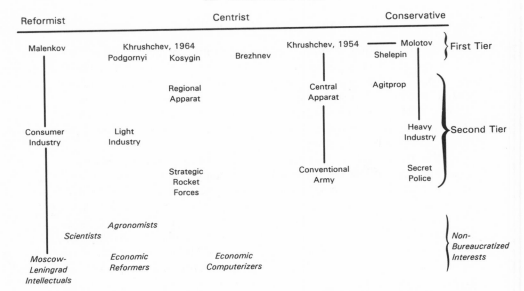

Figure 4.3. The Soviet Policy Spectrum, 1953–1968. Adapted from Zbigniew K. Brzezinski, "The Soviet Political System: Transformation or Degeneration?" *Problems of Communism* 15 (January–February 1966): 10.

Council or later Council of Defense). In later Western analyses the combination of leading positions in the Party, the state, and the military came to be known as the "triple crown."

In clientelism and alliance building, the ploys of first-tier actors included placement of supporters in strategic positions and offers of material incentives to interests who would support them. For example, Khrushchev used both ploys in 1953 and 1954 to consolidate his control in the agricultural sector and to build his authority in this policy realm. Malenkov responded to Khrushchev's Virgin Lands program to grow wheat in Siberia and Central Asia by placing Malenkovites in those state positions responsible for implementing the program—specifically, the ministries of State Farms (A. I. Kozlov) and of Agriculture and Procurement (I. A. Benediktov). Khrushchev countered by both pushing through a reorganization that divided the latter ministry in two and securing the appointment of his own supporter (L. R. Korniets) to the post principally responsible for carrying out the Virgin Lands program (minister of agricultural procurement). Khrushchev appealed for support in the agricultural community by promising that his programs would bring increased investment and greater autonomy to the countryside.[38]

The choice between clientelism and alliances naturally encountered two constraints. First, these techniques often entailed trade-offs between

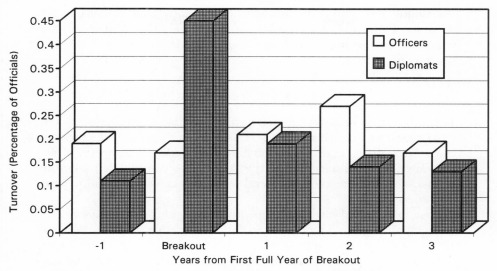

Figure 4.4. Turnover among Senior Diplomats and Military Officers, 1953–1989. Data collected by Barton Fisher.

control and efficiency. A leader had to choose between reliance on loyal clients, who faithfully followed the chief executive's political direction but brought less experience to the job, and reliance on expert allies, whose ties and experience in the bureaucracy promised greater efficiency but less responsiveness to political direction.[39] Similarly, the choice between clientelism and alliances was constrained by the extent to which subordinate bureaucrats had developed specialized skills or constituencies that made removing them difficult and costly. Second, the choice was constrained by the extent to which bureaucracies could resist intervention from outside the bureaucracy. For example, the foreign ministry was more open to intervention by the general secretary in personnel changes than was the defense ministry. Figure 4.4 shows the turnover among senior diplomats assigned to NATO countries and among senior military officers for one year preceding and three years following the beginning of a consolidation drive by the general secretary. Turnover among senior diplomats jumped significantly with each major attempt to consolidate directive leadership, as well as Khrushchev's victory over the anti-Party group and Brezhnev's consolidation of his foreign policy leadership, but changes in military personnel did not so clearly parallel the general secretaries' fortunes.[40] Indeed, the military was often one of the last bureaucracies to submit to clientelistic control as a general secretary consolidated directive rule. Both Khrushchev and Brezhnev initially had to be content with alliances forged with the minister of defense—

Voroshilov and Zhukov for Khrushchev, Malinovskii and Grechko for Brezhnev. Only later in their administrations were they able to select a minister from among their close associates—Malinovskii in 1957 and Ustinov in 1976.

STRATEGIES OF CONSOLIDATION

The constitution of Bolshevism shaped the general secretary's coalition-building strategy in two significant ways. It induced general secretaries to construct a small ("core") coalition during the period of competitive succession politics and then expand this coalition to consolidate leadership further. It also influenced the general secretary's choice of coalition partners at each stage.[41]

First, in the initial stages of competitive succession politics there was an inclination for general secretaries to focus energies on a narrow core coalition of supporters. As formal theories of coalitions suggest, a general secretary was initially under pressures to keep his winning coalition smaller in size, with as few members as possible.[42] Several pressures converged to favor smaller winning coalitions in the first stages of a consolidation drive: Members of a coalition sought to divide the spoils of victory as narrowly as possible. Coalitions of smaller size were more likely to reduce conflict among their members.[43] A coalition composed of *fewer* partners, usually requiring less negotiation and bargaining to organize, was easier to hold together.[44] The pressures to consolidate leadership quickly in the intensely competitive postsuccession period constrained a general secretary at first to focus on a smaller coalition of fewer core constituents that was just large enough to win.

The structure of Soviet politics made a minimal winning coalition in the strictest sense a risky proposition and induced a general secretary later to expand his coalition beyond the minimal winning size. Uncertainty about the weight of support to be delivered by individual partners, the reliability of that support, and even the amount of support necessary to maintain predominance pushed actors to form oversized coalitions.[45] Expanding the coalition reduced the general secretary's dependence on any individual partner, made less potent any threat of individual desertion from the coalition, and, so, strengthened the general secretary's bargaining position vis-à-vis his coalition partners.[46]

Nonetheless, subsequent expansion beyond the core coalition also came at some risk to the general secretary. By spreading scarce resources more broadly and increasing the heterogeneity among coalition partners, expansion could increase the conflict inside the coalition and the risk of desertion from the coalition.[47] If the general secretary sought to add new partners by redistributing scarce resources or by policies that conflicted with the core's priorities, expansion would give original ("core") members greater incentive to bolt from the coalition. Yet, this motivation to defect might also be deterred by expansion. The inclination to defect might be checked by declining numbers of significant partners outside the coalition. Only when a core coalition partner was assured that other core members would join the desertion would the partner act on its inclination.[48]

Second, in addition to shaping the size of his coalition, the constitution of Bolshevism shaped the general secretary's choice of second-tier coalition partners. His position atop the party apparatus made this the natural starting point in constructing his core coalition and so shaped his subsequent coalition building. The new general secretary moved quickly to control the Secretariat, removing incumbents and appointing new all-union secretaries. General secretaries also moved quickly to replace heads of Central Committee departments. For example, by December 1965, barely one year after Brezhnev had become general secretary, more than half the nineteen CC department heads were new appointees, including Brezhnev's associate in the department responsible for administration (Chernenko).[49]

The general secretary's position atop the Party apparatus constrained his subsequent coalition building in two important ways. First, he was constrained, at least in the initial stages, to seek partners with interests complementing those of the Party apparatus. Robert Axelrod demonstrates that "the less dispersion there is in the policy positions of the members of a coalition, the less conflict of interest there is." He predicts that to minimize this dispersion and conflict coalitions tend to form among parties adjacent in policy space.[50] (For illustration, in figure 4.3, leaders would be inclined to seek allies closer along the horizontal axis.) Studies of interest articulation at the Party Congresses show that the predominant concern of republic and regional officials was economic infrastructure and producer-goods industry, followed by agriculture and only distantly by consumption.[51] These operational responsibilities of republic and provincial party secretaries inclined a general secretary to include others concerned for the primacy of infrastructure, producers' goods industry, and agriculture in his core *connected* coalition. Second, enfranchisement of the armed bureaucracies, particularly in the 1950s, inclined a new general secretary from the very start to attempt to extend his coalition to include military and police. The special role of the coercive arms of the Party in the earlier successions made these essential partners. Even with institutionalization of Politburo accountability to the Central Committee and a declining role for armed coercion in the selection process, the military and police could deliver a disciplined bloc of support that from 1961 to 1981 averaged more than 8 percent of the full members of the Central Committee and by 1986 had surpassed 10 percent. Moreover, they pressed interests that complemented those of the apparatus.

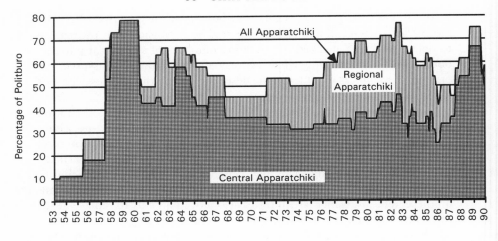

Figure 4.5. Composition of Politburo, March 1953–December 1989: Members from Party Apparatus

The necessary step from coalition formation to consolidation of leadership was cooptation of coalition partners into the Politburo. With support in the Central Committee and Politburo, the general secretary could move to dislodge other leaders and select loyalists. As figure 4.5 shows, general secretaries initially sponsored the cooptation of Party apparatchiki into the Politburo. Khrushchev relied principally on members of the national Secretariat, which by 1957 constituted more than three-quarters of the voting members of the Politburo. Brezhnev relied on party apparatchiki from the republics; thus, by the end of the Brezhnev administration Party apparatchiki from around the country constituted more than two-thirds of the voting membership of the Politburo. As a general secretary continued to expand his coalition, however, the proportionate role of the core coalition partners in the Politburo began to decline. For example, after 1959, the proportionate vote of Party apparatchiki declined.

BUREAUCRATIC POLITICS

Reciprocal accountability between Politburo and Central Committee was constrained in part by the hierarchical subordination of bureaucrats to governors. Indeed, it was a central defining characteristic of bureaucratic reciprocal accountability that these two relationships of politician-selector and governor-bureaucrat were inextricably interlinked. The relationship between governors and bureaucrats abstracted from the relationship of reciprocal accountability was hierarchical: the latter were agents of the former. In its role as policymaking body, the Politburo delegated to bureaucracies significant responsibilities. In both the flow of information and options from bureaucrats to governors and the implementation of governors' decisions, the bureaucrats were the governors' agents to gather intelligence and carry out policy.

Bureaucrats could enjoy considerable discretion: Constraints of limited information led leaders to delegate significant decisionmaking responsibilities within each sector to second-tier bureaucrats.[52] In many sectors this delegation led to what Condoleeza Rice has called "loose coupling": a system "in which the leadership concentrates on setting the broad outlines of policy while option formation and implementation are left to the professional core."[53] This may have been common throughout the economy because the center simply could not deal with all details.[54] Although the Politburo retained the final authority to intervene in any decision, limited capabilities kept it from doing this routinely.

The hierarchical relationship between governors and bureaucrats created a bureaucratic politics dominated by two processes commonly found in polities: First, bureaucrats sought to influence decisions through their control over information. As Jeremy Azrael observes, "experts and specialists inevitably control many of the critical 'premises' on which adequate decisions must be based, and from time to time such control is bound to be utilized to effect official policy choices and aggrandize political influence."[55] Second, governors sought to minimize the constraints of this information by control mechanisms. In short, central to the politics between tiers were problems of hidden information and hidden action and attempts to reduce these.

The two-tier structure of bureaucratic politics assigned different roles and responsibilities to governors and bureaucrats. This constrained each differently and confronted them with diverging incentives. Each approached policy in a different way. For first-tier actors *qua* governors success was defined by their policy leadership; for second-tier actors *qua* bureaucrats, by fulfillment of organizational missions. Governors in the first-tier performed *generalist* roles; they had to balance the needs of a more diverse set of sectors by seeking to reach trade-offs among the goals of these sectors. Bureaucrats in the second-tier performed *specialist* roles—responsible for the organizational missions of a narrower sector or specific organization. For second-tier actors an essential part of sustaining the support of their superiors, essential to their own political survival, was fulfillment of their role-defined responsibilities.[56] Roles, thus, divided bureaucrat from governor, and bureaucrat from bureaucrat.

Bureaucratic Influence

The constitution of Bolshevism magnified the influence of bureaucracies in their respective realms of policy, against both the first tier and other second-tier actors. The forced departicipation of society led to "compartmentalization" of politics in the second tier, which had two important consequences. First, it normally limited second-tier actors' direct or explicit policymaking role to the realms of their officially assigned responsibilities. Bureaucrats usually could influence policy in another sector only indirectly by proposals in their own realm.[57] The struggle *among* bureaucratized interests over resources and policies in many instances was indirect.

Second, it strengthened the hand of bureaucrats within their respective realms by giving individual bureaucracies a monopoly over relevant information. For example, in Soviet civil-military relations, as David Holloway observes, the Ministry of Defense and the General Staff "have a monopoly of expertise in the military field. . . . Even the size of military expenditure is kept secret, and this helps to fend off claims from civilian ministries for scarce resources."[58] Where bureaucrats held a near monopoly over information they could influence policy agendas and induce policymakers to ratify bureaucrats' proposals.[59]

As the providers of intelligence and options, second-tier actors sought to influence policy choices by what Charles Lindblom has called "partisan analysis"—"showing the proximate policy maker how a policy desired by the interest group squares with the policy maker's philosophy, values, or principles."[60] One form of partisan analysis came as competitive ideological appeals to demonstrate that one's policy prescription is "more orthodox" than the alternatives.[61] Much partisan analysis to influence policy used the vehicle of historical reconstruction where analysts reinterpreted the lessons of history to show that these demonstrated the validity of their policy proposals. For instance, in the late 1950s the military sought to wrest control over military doctrine from Party ideologues. They felt that control by nonexperts had led Soviet military strategy to lag behind developments in the West. Military historians argued their position, in part, by addressing the lessons of early World War II, which they claimed showed that the initial reverses at the hands of the Nazi armies were owing to excessive Party intervention. They implied that these reversals might have been avoided if military commanders had been given greater discretion.[62]

Bureaucrats often turned to outright distortion or falsification of expert information. The most common form of this occurred in the planning process as producers routinely understated their production capacity and overstated their resource needs in order to ensure themselves the safety factor (*strakhovka*) that would guarantee they could fulfill their quotas.[63] It was not limited to such minor peccadilloes, however. The Ministry of Timber, Pulp, and Woodworking was caught in flagrant misrepresentation when it started operations near Lake Baikal that violated environmental protection legislation. To meet the law's demanding pollution standards before operations could begin, the Ministry "shopped around" to find a sanitary inspector to certify its compliance. When the chief sanitary inspector of the Ministry of Land Reclamation and Water Management actually refused to certify the plant, the Ministry had to find a second and finally a third inspector to certify plant operation. Later, when the Ministry had to submit pollution reports to continue the plant's operations, it found an analyst to certify that the plant's production met state pollution standards by paying an annual fee of 100,000 rubles to his laboratory, under the guise of retaining the analyst as a consultant.[64]

Interests that could not persuade might attempt to sabotage the implementation of policy. Perhaps the most common form of this was simulating successful fulfillment of the plan by factory managers and ministries that came to be known as *ochkovtiratel'stvo*.[65] By changing the assortment of output, lowering the quality of production, or altering the size of goods, producers could claim to have met the production targets set for them by the leadership. In specific episodes this sabotage could take still more dramatic forms. In 1964, the KGB apparently showed its dissatisfaction toward Khrushchev's rapprochement with West Germany by initiating a campaign of harassment against West German diplomats. This culminated at the Zagorsk Monastery on 12 September 1964 in a nearly fatal mustard gas attack against one German diplomat with covert intelligence responsibilities. According to William Hyland and Richard Shryock, "the KGB apparently had engineered the entire affair, hoping at a minimum to rid itself of a dangerous adversary, and at a maximum to embarrass official relations between Moscow and Bonn at a time when Khrushchev was preparing for a visit to West Germany."[66]

Control of Bureaucracy

The constitution of Bolshevism made these problems of hidden information and hidden action acute. Forced departicipation deprived the regime of many natural checks that might emerge among bureaucracies or in civil society. To combat these problems Soviet leaders *qua* governors relied on institutional mechanisms to expand their control over the behavior of bureaucrats.[67] These levers included institutional checking, selection procedures, compensation schedules, and monitoring. Yet, as in other polities, bureaucrats developed coping strategies that eroded these and produced still other problems of hidden information and action.

Institutional checking divided and sometimes duplicated tasks among organizations so as to make these organizations naturally check the fulfillment of responsibilities by others. For example, the leadership responded to problems of hidden information by multiplying agencies providing information and options. In the areas of foreign policy and defense the Brezhnev administration sought to reduce the monopoly of ministerial think tanks by encouraging the Academy of Sciences to expand its policy-oriented institutes such as the Institute for World Economy and International Relations (IMEMO). Similarly, the leadership sought to prevent the complete vertical integration of production processes by separating construction agencies, production ministries, and end users. Thus, ministerial users of the product of other agencies became in a sense natural watchdogs over the quality and quantity of output. State arbitration (*gosarbitrazh*) provided a mechanism for these disputes to come to light.[68] Institutional checking was eroded, however, by the coping strategies of bureaucrats. Bureaucrats could use their monopoly to deny critical information to alternative agencies. The Academy think tanks, for example, apparently denied access to secret data, were thus eclipsed by the Defense Ministry's think tanks.[69] To overcome the division of production, institutional consumers such as the Defense Ministry sought to isolate themselves from unreliable suppliers by developing their own internal construction and supply agencies—in essence, reunifying tasks.[70]

Selection procedures provided levers to control the type of personnel appointed to bureaucratic posts. The *nomenklatura* system was established to ensure that key appointments in the bureaucracies were approved by higher levels of the Party apparatus. The nomenklatura lists included more than half a million and perhaps as many as three million posts over which the Party apparatus maintained some routine appointment power.[71] Yet, leaders of bureaucracies sought security for their loyalists and technical competence rather than simple political correctness among their subordinates.[72] The consequences of this were growing emphasis on technical competence, routinization of promotion within bureaucracies, and less political intervention from the Party apparatus.

Compensation schedules of bureaucrats were manipulated by governors to direct bureaucrats' activities. As in all complex bureaucracies, the costs of information gathering led the Soviet leadership to manipulate easily observed measures of performance to reward bureaucrats. Thus, success indicators for factories were often expressed in tons of output, for geologists in meters dug, and for truckers in ton-kilometers hauled. These shaped behavior of bureaucrats, but in what has come to be known as "Goodhart's law" these often also induced bureaucrats to develop coping strategies that maximized performance relative to these measures (for example, by producing heavy chandeliers) at the expense of other dimensions of performance.[73]

Monitoring addressed problems of hidden information and hidden action not remedied by these other controls and responded to the new problems the first three types of controls created. Monitoring was institutionalized among bureaucrats by bracketing each bureaucracy with parallel bureaucracies that had as one of their responsibilities supervision of activities.[74] Even monitoring elicited coping strategies from bureaucrats that protected their hidden information and hidden action. For example, the industrial manager and Party secretary in a factory who had similar success indicators and career incentives often formed family circles to provide mutual guarantee (*krugovaia poruka*) between monitored and monitor.[75]

These bureaucratic politics of influence and control bound governors and bureaucrats. Because many of them were also bound as politicians and selectors, bureaucratic politics became tightly intertwined with the "selectoral" politics of accountability. Coalition building became intimately tied to policymaking.

RECIPROCAL ACCOUNTABILITY IN PERSPECTIVE

The decisions that founded the Soviet polity created dual-role elites bound in reciprocal accountability. They defined intersecting games of "selectoral" and bureaucratic politics. These rules constrained the strategic choices of political actors, and the outcome of those games from 1953 to 1986 was further institutionalization of reciprocal accountability.

Western analyses have encountered difficulty as they attempted to cope with the reality of reciprocal accountability. Many of these difficulties have resulted as analysts have attempted to discuss accountability by focusing on one element of reciprocal accountability in isolation and through the conceptual categories of the hierarchical relations normally encountered in a political order with well-defined principles of sovereignty. A common treatment of accountability in the Soviet polity stresses the hierarchical control of leadership over the Central Committee and bureaucracies and ignores (or denies) the accountability of the leadership to the Central Committee. For example, Frederick C. Barghoorn and Thomas F. Remington argue that the Party apparatchiki so fully control the election process that they simply select all incumbents: "Through their monopoly over the personnel selection system, party executives determine the slate of candidates . . . for membership in the party committees, the bureaus, and the secretariats."[76] Thus, the relationship between the Politburo leadership and the Central Committee bureaucrats is simply hierarchical. For example, William Odom argues that the relationship between the party leadership and the military is "fundamentally a bureaucratic matter; and politics within bureaucracies is essentially a struggle by the top leadership to impose its value preferences on the lower bureaucratic levels."[77] Those analysts who stress the importance of leadership conflict or political interest groups in Soviet politics highlight isolated consequences that flow from the relationship of reciprocal accountability without identifying their structural causes. Among the general secretary, Politburo, and Central Committee, John A. Armstrong, for example, notes "four patterns of subordination": Stalin's use of the Politburo to destroy Central Committee members; Stalin's domination of both Politburo and Central Committee; Khrushchev's use of the Central Committee in 1957 to defeat the Politburo majority; and the Politburo majority's use of the Central Committee in 1964 against Khrushchev.[78] Analysts stressing bureaucratic politics, such as Roman Kolkowicz, have noted that bureaucracies compete for resources and employ "a variety of ways of influencing policy and social planning."[79] Yet, typically these do not lead the authors to consider how these patterns may be the result of a unique pattern of accountability.

Closer to the model of bureaucratic reciprocal accountability are studies that stress the interdependence between leaders and bureaucrats. Ken Booth stresses the particular interdependence between Politburo members and armed bureaucrats: "The military looks to the Politburo for backing for its preferred programs and the expenditure to support them, while the party leaders look to the military for support in struggles for succession and in subsequent efforts to maintain authority."[80] Yet, this does not bring together the elements of this interdependence in an embracing concept. One attempt to conceptualize this interdependence is Robert V. Daniels's model of the circular flow of power. Jerry F. Hough makes this a central element in his model of the Soviet polity as a "parliamentary system of a special type," likening Central Committee to parliament, Politburo to cabinet, and general secretary to prime minister. It is special because the general secretary, through the circular flow of power, plays a key role in personnel selection for the posts represented in the Central Committee.[81] The parliamentary metaphor is, of course, inappropriate because a true parliamentary system is embedded within an overall hierarchical political order of popular sovereignty. The circular flow of power is also an essentially hierarchical model that explains the general secretary's dominance over Politburo and Central Committee; it omits the reciprocity that existed between the Politburo as a whole and the Central Committee. To come to grips with the control that the Politburo exercised over the tenure of the Central Committee and the general secretary, the circular flow of power would have to move toward a model of reciprocal accountability. The interdependence of bureaucratic subordination, interest group influence, and leadership accountability requires a model of reciprocal accountability.

CHAPTER FIVE

Balanced Leadership, 1953–1986

A SECOND development in the constitution of Bolshevism after 1953 was the institutionalization of balanced collective leadership. The inequalities among second-tier constituencies and the unequal strategic advantages of first-tier posts in the original design of the constitution of Bolshevism had given rise to the cycling of leadership—the alternation between collective and directive leadership. The first consolidation of directive leadership had destroyed both leaders and bureaucrats in the two tiers of politics, and another consolidation after 1953 might again threaten many incumbents. When given the chance to revise the rules of politics, many in both tiers established greater obstacles to consolidation and stronger guarantees of collective rule.

The institutionalization of balancing was intimately tied to the institutionalization of reciprocal accountability. The consolidation of directive rule had depended on the acquisition of an apex role by the leader—that is, accumulating multiple leadership posts—and the dispersal of policymaking from the Politburo to the separate organs chaired by these posts. The consolidation of directive leadership had shifted the balance of power between tiers and had threatened the accountability of Politburo to Central Committee. Thus, institutionalization of obstacles to consolidation in the first tier would complement the institutionalization of reciprocal accountability between tiers and specifically the institutionalization of the relationship between Politburo and Central Committee.

In arguing that collective leadership was increasingly institutionalized after 1953, I am challenging the literature that documents the cycling of leadership and claims this was an inevitable feature of Soviet politics. According to this literature on succession crises, these cycles were likely to recur until there was substantial institutional change to remedy two constitutional flaws: first, establishment of a stable policymaking center, and, second, creation of rules for an orderly succession.[1] The analysis in chapter 4 shows that after 1953 the institutionalization of reciprocal accountability between Central Committee and Politburo was a major step toward precisely these types of constitutive rules. In making the case for the institutionalization of collective leadership, I am arguing that failure to recognize that the cycles of leadership took place in a changing institutional context led significant parts of western Sovietology to a form of procrusteanism in which succession "crises" were made to appear alike and consolidated leadership was treated as identical.[2] Yet, the directive leadership of Leonid Brezhnev was not identical to that of Nikita Khrushchev, and neither was identical to that of Joseph Stalin; most important, as I argue in the conclusion to this chapter, the consolidation of Mikhail Gorbachev was unlike that of his predecessors. Nor were the succession politics of 1983 identical to those of 1953 or 1923. The cycles of alternating collective and directive leadership were themselves undergoing change.

This chapter is divided into five main parts: The first section surveys the processes of cycling of leadership and institutionalization of balancing. The next three sections present case studies analyzing the development of balancing rules in the post-Stalin, post-Khrushchev, and post-Brezhnev successions. The conclusion examines how this constitutional development by the 1980s produced carefully balanced leadership.

CYCLES AND INSTITUTIONALIZATION

The alternation of collective and directive leadership has long been a standard article of Western wisdom about the Soviet political system. Yet this captures only half—the less dynamic half—of the changes that took place in Soviet leadership over time. Soviet political actors responded to this cycling with strategic moves in the game of constitutional politics to revise the rules of politics. A result of these revisions was the institutionalization of a balancing mechanism among leaders and a fundamental change in leadership cycling.

Cycles of Leadership

The alternation of collective and directive leadership originated with the Soviet political system or at least with its first succession. These oscillations produced profound shifts in the distribution of power in the first tier and in the balance of power between tiers. It also led to a cycle in the strategic behavior of political actors shifting between balancing and bandwagoning. Nonetheless, the cycling of leadership did not itself lead to long-term change in the rules of the constitutional order.

These cycles were rooted in the original constitution of Bolshevism. Failure to assign precise policymaking responsibilities to roles in the first tier and the absence of rules for its transfer allowed oscillations in the power of all first-tier actors. Most important, in the original constitutional design the post of general or first secretary was not fixed in the political landscape; it did not possess defined or guaranteed powers; mechanisms for transferring this post were fluid; and its term was indeterminate. No first-tier actor stepped into the full powers that his post might ultimately exercise; he had to consolidate his hold on these powers. The indeterminacy of power in the first tier impelled leaders to consolidate their power against the efforts of others to consolidate their own.

In the second tier the distribution of power gave an advantage to the coalition-building strategies associated with the post of general secretary. The *kontrol'* and personnel responsibilities of the Party apparatus favored the first-tier actor who began his coalition building there. Other leaders had to build their coalitions within other segments of the narrow bureaucratic elite represented in the selectorate, but these coalitions could seldom match that of the general secretary. For example, in competition with Nikita Khrushchev for preeminence within the leadership, Georgii Malenkov appealed to technocrats and members of the intelligentsia, who represented some of the brightest minds and finest talent of the country. Yet, this constituency was not an organized force that could contend with Khrushchev's loyalists in the Party apparatus. Because the original constitution of Bolshevism imposed few limits on the general secretary's hold within the party apparatus, competitive consolidation efforts were likely to produce a strategic breakout by the general secretary and a breakdown of collective leadership. Collective leadership often gave way to directive rule by the general secretary.[3]

Consolidation by a general secretary influenced the strategies of other leaders in the first-tier. The expansion of a general secretary's coalition brought a shift from balancing to bandwagoning. By applying the theories of structural realism developed in international politics to the domestic politics of China from 1949 to 1978, Avery Goldstein demonstrates how the structural constraints found in a Leninist polity create shifting coalition strategies among political actors. Goldstein argues that when power is more evenly distributed in the first tier "the growing power of one actor or coalition will call forth a countervailing response from those to whom such strength poses a potential threat." After a single leader has consolidated significant policy leadership, however, the response of others may not be further counterbalancing but rather bandwagoning behind the emerging victor or rising hegemon. Owing to the effects of imperfect information the transition from balancing to bandwagoning strategies may begin in anticipation of such a coalition, well before a dominant coalition has actually formed. On the eve of victory, individual leaders may rush to join so as to be rewarded as the critical contributors to the coalition.[4]

Because this balancing and bandwagoning in the first tier took place within a larger constitutional order of reciprocal accountability, however, potentially a third phase followed the shift from balancing to bandwagoning—renewed counterbalancing. The growth of an oversized coalition could lead to the disaffection of second-tier constituencies in the general secretary's coalition—particularly among the original coalition partners of Party apparatus, heavy industry, armed forces, and police. The spreading of scarce policy resources among the constituencies of an enlarged coalition could lead to desertion by these core constituencies. This was sometimes tempting for ambitious first-tier leaders—such as Leonid Brezhnev in 1964—who believed they could bring these disaffected constituencies together in a new selectorate majority and on this basis convince other Politburo members to join in counterbalancing.

Consolidation by a general secretary also influenced the balance of power between tiers. The extent to which the second tier could influence political outcomes rose with collective leadership and declined with directive leadership. Collective leadership brought greater competition to the Politburo. This increased the incentive of losing minorities in the Politburo to appeal outside it, tempting them with both the hope of winning in a larger arena and the expectation that a divided leadership would not impose penalties for such appeals. In this competition, first-tier actors were more dependent on second-tier actors as leaders sought to promote their power aspirations through alliances with selectors. This permitted selectors greater opportunity to press their policy preferences.[5]

The balance between tiers also shifted because collective leadership increased the coordination problems of the first tier and led it to delegate choices to the second. Political opposition and policy divisions within the Politburo rendered it less able to reach decisions—many policy issues were left unresolved and authoritative decisions unmade—and many were deferred to the second tier.[6] For example, the leadership vacuum during Yurii Andropov's illness permitted the military to play a greater role. During the KAL-007 crisis, military officers were highly visible, speaking for the leadership in televised press conferences. Indeed, for twenty-nine days the civilian leadership was unable to publicly contain the diplomatic consequences of this tragedy, while military officers played a leading and largely ineffective role in explaining the incident. In private, civilian officials criticized military handling of the crisis, but at the top the political will to handle the crisis was lacking.[7]

Institutionalization of Balancing

Cycles changed with the institutionalization of rules for collective leadership in the first tier. Each succession was an opportunity to not only reaffirm the accountability of Politburo to Central Committee but also establish new rules that would reinforce collective leadership and the balancing mechanism. Institutionalization included three developments: demarcation of leadership offices, establishment of mutual checking, and creation of procedural norms. *Demarcation* of the office of general secretary meant that its powers were more clearly defined over the decades from 1953 to 1986. In March 1953 no general or first secretary was designated (leaving open the possibility of a return to the 1917–1921 pattern), but by 1982 experience had reinforced the expectation that the selection of general secretary was the selection of the leader of the Communist party and Soviet society. *Mutual checking* in the first tier limited the power of each leader, and particularly the general secretary, by balancing their institutional bases against one another. As I illustrate in the next sections, rules evolved so as to divide ever more finely key posts and to block the accumulation of posts. *Proceduralism* reinforced collective responsibility by establishing stable norms for interaction among Politburo members.[8] Most important, proceduralism established "verifiable" early warning signals of impending threats to collectivism; violation of procedures could be taken as prima facie evidence of such a threat.

These three developments in the first tier checked the twin threats contained within collective leadership: *disqualification*, that is, the temptation to disqualify losing first-tier actors from further participation; and *defection*, that is, the temptation to defect from the oligarchy by appeals to outside constituencies, either to involve the selectorate in first-tier policymaking or to expand the constituencies represented in the first tier. Disqualification sought to constrict participation by eliminating first-tier actors, defection to enlarge it. The former tended to be a strategy of winning first-tier actors, the latter of the losers. Disqualification and defection threatened the balance within collective leadership by changing the essential players. Demarcation, mutual checking, and proceduralism improved the balancing mechanism by preventing disqualification or defection. Much like the balance of power in international relations, competitive efforts at self-aggrandizement within collective leadership created a form of balancing that preserved the collectivity.

The recurring occasion for significant steps forward in the process of institutionalizing balanced collective leadership was the succession. At each succession the rules governing a new collective leadership were renegotiated and the guarantees of balancing improved. In these negotiations the interacting strategic choices of leaders and selectors produced demarcation, mutual checking, and proceduralism—the bases of institutionalized balanced leadership. To illustrate, members of the first tier needed leadership to solve the collective action problems of the Politburo and to protect the leading role of the first over the second tier. Within the second tier the Party apparatus needed the general secretary to maintain its prerogatives relative to other bureaucracies; these came together to institutionalize the post of general secretary and many of its prerogatives. At the same time both groups shared an interest in limiting the self-aggrandizement of the general secretary because both became more vulnerable as a general secretary consolidated directive rule. Thus, in successions these groups also joined to limit the leader's prerogatives.[9] Limits on patronage power were exacted in bargains by first-tier actors seeking to minimize the threat of break out and by second-tier actors seeking to reduce their vulnerability to manipulation for purely political purposes.

All Soviet successions initially led to collective leadership founded on a settlement dividing posts and responsibilities in such a way as to balance power and maintain the collective leadership. These agreements have been called the "gentlemen's agreement" of 1953, the "compact" of 1964–1965, and the balancing acts of 1982–1985. With each succession the leadership built on existing rules and further adjusted the obstacles to the consolidation of directive leadership, strengthened the balancing among first-tier posts, and expanded the norms of collective responsibility so as to make collective leadership more secure with each succession. The evolution of the constitution grew out of competitive efforts to accumulate power and build authority within the structures of reciprocal accountability. The potential for these developments, but not the specific trajectory, was inherent in the original constitutional structure.

THE "GENTLEMEN'S AGREEMENT" OF 1953

In the period from 1953 to 1986 the months that followed the death of Stalin were characterized by the greatest equality among leaders and between tiers. At few times was the position of key Politburo members so evenly balanced or the relative power of elites in Party, state, military, and police so equal as in the months that followed Stalin's death.[10] The dogmas of the new leadership denigrated the role of individuals and stressed collective responsibility. On 16 April 1953 *Pravda* proclaimed,

> The entire work of the Central Committee is the embodiment of the wisdom of the party, of the enormous experience of its collective leadership. . . . No matter how experienced leadership may be, no matter what their knowledge and ability, they do not possess and they cannot replace the initiative and experience of the whole collective.[11]

Pravda called collectivism "the highest principle of party leadership." From 1953 to 1955 the leadership remained fluid, passing from a collectivity led by Malenkov and Beria, to one led by Malenkov, and then by Khrushchev, but in this period leadership remained collective.[12]

Separation of Powers

The balance was the result of what the *Economist* called a "gentlemen's agreement" reached among top leaders from the Politburo, Council of Ministers, and Presidium of the Supreme Soviet to allocate key posts.[13] Public announcements of this decision stressed that the distribution of positions was to preserve unity among leaders and public order: "the most important task of the Party and the government is to ensure uninterrupted and correct leadership of the whole life of the country, which in turn demands the greatest unity of leadership and prevention of any kind of [public] disarray and panic."[14] The principals agreed to a collective leadership that included (in initial order of precedence) Georgii Malenkov as premier (chairman of the Council of Ministers), Lavrentii Beria as head of the unified police (minister of internal affairs, uniting the former MGB and MVD), Viacheslav Molotov as minister of foreign affairs, Kliment Voroshilov as chief of state (chairman of the Presidium of the Supreme Soviet), Nikita Khrushchev as a central party secretary, and Nikolai Bulganin as minister of defense. The agreement sought to ensure the survival of collective leadership (unlike the experience three decades earlier) by a more careful balancing of posts, new rules to limit disqualification and defection, and more attentive balancing.

To avoid threats to the balance among posts the leadership did not appoint a general or first secretary. The decision to award Khrushchev the title first secretary came only in September 1953, and then only because the coalition developing against Malenkov needed a counterweight to Malenkov's authority as premier. Nonetheless, by designating Khrushchev "first secretary" (the title commonly used for each head apparatchik at lower levels of the Party) rather than "general secretary" (a post only Stalin had held), the leadership signaled that there would be limits on the powers of this office.[15]

New proceduralism limited disqualification among leaders by establishing rules that restricted use of the purge among first-tier actors. This rule made it more difficult to remove Politburo members, and, in particular, to expel them from the Party: For example, the defeat of Malenkov and Molotov in 1955 led to their removal from the premiership and foreign ministry, but did not precipitate their removal from the Politburo. Even after their removal from the Politburo in 1957 as punishment for their parts in the Anti-Party Group, they remained in the Communist party. Significant evidence suggests that Khrushchev subsequently pushed to have Malenkov, Molotov, and Kaganovich expelled from the Party and possibly tried for complicity in Stalin's crimes, but for some years the norms governing first-tier relations blocked this. Members of the Politburo and Central Committee apparently opposed measures that might place in Khrushchev's hands the dangerous weapon of the purge, which might in the future be turned against them.[16]

The post-Stalin collective leadership also reinforced norms against defection by establishing new barriers to potential defectors who might appeal to larger constituencies. Factional activity had been proscribed in the first succession following Lenin's incapacitation. The post-Stalin collective leadership adopted a powerful mechanism to give this prohibition teeth and limit the opportunity for its members to reach outside the oligarchy with policy appeals. According to an official Party history, "a strict procedure was established in the CPSU Central Committee whereby no important measure and no speech (to be published in the press) by a member of the Presidium or Secretary of the CPSU Central Committee was undertaken without preliminary group discussion."[17]

In this period the balancing mechanism of fluid alliances among leaders operated more successfully than in the first succession thirty years earlier to contain threats to collective leadership. The first success of the post-Stalin balance was in blocking Malenkov. The initial division of posts on 6 March 1953, apparently concentrated too much power in Malenkov's hands and necessitated a new agreement to adjust the balance. Within a week the leaders agreed to a second division of posts to avoid the dangerous overlap that could permit one of their number to disrupt the balance.[18] As a result of the new adjustment of the balance no one person sat in all three centers of policymaking—Presidium of the Council of Ministers, Secretariat, and Politburo.

A second threat to balance was the concentration of the police power in Beria's hands. Khrushchev's pleadings with minister of defense Bulganin to help prevent Beria from becoming head of a unified police apparatus illustrate the balance-of-power logic. Khrushchev claims to have tried to convince Bulganin that unification of the police under Beria would create a dangerous concentration of power: "No matter what happens, we can't let him do this. If he becomes minister of state security it will be the beginning of the end for us. He'll take that post for the purpose of destroying us, and he will do it, too, if we let him."[19] Beria's move to use the police organization to extend his hold over parts of the Party and state brought his removal. As Merle Fainsod observes, Malenkov's explanation of this removal contained much "typical communist hyperbole," but "the one accusation which carries conviction is that Beria sought to utilize his base in the MVD to attain a position of undisputed supremacy."[20] This threat to the balance brought his removal.

To prevent a replay of Beria's strategy, the leadership divided the police organization and balanced control over its parts. In March 1954 the police apparatus was once again divided between Ministry of Internal

TABLE 5.1
Personnel Change in the Politburo, 1953–1985
(Annual Rates)

Period	Terminated	Appointed
March 1953–May 1957	0.24	0.48
June 1957–September 1964	1.91	2.05
November 1964–December 1970	0.50	1.06
January 1971–October 1982	0.51	1.01
November 1982–February 1985	0.43	0.86

Note: Rates are calculated as (total changes for period/months in period) × 12.

Affairs (MVD) responsible for the uniformed police and a Committee for State Security (KGB) responsible for security police. Control of these two organs was balanced so no one leader dominated both. Khrushchev was able to win appointment of his close associate General I. A. Serov to head the KGB in April 1954, but he could not initially control the MVD.

Balancing between March 1953 and May 1957 brought stability to the Politburo. With a logic akin to that of the Concert of Europe, the leaders prevented expansion of the political process and removal of essential players from the Politburo, for either would have upset the balance. The post-Stalin collective leadership saw no changes in the voting membership of the Politburo between March 1955 and June 1957, with the exception of Beria. Additions did not begin until after February 1955, when Khrushchev began his breakout, but only two additions were made before June 1957. As table 5.1 shows, the early years of the Khrushchev administration (1953 to 1955) brought unusually low turnover among voting members of the Politburo.

Breakdown of Balancing

Nonetheless, the balancing mechanism failed to constrain a third threat—from Khrushchev himself. The failure to limit further the powers of his office and to take timely measures to check his use of this post to expand his control to other bureaucracies rendered the balancing mechanism ineffective, and remedial balancing attempts came too late. At the December 1956 CC Plenum a majority of the leadership joined in a scheme to check Khrushchev's growing consolidation by strengthening central state bodies against Khrushchev's Party apparatus. The Supreme Soviet on 12 February 1957 adopted a reform to broaden the powers of the State Economic Commission; this would make its new chair Mikhail Pervukhin an "overlord of overlords" in economic administration. Yet, Khrushchev struck back the next day by winning Central Committee agreement to eliminate almost entirely the ministries on which the State Economic Commission's control of the economy would depend.[21] Having failed in this attempt to counterbalance the first secretary, the Politburo members made a last attempt at balancing with the ill-starred coup in June 1957 that earned the defeated Politburo majority the label Anti-Party Group.

Khrushchev's directive leadership after 1957 was structured by his apex role within the Politburo. The strategic objective of a first-tier actor intent on directorship was to gain exclusive simultaneous membership and then leadership in all potential policy centers and to disperse policymaking among these. Stalin had relied on his apex role among small committees within the Party leadership such as the "sextets" to ensure his strategic dominance of the policy process. For Khrushchev the strategic objective was to gain control of the Secretariat of the Communist party and the Presidium of the Council of Ministers alongside the Politburo. In this apex role, Khrushchev could disperse policymaking among organs and play the critical coordinating, leadership role.[22]

Khrushchev's control of the Secretariat came with appointments beginning in 1955. In the next three years Khrushchev made eight new appointments to the Secretariat.[23] The separate Bureau of the Central Committee for the Russian Republic created in 1956 provided him direct control over the Russian party apparatus that could circumvent the mediating influence of the all-union Secretariat and apparatus. To further consolidate his control over the Secretariat, at the May and July 1960 CC Plena Khrushchev purged it once again; he replaced the colleagues who had supported him in his rise with more dependent clients. The Secretariat was cut from ten to five members by removing six of his former protégés from 1957 and appointing the man he had selected as his heir apparent, Frol Kozlov.[24]

Khrushchev's assumption of the premiership (chairman of the Council of Ministers) gave him a second forum in which to make policy—the state cabinet. In June 1957, the removal of the Anti-Party Group terminated five members of the Council of Ministers Presidium (including Molotov, Kaganovich, and Pervukhin), but only one new appointment was made, so that Khrushchev did not control the body at the end of 1957. The removal of Bulganin, Khrushchev's election to the premiership, and three new appointments in 1958 gave Khrushchev and his four close associates dominant position on the seven-member CM Presidium.[25] As Khrushchev dispersed policymaking among the separate organs he led, the Presidium of the Council of Ministers took on new life.

As a consequence of these moves, Khrushchev had acquired an apex role that permitted him to play the critical coordinating functions among separate centers of policymaking: (1) Membership in the Politburo was evenly distributed among secretaries, members of the Council of Ministers Presidium, and members of the Russian Bureau; (2) Members of the separate policy centers—Secretariat, Council of Ministers Presidium, and Russian Bureau—did not serve concurrently on more than two of these bodies; (3) Khrushchev chaired all four bodies.[26]

With Khrushchev's assumption of the apex role, much of the enforcement of mutual checking among leaders and many norms of collective leadership eroded. For example, divided control of the police broke down. On 1 February 1956, appointment of his close associate N. P. Dudorov as minister of internal affairs and in December 1958 the appointment of Aleksandr Shelepin to head the KGB gave Khrushchev tight control over both police organizations.[27] The breakdown of collective leadership also weakened norms against purges. In 1961 Khrushchev succeeded in expelling the Anti-Party Group from the Party, although he did not try them for complicity in Stalin's crimes.[28]

Removal of the Anti-Party Group from the Politburo, by breaking the balance in the first tier, opened the flood gates for rapid turnover in the Politburo. As table 5.1 shows, turnover in the Politburo was significantly higher from this point until the end of the Khrushchev administration. Between June 1957 and September 1964, there were fourteen terminations and fifteen new appointments. In June 1957 alone four voting members associated with the Anti-Party Group, including Malenkov, Molotov, and Kaganovich, were removed and Pervukhin was demoted to a nonvoting (candidate) member; moreover, expansion of its voting membership from eleven to fifteen permitted Khrushchev to pack the body with loyalists. These included six new voting members brought in from the party apparatus, so that in July 1957 eleven of the fifteen members were Party secretaries (see figure 4.5).[29] The rate of terminations remained high after 1957. While Khrushchev used the first wave of changes in June 1957 to tip the balance in favor of his dependent secretaries, in subsequent shifts he sought to establish a new balance between the Secretariat and other institutions that he now dominated.

THE "COMPACT" OF 1964–1965

The removal of Khrushchev brought a new division of posts with Leonid Brezhnev as general secretary, Aleksei Kosygin as premier (chairman of the Council of Ministers), Nikolai Podgornyi, Aleksandr Shelepin, and Mikhail Suslov as central Party secretaries. Khrushchev's removal also brought a new opportunity to build more effective guarantees of collective leadership. This team reached an agreement on powersharing and, with the experience of Khrushchev's breakout, established stronger checks on the consolidation of autocratic power. These included more thorough balancing of the posts and powers among members of the collective leadership to facilitate mutual checking, higher obstacles to defection and disqualification, and more vigilant enforcement of the norms that would serve as early warnings of threats to balance.

Mutual Checking

Predicated on the presumption, as the General Staff's newspaper *Krasnaia zvezda* put it, that "two heads are better than one,"[30] the post-Khrushchev balancing agreement led to what Rigby has called an "implicit compact." As before, its provisions (1) divided the posts of premier (chairman of the Council of Ministers) and general secretary between two leaders, (2) distributed seats in the Politburo, Secretariat, and Presidium of the Council of Ministers so "as to avoid dangerous patterns of overlap," and (3) established "countervailing power between top-most leaders." It went beyond the previous agreements, however, in that it (4) significantly reduced opportunities for patronage in the second tier, particularly by limiting the general secretary's personnel powers.[31] The first three parts of this compact were part of the 1953 settlement, and the leaders may have hoped that by more careful monitoring the 1965 compact would succeed where the 1953 gentlemen's agreement had failed. Yet the new limits on patronage suggest they did not trust to this alone.

The division of posts was done with fine attention to reestablishing balance and blocking the concentration of excessive power in the hands of any one person. To prevent a new consolidation, the day after Khrushchev's ouster the Central Committee Plenum adopted a resolution to keep the posts of general secretary and premier (chairman of the Council of Ministers) in separate hands.[32] An essential structural foundation for the balance between general secretary and premier was reestablishment of the ministries that had been dismantled under Khrushchev. Beginning in March 1965 a growing number of state committees were transformed into ministries—first in the area of defense production. In September 1965 the regional economic councils (*sovnarkhozy*) that Khrushchev had used to assume ministerial responsibilities were abolished. By 1967, twenty-five all-union and twenty-seven union-republic ministries had been reestablished. These would be balanced against the Party apparatus.

Control of the police was once again divided. In September 1966 Brezhnev moved to establish his control over the uniformed police by appointing his long-time associate Nikolai Shchelokov as minister of internal affairs, but the security police remained outside his control. In 1967 removal of Aleksandr Shelepin from the Secretariat where he supervised the police and removal of close associate Vladimir Semichastnyi from the KGB gave Brezhnev the opportunity in 1967 to purge the police of *Shelepintsy* (allies of Shelepin), but he did not gain control of the secret police. Control was balanced by the collective leadership through the alternating layering of associates. Brezhnev's associate Nikolai Savinkin became head of the Party department supervising the police (Administrative Organs Department), and Brezhnev's brother-in-law (Semen K. Tsvigun) became first deputy chair of the KGB and associates Viktor M. Chebrikov and Georgii Tsinev became deputy chairmen of the secret police organization. Yet, to keep control of the police divided and to block any threat to the first-tier balance, the leadership placed the chairmanship of the KGB, situated between the layers of Brezhnev associates, in the hands of independent political figure Yurii Andropov, who was not a dependent client of the general secretary.

Key to the success of the balance after 1964, where previously it had failed, were limits on the general secretary's control over personnel. Beginning with the very first succession in the 1920s, the greatest threat of breakout had come from the general secretary's control of the Party apparatus. In 1922 and in 1953 the collective leadership established inadequate safeguards against patronage within the Party apparatus. Thus, by consolidating control within the apparatus, a general secretary could confront other leaders with a fait accompli in a Central Committee showdown. Indeed, between 1953 and the 1956 Party Congress, Khrushchev had replaced seven of the fourteen union-republic secretaries and thirty-nine of the sixty-nine Russian Republic provincial first secretaries. He replaced them with a dependent clientele: Three of the new union-republic secretaries and six of the new Russian provincial secretaries had previously served with Khrushchev in the Ukraine. By the 1961 Party Congress in October, all but two of the Russian Republic's provincial secretaries had been replaced.[33]

The post-Khrushchev leadership limited the general secretary's patronage power by separating and balancing control over the apparatus. Initially Brezhnev shared control over the patronage machine with Podgornyi. Thus, at the critical moment (November–December 1964) when the provincial party organizations were being reorganized in order to undo a reform previously introduced by Khrushchev, no one leader was in a position to use this to break out from collective leadership by appointing a clientele among the first secretaries. Reflecting the balance within the Secretariat, the leadership relied on the solution of bringing back previous incumbents to fill the first secretary posts in the reunified organizations—or where one was no longer available, promoting the ranking party official in the provincial organization. When Brezhnev succeeded in gaining the transfer of Podgornyi from the Secretariat, the

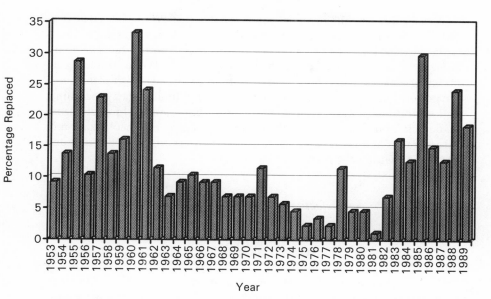

Figure 5.1. Turnover among First Secretaries of Union Republics and Russian Provinces, 1953–1989. Data provided by John P. Willerton.

collective leadership still checked Brezhnev's control of Party personnel policy by bringing up Ivan Kapitonov to counterbalance Brezhnev's associate Andrei Kirilenko. Limitations on the general secretary's patronage powers reduced opportunities for consolidation within the second tier. According to a provincial first secretary speaking to the 1966 Party Congress, between late 1964 and April 1966, "the Central Committee has made a most important turnabout in its work with personnel and has ended mass transfers."[34] The 1966 Party Congress removed the provision in the 1961 Party Statutes mandating turnover of one-third of the membership of Party committees at each election, a provision Khrushchev had used to justify removal of disloyal Party personnel. As a consequence, the rate of annual turnover among union-republic and Russian Republic provincial first secretaries was significantly lower in the Brezhnev years. Figure 5.1 shows that in each administration the breakout of each general secretary brought greater turnover, but this was far less pronounced under Brezhnev than his predecessors. It shows that this difference between administrations was far greater than any difference among time periods within the same administration.[35]

The general secretary's ability to translate a constituency within the Party apparatus into control over the Central Committee was also limited. Outside political intervention in personnel matters decreased as leaders of key bureaucracies asserted greater professional control over their subordinates. As Robert Blackwell observes, Khrushchev's "heirs replaced their patron's freewheeling cadres policy with a far less politicized approach in making personnel decisions."[36] For example, commanding officers at the highest levels of the Soviet armed forces gained greater professional and institutional autonomy, limited Party meddling, and established a more traditional chain of command.[37] In civilian bureaucracies, one concomitant of this trend was growing specialization of career tracks and professionalization of the criteria for appointment and promotion within the respective hierarchies.[38]

Defection and Disqualification

Norms against defection and disqualification were reinforced in the compact of 1964–1965. Sanctions against defection limited most airing of differences outside the Politburo and blocked most appeals to enlarge the arena of conflict. The Brezhnev Politburo enforced this with great vigilance, punishing three of its members guilty of attempts to widen the arena of debate—Gennadii Voronov, Alexander Shelepin, and Petr Shelest—by stripping them of posts.[39]

Norms against disqualification were reinforced by limiting piecemeal disqualification that could dislodge first-tier actors from their second-tier bases. Balance in the first tier depended on the balancing of coalitions that stretched across tiers. A key to Khrushchev's success had been to break the institutional ties of first-tier actors to second-tier constituencies in preparation for a showdown in the Central Committee. In February 1955 the resignation of Malenkov and appointment of Bulganin to assume the premiership—chairman of the Council of Ministers—cut both off from their original bases of support. In the Ministry of Defense Marshal Georgii Zhukov brought in his loyalists to replace those put in place under Bulganin. In that same year, Khrushchev began a campaign to remove Molotov from the foreign affairs establishment, and on 2 June 1956 Molotov stepped down as foreign minister. Thus, on the eve of the defeat of the Anti-Party Group, with the exception of Khrushchev, all the original leading members of the collective leadership had been cut off from major second-tier constituencies. Beria was dead. Malenkov controlled only the Ministry of Power Plants and Electric Industry. Molotov was minister for state control. Bulganin as chairman of the Council of Ministers presided over a much diminished administration after ministries were dismantled in the sovnarkhoz reform.

After Khrushchev the balance survived because the leadership blocked this type of piecemeal disqualification.[40] While a few leaders, such as Shelepin, whose accumulation of power threatened the balance, were dislodged from their second-tier constituencies and ultimately from the Politburo, those leaders such as Suslov and Kosygin who were essential to maintaining the balance retained their critical roles atop their constituencies until virtually the end of the Brezhnev administration.

Brezhnev's push to dislodge Kosygin from the economic apparatus failed. At the December 1969 CC Plenum, as John Dornberg reports, Brezhnev "delivered a secret speech which was violently critical of the state of the economy and called for draconian, orthodox measures to deal with it."[41] Brezhnev blamed Kosygin's methods and the ministries for economic problems and pressed for greater reliance on the methods of the Party including "moral stimulants," discipline, and mobilization. The issue came to a head in early 1970, when Brezhnev apparently sought to unseat Kosygin and secure his own appointment or that of a proxy as premier, but a majority of the Politburo blocked this.[42] The following year this issue again surfaced along with rumors that an organizational compromise was in the works to create a new state council on the model of Romania and the German Democratic Republic, whereby the general secretary could become president with direct control over the premier and council of ministers.[43] In this Brezhnev clearly failed; he had to be content with a set of lesser appointments that hemmed in, but did not dislodge, Kosygin. In 1970 changes in the seconds-in-command in both the State Planning Committee and State Committee for Science and Technology increased Brezhnev's "presence" within Kosygin's state economic bureaucracy, leading once again to mixed control through alternating layers of protégés. Replacement of government heads by party apparatchiki in four union-republics—Kazakhstan, Moldavia, Azerbaidjan, and Latvia—further expanded Brezhnev's presence at lower levels of the state apparatus. Yet, by preventing the dislodgment of Kosygin, the leadership maintained a cornerstone of collective rule.

Norms of the implicit compact were given weight by the precedent of Khrushchev's removal, which established that the general secretary could be removed.[44] It also established, however, that removal was not likely to take place unless the incumbent violated these norms.

Balancing Mechanism

In the Brezhnev administration balancing worked with far greater success than previously to prevent breakdown of collective leadership. The most significant threat to collective leadership in the post-Khrushchev succession came from Aleksandr Shelepin, who emerged from the 1964 succession as chair of the Party-State Control Committee, deputy chair of the

Council of Ministers, all-union Party Secretary, as well as member of the Politburo. Shelepin held a unique position at the juncture of party and state. He supervised the Administrative Organs Department, the Party apparatus department monitoring the police, and his hand-picked successor atop the KGB gave him a base in the police. In the first half of 1965 Shelepin's supporters circulated rumors that Brezhnev would soon be replaced "by a man with a little more dynamism and natural authority." His obvious ambition, his control of the police, and his attempt to use the Party-State Control Committee to gain leverage over the Party apparatus threatened to upset the balance in the leadership and spurred balancing behavior into action. To contain Shelepin, Brezhnev brought together an overwhelming majority that included even Brezhnev's other significant competitor for control of the Party apparatus—Nikolai Podgornyi. The leadership rapidly moved to expel Shelepin from the Party-State Control Committee (1965) and then more slowly from the Secretariat (1967). To prevent anyone else attempting to repeat his strategy from the Party-State Control Committee, the Party dissolved the Committee on 6 December 1965, with the admonition that "the organs of peoples' control do not control the work of party organs."[45]

Again balancing brought stability to the Politburo. Only three voting members were removed before January 1971, and only four were added.[46] The stronger rules of balancing meant that even after Brezhnev's emergence as a first among equals the Politburo did not undergo significantly higher turnover. After 1970 the rate of termination and new appointments was no greater than during the first years of collective leadership (see table 5.1): in almost twelve years there were only six terminations and a dozen appointments.[47]

Balancing prevented Brezhnev from achieving the apex role held by his predecessors. Although leadership under Brezhnev was apparently structured by a set of subcommittees within the Politburo, Brezhnev neither chaired nor even sat on all these policy centers that he would need to establish directive leadership.[48] Simultaneous with his election as general secretary, Brezhnev apparently became civilian commander-in-chief of the armed forces (chairman of the Defense Council), although his tenure was not discussed publicly until 1976.[49] He failed in his attempts to assume the premiership (chairman of the Council of Ministers) and managed to add only the more honorific post of chief of state (chairman of the Supreme Soviet Presidium), only after more than a decade in office (1977). Brezhnev enjoyed a strategic advantage over other leaders by virtue of chairing the Politburo and two significant committees of the leadership—the Secretariat and Defense Council. Yet, Brezhnev was not the only Politburo member to sit concurrently on more than one such committee; Kosygin sat on the Defense Council and CM Presidium, Suslov on the Defense Council and Secretariat. Brezhnev remained excluded from the Presidium of the Council of Ministers. As a consequence, each committee was balanced between at least two significant members of the leadership, which blocked the emergence of an apex role and maintained divided authority.

THE "BALANCING ACTS" OF 1982–1985

By the time of Brezhnev's death on 10 November 1982, norms of the gentlemen's agreement and the implicit compact were well established. Growing institutionalization guaranteed stability of collective rule in the Politburo. In 1982 a balanced leadership assigned major roles not only to Yurii Andropov as general secretary and Konstantin Chernenko as a party secretary, but also to Mikhail Gorbachev as a party secretary and Dmitri Ustinov as minister of defense. Subsequently, major visible roles were assigned to Viktor Grishin as the Moscow city first secretary and Grigorii Romanov as the Leningrad province first secretary (later, a national party secretary). The balancing mechanism worked with still greater efficiency—in particular, owing to the increasingly careful definition of the role of the general secretary and the layered control within the Party apparatus itself.

Checks and Balances

An important step forward in the institutionalization of collective leadership was increasingly precise definition of the role of the general secretary, so as to establish both lower and upper bounds to its powers. On the one hand, institutionalization of the role guaranteed it certain powers. By 1982 actors in both tiers shared an expectation that the general secretary would serve as the "head of the Politburo" rather than just one member in a collectivity. The label "head of the Politburo" had not been used to describe Brezhnev until 1969; but people used it to describe the role of Andropov and Chernenko immediately upon election, and a Central Committee resolution used it within eight months of Andropov's election.[50] On the other hand, institutionalization of collective leadership placed upper bounds on those powers and created further obstacles to consolidating directive leadership.

The Brezhnev administration set the pattern whereby the general secretary served as chairman of the Defense Council and chairman of the Presidium of the Supreme Soviet ("president"). The former was granted to general secretaries almost automatically or with only slight delay in all three of the next successions. Confirmation that the general secretary served as defense chair came within six months of Andropov's succession, one month of Chernenko's, and five months of Gorbachev's. The head of the Party's International Department, Leonid Zimyatin, confirmed that there had been an unpublished provision under which the general secretary would serve simultaneously as chair of the Defense Council.[51]

Yet, the post of chief of state—that is, chairman of the Supreme Soviet Presidium—was not the automatic prerogative for all general secretaries. Andropov was apparently at first blocked from adding the post; reportedly this had been promised to Chernenko in the leadership settlement of October 1982. A month later Andropov had reneged, deciding to block Chernenko's election; thus, the November Supreme Soviet session left the post vacant. Within six months, however, the general secretary was able to win election for himself. In 1984 Chernenko was elected to the post almost automatically—within two months of his succession. At the April 1984 parliament (Supreme Soviet) session that formally elected Chernenko, Gorbachev created the expectation that combined party and state posts would be normal in the future: "Simultaneous performance by the general secretary . . . of the functions of the chairman . . . is of great importance for pursuing the foreign policy of the Soviet Union."[52] Yet, just a year later general secretary Gorbachev was denied the chief of state post, and at the 2 July 1985 Supreme Soviet session that elected Andrei Gromyko instead, Gorbachev seemed to contradict his earlier logic. While defending the previous decision to combine posts as "justified under the conditions of the time," he argued that the tasks of domestic restructuring would "demand greater intensity in the work of the CPSU Central Committee and its Political Bureau." "Under these concrete conditions and with due account taken of the present state, the plenum of the CPSU Central Committee found it advisable that the general secretary of the CPSU Central Committee should concentrate to the maximum on organizing the work of party central organs."[53] The demands of mutual checking in 1985 led the collective leadership to contain Gorbachev's power by denying him the office of chief of state.

Mutual checking also led the leadership to enforce the 1964 Central Committee resolution that separated the general secretary and chair of the Council of Ministers. The leadership continued to balance control of the police, despite Andropov's long association with the KGB. When Andropov removed Brezhnev's client as minister of internal affairs and appointed his own associate from the KGB to succeed him, the KGB chair was then given to Viktor Chebrikov, a longtime associate of Brezhnev and Chernenko. In January 1986, the collective leadership replaced the minister of internal affairs but left Chebrikov in his post as chairman of the KGB.[54]

Balancing within the Apparatus

Most important, this elaborate balancing took the next step necessary to block consolidation of directive leadership by a general secretary—by balancing control within the Party apparatus itself. The balancing acts of 1982–1985 gave special attention to this through cohabitation within the Secretariat and through layering of control in the personnel machine. After Andropov's election, Chernenko remained within the Secretariat and retained his close associations with the Brezhnevite cadres. After Andropov's death, Chernenko's control of the apparatus was balanced by appointment of Gorbachev as his second in command within the Secretariat, a position charged with oversight of personnel matters. After June 1983, they cohabited the Secretariat with Romanov. When Gorbachev assumed the general secretaryship, operational control of the Secretariat was taken from him and placed in the hands of Egor Ligachev. In an interview published on 4 December 1987 with *Le Monde* writers Michel Tatu and Daniel Vernet, Ligachev explained, "I chair the Central Committee Secretariat's meetings and, at the request of the Central Committee Politburo, I organize its work."[55] He suggested that he kept the general secretary, who did not attend, informed of Secretariat meetings. In particular, Ligachev retained a significant role in cadres policy. In April 1985 appointment of Gorbachev's associate Georgii Razumovskii to head the Organization Party Work Department (OPW), which was responsible for work with local Party organizations, gave Gorbachev some leverage in personnel matters to check Ligachev's control over cadres. The presence of Ligachev's appointee Evgenii Razumov as first deputy chair of the same department, however, meant that control over personnel remained balanced among Politburo members with their partisans at alternating layers of authority in the personnel machine.[56]

This balancing checked each general secretary's ability to remake the Secretariat. In his brief tenure Andropov presided over the removal of only Kirilenko, and even this had apparently been decided before Brezhnev's death. Andropov did oversee appointment of Nikolai Ryzhkov, Grigorii Romanov, and Egor Ligachev. During Chernenko's tenure as general secretary neither removals nor appointments were made to the membership of the Secretariat.

After March 1985 turnover rose dramatically, but balancing prevented general secretary Gorbachev from turning this opportunity into control of the Secretariat and apparatus. Between March 1985 and December 1986, five incumbent secretaries were terminated, and seven new secretaries were appointed, in addition, an eighth appointee was terminated before the end of this period. Gorbachev's gains in appointments of allies to the Secretariat and Central Committee apparatus were balanced by appointments not beholden to him. In April 1985 the Central Committee elected Gorbachev's associate Viktor Nikonov, but two months later it made the paired appointment of regional party secretaries Lev Zaikov and Boris Yeltsin, who balanced more moderate and more radical members. Immediately following the 1986 Party Congress, five new secretaries were added—Georgii Razumovskii, Aleksandr Yakovlev, Vadim Medvedev, Anatolii Dobrynin, and Aleksandra Biriukova—but only the first three were commonly counted as Gorbachev protégés. This balancing in the Secretariat was reflected in the control of apparatus departments. From the time of the Party Congress until early 1987, as Thane Gustafson and Dawn Mann note, in appointments to Central Committee department heads, with one exception it was "difficult to detect Gorbachev's personal touch."[57]

Balanced control of the Secretariat and apparatus departments meant that all three general secretaries had little opportunity to build a lower-level clientele in the Party apparatus. Andropov made only a small step toward consolidating a hold on the apparatus of Brezhnev appointees; only one-seventh of the regional first secretaries were replaced during his rule.[58] Gorbachev was unable from March 1985 until early 1987 to build the personal clientele within the Party apparatus that had been essential to the early breakout of former general secretaries. At the April 1985 Central Committee Plenum Gorbachev announced a campaign to begin renewal of party personnel. He argued against "any kind of stagnation in the movement of cadres" and urged that "we must look for ways to achieve more active movement among our leadership cadres."[59] The pace of turnovers among regional party secretaries increased, and in the year from Gorbachev's appointment leading up to the 1986 Party Congress, 46 of the 157 province secretaries had been replaced.[60] Nonetheless, operational control of this personnel change was entrusted to the balanced Secretariat.[61] Not surprisingly, the purge did not bring a narrow consolidation for one leader or other, but a professional renewal in the apparatus. The ousted first secretaries tended to be the oldest apparatchiki: almost all were appointments originally made under either Khrushchev or Brezhnev. The newly appointed secretaries for the most part were not partisans sent in to help the general secretary consolidate control, but promotions within the respective regional organizations.[62] The replacements, younger than their predecessors, did not differ from them in their recent careers.

Collective leadership was reflected in the Central Committee. Turnover in the Central Committee was high: At the 1986 Party Congress 46 percent of the incumbent voting membership was not reelected, and in the new (slightly smaller) Central Committee 44 percent of the full members were new. Although this was higher turnover than in the "first" Central

Committee of previous general secretaries, it did not bring consolidation. Much of the turnover was simply occasioned by the superannuation of the apparatus. As Baruch Hazan observes, "the composition of the new Central Committee reflect[ed] intensive bargaining and compromise by both Gorbachev's faction and the conservative wing of the Party."[63]

Balancing

The balancing mechanism worked with remarkable efficiency by the time of the post-Brezhnev succession. The greatest threat to the balance in the post-Brezhnev succession appears to have come from the second tier— Chief of the General Staff Nikolai Ogarkov. The Marshal's challenge to civilian leadership of the military brought his swift removal in September 1984. As Dale R. Herspring observes, "Moscow's primary concern was not so much to discipline him as to assure that he would no longer be involved in Kremlin politics."[64] Ogarkov's moves threatened the balance within the leadership due to his close association with Politburo member Grigorii Romanov. The reaction to Ogarkov's moves, as Ilya Zemtsov describes, was a classic balancing act: "Chernenko understood that once Romanov had his man as minister of defense, he would have had sufficient power to threaten not only Gorbachev but also him. He feared that unlike Gorbachev, Romanov would not patiently await his death but might seize the first opportunity to topple him from power. Thus, against Romanov's ambitions Chernenko mobilized all his associates."[65] The threat from Ogarkov grew with defense minister Ustinov's advancing age, declining health, and impending retirement or death. The issue of Ustinov's replacement could no longer be postponed when he died at the age of seventy-six on 20 December 1984. Appointment of a first-tier actor, appointment of a first-tier actor's ally, or appointment of an ambitious military leader to be minister of defense could threaten the leadership balance. To forestall this, the leadership appointed Marshal Sergei Sokolov, an elderly military professional with no known political ambitions. The leadership bowed to pressure from the military to appoint a military professional after eight and a half years of civilian leadership in the Ministry, but it did not appoint one who would actively press military claims or was likely to swing the weight of the military in leadership disagreements.[66] In particular, they did not elevate either of the most obvious successors—Chief of the General Staff Marshal Akhromeev nor Commander-in-Chief of the Warsaw Pact's Joint Forces Marshal Kulikov— who were likely to be tougher spokesmen.

As a consequence of successful balancing, changes in the voting membership of the Politburo did not bring consolidation for the general secretaries. Under Andropov and Chernenko changes were limited and occasioned for the most part by infirmity or death. In November 1982, one retirement from ill-health (Andrei Kirilenko) permitted Andropov to win promotion of his ally Geidar Aliev to full membership. The death of Arvid Pel'she in May 1983 permitted elevation of Mikhail Solomentsev and Vitalii Vorotnikov from nonvoting to voting membership at the December Central Committee Plenum. Throughout the tenure of Chernenko no additions were made to the Politburo. As table 5.1 shows, the rate of terminations was the lowest since the collective post-Stalin leadership.

Under Gorbachev balanced collective leadership limited his ability to shape the Politburo. Between March 1985 and December 1986, three full members of the Politburo were terminated, and five new full members were appointed. With only one exception, these did not represent a step forward for Gorbachev's personal consolidation. One month after Gorbachev's election the Central Committee elected to the Politburo three new full members who were not clients of the general secretary—KGB chair Viktor Chebrikov and Central Committee secretaries Egor Ligachev and Nikolai Ryzhkov. In July it removed Romanov and elected to voting membership Eduard Shevardnadze, the one clear gain for the general secretary. In March 1986 the Central Committee removed Grishin and elevated Lev Zaikov to full membership. Thus, one year after his succession, the Central Committee had eliminated Romanov and Grishin, the two men who most threatened Gorbachev's candidacy during the succession, offered him a solid majority for some form of reform, and disallowed him a solid majority of dependent clients. Only Shevardnadze was beholden to Gorbachev for his position on the Politburo; the majority was composed of colleagues who had helped Gorbachev rise to general secretary and on whom he continued to depend.[67] By the end of 1986 balancing still prevented the general secretary from consolidating power with a majority of dependent clients on the Politburo.

INSTITUTIONALIZED COLLECTIVE LEADERSHIP

The evolution of the rules of collective leadership in successive successions inched toward a form of institutionalized leadership in which the general secretary increasingly played the strategic role of chair and "balancer." By 1985 the general secretary served as chair of the Politburo on which the major organizational leaders of the Central Committee enjoyed representation. The general secretary exercised enormous influence as a consequence of not so much his "organizational tail," as was true in the past, but his balancing role among organizational leaders.

The growth of the "institutional general secretary" meant the office and its powers were more firmly fixed in Soviet politics. The powers of the office of general secretary and the rules for their transfer were so well established that even though both Andropov and Chernenko were incapacitated, not one of their colleagues attempted a breakout. Within eight months of his election Andropov's health limited his activities, and he made his last public appearance on 18 August 1983. Within five months of his election Chernenko fell seriously ill, disappearing from public view for two months in the summer of 1984 and in subsequent public appearances his role was often brief and well choreographed to mask his physical decrepitude. Yet, unlike the mounting leadership conflict that burst out following Lenin's first stroke, the vulnerability of these general secretaries did not bring a breakdown of the well-balanced collectivity.

The "institutional general secretary," nonetheless, placed limits on the powers of its incumbent. It meant that Gorbachev was hemmed in by other first-tier actors who checked his powers. The chief of state, chairman of the Supreme Soviet Presidium, was assigned to Andrei Gromyko. Ligachev directed the Secretariat and chaired its meetings. In September 1985 Nikolai Ryzhkov became premier (chairman of the Council of Ministers). Gromyko, Ligachev, and Ryzhkov were not junior partners, but colleagues of the general secretary.[68] Gorbachev's position permitted him to bring them together behind his proposals by persuasion and balancing. Because they were not "his men," when persuasion or trickery would not work, Gorbachev had to compromise or simply retreat.

The growth of the "institutional general secretary" brought a decline of patronage in politics. The last three general secretaries relied less on clients and more on formal institutional relations to govern. Khrushchev had worked hard to install his "Ukrainians" at all levels. Brezhnev had promoted to the highest levels former associates and subordinates from his earlier posts in Moldavia, Kazakhstan, and the Ukraine. Yet, among the post-Brezhnevian leaders none appointed an extensive clientele. Andropov appears to have had little outside the KGB. Chernenko relied on Brezhnev's appointees. Gorbachev brought to prominence few former associates and still fewer former subordinates. Vsevolod Murakhovskii, Gorbachev's early patron in the Stavropol Komsomol Organization, who then became his successor as Stavropol province first secretary, became chair of the State Agro-Industrial Commission under Gorbachev. Stavropol province secretary V. I. Kalashnikov rose to Volgograd province first secretary. The head of the Stavropol province department for organization party works (OPW), who had served as a province cadres secretary under Gorbachev, rose to an all-union post in OPW supervising appointments in Moldavia and parts of the Ukraine. Gorbachev's schoolmates from the Moscow State University rose to head the Party's General Department, edit *Sovetskaia Rossiia* and *Kommunist*, and assist the editor of *Pravda*. The numbers of such appointments pale by comparison with the Khrushchev and Brezhnev cohorts. The appointments from Stavropol province do not exceed random chances of advancement from any such province.[69]

This view of the institutional general secretary sets this analysis apart from much of western Sovietology. Accounts of Gorbachev's rule as though he duplicated Khrushchev's consolidation failed to see the changed institutional environment in which Gorbachev worked. Attempts to use the models of a static institutional context led to hollow procrusteanism. For example, by missing the institutional development of balanced control over personnel policy, a number of analysts continued to view the Party cadres apparatus as the general secretary's machine. This led to attempts to apply old counting rules to turnover, all based on the assumptions that the old circular flow of power had remained firmly in tact thirty years after the death of Stalin and that new appointments must be the general secretary's people.[70]

This experience illustrates how important our models can be in shaping our interpretation of the ambiguous data that is so often the mainstay of our craft. By failing to note changed institutional constraints the previously fashionable Western approach led us to view later events as simply anomalous rather than important steps in an ongoing constitutional development. For example, it did not lead these analysts to ask why in 1988 Gorbachev would begin to trade autocratic control as general secretary, as they saw it, for the awkward balancing act of democratizing politics as president of the Soviet Union. (Indeed, the formerly fashionable view interpreted this as just further consolidation.) The argument I present here leads to a different conclusion, as I develop more fully in chapter 9, only if we recognize that Gorbachev did not have autocratic control of the Secretariat or Central Committee can we understand why he would seek to marginalize these bodies through constitutional reforms. He did not trade autocratic leadership for the balancing of democracy; rather he changed the actors among whom he had to balance and the institutional setting in which the balancing occurred. The prevailing view blinded us to this important change and, in fact, continued almost to the end, to contend that Gorbachev was getting stronger as his consolidation continued.[71]

CHAPTER SIX

Institutionalized Stagnation

WITHIN the developing constitution were keys to unlocking one of the puzzles with which this book began: Why did a dynamic polity that engineered fundamental transformation in society then stagnate, unable to either sustain this transformation or adapt to the changes it had engineered? Reciprocal accountability and the cycling of leadership made sustained reform difficult. The institutionalization of these left the Soviet polity virtually unable to adapt to social change.

Reform in the Soviet Union after 1953 referred to attempts to reduce or eliminate the special place of the iron triangle of Party apparatus, economic administration, and coercive arms. Reform is an inherently redistributive enterprise, as defined in chapter 1, "a shift in power and wealth from one group to another."[1] The prospects for such reform in the Soviet polity were limited by the constitution of Bolshevism that enfranchised the bureaucracies of early state building and modernization. Forced departicipation made changes in these selectors or their missions difficult. The bureaucratic nature of the selectors made it unlikely they would autonomously develop new missions. The institutionalization of reciprocal accountability and balanced leadership made it increasingly difficult to challenge their special place in the selectorate. Indeed, from 1953 to 1986 significant changes in either the dominant actors of Soviet politics or their policies became more and more unlikely.

Chapter 6 examines this problem of institutionalized stagnation. The discussion is informed by the model introduced in chapter 1: The roles and relationships defined by the constitution of Bolshevism created a policy process; this process, in turn, shaped policy outcomes.[2] The first part of this chapter examines the structural features of this policy process, stressing the constraints of reciprocal accountability and the cycling of leadership on the formation of policy coalitions across tiers. The second part argues that the structure of policymaking limited the opportunities for reform; moreover, institutionalization of reciprocal accountability and balanced leadership led to increasing policy dysfunction and growing inability to adapt to social change. The conclusion to this chapter compares this analysis of the policy process with earlier studies by western Sovietologists.

THE BOLSHEVIK POLICY PROCESS

The model of the constitution of Bolshevism developed in previous chapters focuses our analysis of the policymaking process on three consequences: Reciprocal accountability shaped the role of policy in the formation of coalitions between leaders and bureaucrats. The cycling of leadership in the first tier led to recurring shifts in the publicly articulated positions of individual leaders and in the level of policy contestation among them. Yet, the institutionalization of the rules of the Soviet constitution led to a long-term decline in these recurring shifts of positions and contestation. The following discussion addresses each consequence in turn.

Reciprocal Accountability and
Policy Coalitions

The "selectoral" politics of accountability under the constitution of Bolshevism was a powerful constraint on policy formation. Coalition building under reciprocal accountability demanded *policy entrepreneurship*. In building coalitions within the first tier, leaders offered policies that enhanced their partners' power and authority. In appealing to constituencies in the second tier, leaders offered policies that permitted bureaucrats to fulfill their organizational missions. Policy was a currency with which first-tier actors gained support and consolidated leadership.[3] Coalition maintenance demanded *entrepreneurial aggregation*. The leader of a coalition had to not only articulate the policy positions of his coalition partners and constituents, but also, given the incompatible and sometimes conflicting nature of these, mediate among their policy preferences and integrate these in a larger program. Competing demands of coalition partners and constituents gave rise to a *centrist advantage*. Each leader did not need to occupy the center position in the policy space of his coalition, but there was an advantage to such a position insofar as there were trade-offs among constituents' policy priorities.[4]

Thus, the publicly articulated policy positions of first-tier actors tended to reflect their coalitions. During successions, for example, premiers (chairmen of the Council of Ministers) were more inclined to favor diminishing the Party's role in economic administration and expanding the autonomy of ministries; general secretaries were more inclined to stress the importance of Party leadership. Between March 1953 and the end of 1954 Georgii Malenkov attempted to expand the prerogatives of his ministerial agencies against Nikita Khrushchev's Party apparatus; this led to the subsequent indictment from the Party that he violated "the Leninist understanding of the leading role of the Party in the system of the dictatorship of the proletariat" and promoted "the primacy of the state organs over the Party."[5] Similarly, during collective leadership the critical role of the military in their coalitions led general secretaries to show greater concern for its resource demands. In the post-Stalin succession Khrushchev resisted Malenkov's attempts to cut the military budget. In the post-Khrushchev succession Leonid Brezhnev pressed a major buildup of military forces.[6]

The reciprocal nature of accountability between tiers could facilitate leaders' efforts at coalition formation because in some instances leaders could shape parts of the selectorate and their preferences. Thus, first-tier leaders did not rely on policy incentives to the same extent with all bureaucracies or at all times. To the extent a leader could rely on clientelism to establish control within a specific bureaucracy he had less need to offer policy payoffs, for the threat of removal could bring quick compliance from bureaucrat-constituents. Thus, bureaucracies such as the foreign ministry were much less likely to exact policy payoffs than the military. In addition, when a leader had consolidated power, he had less need to make policy payoffs to specific coalition partners or constituencies, for the shift from balancing to bandwagoning that accompanied the consolidation of power reduced pressures for policy payoffs.

Yet, the essential difference between the leaders' generalist roles and their constituents' specialist roles complicated the leaders' efforts at coalition maintenance. Among the policy preferences of constituents within their coalitions, first-tier leaders of coalitions often faced trade-offs, which could create tensions between leaders and individual constituencies.[7] In addition, leaders as generalists—particularly those who aspired to directive leadership—could be judged by the success of many sectors, even some outside the immediate supporting coalition. To the extent the aspiration to consolidate leadership depended on demonstrating an ability to enable numerous bureaucrats to fulfill their responsibilities, a leader could not completely ignore the resource demands of bureaucrats outside his coalition, even unenfranchised bureaucrats. Each leader had to balance between policy as a payoff to coalition partners and policy as a demonstration of leadership abilities. Thus, the leader had to balance policy payoffs to existing clients and allies, to prospective allies, and even to bureaucrats likely to remain outside the leader's coalition. This limited the resources available to leaders for payoffs in coalition building and inclined leaders to be more centrist than their coalitions.[8]

Leadership Cycling and Policy Positions

The recurring cycles of collective and directive leadership had two profound consequences: (1) they induced first-tier leaders to change their policy positions over time, and (2) they shaped the policy conflicts among leaders. The publicly articulated policy positions of leaders were not static; they shifted with changes in the composition of the leaders' coalitions. Changing coalitions demanded *dynamic centrism*: As each leader's coalition grew or shrank, his publicly articulated positions were likely to shift in the direction of the moving centrist position.[9] For example, an expanding coalition demanded new policy payoffs for new constituents, and when these new constituents were not added equally on both sides of the leader's previously articulated policy position—that is, in situations involving trade-offs among policy preferences of coalition constituencies—that position was likely to shift along the policy space to maintain the center of the coalition.

The heuristic device introduced in figure 4.3 illustrates this link of coalitions to policy positions and the consequence of a changing coalition for the general secretary's declared policy position. The most successful coalition-building strategy for a new general secretary after 1953 was to begin on the conservative side of this spectrum with the vested interests of the iron triangle. This constrained a new general secretary to defend the priorities of these vested interests. In expanding his coalition further the general secretary at first sought constituencies with priorities complementary to those of the original coalition. Thus, a prudent coalition-expansion strategy initially added new constituencies on the conservative side of the spectrum, but these were frequently nearer the center of the political spectrum than the general secretary's original constituencies. Further expansion added constituencies with still more reformist preferences. To occupy the policy center in his broadening coalition of supporters, the general secretary began to challenge some priorities of the original constituencies. Throughout a career a general secretary's publicly articulated positions, beginning at a more conservative position upholding prerogatives of the iron triangle, would then shift to more reformist positions as his coalition expanded.[10]

The recurring cycles of leadership consolidation had a second significant consequence for the policy process: it constrained the level and nature of policy conflict in the two tiers.[11] Open policy contestation was a sign of the breakdown of norms in the first tier against defection. Enforcement of these norms was more certain under either well-balanced collective leadership or stable directive leadership. Enforcement weakened and contestation rose when either stage of the leadership cycle began to break down: when collective leadership was assaulted by a general secretary's breakout attempt, or when directive leadership was assaulted by disaffected members of the general secretary's original coalition. Yet, these two periods of public contestation were characterized by different forms of conflict, policy contestation under collective leadership was usually conflict *among* coalitions, and that under directive leadership often involved conflict *within* the dominant coalition.

The level of policy contestation under collective leadership reflected a tension between competing centrifugal and centripetal policy pressures. The imperatives of exclusion and differentiation in coalition formation (discussed in chapter 4) encouraged divergence in policy positions among first-tier actors. Competitive coalition building inclined Politburo members to offer diverging policy proposals for and against reform. The pressure to build authority encouraged leaders to distinguish themselves from one another in the policy arena; they often exaggerated their differences in the confrontation of bold reform proposals and an equally bold defense of iron triangle priorities. This *imperative of policy differentiation*, as George Breslauer and Richard Anderson have labeled it, was the natural consequence of the coalition dynamics of exclusion and differentiation.[12] In constant tension with this imperative of policy differentiation were intense pressures to contain first-tier conflict—the *strain toward agreement*.[13] To preserve its policy leadership the first tier had to limit this public differentiation. Seeking to preserve the Politburo's role, the leadership developed norms to prevent individual defections among its members by establishing sanctions against public contestation (discussed in chapter 5). Yet, these norms were only as successful as the vigilance of collective leadership in enforcing sanctions. Limits on contestation were particularly fragile when a potential hegemon—particularly a general secretary who had completed his consolidation within the Party apparatus— thought he might escape the sanctions of the collectivity. Indeed, levels of policy conflict might rise significantly toward the beginning of a "breakout" attempt as the emerging hegemon sought to discredit the policies of his opponents.

Directive leadership at first reduced the incentives and opportunities for policy differentiation and thereby reduced public contestation among leaders over policy. The exclusion of alternative leaders from the first tier and the shift from balancing to bandwagoning as leaders followed the policy initiation of the hegemon reduced public airing of opposing policy proposals. Interests inside the general secretary's coalition at first had little incentive to protest his priorities; interests outside the coalition were at an increasing disadvantage if they sought to protest the policies of the general secretary. Yet, if a general secretary continued to consolidate and developed an oversized coalition, contestation might increase again, but

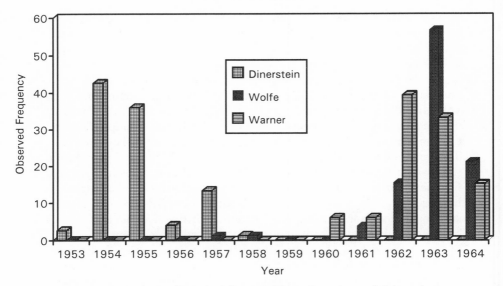

Figure 6.1. Frequency of Key Articles on Military Doctrine and Science by Military Officers, 1953–1964. *Sources*: H. S. Dinerstein, *War and the Soviet Union* (Westport: Greenwood Press, 1962); Thomas W. Wolfe, *Soviet Strategy at the Crossroads* (Cambridge: Harvard University Press, 1965); Edward Warner, *The Military in Contemporary Soviet Politics* (New York: Praeger Publishers, 1977). Tabulations by Michael Tierney.

this time from within his own coalition. As the general secretary's enlarged coalition required broader distribution of policy resources, his original coalition constituencies might begin to challenge his policies and their loss of resources. The policy priorities necessary to keep an enlarged coalition together could bring voices of reaction from the iron triangle—particularly from heavy industry and the military, which were more difficult to silence than other second-tier actors.

An illustration of this wavelike pattern of policy contestation, rising with the breakdown of both collective and directive leadership, can be seen in the public debate over military policy in articles by senior military figures during the Khrushchev administration. Figure 6.1 plots the number of such articles identified by three Western "expert coders."[14] Collective leadership initially saw little public contestation, but as Khrushchev began his breakout, military professionals began challenging the collective leadership's military policies in articles published in 1954 and 1955. Once Khrushchev had established his directive leadership after 1957, however, this public contestation rapidly declined. As Khrushchev began to push reforms in military policy in 1960, disaffection among his original coalition partners grew, and public contestation rose once again.

Institutionalization and
the Regime Spiral

Owing to the institutionalization of reciprocal accountability and balanced leadership, the cycles of policymaking never exactly repeated one another. With each succession, the divergence among Politburo members under collective leadership became less extreme, and the consolidation under directive leadership was less complete. In 1953 and 1954 the public divergence between reformers and conservatives was greater than in any subsequent succession of the post-Stalin period, yet it paled by comparison with the differences between Left Opposition and Right Opposition in the post-Lenin succession. Similarly, while Khrushchev's consolidation was more complete than Brezhnev's, it was a weak reflection of Stalin's autocratic rule.

Useful in analyzing these different stages within changing cycles is the concept of a domestic political *regime*. This designates different modes of policymaking, distinguished by the level of leadership consolidation and policy contestation.[15] Consolidation brings shifts along a spectrum of policymaking modes—the poles of which represent collective decision-making and individual choice. Different levels of consolidation can be accompanied by either high or low contestation.[16]

Regimes represent primarily different stages of the cycling of collective and directive leadership. Each succession began from comparable starting points of collective rule and low contestation. From there, owing to the strategic constraints of the constitution of Bolshevism, the succession-consolidation cycle could proceed through four stages: First, collective leadership created a balance of power among competing leaders that checked public contestation. Policymaking emerged through bargaining among more or less equal members of the Politburo concerned to provide policy payoffs to their constituencies in the second tier. Second, under the breakout of the general secretary the checks on public contestation began to break down as at least one member of the collective leadership began to attack the balance of power. Third, directive leadership under the general secretary freed him from the policy compromises of collective leadership and placed a lid on public contestation over policy. Fourth, further expansion of the directive leader's coalition could usher in a period of heightened policy challenges to the general secretary as his original constituents grew disaffected and, to quote Ilya Zemtsov, as "the general secretary's hitherto subservient colleagues begin to feel they are his full-fledged partners."[17] This attitude might even culminate in removal of the leader.

Regimes also represent different points along the longer-term process of institutionalizing balanced leadership and reciprocal accountability.

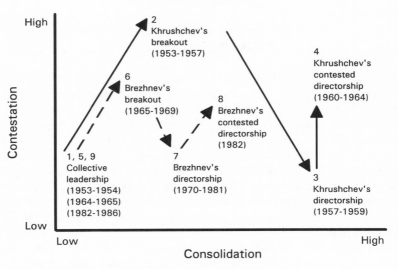

Figure 6.2. Soviet Political Regimes, 1953–1986

Each period of collective decisionmaking was unlike its predecessor, as was each period of directorship. Institutionalization changed the strategic behavior of first- and second-tier actors. Institutionalization of Politburo accountability to the Central Committee increasingly focused succession on the "selectoral" politics between these two organs. With institutionalization of the post of general secretary, actors in both tiers were more likely to grant a new general secretary policy leadership in some realms at the beginning of his term. Yet, with greater institutionalization of balancing, consolidation of directive rule and expansion of control to other policy realms became more difficult. Institutionalization of balancing reinforced norms against policy contestation. In short, these developments changed the cycling of leadership so that it always recurred at a higher stage of institutionalization—producing not simply cycles, but a spiral of regimes.

Measuring shifts in Soviet decisionmaking processes precisely along the two dimensions of consolidation and contestation is, of course, a problematic task. Consolidation can be measured by the number of positions accumulated by a general secretary, by his appointments to key posts, and by his alliances with strategic elites.[18] Policy contestation is gauged by the public debate among leaders. By plotting the regimes of Soviet politics from 1953 to 1986 against the two dimensions of policy consolidation and contestation, the result is figure 6.2.[19] The figure shows not only the relative position of each regime (in rank order) but also the path of each administration and the declining amplitude of the oscillations between collective and directive leadership. I briefly discuss each of these nine policymaking regimes in turn.

THE POST-STALIN ADMINISTRATIONS

The years from the death of Joseph Stalin to the removal of Nikita Khrushchev saw four distinct regimes. From the death of Stalin (March 1953) to the removal of the Anti-Party Group (June 1957), policymaking was a collective enterprise. From June 1957 to October 1964 Khrushchev exercised directive leadership in policymaking. Each of these periods was further divided into two distinctive regimes by the rise of contestation—with the breakdown of collective rule under Khrushchev's breakout attempt and the assault on directive rule as core constituencies grew disaffected.

In the post-Stalin succession, competing efforts to build constituencies and authority brought diverging positions on major policy issues and competing reform programs.[20] Yet, for about a year after Stalin's death public contestation was submerged by collectivism and the strain toward agreement. In offering his "New Course" Malenkov was torn between two pressures of centrism—between the reformist pressures of his constituency and the more conservative position of the dominant actors in the selectorate. As a consequence, his policy pronouncements gave the impression that the premier sought to be all things to all constituencies. On 8 August 1953, in formally announcing his New Course, the chairman attempted to balance the demands of reformers and conservatives: He announced a significant increase in investment funds for light and food industry as well as agriculture and fishing, while stressing the continued importance of capital goods industry as "the main foundation of our socialist economy" and calling for its continued development "by all means."[21] Norms against defection at first limited criticisms of the New Course from more conservative members of the collective leadership, who resisted major shifts in resources from producer-goods to consumer-goods industry. Until 1954 these other leaders offered only different shadings of emphasis in their statements rather than direct debate. Kliment Voroshilov, for example, pressed the importance of investment in producer-goods industry; he described it as "the main basis of the socialist economy, of the increased well-being of the people and of the strengthening of the defense capacity of the country."[22] Even Malenkov could agree with this statement. Similarly, Khrushchev warned against cutting investment in producer-goods industry, but he balanced this by asserting the demands of food and light industry. In his election speech in March 1954, for example, Khrushchev admonished his listeners that "speeding up development of light and food industries" should be done "without relaxing attention to the further development of heavy industry, which is the very foundation of the Soviet economy."[23]

A turning point in collective rule came with the start of Khrushchev's breakout in the latter half of 1954.[24] As Malenkov lost ground, public criticism from other members of the Politburo became more direct. By the time of the January 1955 Central Committee Plenum Khrushchev took the extreme position of denouncing the call for greater attention to consumer goods as "right-wing deviation" akin to the ideological error of the Right Opposition of the 1920s: "These wrong views contradict the law of Marxism-Leninism. They are nothing but a slander of the Party. They are a belching forth of the right deviation, a belching forth of views hostile to Leninism, which in their time were preached by Rykov, Bukharin, and their ilk."[25] Khrushchev's response to the New Course was different—the Virgin Lands Program to extend agricultural cultivation in Siberia and Central Asia. A program of this magnitude made enormous demands on labor and required diversified industrial production.[26] Although expanded agricultural output would ultimately satisfy consumer demand, in the short run it limited growth of consumer-goods industry.

Khrushchev's victory over the Anti-Party Group (June 1957) and accession to Nikolai Bulganin's post as premier (March 1958) ushered in a period in which the first secretary dominated policymaking. Khrushchev enjoyed about two years of virtually uncontested—at least publicly uncontested—leadership. The plenary sessions of the Central Committee offered a barometer of this changed mode of decisionmaking. Beginning at the December 1958 plenum, as Thomas H. Rigby observes, Central Committee "sessions took on the form of a dialogue between Khrushchev and the others present, with the first secretary interrupting himself and other speakers to elicit information, pass judgment or give spot directions to all and sundry, including the highest officials."[27] Beginning in early 1960, however, Khrushchev was increasingly besieged by challengers to his policies from among his original iron triangle constituencies. This ushered in a phase of contested directorship characterized by increasing policy contestation. Directive leadership remained in tact in this period. Apparently Khrushchev exercised enough power to take policy initiatives on his own, without the approval of the full Politburo.[28] What had changed in 1960 was growing disaffection within his original constituencies to his policy innovations. Iron triangle bureaucrats objected, and some leaders were willing to exploit these political opportunities, over proposed reductions of one-third in armed forces, a shift in investment from the "steel-eaters" toward consumer goods and agriculture, and reorganization of the lower Party apparatus into separate industrial and agricultural hierarchies.[29] Khrushchev's policies alienated virtually every constituency that had been the very core of his coalition.[30] Khrushchev's disproportionate power did not protect him from growing policy disputes.

THE POST-KHRUSHCHEV ADMINISTRATION

Leonid Brezhnev's tenure as general secretary lasted nearly two-thirds longer than that of his predecessor, yet he never consolidated the same directive policy leadership as Khrushchev. With different timing his administration shows a similar pattern of four distinctive regimes, but they never reached the same levels of consolidation nor contestation. The removal of Khrushchev in October 1964 established a half-decade of collective leadership characterized by balancing among competing leaders. The common policy position of this collective leadership began to break down in the summer of 1965 as Brezhnev started his breakout, but stronger norms against defection limited this policy differentiation under collective leadership. Leaders engaged in far less overt public contestation; the proposals they offered diverged far less than those in the previous two successions. Stronger guarantees of balancing limited the general secretary's personal rule. By 1970 Brezhnev had established a form of limited directorship, but the culmination of this consolidation did not come until 1976. The fourth regime of the Brezhnev administration (contested directorship) came in his last year, as his health and hold on office began to slip.

Collective leadership once again elicited proposals for and against reform, but the stronger constraints on differentiation meant these were less divergent than in previous successions.[31] Aleksei Kosygin and Nikolai Podgornyi were the most outspoken proponents of policy innovations that would shift priorities from the iron triangle to either consumer-goods industry (Kosygin) or social programs (Podgornyi), yet their arguments were tepid compared to Malenkov's plans for the "New Course." Podgornyi spoke in Baku in May 1965 for expansion of the "social funds of consumption," including "housing construction, urban amenities, health care, and services for the daily needs of the people." He argued that restrictions on consumer welfare and national sacrifices by the population to allow for priority development of heavy industry and strengthening of defense were things of the past.[32] Kosygin was not so bold in his proposals for development of light and food industry and satisfaction of the population's demand for a varied assortment of goods. Yet, speaking in Minsk in February 1968 he called for accelerated growth in light industry in order to reduce the imbalance in growth rates with heavy industry.[33] Brezhnev chose to build a constituency within the iron triangle, and in reaching out to this constituency he resisted reforms that would impinge on its priorities. Thus, his speeches pressed for strengthening defense, while he remained virtually silent on the need for investment in light industry. He attacked Kosygin's reforms for their emphasis on material incentives to increase productivity rather than Party apparatus leadership: "It would be wrong to reduce everything to material incentives; this would impoverish the inner world of Soviet man."[34] Like his predecessor's first policy initiatives, his innovations focused on agriculture. At the March 1965 CC Plenum Brezhnev introduced an agricultural program that would give greater autonomy to collective farms through a new system of deliveries.[35] In addition, he promised lower prices for farm equipment, pensions and minimum monthly incomes for collective farmers, and reduced taxes on private holdings.

Institutionalization of balancing made Brezhnev's breakout a more protracted process and his directive rule less complete. By early 1970 he had established his policy leadership in some issue areas, particularly in foreign policy, yet for the next decade this remained a limited or compartmentalized directorship.[36] With time it also brought diminished levels of policy contestation as Brezhnev eased out some of the original collective leadership that had come to power with him, including Aleksandr Shelepin (1975) and Podgornyi (1977). Because he never achieved the apex role of his predecessors, his directorship never completely supplanted the policy processes of collective bargaining. Brezhnev's directorship lasted until the end of 1981, when his growing infirmity brought a contested directorship with growing challenges to his policy initiatives. Challenges from the original coalition constituencies grew—particularly from military leaders such as Marshal Nikolai Ogarkov who objected to the new stringency in military spending. As first-tier leaders became more willing to exploit these opportunities, these challenges became part of the impending succession.[37]

THE POST-BREZHNEV ADMINISTRATIONS

The years from November 1982 to December 1986 suggest the Soviet Union was about to begin another cycle of regimes. The death of Leonid Brezhnev brought new collective decisionmaking with emphasis on consensus and limited policy differentiation. Collective decisionmaking and norms against defection limited the public debate over priorities within the first tier. The period of collective leadership without contestation lasted far longer than in either of the earlier successions.

In the post-Brezhnev succession, norms of collegiality seemed to all but kill policy divergence. The post-Brezhnev succession saw few if any significant reform proposals from within the first tier. Although Yurii Andropov's administration appears to have been more activist than Konstantin Chernenko's, the new general secretary avoided hard issues of changing priorities.[38] Whatever his personal preferences for reform, his presentation of the 1983 Plan on behalf of the collective leadership repeated the priorities of the late Brezhnev years and added only one innovation—a new emphasis on labor discipline to increase productivity.[39]

Chernenko's first address to the Central Committee as general secretary also gave little reason to expect major reforms. He avoided hard choices among spending priorities by seeming to suggest that the Soviet Union could have all things simultaneously. In his March 1984 speech to his constituents before the Supreme Soviet elections, Chernenko noted that international tensions had required diversion of considerable resources to defense in preceding years. While he claimed that the leaders would not curtail social programs, increases in food and consumer goods were to depend on greater labor efficiency.[40] In April 1984 Chernenko made a plea for conservative approaches to organizational reforms as well: He told the Central Committee members "putting existing capabilities fully into action will be enough" and warned that searching for "new forms and activities of economic activity" should not "divert us from the more effective use of existing managerial institutions."[41]

Gorbachev as well did not rock the boat in his initial policy statements. In light of what followed later, it is easy to lose sight of the fact that his initial pronouncements were timid and disappointing.[42] In his acceptance speech Gorbachev pledged to continue the policies of his two predecessors—"acceleration of socioeconomic development and perfection of all aspects of social life." He indicated his policy priorities would emphasize producer-goods industry. He argued that the standard of living would rise through greater labor productivity rather than shifts in investment to consumer-goods industry: "the improvement of man's living conditions would be based on his growing contribution to the common cause."[43] In June 1985 he argued against further increases in agricultural investment, and he stressed that investment should focus on machine building and electronics.[44] According to one analyst's count, none of Gorbachev's subsequent seventy-nine speeches even used the term *reform* when addressing the Party's plans.[45] The new general secretary astutely played the game of normal politics according to the increasing constraints of balanced leadership within bureaucratic reciprocal accountability.

POLICY DYSFUNCTION AND STAGNATION

Among the most perverse consequences of this political process under bureaucratic reciprocal accountability and of its institutionalization were increasing policy dysfunction and institutional maladaptation. Once the bureaucracies of state building and early industrialization were enfranchised, coalition politics made significant reform of these bureaucracies and their missions unlikely. The subsequent political process revolved around attempts of leaders *qua* politicians to provide these bureaucrats with the means to fulfill these missions and attempts of leaders *qua* governors to force adaptations in these missions. In the long run the structure of Soviet politics worked against the latter. The cycling of collective and directive leadership led to a pattern of recurring reform attempts without significant actual reform. Collective leadership encouraged the clash of alternative programs of innovation and preservation, and directive leadership brought opportunities for real innovation. Yet, in both periods the constitution of Bolshevism tended to work to the disadvantage of reform. In successions, the forces of preservation typically defeated reformers. Reforms introduced under directive leaders were limited and subjected to being turned back in the next succession. With the institutionalization of the constitution of Bolshevism even this limited reform became more difficult: Institutionalization of reciprocal accountability and balanced leadership meant that the brief episodes of innovation became briefer and fewer. As oscillations between collective and directive leadership became less extreme, in normal politics motivations and opportunities for reform declined. This brought increasing policy dysfunction as the polity was unable to adapt to its changing social and economic environment.

Innovation and Dysfunction

The problem of sustained reform was a problem of both the reformist content of policy and the coherence and consistency of a reform program. Bolshevik policy dynamics made significant reform unlikely and still more difficult to sustain. The prospects for reform rose with the general secretary's consolidation of directive leadership because consolidation increased the general secretary's incentive to force sacrifices on iron triangle interests, his chances of gaining approval for these reforms in the Politburo, and his opportunities to force these changes on the second tier. Conversely, collective rule and policy contestation subverted these.

First, consolidation shaped the general secretary's "selectoral" incentives. The constraints of policy entrepreneurship, aggregation, and centrism shaped the position of all leaders in the first tier with regard to policy innovation: The "selectoral" incentive for a leader to introduce reforms depended on the relation of affected interests to his coalition.[46] A leader was less likely to favor reforms adversely affecting an interest within his coalition and particularly interests making the greatest contributions to his coalition. (By extension, he was more likely to oppose reforms adversely affecting the interests of his constituents when his coalition was smaller.) Instead, a leader would be more likely to favor reform if the interests benefiting were within his coalition and made a more significant contribution to its success. Thus, low consolidation of leadership tended to deter general secretaries from supporting reform: because he was inclined to begin coalition building from the iron triangle a general secretary initially tended to oppose reform at the expense of the iron triangle. This constraint was acute at the beginning of the general secretary's coalition building when his coalition was smaller because the relative importance of the iron triangle to his coalition was greater. It was a particularly strong constraint on his policy positions affecting an institution, such as the military, that was better able to resist clientelistic control.

High consolidation reduced the coalition-based constraints that deterred the general secretary from supporting reform and actually gave him a "selectoral" incentive to support it. As a general secretary consolidated his coalition the relative contribution of the iron triangle to his coalition declined and the pressure to resist reform receded. The shift from balancing to bandwagoning reduced particularistic pressures on the general secretary, and consolidation made threats to his tenure less immediate. The directive leader enjoyed significantly greater freedom to define the policy agenda and attend to systemic problems that transcended particular interests. In addition, consolidation of directive leadership actually gave a general secretary a "selectoral" incentive to initiate policy innovation. That is, expansion of the general secretary's coalition transformed his policy problem. To expand his coalition beyond the iron triangle it was imperative to extend policy payoffs to interests outside this core. As he balanced the priorities of an ever larger set of interests, dynamic centrism demanded he support more reformist policies. Moreover, reform was an invaluable means by which a general secretary might further consolidate his position. Having consolidated directive rule a general secretary might see reform as a way to rid himself of limitations on his personal power imposed by his original coalition constituencies. The general secretary's incentive to reform rose with consolidation as he saw forcing sacrifices on the iron triangle as a means to meet the competing demands of an enlarged coalition and to clip the constraints on his leadership imposed by his original constituencies. Yet, even with directive rule the general secretary was likely to press only moderate reform. The oversized coalition of the general secretary during directive leadership was likely to be more centrist in its policy orientation than the coalitions of reformers during collective leadership. The defeat of reformers in the succession reduced pressures for reform from progressives outside the leader's coalition. The general secretary was constrained by the threat that reform would prompt desertion from iron triangle constituencies.

Second, the prospects for reform increased with consolidated directorship because it increased the chances the general secretary could gain support for reform within the first tier. Low consolidation of policy leadership worked to the disadvantage of reform—particularly, significant and sustained reform—by complicating the decision process within the first tier. Under collective leadership reformers were typically unable to secure agreement in the Politburo for the redistribution entailed in real reforms. Policymaking under low consolidation tended to be slow and prone to delays; it led to avoidance of choices among clear-cut alternatives, encouraged deferring choices to other bodies for resolution, and often produced either no policy owing to stalemate or compromised outcomes.[47] Thus, collective leadership was often unable to agree on reform.

Collective leadership, in particular, eroded the coherence and consistency of reform attempts; this left the innovations that were adopted less significant and unsustained. *Coherence* across policies is the extent to which policies in different areas (e.g., pricing policy, agricultural production goals) are reinforcing, while incoherence cancels initiatives by actions at cross-purposes. *Consistency* over time is the extent to which actions in a specific policy area are reinforced by subsequent actions, with inconsistency subverting a state's ability to pursue stable objectives.[48] Under low consolidation, leaders had to rely on one another to initiate policies, particularly when these entailed coordination of policy realms. Collective decisions often resulted from ad hoc compromises without agreement on longer-term goals. The parties to a compromise in one issue area might be very different from those in another, and so the compromises reached in each might work at cross-purposes. Under collective leadership, individual leaders could push policy initiatives within their respective realms of authority that were at odds with the initiatives pushed in other realms. Changing ad hoc groupings among leaders led to changing policies; initiatives taken in one compromise could be countered in the next. All these subverted the coherence and consistency of reform efforts.

At most, collective leadership led to a kind of paper reform: The contradictory pressures of differentiation and collegiality in the first tier could lead to logrolling among the policy priorities of different members of the collective leadership without agreement on the redistributive issues these entailed. The logrolling without agreement on trade-offs was papered over by ignorance (feigned or real), obfuscation, and wishful thinking. Leaders sometimes adopted policies with competing demands on scarce resources and simply ignored the trade-offs. Leaders could mask conflicts by "expressing policies in vague generalities representing the 'lowest common denominator' of agreement in which all can acquiesce."[49] They sometimes based policy on unrealistic assumptions; for example, economic growth or government revenues would accelerate so as to permit all rival programs to be funded.

Third, the prospects for reform rose with consolidated directorship because consolidation increased the ability of the first tier to enforce reform on the second tier. Conversely, collective leadership subverted the prospects for reform by expanding the autonomy of second-tier bureaucrats and so increasing their ability to resist policy direction from the leadership.[50] For example, collective leadership following the death of Stalin and again after the removal of Khrushchev gave the military greater autonomy from first-tier control. Between March 1953 and January 1955 the military threw its weight behind Party leaders who supported priority investment for heavy industry and high budgetary allocations to defense. Under the leadership of Marshal Zhukov between February 1955 and October 1957, the military sought to limit political intrusion in its professional domain by circumscribing the role of party organizations within military units and giving the military a greater voice in military strategy. Roman Kolkowicz observes, "The Party leadership had little choice but to tolerate the military's growing voice in the hope of reasserting the Party's dominance at that point in the future when the ineffective collective leadership would have been replaced by a single, strong leader."[51] Only after defeat of the Anti-Party Group did the opportunity return to shift the balance between tiers. In October Khrushchev removed Zhukov and began a campaign to expand both Party controls within military units and Party leadership in the development of military thought.

In addition to low consolidation, policy contestation eroded the ability to pursue coherent and consistent reform. In particular, the combination of consolidated leadership and contestation could lead to unusually erratic policy. Contestation made it expedient for a general secretary to take dramatic initiatives or make sharp changes in the direction of policy in order to keep his opponents "politically off balance." For example, the growth of competition within the central elite in reaction to Khrushchev's reformist initiatives undermined the continuity of policy. This helps explain the zigzag course in Khrushchev's foreign policy from 1959 to 1964—from the spirit of Camp David in 1959 to the Berlin ultimatum, missile rattling, and Cuban Missile Crisis of the next three years, and then after 1962 to the détente of the hot-line and test ban agreements. The swings in policy during this period grew from a cycle of Khrushchevian initiatives, mounting criticism, and a tactical retreat by the first secretary.[52] He sought to propitiate key critics by initiatives that contradicted the general line in policy. The first secretary's maneuvers resulted in contradictory initiatives and rapid changes in the direction of policy. The combination of directive leadership giving a single leader the power to make bold policy moves and the policy contestation that gave him an incentive to respond to contradictory political pressures fed this unusually incoherent and inconsistent policy.

The cycling of leadership gave rise to a reform-retreat cycle that made reform difficult. Only moderate reform was likely. Reformist proposals flourished with the pressure toward policy divergence under collective leadership, yet reformers were defeated by balancing during successions. The opportunity to pass reform reached its peak under directive rule, but by then the flowering of reform proposals had wilted and prudence dictated moderation even by a directive leader. The power of the iron triangle in the selectorate and its strategic place in the leader's coalition checked reform under both collective and directive leadership. With the next succession, reforms adopted under a directive leader could be turned back under new collective leadership.

The spiraling of regimes made reform still more difficult, for inherent in the institutionalization of this constitutional structure were declining policy divergence within collective leadership and dwindling opportunity to force reform under directive leadership. As difficult as reciprocal accountability had made sustained reform, the oscillation of leadership held some opportunities for progress. Reversals in policy were seldom complete; while they brought one step back, they often came after two steps forward. The alternation between reform and retreat was not simply cyclical; it was dialectic. Successions were invaluable insofar as they could bring a flowering of reform proposals; the imperative of differentiation during successions brought *intellectual* renewal in politics through widening the menu of options discussed in the first tier. Opposition between ideas of reform and preservation under collective leadership could lead to a synthesis of moderate reform actually implemented under a directive leader.[53] Yet, over the longer term, as oscillation between collective and directive leadership declined, obstacles to even this limited renewal grew. With institutionalization of balancing and of norms against defection, each succession saw less differentiation and contestation in the first tier. Thus, each succession was less likely to bring the flowering of reform proposals. With institutionalization of mutual checking and limits on disqualification in the first tier and routinization of appointment and promotion in the second tier, consolidation brought fewer opportunities for a leader to establish directive rule and so fewer opportunities to impose change. Reform proposals became less common; sustained, coherent reform programs became rarer still; policy stagnated. The consequence of these trends was growing policy dysfunction.

Institutional Maladaptation

The root of this increasing inability to innovate—institutional maladaptation—was a more fundamental problem that grew with time. That is, the constitution of Bolshevism itself was unable to accommodate social change—paradoxically, changes the regime had itself engineered. The missions of the regime were fixed at its creation and institutionalized in its chief bureaucratic constituencies. Policy innovation required changing the missions of the chief constituents or changing the constituents altogether, but the constitution of Bolshevism stood as an obstacle to either change. Most important was the resistance of this restrictive, bureaucratic selectorate to the infusion of new social forces created by the processes of modernization.

Adaptation was hypothetically possible, but institutionalization of reciprocal accountability and collective leadership made this inordinately difficult. In ascending order of assault on the existing political order, the hypothetical adaptations included: First, new incumbents in existing job slots might adapt their bureaucracies' missions; yet, the routinization of promotion, with its emphasis on steplike promotion up the bureaucratic ladder, limited the chances that even new bureaucrats would bring fresh perspectives and a redefinition of missions. Second, adaptation might come through direct incorporation of new social forces into the Central Committee; however, the barriers to entry into the Central Committee were high, and with the institutionalization of job-slot representation they were being reinforced. Third, the first-tier leadership might seek to create alternative centers of accountability outside the Central Committee, but institutionalization of reciprocal accountability between Politburo and Central Committee prevented this.

Cycling of leadership had held the promise of renewal. Leaders might seek advantage by expanding the political process when either collective sanctioning against defection was paralyzed or enough power to resist sanctions had been consolidated.[54] On the one hand, intense conflict under collective leadership could leave the first tier vulnerable to paralysis in which the leaders could not enforce sanctions against defection from the oligarchy. As the experience of the 1920s demonstrated, without enforcement of sanctions, ambitious leaders might organize constituencies either in the unenfranchised bureaucracies or outside the bureaucracies to assault the exclusive positions of the enfranchised in the Central Committee. On the other hand, high levels of consolidation could allow a directive leadership to impose change on the second tier. As the experience of the 1930s showed, an autocrat could refashion the configuration of forces in the selectorate. Yet, institutionalization of balanced leadership had made either of these possibilities less likely. Guarantees of powers and authority to the general secretary and the institutionalization of a procedure to transfer these powers reduced the dispersion of power during the succession. Greater institutionalization of balancing reduced the opportunities to consolidate the directive leadership that could be turned against the constitutional equilibrium.

Even the small attempts by leaders to expand the policy process were constrained by collective rule and reciprocal accountability. For example, during his directive rule Khrushchev sought to expand popular involvement in administrative tasks through volunteers working in administration and transfer of administrative functions to public organizations like the Communist youth league (Komsomol) and residence committees. The impact on policymaking was limited: at most some decisionmaking shifted to levels of the Soviet system where popular opinion might be given greater weight; administrative responsibilities devolved upon soviets and public organizations, with some possibilities for popular influence over administration; and electivity and accountability of the soviets modestly expanded. These changes did not threaten the composition of the selectorate. Indeed, Khrushchev's policies especially emphasized preventing the involvement in administrative tasks from subverting the enforced departicipation of society. His policies used such instruments as popular militia and comrades' courts to check the expanding popular involvement with heightened emphasis on social control, discipline, and homogeneity in the population. These elements prevented this expanded popular involvement from taking a real share of policymaking power or threatening the existing lines of accountability.

As timid as these changes may have been, they provoked a reaction from the iron triangle. The early Brezhnev administration reversed many of these practices. Its policies limited popular involvement in administration by reducing the intrusion of volunteers in the implementation of policies, dismantling the Party-State Control Commission, and curbing the devolution of administrative responsibilities to public organizations. As popular involvement in the implementation of policies was limited, bureaucratic participation in policymaking was further routinized. Breslauer notes that in Brezhnev's early speeches as general secretary, "specialists were accorded extensive recognition and praise . . . , and were assured that their advice would be heeded by decisionmakers."[55] The expanded use of think tanks and experts drawn from the bureaucracies into the policymaking process was a natural consequence of reciprocal accountability, which institutionalized the role of the second tier in policymaking without threatening the restrictive selectorate. Renewed pressures to reinforce departicipation prevented this from both spilling outside the enfranchised and empowered bureaucracies and changing the selectorate: Brezhnev checked expanding elite participation with new pressures against dissidents within the elite, including campaigns for "iron discipline" within the Party, intensified political indoctrination and Party *kontrol'* within the scientific community, and heightened vigilance against dissidence within the cultural intelligentsia. This kept the institutionalization of bureaucratic involvement in policymaking from threatening an expansion of selectoral politics.[56]

A consequence of this inability to include new social forces in the political process was the petrification of the selectorate. The criteria for inclusion in the political process had been defined by the missions of early industrialization and regime building. Yet, as the early tasks were completed, new social forces were created, and new missions became necessary; however, the political system could not incorporate these forces or missions.

One superficial manifestation of this petrification of the selectorate was the growing stability of personnel and the difficulty of bringing younger generations into the leadership. The growth of collective leadership had led to not only stability within the first tier but also guarantees of the tenure of second-tier bureaucrats that supported that administration. Thus, under the Brezhnev administration the average tenure of office-holders lengthened. Between January 1964 and January 1982 the average term of union-republic first secretaries jumped from 6.6 years to 11.5 years. A consequence of this was the aging Soviet bureaucracy. For example, compared with the last years of Stalin's rule (March 1950), the average age of Council of Ministers members in the late Brezhnev administration (March 1980) rose from forty-six to sixty-five years.[57] The growing stability of second-tier personnel was reflected in declining turnover in the Central Committee. After 1965 the proportion of voting members of the Central Committee that survived to be returned as voting members by the next Party Congress increased from only half (1961) to about four-fifths for the next four elections.[58]

Stability of personnel was only a superficial manifestation of the petrification of the selectorate, however, and not the heart of the problem. Even with rapid turnover, the problem of stagnation remained. First, with institutionalization of promotion, turnover did not necessarily bring renewal. A new incumbent was often the previous incumbent's second-in-command—often an approved or handpicked heir. For example, in the turnover among first secretaries from March 1985 to the end of 1986, most new provincial secretaries were simply promotions from within the respective organizations.[59] Second, the deeper problem was the inability to expand the franchise beyond existing job-slots. Norms governing the creation of new Central Committee seats limited the ability to shift the balance among institutions or bring in representatives of new institutions. As Robert V. Daniels observes, "while it might appear that expanding the Central Committee . . . would offer the leadership an opportunity to pack it with individuals of their choice, the network of unwritten rules and expectations about Central Committee rank and job status very narrowly restricts the options of the leadership in opening up new membership slots."[60] With each general secretary after Stalin, institutionalization reduced the discretion of even directive leaders to change this representa-

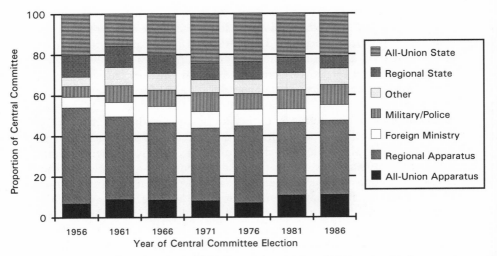

Figure 6.3. Job-Slot Representation in the Central Committee, 1956–1986.
Sources: *Pravda*, 26 February 1956, 1 November 1961, 9 April 1966, 10
April 1971, 6 March 1976, 4 March 1981, 7 March 1986.

tion of job-slots. Central Committee members not holding office—that is,
workers and managers—averaged only 5.1 percent of the voting membership and never exceeded 10 percent between 1956 and 1986; moreover,
these members in non-job-slot seats played largely honorific roles in Central Committee proceedings. As figure 6.3 shows, the proportionate positions among bureaucracies in the Central Committee shifted very little
after 1961. After 1961, Party apparatchiki averaged 30 percent of the
job-slot seats in the Central Committee, never fluctuating more than 3
percentage points from this; armed forces and police officers averaged 8.9
percent, fluctuating within 1.1 percentage point; Foreign Ministry officials averaged 7.7 percent and never fluctuated more than 1 percentage
point; and other ministerial and local state administrators averaged 45.8
percent, with the maximum fluctuation under 2 percentage points in all
five elections. With institutionalization of the rules of reciprocal accountability, the proportionate shares in the selectorate became fixed.

In short, the institutionalization of balancing had a most perverse consequence: it increased the stability, but limited the adaptability of the political system. Institutionalization of reciprocal accountability and balanced leadership limited the ability of the Soviet political system to
change. Together they created the paradox of institutionalized stagnation—stability without adaptability.

INSTITUTIONS AND THE POLICY PROCESS

In stressing the policy consequences of the constitution of Bolshevism, this analysis seeks to add an important element that has been missing in the last decade and a half of intensive and very fruitful Western analysis of the Soviet policy process. Previous studies have largely ignored the role of institutional constraints on the policy process and policy outcomes. Valerie Bunce's pioneering analysis of the link between successions and domestic policy priorities in *Do New Leaders Make a Difference?* examines the link between policy process and policy output, but in a context largely devoid of institutions.[61] George W. Breslauer's analysis of authority building in *Khrushchev and Brezhnev as Leaders* focuses (to use his terminology) on the "man" rather than the "system" and, therefore, excludes (except as almost an afterthought) any consideration of institutional constraints. For example, in explaining the differences between Khrushchev's and Brezhnev's authority-building strategies, he stresses the personality of each leader, the climate of opinion in each administration, and the state of knowledge; institutions are secondary.[62] More recently, Jack Snyder in *Myths of Empire* has made an important step forward in introducing institutions into our analysis of Soviet policymaking, by examining the political context that gave rise to the domestic policy coalition fostering the Soviet foreign policy of overexpansion.[63] Yet, Snyder's purpose is not to elaborate an institutional model of authoritarianism or a coalition model suitable for analysis of domestic policy. That is the project of this book.

This chapter has argued that consideration of institutional constraints should shape the way we think about the policy process. For example, if Bunce had considered the institutional differences between democracies and authoritarian polities, she might not have begun her analysis from the premise that Soviet successions are fundamentally similar to those in Western democracies. Consideration of institutional constraints leads us to suspect that the honeymoons that may be important for newly elected American presidents did not exist for new Soviet general secretaries caught in a succession struggle within a collective leadership. In 1953, for example, the institutional roles of American president and Soviet first secretary were not identical; indeed, from March to September of that year the latter post did not even exist. Attention to institutional constraints also led us to introduce a concept of leadership consolidation into Bunce's analysis—a phenomenon driven by the institutional context of bureaucratic reciprocal accountability that does not exist in the same form within western presidential democracies. These amendments to the Bunce model would fundamentally alter the a priori predictions one derives.

In drawing our attention to the context in which individuals must act, institutional analysis stresses problems of collective action, conflict, and coalitions. These are important themes in works such as Snyder's, which stresses the importance of coalitions and logrolling to hold them together. Yet, institution-free analysis has largely chosen to overlook these elements of the policy process. Concerns for collective action problems (and free riders) lead us to look skeptically at claims, such as Bunce's, that the collective interest of the leadership during successions led them to submerge individual differences in a common effort to shift spending toward consumer spending. Collective leadership would require a special institutional environment for this imperative (the strain toward agreement) to triumph over the contradictory imperative toward differentiation. This concern with group processes also leads to a very different view of the relationship between the stages of Soviet administrations and reform. Bunce identifies a simple two-stage cycle of succession and postsuccession politics in which the former favor reform and the latter leads to "politics as usual" and "incrementalism."[64] The institutionalist concern for conflict and coalitions leads us to view the "pumping-up" of consumer spending that Bunce highlights as actually only a part of logrolling. Yet, logrolling under collective leadership leads to paper reforms that are diminished by incoherence and inconsistency. Only consolidated leadership can impose the priorities needed for a real shift in what we would call reform. Breslauer's three-stage analysis of a general secretary's changing incentives is much closer to the present analysis: successions bring competing proposals and logrolling of programs; "ascendancy" brings reformist programs from the general secretary; but the failure of these reforms may later heighten pressures for an alternative program.[65] The present chapter has extended this line of analysis by examining the ways in which institutions constrain individual policy preferences and bring these together in collective outcomes.

The institutionalist focus also draws our attention to institutionalization as a source of longer-term change. The institutionalization of reciprocal accountability and balanced leadership is consistent with Snyder's concept of growing cartelization of leadership under Khrushchev and Brezhnev, but Snyder does not develop these themes.[66] For Breslauer, in the absence of serious consideration of the system, changes in the policy process and policy outcomes are attributed to differences between Khrushchev and Brezhnev (and perhaps the growth of knowledge), but not to longer-term institutionalization of structural constraints. The theme of long-term changes in the Soviet polity leading to greater stability pervades much analysis of the Soviet policy process. The institutionalist perspective presented here explains why this development, usually seen as positive, had such a perverse consequence.

The contribution made by this institutionalist model of the policy process can only partially be judged by its theoretical rigor. It must also be assessed by the range of empirical questions it permits us to address and the number of tenable relationships it suggests. The next three chapters explore some aspects of the fruitfulness of this model through the form of case studies of reform in the Soviet polity. Chapter 7 examines reform in domestic policies—in governmental spending priorities and procedures from 1953 to 1986. Chapter 8 presents a case study of change in foreign policy—military planning from 1953 to 1986. Chapter 9 analyzes the effort beginning in January 1987 to reform the constitutional foundations of Soviet politics and its failure. Through these case studies I seek to assess the extent to which this institutionalist approach gives us analytic leverage in empirical study of reform under bureaucratic reciprocal accountability.

CHAPTER SEVEN

The Domestic Policy Spiral

THE SOVIET inability to adapt its policies and procedures to the changing demands of an industrializing society stands as a monument to the self-limiting qualities of bureaucratic reciprocal accountability. The constitutional order was not unique in leading political actors to assess policy innovations from a partisan perspective, but, as a constitutional order based on bureaucratic reciprocal accountability, it restricted those with a meaningful opportunity to participate in this assessment of innovations to a narrow selectorate with relatively static role-defined missions. Policy innovations that might threaten these missions and reforms that threatened the privileged position of these actors in the assessment of innovations and the making of policy were unlikely to succeed.

Reform—as an innovation that redistributes wealth, power, or both—can come in the form of changes in the policy outputs of the polity or in the processes and procedures by which the polity distributes these. In the following discussion *policy reform* refers to efforts to redistribute privileges and wealth by changing the policy outputs of government. For example, these include shifts in government spending among such budget categories as defense or social programs. In a command economy this also includes shifts of investment and production among priorities such as producer goods or consumer goods. *Procedural reform* refers to efforts to redistribute power and wealth by changing the processes of policymaking. This can include transfers of decisionmaking among previously existing organs or changes in the configuration of formal organs themselves.

This is the first of three chapters that analyze cases of policy reform. These cases illustrate how the constitution of Bolshevism limited the opportunities for either policy or procedural reform. The coalition politics favored by the constitutional order defeated significant redistribution of policy outputs. In particular, it blocked changes in the procedures that had guaranteed the iron triangle a privileged position in the policymaking processes by which these allocations were made. Over time, with the institutionalization of bureaucratic reciprocal accountability and balanced leadership, these obstacles to reform became more severe.

This chapter, divided into two parts, examines domestic policy reform from 1953 to 1986. The first half examines the central recurring issue of spending priorities in these years. The politics of the budget and plan were the central theater for setting policy priorities. The second half of this chapter examines attempts to change decisionmaking procedures and organizations. The research strategy in both halves is designed to assess the analytic leverage of the new institutionalism by confronting its expectations with different types of reform and various types of evidence. Thus, in the following case studies I employ close textual analysis of official statements, case studies of individual reforms, and aggregate statistical analysis. The more we discover that the evidence confirms the insights of the model presented in this book and the tenability of its expectations, the greater the utility of this analytic approach.

REFORM OF SPENDING PRIORITIES

The greatest policy problem facing the Soviet leadership after 1953 was economic growth, and the greatest *policy reform* was how to allocate spending to achieve higher rates of growth. Since the first five-year plan in 1928, the pursuit of accelerated growth has influenced the allocation of resources within a distinctive Soviet developmental strategy. This strategy assigned priority to investment over consumption and to investment in the producer-goods sector over the consumer-goods sector.[1] By the end of the Stalin era this had become a bit of a dogma: Joseph Stalin admonished the generation that would succeed him that to build communism the Soviet Union must engage in "continuous expansion of all social production, *with a relatively higher rate of expansion of the production of means of production.*"[2]

Government spending was an intensely partisan issue because it went to the heart of the iron triangle's privileged position in the receipt of scarce resources. Central to the debates between conservatives and reformers after Stalin's death were issues of spending priorities.[3] The precedence of producer goods over consumer goods established disparities in the status, power, and resources of institutions that reformers attacked. Conservatives—particularly, those associated with the iron triangle— defended prevailing economic priorities against reformers' pressure to devote more to the growth of consumption and social amenities.

Spending priorities from 1953 to 1986 were sensitive to the shifting political fortunes and coalition strategies of major political actors. The success of conservatives and reformers and the actual priorities of economic policy between 1953 and 1986 reflected the cycling and institutionalization of politics. Reform in economic priorities shifted over time with oscillation between collective and directive leadership and as the level of contestation within the first tier rose or fell. Over a still longer term, the prospects for reform in spending priorities declined as institu-

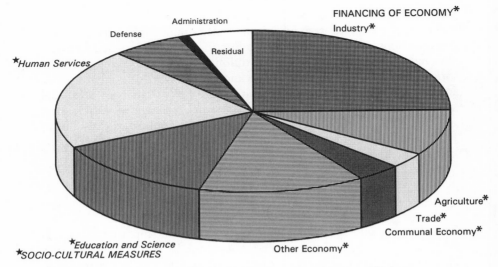

Figure 7.1. Allocation of Unified State Budget, 1980. *Sources*: Ministerstvo
Finansov SSSR, Biudzhetnoe upravlenie, *Gosudarstvennyi biudzhet SSSR
i biudzhety soiuznykh respublik, 1976–1980 gg.* (Moscow: Finansy i
statistika, 1982), 22–23.

tionalization reduced the amplitude of these oscillations between collective and directive leadership. The pattern of spending priorities illustrates
well how the regime spiral slid into growing policy dysfunction.

In Soviet spending debates the major trade-offs involved the familiar
tug-of-war over spending on defense, social-cultural measures, and the
economy. Yet, because the economy was an elaborate state undertaking,
an equally important issue was the production and investment priorities
for the whole economy and the trade-off among sectors such as producer-
goods (Group A) industry, consumer-goods (Group B) industry, and agriculture. A majority of this spending was channeled through the Unified
State Budget, which allocated funds gathered from taxes on the profits of
state enterprises (30 percent of 1980 revenues), turnover or value-added
taxes (31 percent of revenues), income taxes (8.1 percent of revenues),
and other revenue sources. The Unified State Budget included the spending of not only the national (or all-union) government but also all lower
levels of government. Yet, not all spending controlled by the authorities
passed through the budget. In the command economy, leaders also allocated funds (such as the retained earnings of the state-owned enterprises)
that did not enter the budget but were part of the financial plan for the
economy. Both the budget and nonbudgetary allocations were parts of an
integrated plan, and I analyze them below.

TABLE 7.1
1980 Unified State Budget and Financial Plan
(Billions of Rubles)

	Unified State Budget	Financial Plan
TOTAL	294.6	Unknown
Including:		
Social-Cultural Measures	98.8	123.3
Financing of National Economy	161.0	291.9
Including:		
Industry and Construction	74.1	(157.6)
Heavy Industry		(129.4)
Light Industry		(28.2)
Defense	17.1	Unknown
Administration	2.5	Unknown

Source: Ministerstvo Finansov SSSR, Biudzhetnoe upravlenie, *Gosudarstvennoe biudzhet SSSR i biudzhety soiuznykh respublik, 1976–1980 gg.* (Moscow: Finansy i statistika, 1982), 22–23; Tsentral'noe Statisticheskoe Upravlenie, *Narodnoe Khoziaistvo SSSR v 1980 g.* (Moscow: Finansy i statistika, 1981), 522–23; V. F. Garbuzov, "O Gosudarstvennom biudzhete SSSR na 1982 goda i ob ispolnenii Gosudarstvennogo biudzheta SSSR na 1980 goda," *Pravda,* 18 November 1981.

Note: Parentheses indicate planned or authorized expenditures.

To illustrate this allocation of expenditures in budget and plan, consider the 1980 Unified State Budget and financial plan:[4] As figure 7.1 shows, the Unified State Budget allocated more than half of its expenditures that year to the financing of the national economy (FNE) for such purposes as capital investment. It allocated another one-third to social-cultural measures (SCM) including education, science, health, and social welfare programs (e.g., pensions, aid for dependent children). The defense category, which accounts for only 5.8 percent of the budget, quite obviously did not include all military expenditures; some financing of hardware procurement was included in the totals for the economy, and some personnel costs were included in social-cultural expenditures. Much financing of defense may have been outside the Unified State Budget. United States intelligence estimates suggest the total costs of defense in 1980 may have been as much as five times the official budget figure. The budget also had a small, but significant residual that was simply not explained.

The financial plan included both these budgetary expenditures and allocations that were formally outside the budget. In 1980, as table 7.1 shows, nonbudgetary allocations such as internal financing of the economy from enterprise revenues brought total spending on the economy to 195.4 percent and total spending on social-cultural measures to 121.2

percent of the budget figure. Thus, the leadership controlled the allocation of significant sums outside the budget. (The leaders could shift these nonbudgetary funds into and out of the budget or simply credit them against budgetary allocations.) The total spending on the economy from budget and all other sources in 1980 was slated to be apportioned 44.3 percent to producer-goods industry, 17.4 percent to agriculture, and 9.7 percent to consumer-goods industry.

The following analysis of changing budgetary priorities permits us to examine the expected effects of both the short-term cycling of leadership and longer-term institutionalization by making two comparisons. Cyclical changes in spending priorities associated with the recurring shift from collective to directive leadership show up in the comparison of regimes within administrations—a comparison that emerges across the next two sections. Longer-term changes in policy associated with the institutionalization of politics show up in the comparison of administrations at similar stages of consolidation—a comparison within each of the following sections. This analysis draws on a systematic examination of the thirty-five annual budgets (and financial plans) adopted by the Soviet Union from 1953 to 1987. The evidence is drawn from both close textual analysis of the formal budget plan reports and statistical analysis of aggregate trends in spending.

Collective Leadership and the Defeat of Reform

During successions pressures for reform in spending priorities were defeated by coalitions of leaders and iron triangle interests. The iron triangle initially suffocated reforms in logrolling and inconsistent policies and then simply reversed the paper reforms. Logrolling and paper reforms were the momentary consequence of a collective leadership still sorting out positions of power; the defeat of reform accompanied the emergence of a new leader—the general secretary's breakout from collective leadership with the assistance of the iron triangle. In the momentary balance among uncertain heirs the tension between the "imperative toward differentiation" and the "strain toward agreement" might lead to compromise, but it also led to stalemate when it came to the hard trade-offs represented by reform. The emergence of a new leader ended this paper reform. One continuity holds across all three successions: With a new leader reforms were defeated and conservative economic priorities prevailed.[5]

Over time, however, elements of this pattern slowly changed. With the institutionalization of power, there was less divergence, less flowering of reform ideas, and less logrolling. The strength of reformist pressure depended on the imperative toward differentiation among leaders. The decisiveness with which these reform proposals were reversed in the conservative triumph depended on the extent to which the general secretary could make a decisive breakout. These all declined with each succession. The following three studies of the spending priorities in each succession show this clearly: In the post-Stalin succession, conservative priorities prevailed after defeating a reform experiment. By the post-Brezhnev succession, bold reform proposals were simply not presented by leaders; virtual stasis had set in.

THE POST-STALIN SUCCESSION

The most extensive logrolling and most decisive conservative rebuff to reform came in the post-Stalin succession. Malenkov's leading position within the collective leadership should have given reform an advantage, but balancing checked any attempt to produce real shifts in spending priorities at the expense of the iron triangle. The breakout by Khrushchev brought an iron triangle triumph and reversed reform.

Balancing among leaders who had differentiated themselves from one another led to a collective outcome of stalemated, incompatible commitments. The new leadership as a collectivity was committed simultaneously to expanding consumer-goods output (the New Course), raising investment in agriculture (the Virgin Lands Program), maintaining high investment in heavy industry, and keeping defense strong. Virgin Lands and the New Course could not be pursued simultaneously, let alone while maintaining heavy industry and defense. Yet, the collective leadership could not sort out its priorities. In the end agriculture was promised more tractors, and consumers were promised more washing machines, but the iron triangle prevented these from threatening its own spending and investment plans.

The collective leadership's State Budget for 1954 made this balancing clear: The minister of finance summarized the spending priorities of the budget in the following words: "the overwhelming majority of state budget funds is being directed to developing industry, agriculture, transport, trade, and other branches of the national economy, to raising the material and cultural well-being of the Soviet people."[6] That is to say, virtually every sector of the economy as well as social-cultural programs were to be priorities. It projected a 10 percent increase in expenditures on social-cultural measures and even higher growth in expenditures on the economy. Both heavy industry and light industry continued to receive levels of investment at least as high as those promised under Stalin's Fifth Five-Year Plan.

The plans to expand previously neglected sectors did not come at the expense of heavy industry. In this regard three features of this budget and plan stand out. First, the minister made it clear that heavy industry would continue to receive precedence in economic growth plans. He opened his discussion of the 1954 budget by noting that "major appropriations have been made in the draft budget for financing heavy industry, which has been and is the fundamental basis for developing every branch of the socialist economy and strengthening our homeland's defensive strength, and the foundation of the people's well-being." In summarizing the spending priorities he once again underscored the priority and fundamental role of heavy industry: "The budget reflects the policy being pursued by our party and government, a policy for further developing heavy industry and realizing on this basis the all-round development of agriculture and a considerable increase in the production of consumers' goods."[7] Growth in heavy industry was the key to development in other sectors. Second, in the budget proposed for 1954, heavy industry was not asked to sacrifice for the new expenditures in other sectors. Capital investment in metallurgy, power stations, coal, oil, and chemical industry, and construction and building materials industry continued to increase at the rate projected by the Fifth Five-Year Plan adopted under Stalin—12 percent per year. In the investment plans, the minister did not predict a shift in investment from heavy industry to light industry, but he urged the creation of new funds to be given to previously neglected sectors.[8] Third, in the actual implementation of the spending plan apparently heavy industry made no sacrifice to consumer interests. In the post-Stalin succession both heavy industry and light industry received investment funds at least equal to the rates of the late Stalin era. As a consequence, in 1954 output of producer goods was reported to be up 13.6 percent over 1953, a higher growth rate than the last year of Stalin's rule when it stood at 12.2 percent; consumer-goods production was up by 12.9 percent, again above the 10.4 percent growth rate for 1952.[9]

Unable to win agreement on actual reforms that entailed redistribution of resources, the collective leadership settled on paper reforms. This is the real story hidden behind the public show of pumping up consumer-oriented spending. In many instances the collective leadership increased funds, which could be expanded rapidly and with great public flourish, but it did not reallocate the physical resources for production. For example, the leadership, while pumping up the population's disposable incomes, did not commensurably increase the supply of consumer goods. Four actions to increase these incomes were particularly significant. First, in 1953 and 1954 the leadership continued the price reductions in consumer goods begun in 1948. This increased the purchasing power of consumers. The 1 April 1953 cuts, although significantly lower than those from 1948 to 1950, brought 67 percent greater savings to the population than the cuts in either 1951 or 1952.[10] Second, the turnover tax was reduced so that the effective price of goods fell still further. Third, the leadership cut by half the "voluntary" bond purchases by workers. These mandatory annual deductions from each worker's wages to purchase bonds from the state were cut from the equivalent of four-weeks to only two-weeks income.[11] This put more rubles in consumer's pockets. Fourth, taxes on the private plots of collective farmers were cut.[12] Peasants would have more money. Yet, without a shift in real output, none of these measures gave consumers a real increase in purchasing power.

A consequence of logrolling was a dramatic jump in state expenditures and a growing de facto deficit. Indeed, one recurring pattern of the post-Stalin years was that divided government brought deficits. Budgetary expenditures during 1953 and 1954 show the highest rate of growth for the period of the Five-Year Plan. While the average growth for the five years was 5.6 percent per year, in 1953 state expenditures jumped a whopping 11.8 percent and in 1954, another 7.6 percent. While expenditures were rising, cuts in prices, taxes, and bond sales reduced the revenues of the state. In 1953, according to the minister of finance, all revenue collections from citizens were down 24.4 percent (to 65 from 86 billion rubles) from 1952.[13]

With increased expenditures and cuts in the usual sources of revenues, how would the budgetary shortfall be filled? Politburo members had foreseen the consequences of this logrolling between the priorities of reformers and conservatives, but reformers (as wishful thinkers) argued the gap would be filled by the new economic efficiency, growth, and expanded sales that their policies would bring. Even under lower tax rates, they reasoned, higher profits and sales would generate expanded revenues.[14] The logroll between reformers and conservatives appears to have the markings of a deal that permitted reformers their policies on their promise they could generate their own funding.

Yet the Soviet economy did not generate these new revenues and did not close the gap between expenditures and revenues. In August 1953 the chair of the Budget Committee for one of the legislature's chambers (Soviet of Nationalities) complained that machine-building industry was not meeting its full tax obligation in 1953.[15] At the end of the first quarter of 1954 the new chair of this Committee complained that revenues from taxes on the profits of transportation, building materials industry, and coal and oil industries fell short of obligations in 1953, and he warned that these revenues plus the revenues from the turnover tax of the food industry and consumers' cooperatives were falling behind in 1954 as well.[16]

To a significant extent the leadership simply did not fill the gap between expenditures and revenues.[17] The manifestations of this deficit included lengthening queues of consumers, inflation in the private markets, and galloping savings. The rise in disposable incomes without commensurate increase in the output of consumer goods aggravated the disequilibrium between supply and demand. Because fixed prices in government stores did not fluctuate according to the new demand, queues of consumers with extra rubles in their pockets reportedly lengthened.[18] In early 1954 the minister of trade admitted: "The increased real wages of workers, the rise in the living standard of the rural population, and the systematic reduction of prices have all occasioned a rise in demand for consumer goods which has outstripped production of certain items such as meat and animal fats. Some people even have the impression that there are fewer goods to be had now than there were several years ago."[19] Prices reportedly jumped significantly in the markets where collective farmers could sell the items from their private plots. Yet inflation in this small segment of the economy did not compensate for expanded purchasing power, so citizens simply socked away their rubles in idle accounts: While savings accounts grew an average of 19 percent in 1951 and 1952, they soared 46 percent in 1953 and grew another 25 percent in 1954.[20]

The iron triangle could not for long accept the fiscal mismanagement that resulted from logrolling. Khrushchev's breakout provided their opportunity. On 24 December 1954, a published interview with the first secretary announced that heavy industry would be given still greater precedence in Soviet budgets and plans.[21] Replacement of Malenkov as premier in early 1955 and denunciation of the New Course as the "belchings" of right-wing deviation sealed the fate of the logroll. The 1955 budget revealed the triumph of the iron triangle's spending priorities. The minister of finance opened his presentation of the budget by bluntly explaining its major emphases:

> The budget provides the funds necessary for further expanding industry—primarily heavy industry. The rapid development of heavy industry has been and remains the decisive task in building socialism and successfully advancing our country toward communism. Heavy industry, the basis for strengthening the might of the Soviet state, has been and will always be an object of particular concern to the Party and government as the material and technical foundation of our entire national economy, the basis of the country's uncrushable defensive capability, and the source of the steady rise in the people's well-being.[22]

Planned state investment in light industry dropped by 23 percent from the previous year. Appropriations for expansion of manufacturing capacity for consumer goods dropped by 16 percent and for expansion of retail trade by nearly 50 percent. Alternatively, heavy industry received 27 percent more in planned state investment, and planned defense spending jumped by 12 percent. As a consequence of these spending priorities, con-sumer-goods industry in 1955 showed its slowest growth for the plan period—only 8 percent against a 13 percent rise in 1951–54; yet pro-ducer-goods production rose 14 percent against an average of 13 percent for 1951–54.[23]

The conservative victory also brought harsh criticism of the budgetary deficit that had emerged during the logroll of 1953 and 1954. The 1955 budget was actually 2.6 percent below the expenditures of 1954—the only decline in spending in the decade. *Pravda* pointed out that wages had risen too rapidly in previous years, faster than the increase of labor pro-ductivity.[24] To sop up the increased purchasing power of consumers, mandated bond purchases for each worker doubled in 1955, a return to the equivalent of four weeks take-home pay. Retail prices were not re-duced for the first time since 1949. Wages rose at their lowest rate for the five-year plan period—1.5 percent against an annual average of 8 percent for 1951–54.[25] With the patronage of the new emerging leader the iron triangle had reimposed its own form of fiscal responsibility.

THE POST-KHRUSHCHEV SUCCESSION

Compared to previous successions the early Brezhnev administration did not bring the same extremes of policy divergence and logrolling or conservative triumph. It brought neither pressures for reform as in-tense as in 1953 nor reform programs as comprehensive as the New Course; it also did not bring the same decisive rebuff to reform from conservatives. Nonetheless, policies underwent the same pattern of early inconsistency, paper reforms warring with established priorities, and then a triumph of the conservative priorities championed by the emerging leader's coalition.

Collective leadership after Khrushchev's ouster once again brought in-consistent policies. The balanced leadership sought to expand investment in defense, agriculture, and consumer goods, while maintaining con-stantly rising investment in heavy industry. It sought to satisfy virtually all claimants.[26] As in the previous succession, this led to paper reform and de facto deficits. To increase the money in citizens' pockets, wages were increased at a faster rate. While they grew by an average of 3 percent in 1961 through 1964, they jumped at more than twice that rate (7.1 per-cent) in 1965 and continued to grow at an accelerated rate (4.9 percent) in 1966 through 1969. The effort to increase incomes also led to a cut in collective farm income taxes: in 1966 projected revenues from this source fell from 1.2 billion to 700 million rubles.[27] Once again this did not bring a real shift in resources. As before, savings began to grow at an accelerated rate: While from the beginning of 1960 until the end of 1964 savings deposits grew by 56 percent, from the beginning of 1965 to the end of 1969 they grew by 144 percent.[28]

Its first budget, presented in December 1964, reflected the costs of indecisiveness in the new balanced leadership. In the short time available to it, the collective leadership lacked the resolve to thoroughly shift Khrushchev's spending proposals. They presented Khrushchev's budget, but with additions. As in the previous succession the collective leadership brought logrolling and a rapid increase in spending. While in the four years at the beginning of the decade (1960–63) budget expenditures rose at an annual rate of 5.4 percent, in 1965 they jumped 10.2 percent.

The emergence of a new leader within the collective leadership, however, reasserted the conservative priorities of his iron triangle constituents. At the beginning of his breakout drive, like his predecessor a decade earlier, Brezhnev defended the privileged budgetary position of heavy industry and defense, followed by agriculture.[29] In five major speeches in 1965 Brezhnev particularly stressed the need to invest in defense, calling for "ceaselessly strengthening" Soviet armed forces of all services.[30] The budgets from 1966 to 1968 were similar to the budget of 1955; they included new payoffs to the iron triangle for its support of the general secretary. The official presentation of the budget each year was filled with verbal reminders of the precedence of heavy industry. In presenting the 1966 budget the minister of finance proclaimed, "the stipulated allocations ensure the preponderant development of power generation, machine building and metalworking, and the chemical industry—that is, the branches that determine technical progress in the national economy."[31] In presenting the 1968 State Budget, he announced, "the priority development of heavy industry is our party's general line, the foundation of the entire national economy's progress."[32] These were also years of some of the most rapid growth in defense spending. Even Soviet budgetary figures show that defense grew at a significantly accelerated rate—an average of 8.5 percent in the four budgets from 1966 to 1969, compared with 2.7 percent and 0.3 percent, respectively, for the four years preceding and following.[33]

Nonetheless, greater balancing within the leadership and the checks on Brezhnev's breakout meant that throughout much of the late 1960s collective leadership continued to logroll to a greater extent than in Khrushchev's breakout; more incoherent and inconsistent policies followed. This was hidden at the time in Soviet presentations of annual budgets by covering embarrassing shifts in consumer-oriented spending with silence. Yet, by placing these budgets end to end the following picture emerges: As figure 7.2 shows, in the post-Khrushchev succession, spending on heavy industry grew at a faster rate than spending on light

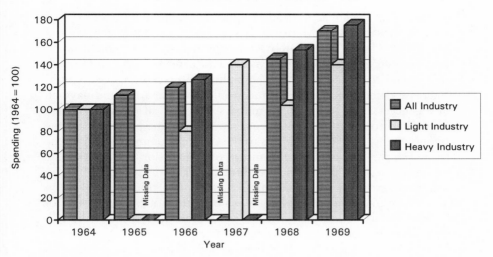

Figure 7.2. Spending on Industry, 1964–1969: Light vs. Heavy Industry.
Sources: *Pravda*, 17 December 1963, 10 December 1964, 8 December 1965, 11 October 1967, 11 December 1968, 17 December 1969.

industry. Indeed, compared to the last year under Khrushchev, the leadership actually spent 20 percent less on light industry in 1966 and only 4 percent more in 1968. Growth in spending on heavy industry appears to have been far more stable over time. This is shown by the figures for heavy industry and the figures for all industry of which heavy industry was the major part. As in the previous succession the pumping up of consumer-oriented spending reform did not come in redistributive reform at the expense of the iron triangle's priorities. It appears to have been funded when reformers could generate budgetary surpluses through economic growth or efficiency; thus, spending on light industry not only lagged behind, but it was also quite erratic.

THE POST-BREZHNEV SUCCESSION

In the post-Brezhnev succession, with still greater balancing and mutual checking among leaders, divergence in their policy positions and the pressure for reform were far less acute. Each new general secretary prudently reached out to the conservative constituencies of the iron triangle, but in the absence of strong reform pressure or a decisive breakout attempt in the period, none led a sharp conservative backlash against reform. Nonetheless, consistent with the strong role of the iron triangle under collective leadership, throughout this period there was a steady increase in conservative priorities and retreat from the reforms of Brezhnev's last years.

Balancing in the collective leadership led to a continuation of existing priorities, what Boris Meissner has called "Brezhnevism without Brezhnev."[34] Almost immediately Andropov reached out to the iron triangle. The new general secretary reassured the armed forces that the leadership would continue Brezhnev's commitment (made in his last month) to increase defense expenditures and would give the army and navy all that was necessary.[35] Within a few months Andropov also began to reach out to other iron triangle constituencies with spending proposals for the economy: In his May 1983 address to the Central Committee Plenum, he retreated from the mildly reformist economic priorities of the late Brezhnev years. Yet, policy changed little under Andropov. The Plenum resolutions, avoiding the hard issues of investment priorities, dwelt on management and labor discipline as major causes of the poor state of consumer goods.[36] Under Chernenko the leadership continued the balanced effort to proceed on all fronts, but with an increasingly conservative tilt as the pressure from the iron triangle mounted. In the general secretary's last speeches, Chernenko attempted to satisfy these pressures from the iron triangle with proposals on spending priorities—new investment in infrastructure and producer goods. At an enlarged Politburo session he defended the plan proposed for 1985 as a means to balanced modernization of the producer-goods and consumer-goods sectors, but stressed the priority of technological reequipment in the former—particularly, in energy production, metallurgy, and machine building.[37] The budget proposed for 1985 actually mandated an 11.8 percent increase in defense spending.[38] The increase signaled a slow shift in spending and publicly committed the leadership to more conservative priorities.

Under the next general secretary the collective leadership continued with spending that attempted to be different things to many constituencies. The comprehensive program for consumer-goods production issued in October 1985 confirmed these priorities: It projected a 30 percent increase in consumer goods in the next five years, but this would be achieved through greater efficiency rather than investments.[39] These priorities were confirmed in the plan for 1986 and in the speeches of Gorbachev and Ryzhkov at the 1986 Party Congress. The plan, while giving priority to machine building, called for expanded investment in agriculture. But the plan failed to make clear where the economy would find additional resources for agriculture and pinned hopes once again on improved labor productivity.[40] Gorbachev's initial speeches as general secretary sought to reach out to the iron triangle; he called for greater investment with particular emphasis on machine tool industry, computers, and electronics.[41] As Marshall Goldman notes, "Instead of giving higher priority to the consumer he poured more money into machine tools, continuing the traditional pre-eminence of heavy capital investment. Rather than cutting back in this area when faced with a 30 percent drop in oil and gas revenues, he cut food and other consumer imports instead."[42] The budgets permitted defense to grow faster than the entire economy: United States government estimates show an actual increase in the rate of growth in defense expenditures after Gorbachev came to power; and a deputy chief of Gosplan has indicated that only in early 1988 did this begin to decline again.[43] Prudent new leaders favored the iron triangle in spending priorities.

Directive Leadership, Reform, and Reaction

In contrast to the logrolling and conservatism of early administrations, consolidation of policy leadership brought real reform in budgetary priorities. The directive leader reached out to new constituencies of his expanding coalition with financial resources. The directive leader held a position that permitted him to find these resources by setting budgetary priorities. Yet the reaction and threatened desertion of iron triangle constituencies could constrain even a directive general secretary to temper his reforms with obeisance toward their conservative priorities. Moreover, with time greater checks on the directive leader meant there were fewer of these opportunities for reform. While Khrushchev's directorship brought a significant shift in budgetary priorities, Brezhnev's limited directorship brought notably less.

KHRUSHCHEV'S ASCENDANCY

In budgeting, Khrushchev's ascendancy brought a new concern for the consumer—almost as though he had embraced many of the reforms of Malenkov.[44] This did not happen overnight, however, and it became increasingly harder to sustain in the face of iron triangle resistance.

Immediately after his victory over Malenkov in February 1955, Khrushchev continued to build his coalition on the iron triangle; only cautiously did he begin to reach outside. The dominant priorities in spending at first remained conservative. The budget proposed for 1956 projected a jump of capital investment in producer goods to 60 percent (compared to 53.3 percent in 1954) and a drop for consumer goods to 4.8 percent of the total (compared to 8.3 percent in 1954). As a source of revenue turnover tax, a major part of the price of consumer goods, was to jump to 45 percent of the total; forced state bond purchases, a major deduction from consumers' incomes, were to remain at their 1955 levels.[45] The Sixth Five-Year Plan (1956–60) adopted at the 1956 Party Congress in February, reasserted the priority of heavy industry, and, in the words of Merle Fainsod, "appeared basically Stalinist in its emphasis."[46] Yet, there were also signs of change: In projected spending for 1956 industry would suffer a cutback in total spending in 1956, and the cutback of 490 thousand rubles would be borne entirely by heavy industry; light industry was projected to hold its own in expenditures compared with 1955, but heavy industry would fall by 3.0 percent. Moreover, defense expenditures were cut in 1956 by 9.4 percent—the beginning of a steady decline that continued for the next four years.[47] By May 1957 Khrushchev ventured to propose a new commitment to consumer goods: the Soviet Union should seek to overtake American production in meat, milk, and butter within three to four years.[48]

During the two years after his victory over the Anti-Party Group Khrushchev shifted to a more ambitious reform program. At the 1959 Party Congress (January–February) Khrushchev introduced an ambitious seven-year program to force technical development necessary for the transition to communism. The Seven-Year Plan adopted on 5 February 1959 was initially orthodox in its spending priorities. It envisioned that producer goods would still grow at annual rates higher than consumer goods—9.3 percent versus 7.3 percent.[49] Yet, within months the plan was being revised to give greater attention to consumer goods. On 16 October a decree "On Measures to Raise Production, Increase Variety, and Improve Consumer and Household Goods" chided the regional economic administrations, the sovnarkhozes, for neglecting consumer-goods production.[50] In the last quarter of 1959 a revised plan called for growth in consumer-goods production to jump from the 7 percent annual rate originally projected to 12 percent per year.[51] At the May 1960 Supreme Soviet session Khrushchev announced that 25 to 30 billion rubles in addition to the sum allocated by the Seven-Year Plan would be invested in consumer-goods production.[52] By January 1961, Khrushchev was announcing that part of the investment originally planned for producer-goods industry would be diverted to agriculture and consumer goods.[53]

As his policy proposals became more reformist they provoked growing criticism. For example, in November 1960 Politburo member Frol Kozlov slighted the new emphasis on consumer goods and asserted that "everyone knows" steel production is the basic index of "a country's economic strength."[54] Khrushchev responded to this challenge the next January by underscoring that the strength of a state is measured by not only metal production but also "the amounts of production man receives and eats." He criticized "some comrades" with "an appetite for metals" who would unbalance the economy.[55] From late 1960 to late 1964 this policy contestation would be an important constraint on policy. The results were dramatic reversals in a zigzag of shifting budgetary priorities.

With growing contestation policy became less coherent and less consistent. In part to respond to these pressures Khrushchev made incompatible policy commitments that he could not sustain simultaneously. For example, while pressing for defense cuts, the first secretary began a more assertive foreign policy. From the summer of 1961 through early 1963 these incompatible commitments, occasioned by new pressures from the iron triangle, forced a retreat from the spending reform. In particular, his activist policies in Berlin and Cuba made it difficult to sustain his cuts in defense. While the 1961 budget adopted on 22 December 1960 had cut the defense allocation by 0.5 percent, these plans were reversed in 1961, and actual defense spending rose by 24.6 percent.[56] Resolutions adopted at the 1961 Party Congress in October reasserted the priority of heavy industry.[57] By the end of 1962 Khrushchev faced broad resistance to spending reform from within his own coalition.[58] In his February 1963 election speech to his constituents, Khrushchev announced that his consumer program had been postponed in favor of the claims of producers goods and defense production.[59]

Yet in 1963 the first secretary struck back and began a new push for dramatic reforms in spending priorities. The budget proposed for 1964 would cut the allocation to defense by 4.2 percent from 1963 spending levels, and in 1964 Khrushchev pressed for new troop cuts and defense economies.[60] In late September 1964 to a joint meeting of the Politburo and Council of Ministers he proposed a revolution in spending priorities for the economy where consumer-goods production would be given precedence over producer goods: "Our country is now at the state of its development when we should advance the satisfaction of the growing material and spiritual requirements of man into first place in working out the long-range plan for the development of our economy." Indeed, in designing economic priorities for the next five years, he told this meeting:

> The chief task of [the next five-year plan] is a further rise in the living standard of the people. Whereas during the period of the first five-year plans and in the postwar years we laid chief stress on the development of heavy industry as the basis for an upsurge of the economy of the entire country, and on strengthening its defense capability, now, when we have a mighty industry, when the defense of the country is at the proper level, the Party is setting the task of the more rapid development of the branches that produce consumer goods.[61]

As Khrushchev continued to press his reforms, resistance from his original coalition constituencies grew. In his choice to force his policy reforms, he provided a basis for the overwhelming coalition that removed him.

BREZHNEV'S LIMITED DIRECTORSHIP

Economic priorities in Brezhnev's drive for consolidation made the same shift as they had in Khrushchev's rise. As the general secretary's consolidation progressed, the conservative priorities in spending were moderated and then slowly reversed. Yet, Brezhnev's limited directorship brought far more limited reform in spending. It did, nonetheless, elicit resistance from the iron triangle.

The 1969 and 1970 budgets presented the first small signs of a change in priorities. Both provided for declining growth in defense spending: Although it had jumped by 15 percent in 1968, it increased by 6 percent in 1969 and only 1.1 percent in 1970. Nonetheless, the priorities of these budgets were for the most part still conservative. They increased allocations to heavy industry by 19.7 percent and 26.1 percent, respectively.[62] Brezhnev's attacks on the Kosygin reform stressed that spending on consumer goods would remain a lower priority. Even in June 1970 he told his constituents in a pre-election rally, that in designing the priorities for the next five years producers goods would have precedence: "Work on the five-year plan is continuing and it would be premature to speak of concrete figures and targets, but I can assure you that further important industrial growth is envisaged primarily for those branches that produce the means of production."[63] Evidence in the autumn suggests that this was still the priority.

In 1971 the shift in priorities was more pronounced. Although the first steps toward a more reformist budget were underway by 1970, the shift appears to have been accelerated by the riots among Polish shipyard workers in December 1970.[64] In the Soviet press, calls for labor discipline and austerity were muted; criticism of government officials for insufficient consumer goods became more common. The Ninth Five-Year Plan (1971–1975), published on 14 February 1971, showed a dramatic movement in priorities. It forecast the rate of growth in consumer goods (44 to 48 percent) would be faster than the rate for producers goods (41 to 45 percent). It proclaimed the "main task" was "to ensure a significant increase in the material and cultural standard of living."[65] To the 1971 Party Congress six weeks later Brezhnev proclaimed that long-established priorities would begin to change: "The long years of heroic history when millions of Communists and non-Party people deliberately made sacrifices and underwent privation . . . lie behind us. . . . What was explicable and only natural in the past when other tasks stood in the foreground is unacceptable under present conditions."[66] The change in spending that followed was not a momentary response to a foreign crisis, but a broad shift in priorities that persisted through the end of the Brezhnev administration.

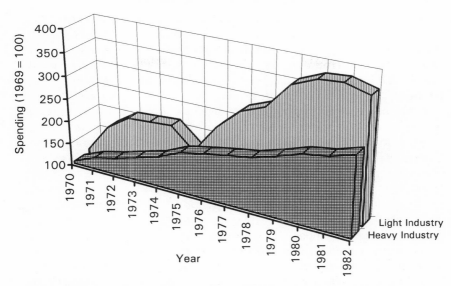

Figure 7.3. Spending on Industry, 1970–1982: Light vs. Heavy Industry.
Sources: *Pravda*, 17 December 1969, 9 December 1970, 25 November 1971,
19 December 1972, 13 December 1973, 19 December 1974, 3 December 1975,
28 October 1976, 15 December 1977, 29 November 1978, 29 November 1979,
23 October 1980, 18 November 1981.

The pattern begun in the Ninth Five-Year Plan (1971–1975) continued in the next two plans adopted under Brezhnev—a moderate reformist orientation in contrast to the priorities of the first five years of collective leadership and Brezhnev's breakout (1966–1970). The 1976–1980 Five-Year Plan promised increases in consumption and stable growth in agriculture while slowing the growth in military expenditure.[67] Indeed, beginning with 1977, defense allocations actually declined as a portion of total spending.[68] The 1981–1985 Plan promised to accelerate these trends. The "Food Program" adopted at the May 1982 Central Committee Plenum promised substantial additional investment in rural amenities and agricultural infrastructure, including transport and storage.[69] As figure 7.3 shows, from 1970 to 1982, the shift in spending priorities characterized all three five-year plans: Planned budget and nonbudget allocations to light industry grew more rapidly than allocations to heavy industry.[70] Yet, it was a more moderate shift than that championed by Khrushchev: Although the trend in spending was more reformist than the priorities of the post-Khrushchev collective leadership, Brezhnev's limited directorship brought only a moderate shift in spending.

Even though Brezhnev made only small assaults on the privileged position of the iron triangle, these pinched hard in the tight economy of the early 1980s. As the previous data show, the continued and steady growth of allocations to heavy industry was not threatened. Nonetheless, in tight times, as Bruce Parrott observes, "bruising budgetary conflicts broke out over military policy, investment in heavy industry, and investment in agriculture and consumer-goods production."[71] For example, the new spending on light industry brought strong objections from Party secretary Andrei Kirilenko responsible for machine building.[72] The failure to keep up growth in defense spending brought even more vociferous objections from the armed forces (discussed in chapter 8).

Aggregate Trends

Data that permit comparisons of spending priorities across the entire post-Stalinist period (or even most of it) are extremely rare. Missing data in many years, aggregation into categories that obscure the sorts of priorities likely to involve political controversy, and frequent changes in the definition of statistical categories all work to the analyst's disadvantage when using Soviet sources. Even Western data are often controversial, and any one data set is likely to produce objections of severe bias. Nonetheless, Soviet and Western data do permit a few good "tests" of the trends discussed above. The strategy here is to use multiple sources of data not likely to agree in their biases. If these alternative data sets converge in supporting the hypotheses of this book, which are not among the biases that have shaped any of these data sets, we have greater confidence in these propositions.[73]

The expectation that reformist orientation in spending closely paralleled the consolidation of power is borne out by the pattern of social spending. For example, capital investment in social programs shows this pattern. United States Central Intelligence Agency (CIA) estimates of Soviet gross fixed capital investment from 1960 to 1980 show the following: At the peak of directive leadership, allocations to health and human services (social insurance, physical culture, communal economy, and personal services) grew more rapidly than other investments.[74] Moreover, it grew more rapidly during Khrushchev's ascendancy than Brezhnev's. In the years from 1960 to 1964, the average annual rate of change of this proportion was 9.7 percent, and in the years from 1976 to 1980 it was 1.6 percent. Alternatively, in the intervening years as Brezhnev sought to consolidate leadership (1965–1975) the average annual change in the proportion was negative (–2.4 percent).

Similarly, using Soviet budgetary data for 1950 to 1987, the ratio of spending on social-cultural measures to defense spending was lower

TABLE 7.2

Regression Results: Social-Defense Spending Ratio,
1953–1987

SMC/Defense = f(collective leadership, time)

	Coefficient	t
Breakout by General Secretary	−0.485[a]	−3.54
Time	0.171[a]	26.39
Constant	0.477[a]	3.03

Note: n = 35; R^2 = 0.96; F = 348.34.
[a] Significance: 0.01 (one-tailed t-test).

when the general secretary was pressing his breakout attempt to consolidate leadership than under directive leadership.[75] Table 7.2 reports the results of a regression equation in which these effects are tested. In this equation any long-term trend that might hide shorter-term shifts is "controlled for" by inclusion of the time variable. In the equation, years characterized by a breakout attempt by the general secretary that brought the transition from collective to directive rule (1953–1955, 1965–1975, 1985–1987) are associated with lower relative effort on social expenditure (indicated by the significant negative coefficient estimates).

The conservative orientation in spending associated with breakouts is shown by the pattern of defense spending. The critical role of the military in successions led to greater relative defense spending at these times of first-tier struggle. To cross-check results, I have analyzed three separate measures of defense spending: Soviet budgetary figures and two Western estimates of Soviet defense expenditure reported by the U.S. CIA and the Stockholm International Peace Research Institute (SIPRI).[76]

Table 7.3 reports the results of these three tests of this hypothesis about defense spending. The dependent variable is the natural logarithm of defense spending, and the time variable permits us to "control for" the growth in defense over time and examine deviations from normal growth. Equation 1 reports the results based on Soviet data for 1950 to 1987. In Equation 2, CIA estimates reported to the U.S. Congress Joint Economic Committee cover the period from 1950 to 1976 in five overlapping series (104 data points for twenty-six years). Equation 3 reports the results based on SIPRI data for 1948 to 1985 from seven overlapping series (128 data points for thirty-five years). In all equations periods of breakout and consolidating leadership show significantly higher rates of defense spending, as indicated by the significant positive coefficient estimates in each equation.

Closer examination of the data shows even stronger correspondence to the predicted patterns; within these periods of conservative priorities in spending, as the general secretary's coalition grew a shift was beginning

TABLE 7.3

Regression Results: Defense Spending, 1948–1987

log[defense] = f(collective leadership, time, series)

	Coefficient[a]	t
Equation 1. Soviet Data, 1950–1987.		
(n = 35; R^2 = 0.86; F = 97.75)		
Breakout by General Secretary	0.136	4.01
Time	0.021	12.88
Constant	2.105	47.54
Equation 2. CIA Data, 1950–1976.		
(n = 104; R^2 = 0.97; F = 453.13)		
Breakout by General Secretary	0.065	2.65
Time	0.044	24.31
Series 1	−0.652	−16.41
Series 2	−0.555	−16.28
Series 3	−0.684	−20.06
Series 4	0.280	8.98
Constant	2.594	68.55
Equation 3. SIPRI Data, 1948–1985.		
(n = 128; R^2 = 0.99; F = 1180.67)		
Breakout by General Secretary	0.095	5.71
Time	0.032	23.98
Series 1	−1.722	−41.29
Series 2	−0.952	−23.73
Series 3	−0.605	−16.47
Series 4	−0.573	−16.21
Series 5	−0.163	− 4.37
Series 6	−0.089	− 2.34
Constant	3.755	73.89

[a] Significance of Coefficient (all entries in column) is 0.01 (one-tailed t-test).

to take place in priorities. Figure 7.4 reports the deviation of actual spending from the long-term trend in defense spending according to the Soviet, American, and Swedish sources.[77] These show relatively increasing defense effort during the early years of the breakout by Khrushchev (1954–1955), but a decreasing rate of growth from 1956 to 1960 as Khrushchev began to expand his coalition. The last Khrushchev budgets (1961–1965) show the erratic turnaround of Khrushchev's embattled directorship with a quick rise in the first three and then a decline in the last two budgets. The earliest years of Brezhnev's rise also brought an increase in relative defense effort with an above-trend increase each year from 1966 to 1969. As Brezhnev expanded his coalition this relative effort slackened beginning in 1970; this slackening growth continued through

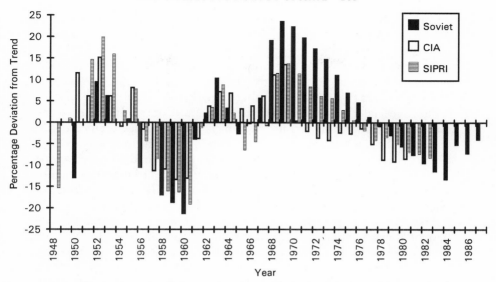

Figure 7.4. Cycles of Defense Spending, 1948–1987. Deviations from trends in table 7.3 are shown; percentages are calculated from antilogs of residuals and predicted values in table 7.3 equations.

Brezhnev's last budget (1983). With balanced collective leadership under increasing iron triangle pressures, the defense budgets began to rise at a faster rate once again (1985–1987).

In short, the data show the following pattern: Spending was more likely to favor the iron triangle during the period of breakout and consolidation, which brought the shift from collective to directive rule. Because the new leader initially "pumped up" the iron triangle, these conservative priorities were more favored throughout this initial period than in later periods. Yet, within this initial period of each administration, an important shift was taking place. As his coalition expanded and the leader reached out to new constituencies, the leader did not continued to "pump up" iron triangle budgets at the original pace. With directive rule the general secretary was able to shift spending to reformist priorities.

POLITICS OF PROCEDURES AND ORGANIZATION

This expectation is also confirmed by the pattern of procedural reforms. Soviet policy between 1953 and 1987 was characterized by nearly constant tinkering with the processes of policymaking. Procedural reform was a means by which leaders and bureaucrats sought political or policy advantage in normal politics. The most important manifestation of this was the continuous development of the rules of reciprocal accountability and balanced leadership.

Reforms of procedures and organization were intimately tied to the cycling of leadership in the context of bureaucratic reciprocal accountability. Reforms that might redistribute powers required directive leaders. A directive leader could gain Politburo acceptance of reform and press the innovation against bureaucratic resistance. Indeed, in such reforms a directive leader might find political advantage against the iron triangle. Yet, a new collective leadership, sensitive to pressures from their bureaucratic constituents, were inclined to reverse such reforms. The procedural innovations adopted in the logroll of collective leadership were more likely to reinforce balancing among established constituencies and leaders.

For their impact on the balance of power between and within the two tiers of Soviet politics, six organizational changes stand out in the years from 1953 to 1987. The 1953 decision to reinstate the Politburo and reverse Stalin's expansion of the Party Presidium may be singly the most important, for Stalin's innovation appears to have been designed to break the corporate power of the Politburo. The 1957 sovnarkhoz reform of the state economic structure eliminated most ministries and delegated many of their decisionmaking responsibilities to regional economic councils (the sovnarkhozes). The 1962 bifurcation of the Party structure divided the Party apparatus below the union-republic level between separate industrial and agricultural hierarchies. In 1965 two decisions, reversing these last reforms, brought reunification of the Party apparatus and reinstatement of the ministries. The 1973 production association reform sought to create interindustry associations (*obedineniia*) that would encourage cooperation in supplies and sales. These decisions fell short of constitutional reform; they redistributed power among existing political actors, but they changed neither the selectorate nor the relationship of reciprocal accountability between selectorate and effective decisionmakers. By changing formal structures, all six decisions changed the distribution of decisionmaking prerogatives among major political institutions.

These six organizational changes are closely associated with the political processes of cycling and institutionalization. All changes responded to real problems such as economic inefficiency, but each was only one of several solutions to the problem at hand. The change adopted in each instance had a political logic as well. The changes were shaped by the configuration of power in the first tier and its relationship to key constituencies in the second tier. All six organizational changes conform to the pattern predicted by the spiraling of regimes. First, the changes divided in their political logic between those adopted to balance political power under collective leadership and those used to consolidate the hold of an emerging or dominant director. The sovnarkhozes, party bifurcation, and the production associations were all involved with the attempt of a general secretary to consolidate his power. The reinstatement of the Politburo, reunification of the Party apparatus, and reinstatement of the ministries were associated with efforts to reestablish balance among first-tier actors and between Party and state. This political logic meant that reforms could be undone by retreats and then repeated as the cycling of leadership recurred. Indeed, four of these procedural innovations are reforms (sovnarkhoz and party bifurcation) paired with a later retreat (reinstatement of ministries and party reunification, respectively). Second, these changes divide between reforms that sought to limit the powers and prerogatives of the iron triangle and innovations that sought to reestablish those prerogatives. The sovnarkhoz and party bifurcation reforms, in particular, changed the balance of power among institutions. The other four changes reasserted these powers and prerogatives either against a previous directive leader or against the equality of collective leadership. Third, all changes emerged from and were shaped by the processes of building coalitions within and across tiers. The design of each organizational innovation reflected the political constituencies of the leaders who pressed the change. In building support for the innovation among constituencies, leaders had to consider the claims of these coalition partners. Fourth, long-term institutionalization brought fewer opportunities for consolidating reforms and less need for balancing innovations. Thus, over the longer term, institutionalization of leadership meant organizational innovation after 1970 was rare; like policy reforms, procedural reforms were less frequent in the latter half of the 1953–1986 period.

Reinstatement of the Politburo, 1953

One of the most important organizational changes engineered in Stalin's last years was the displacement of the Politburo. If left to stand, this could have fundamentally changed the pattern of post-Stalinist constitutional development by threatening both collective leadership and the privileged position of the iron triangle. As a first step toward reestablishing balancing, the new collective leadership reinstated the Politburo.

At the 1952 Party Congress Stalin had introduced a broad expansion of the leading Party organs. In these changes, the Politburo of eleven members and one candidate was replaced by a Presidium of twenty-five members and eleven candidates. This reform may have been a transitional arrangement in preparation for a purge: According to Khrushchev, "his proposal . . . was aimed at the removal of the old Political Bureau members and the bringing in of less experienced persons. . . . We can assume that this was also a design for the future annihilation of the old Political Bureau members."[78] In practice the powers of the enlarged Presidium appear to have been exercised by its secretive Bureau of ten to twelve members, but the provisions adopted by the Congress involved no such inner working body. The organizational innovation was a step toward institutionalizing Stalin's apex role that depended on the practice of handpicking the inner-working bodies within the Politburo.

Even after Stalin's death this new arrangement could have served to unbalance collective leadership. It could have freed the leader—either the premier or first secretary—from many constraints on his leadership from fellow Politburo members: The enlarged body was more unwieldy and less able to act except under direction from its leader. The informal Bureau, for which there was no statutory basis, could give the leader discretion to select the inner body to which he turned for discussion of policy. From the perspective of the balance among constituencies, the enlarged Presidium threatened the leaders of the iron triangle with being submerged in a larger body of more diverse composition.

Among the most important balancing decisions made by the successors in the collective leadership was reinstating the Politburo, although the leaders chose to keep the new label Party Presidium. The new collective leadership defended the reversion to the pre-1952 pattern by arguing that reducing its membership to ten members and four candidates would "ensure more operative leadership" from the body.[79] The membership of the Presidium in March 1953 was identical to the Politburo on the eve of the 1952 Party Congress, with only two exceptions—Andreev and Kosygin were replaced by Pervukhin and Saburov. The reinstated Politburo preserved the privileged position of the leaders of the iron triangle.

Creation of Sovnarkhozes, 1957

Among the six cases analyzed here, two were organizational ploys associated with Khrushchev's drive to consolidate his leadership. The first, taken during the period of his breakout while Khrushchev was still constrained by the collective leadership that came to power in 1953, was a reform of the state economic administration. Prior to 1957 the shifting balance of power first toward the state (1953–1955) and then toward the Party (1955–1957) had not yielded significant opportunities to institutionalize this in formal organizational changes. At the February 1957 Central Committee Plenum Khrushchev finally made such a move, when he proposed dismantling much of the central state economic apparatus.

This organizational reform dislodged Khrushchev's major competitors from their power bases, transferred many decisionmaking issues from the Council of Ministers to organs Khrushchev could more readily control, and further cemented the loyalty of Khrushchev's constituents within the Party apparatus and the administrations outside Moscow.

The problem the sovnarkhoz reform sought to solve was departmentalism, but it was only one of two radically different paths proposed by members of the Politburo. Arguing that Moscow could not effectively administer all enterprises, the first secretary proposed replacing ministries by regional economic councils responsible for virtually all production on their territory. Many of Khrushchev's opponents sought to fight departmentalism by further centralization of planning in Moscow's (all-union) state economic agencies. They had used Khrushchev's weakness following the Polish and Hungarian crises to press in December 1956 for concentration of economic decisionmaking in the State Economic Commission.[80]

Khrushchev's strategy countered this by welding a coalition with the two constituencies likely to resist centralization of decisionmaking in the central (all-union) state administration. Against the power of the center Khrushchev played to the republics and provinces (oblasts). Against the prerogatives of the state he played to the Party apparatus.[81] The sovnarkhoz reform strengthened Khrushchev's hand relative to other first-tier actors, by dissolving the organizational bases of their constituencies. Twenty-five economic ministries—ten all-union, fifteen republican—along with the Soviet Economic Commission were dissolved. Many decisionmaking responsibilities of the ministries were delegated to regional economic councils created in 105 provinces and smaller republics. Transfer of central ministry personnel to the sovnarkhozes subordinated them to the republic and provincial party organizations—the Party apparatus where Khrushchev's control was strongest. Of the sovnarkhoz chairmen, 30 percent were former ministers or deputy ministers assigned from Moscow, and another 35 percent were reassigned from union-republic ministries. These were all now subjected to the guidance of republic and provincial party secretaries.[82]

To win the support for this reform, Khrushchev had to compromise with leaders in the republics and provinces. The program adopted at the May 1957 Supreme Soviet session and launched on 1 July 1957, revised the original proposal presented in Khrushchev's "theses." As a payoff to the republic leaders, the presidium of the Council of Ministers was enlarged to grant ex officio membership to the fifteen republic premiers (chairmen of union-republic councils of ministers). Khrushchev abandoned his original proposal to check republic and provincial control over the sovnarkhozes by a second chain of command directly from the central (all-union) authorities. He also permitted republic authorities to determine the number of councils to be formed on their territories and acquiesced in councils that were coextensive with the jurisdictions of existing province party committees.[83] Edward Crankshaw observes that "the leading figures in every district demanded their own economic council—and, indeed, in the end Khrushchev had to break up the country into more and smaller fractions than he had originally proposed."[84]

Bifurcation of the Party Apparatus, 1962

An equally dramatic procedural reform undertaken by Khrushchev came five years later in the division of lower levels of the Party apparatus into two separate hierarchies. This reform did not stand alone; rather, it was part of a comprehensive reorganization of regional and local administration that included Party bifurcation, amalgamation of sovnarkhozes, and consolidation of rural counties (*raions*). This clever maneuver removed some constraints placed on the general secretary by his own core constituencies.

The problem that the reform addressed was the overburdening of provincial and local secretaries. Within their respective territories, the first secretaries were expected to provide, among other things, ideological leadership, long-range planning guidance, and short-term problem solving in diverse sectors of production and administration.[85] Khrushchev's reform was not the only proposal on the table, and the Politburo divided on the wisdom of the general secretary's scheme. "Some Communists" charged that Khrushchev's solution "contradicted established principles of party structure."[86] "Some comrades" countered Khrushchev's reform with the claim that improved economic performance "is not a matter of organizational restructuring but of intelligent use of economic levers."[87] From these charges it appears that opponents sought to keep the party organization unified and to rely on either cost accounting or better direction to lighten the load of provincial secretaries.

The problem for Khrushchev was colored by his ambition to limit the constraints placed on him by his coalition constituents—particularly, the Party apparatus.[88] At the November 1962 Central Committee Plenum Khrushchev won adoption of a scheme to divide the lower reaches of the Party into two parallel hierarchies. The scheme would divide party organizations at the provincial level into separate industrial and agricultural party organizations, each with its own first secretary. Party organizations below the province would be assigned to one or the other province committee depending on the predominant form of production on its territory.[89] From Khrushchev's perspective, bifurcation would increase his control over the party apparatus by expanding his patronage opportunities.[90]

Khrushchev faced the daunting problem of rejuvenating the Party apparatus without being blocked by the apparatus itself. He had to gain approval, or at least acquiescence, from the regional apparatus leaders sitting in the Central Committee. A key to this success was a rule change made a year earlier. At Khrushchev's instigation the 1961 Party Congress had adopted a new statute that mandated one-third renewal of the membership in party organs at all levels.[91] On the eve of local party elections in late 1962 this measure threatened apparatchiki who might now be turned out of office as part of the renewal of their organizations' leading organs; the statute placed them in a position where they might welcome a compromise that permitted them to hold on to their posts. Expansion of party organizations could infuse new talent without removing existing secretaries. Indeed, this was the compromise with incumbents. After the December 1962–January 1963 elections in the Russian Republic and Ukraine more than one-third of the province first secretaries were new, but only three of eighty incumbent first secretaries failed to win reelection or promotion to higher posts within the Party apparatus.[92]

Nonetheless, the reform provided Khrushchev an opportunity to clip the power of incumbent first secretaries and free himself somewhat from the constraints of his constituents. First, it created new province first secretaries: 61 added to the existing 80 in the Russian Republic and Ukraine; 75 added to the nationwide total of 134.[93] The new appointees were likely to be more dependent clients than the incumbents—at least for the near term. Second, the organizational change gave Khrushchev new leverage over the secretaries through the sovnarkhozes. The reorganization announced at the November 1962 Plenum provided for reducing the number of sovnarkhozes from the existing 103 to 47. As a consequence, each sovnarkhoz was now responsible for about three provinces with about five provincial first secretaries. The sovnarkhoz chair exercised fewer powers after the 1963 amalgamations, but these could be counterpoised to the first secretaries in ways that had not previously been possible.[94] Third, in the bifurcated province organizations, the incumbents were disproportionately appointed to the more junior post of first secretary for agriculture. In the sixty-one province organizations of the Russian Republic and Ukraine that were divided, forty of the incumbent first secretaries were assigned to agriculture and only fifteen to industry.[95] Fourth, the apparatus subordinate to the agricultural secretaries was cut back by the amalgamation of rural counties (*raiony*). Thus, in the consolidation of counties, the number dropped by almost half—from 3,421 on

1 January 1962, to 1,833 on 1 April 1963.[96] These changes weakened incumbents and strengthened Khrushchev's control over his most important second-tier constituency.

Reunification of the Party Apparatus, 1964

Just over a month after removing Khrushchev the collective leadership began to reverse his major procedural reforms in order to reestablish balance in the collective leadership. The next two significant changes in Soviet procedures reversed Khrushchev's reforms associated with his consolidation. The first reunified the Party apparatus, and the second reestablished the state ministries.

The November 1964 Central Committee Plenum adopted a decree "On the Unification of the Industrial and Rural Oblast and Krai Party Organizations."[97] The dual party committees in each province were replaced by a single committee, and all lower party organizations were subordinated in a single hierarchy once again. Along with this, rural county (*raion*) party organizations were reinstated. The reunification, in many ways, returned to the status quo of early 1962. In most instances former first secretaries were returned to their posts. Forty-one of sixty-one reunified province organizations were headed by men who had been first secretaries prior to bifurcation. In eighty provinces of the Russian Republic and Ukraine, the turnover rate (28 percent over two years) was even below the normal rate for province first secretaries.[98]

The reversal of the 1962 reform—and the thorough-going nature of this reversal—attests to the power of the Party apparatus in the selectorate during successions. The Central Committee, which had been elected in 1961, was still dominated by province secretaries who lost in the 1962 apparatus reorganization. A new Central Committee including the new secretaries would not be elected until 1966. During the succession, the price exacted by the selectors who had suffered in the 1962 apparatus reorganization was retreat on Party organizational reform.

Reinstatement of the Ministries, 1965

The second step in reversing Khrushchev's consolidating reforms came less than a year later with the dissolution of the sovnarkhozes and reinstatement of the ministries. Khrushchev's sovnarkhoz reform had replaced the problem of departmentalism with localism. It had also changed the balance between Party and state in ways that could threaten the first-tier balance in a succession. For the new collective leadership one solution to both problems was reinstating the ministries.

Reinstatement of the ministries in September 1965, in many ways, represented a return to the status quo of eight years earlier. The structure of ministries resembled that abolished in 1957. Indeed, many leading personnel were the same as in 1957: In thirty-three industrial and construction ministries in late 1965, twenty-two of the ministers had also been either ministers or deputy ministers in 1957.[99] Fully one-fourth of ministers in all sectors held the posts they had held eight years earlier—including, most important, the chair of the state planning committee (Gosplan).

The actual shape of the reform was influenced by the need to construct a supporting constituency in the second tier. Elite opinion was sharply divided on the value of the sovnarkhozes. The province party secretaries that dominated their local economic councils appeared to defend the status quo. The first secretary of the Leningrad city party organization even argued in *Izvestiia* for an expanded role for the sovnarkhozes:

> Of late, an increasing number of voices have advocated the liquidation of sovnarkhozy and return to the former system of management by ministries. In our opinion, such proposals are unfounded. We believe that the system of sovnarkhozy is progressive and has fully vindicated itself. . . . We advocate sovnarkhozy, but with substantially wider rights and prerogatives.[100]

He stressed the importance of the sovnarkhozes for the balance between Party and state: "In practice it is impossible to exert effective Party leadership over the economy unless the principle of territorial-branch management is maintained."[101] Yet not all province secretaries supported this line, particularly those where the consolidation of sovnarkhozes in 1962 and 1963 had placed economic administration outside the control of provinces. State officials were also divided: Although many state bureaucrats and managers strongly supported eliminating sovnarkhozes, sovnarkhoz officials who expected not elevation to higher office but demotion to the enterprises were more skeptical.

The need to build a coalition of support led to close linking of the reinstitution of ministries with a reform to expand the financial resources and decisionmaking prerogatives of the enterprises. Moreover, this close linkage with the cost-accounting (*khozraschet*) reform could prevent the extreme centralization of decisionmaking that had led to departmentalism before 1957. The cost-accounting reform sought to apportion sovnarkhoz powers between ministries and enterprises with significantly greater responsibility in the latter than before 1957. Kosygin told the Central Committee Plenum: "It is necessary to abandon customary notions that in the relations between the guiding economic agencies and the enterprises, the former have only rights and the latter only obligations." Instead, he said, the reforms depended on recognition of "mutual rights and obligations."[102] Under the proposed procedures ministries would give a simplified plan to each enterprise with an emphasis on sales; the material incentive fund for each enterprise would be calculated with consideration for its profitability; enterprise managers would exercise new decision prerogatives in fulfilling these objectives.[103]

In its political logic reinstatement of the ministries was a balancing reform, for it checked the power of the general secretary, which was strongest in the party apparatus and at provincial levels. The combination of ministries and cost-accounting represented both a shift in the locus of decisionmaking and a change of control mechanisms that worked to the disadvantage of the general secretary. Decisionmaking was transferred away from the intermediate levels of the territorial-administrative hierarchy and toward the all-union state economic agencies and enterprises. The new reliance on economic incentives by ministries as levers of control over enterprises further diminished the opportunities for Party intervention.

Creation of Production Associations, 1973

The last significant procedural reform of the period from 1953 to 1986, and the least significant of the six cases examined here, was the introduction of an intermediate layer of economic administration between the ministries and enterprises—the production associations. Reinstatement of the ministries had brought renewed departmentalism, leading to a new search for means to check this. For Brezhnev this problem was compounded by his own personal problem of engineering a breakout. As before, his Party apparatus could best check the economic bureaucracy of the state at the republic and province levels and through political-administrative rather than economic levers. For Brezhnev the answer to both the Soviet economic problem and his own political problem was to invest territorially based interindustry production associations (*proizvodstvennye obedineniia*) with the power to direct the production process in subordinate enterprises.

Taking place in the context of balanced leadership and strong obstacles to another consolidation, the introduction of this reform was more protracted than earlier reforms. On 3 April 1973, the place of the production associations was codified in a Joint Resolution of the Central Committee and Council of Ministers.[104] This measure also created industrial associations that could have all-union jurisdiction. At the 1976 Party Congress Brezhnev urged renewed effort to extend the associations throughout the economy.[105] The production associations united structurally separate industrial enterprises engaged in similar or complementary production;[106] these included shared subsidiaries such as research laboratories. The "economic" logic of this innovation was threefold: It would move bureaucrats who made production decisions (previously in the ministries) closer to the production process in enterprises. Vertical integration of production processes previously divided among ministries would yield new economies of scale. Closer links between the actual production process in enterprises and the research and development institutes would bring technological innovations that could be implemented in the enterprises.[107]

It also had a "political" logic that was part of Brezhnev's continuing efforts to consolidate leadership, for it affected the balance between Party and state. First, it represented a shift in decisionmaking by bringing it back to intermediate levels of the territorial-administrative hierarchy: With respect to ministries, the reform represented decentralization, but with respect to the enterprises it represented recentralization; indeed, both ministry and enterprise officials resisted creation of associations.[108] In many instances enterprises lost their recently won autonomy when a single plan (*tekhpromfinplan*) and incentive fund was assigned to the association to be administered for all its constituent enterprises. Decisionmaking formerly in the hands of enterprise managers, thus, passed to the production associations' councils of directors.[109] Second, the creation of production associations, as Joseph Berliner observes, was "also a vote of confidence in the superiority of 'administrative levers' over 'economic levers.' "[110] The reform represented a reversal of the "cost-accountability" reform that had counted on economic levers such as adjusted success indicators and prices to induce enterprise management to undertake more efficient production. With administrative controls the Party was better able to intervene in the hierarchical flow of economic directives.

RESTATEMENT

The spiraling downward of policy innovation revealed a truly pernicious consequence of institutionalized balanced leadership in the context of reciprocal accountability. The constitution of Bolshevism had shaped the types of reforms that were likely to be introduced and the chances they could succeed. This constitutional order made it difficult to gain acceptance for significant reforms and even more difficult to sustain them. With the institutionalization of this order, these became still more difficult.

These cases of domestic reform conform to the pattern predicted in the previous chapter: Coherent, consistent reform that could threaten the privileged position of the iron triangle required directive leadership and the elimination of policy contestation from the first tier. Khrushchev's directive leadership brought the most significant efforts to change spending priorities. His organizational reforms were the last ones in this period that had any chance of threatening the procedures of reciprocal accountability and balanced leadership. Initiating a coherent reform effort across many policy realms required consolidated leadership; sustaining this in consistent policy required consolidated leadership unthreatened by competition. Khrushchev's directorship did not escape the pressures of iron triangle constituencies, and his reforms were undermined by incoherence and inconsistency. The cycling of leadership tended to force retreats from reform—although sometimes after one step forward, there came only a half step backward. Even Khrushchev's reforms could not survive the next succession in tact. The collective leadership responded to the pressures from the bureaucracies of the selectorate and in particular to the privileged iron triangle.[111]

Leadership cycling meant that reform at best progressed dialectically and at worst was killed in cycles of reform and retreat. The improved balancing of leadership meant that with time even the prospect for dialectical development declined. The limited directorship under Brezhnev brought less reform in either policy or procedure. The balanced leadership that succeeded him brought virtual stasis. The institutionalization of balancing and reciprocal accountability, by raising obstacles to the consolidation of directive leadership, limited the opportunities for reform under normal politics. It led to a polity that could adjust neither its policies nor its procedures to the changing problems of an industrializing society.

CHAPTER EIGHT

The Dialectics of Military Planning

AMONG the most important responsibilities facing the actors in the Soviet political system was development of policies to ensure national security. The stakes were high because the Soviet Union at its peak possessed a military might, if not first in the world, second only to that of the United States. The stakes within the Soviet Union were still greater because the military's claim on resources amounted to about one-eighth of gross national product and affected the health of the entire economy. The stakes for Soviet politicians were enormous because the armed forces comprised one of the most important constituencies in the selectorate.

A powerful lever held by Soviet politicians over military policy was the elaborate set of plans contained in the Soviet grand strategy and military doctrines. Debates over military plans were not simply discussions of abstract doctrine, for military plans were the centerpiece of interdependent policies to ensure national security. These debates were often the most important elements in discussions about the relationship of the Soviet Union to other states. Military plans were powerful means to shape Soviet force posture; they integrated existing forces and directed to the development of future forces.[1] Debates over military plans were often really debates about the allocation of resources in the larger economy.[2]

Military plans were shaped in the coalition politics between leaders and bureaucrats. Military bureaucrats developed their plans in response to the objectives of the state's political leadership as well as their own assessments of international pressures and technological possibilities. Doctrinal intervention by the political leadership was a powerful lever to change the direction of this military planning. Yet, in the routine development of these plans after Stalin's death, "loose coupling" permitted Soviet military professionals considerable autonomy. The Politburo did not develop alternative centers of expertise, parallel monitoring agencies, or supervisory departments to permit it to exercise routine, detailed direction over the General Staff in matters of military science.[3] Reciprocal accountability between political leaders and military elites made doctrinal intervention sporadic and its outcome uncertain.

Doctrinal intervention was a cyclical process of major changes pressed by a directive leader and retreats from those reforms by collective leadership. The timing of doctrinal innovations by the civilian leadership to shift the direction of military planning was constrained by the consolidation process. Only a directive leader had the motive and opportunity to impose a doctrinal innovation on military plans. A new general secretary who began his coalition building with the military as an initial supporter would have little incentive to seek to impose an innovation on the military. The general secretary was more likely to press doctrinal innovations when the military was a less significant source of support within his coalition. Indeed, doctrinal innovations tended to come quite late in the rule of each leader because the military, such a powerful constituency, was so resistant to control through clientelism. Nikita Khrushchev and Leonid Brezhnev developed alliances early in their careers with the minister of defense (Marshal Georgii Zhukov and Marshal Andrei Grechko, respectively), but only later in their administrations did they win the appointment of a close ally (Marshal Rodion Malinovksii in 1957 and Dmitrii Ustinov in 1976) who permitted them to press more forcefully for reform within the armed forces. The cycling of leadership also influenced the extent of the general secretary's success at restructuring military plans. A general secretary was better able to enforce integrating doctrinal guidance on military science when he enjoyed uncontested consolidated authority within the first tier. The autonomy of military elites in the articulation of military science in part depended upon disunity and competition within the leadership.

The cycling of leadership produced alternation between doctrinal innovations under directive leadership and retreats from those innovations under collective leadership. Yet, the development of military plans was not simply cyclical. Because military professionals were prevented from rejecting doctrinal innovations outright without the patronage of the first tier, in periods of enhanced military autonomy they could usually achieve this end only by coopting doctrinal innovations into military science with a very different twist. The shifting balance between first- and second-tier actors resulted in a "dialectics" of doctrine. Developments in military thought did not simply retrace the same intellectual ground, although there are examples of this; instead, it developed in a spiral that resembled Vladimir Lenin's description of the dialectic: "a development that repeats, as it were, stages that have already been passed, but repeats them in a different way, on a higher basis."[4]

Institutionalization of balanced leadership and reciprocal accountability had a profound effect on this spiral. The first process made it easier for the general secretary as commander-in-chief to propound doctrine, but the two processes together made it increasingly more difficult for civilian leaders to impose innovation on the military. Balanced leadership blocked any single leader from consolidating the directive rule necessary

the institutionalization of the reciprocal responsibilities of leaders and military bureaucrats for the articulation of military thought reduced these procedural shifts.

The emergence of the two-tier structure of military thought and its institutionalization were protracted processes greatly influenced by the larger developments of the political order under the constitution of Bolshevism. The concept of doktrina emerged from a spirited debate in the first years of the Soviet republic. Beginning in 1918 in a series of books and articles in the journal *Military Affairs (Voennoe delo)*, military specialists debated whether the Soviet Union should adopt a unified military doctrine and what relationship this would have to military experience. To a significant degree this was a debate over the relationship of civilian leadership to military affairs and the extent to which the political leadership should enforce uniformity in military thought on the armed bureaucrats. The most prominent voices for unity in military thought came from those who would ally themselves with Joseph Stalin—particularly from Marshal Mikhail V. Frunze. In his essay on "Unified Military Doctrine and the Red Army" (June 1921), Frunze argued "the state must define the nature of overall and particular military policy."[9] Specifically, the political leadership must develop a unified military doctrine that would guide the development of the country's armed forces and the methods of combat training of the troops; the unified military doctrine would link the armed forces to the military missions of the state. Critics of the unified military doctrine argued that it would "kill living thought" and stifle innovation in the military. Arguing against greater direction from civilian leadership, critics claimed that military doctrine could only properly derive from the experience of the armed forces. The appointment of Frunze as People's Commissar of War in 1924 and of Kliment E. Voroshilov after Frunze's death the following year ended these criticisms in favor of the unified military doctrine supported by Joseph Stalin.[10]

The concept of military science was at first less well developed in Soviet military thought—even on the eve of the First Five-Year Plan. In 1928, the *Great Soviet Encyclopedia* defined the military sciences as "systems of ideas and knowledge" that included five groups of disciplines: military history, socioeconomic studies of military geography and military statistics, military administration, techniques of combat, and strategy and tactics. Yet it provided little elaboration beyond this.[11] The relationship of military science to doktrina received even less attention. Under Stalin, the distinction between doktrina and military science for all purposes disappeared as the general secretary himself dictated the latter. As in other social sciences such as linguistics and even some natural sciences such as genetics, military science became dominated by Party-imposed dogmas— in this case, the general secretary's views of the winning strategies of World War II formulated as the "permanently operating factors of war."

In the words of General V. V. Kurasov, "By brilliantly discovering the permanently operating factors of victory, Comrade Stalin thereby discovered the direction and basis for further development of Soviet military art and . . . strategy." Because Stalin purportedly "determined these decisive factors of war on the basis of brilliantly applying the method of Marxist dialectical materialism to the phenomena of war," challenges to his military science risked the label heterodox.[12]

Immediately after Stalin's death the decline of autocratic authority permitted the reemergence of the distinction between doktrina and military science. Like researchers in other disciplines, military scientists began to claim greater autonomy in expert investigations—specifically, into the laws of armed combat. Leaders of this movement argued that Stalin's military science focused on political and social conditions for victory, but ignored questions of armed combat. In seeking to carve out an intellectual niche for their expertise, military professionals argued that a clearer distinction must be drawn between the issues of military science and the sociopolitical factors that are legitimately a concern of the Party. They argued for a narrowed and shifted focus for military science that would permit experts the autonomy to study the laws of combat. Major General N. Talenskii, the first of these professionals to go public, stressed that armed combat was as much governed by its own objective laws as by the social and political factors examined by Stalin's dogma and that the distinctive laws of armed combat were the legitimate focus of military science.[13] He argued that study of these laws required the expertise found at the military academies.[14]

By 1955, at a time of the iron triangle triumph in the succession struggle, this debate was resolved in a lopsided compromise that accepted Talenskii's proposal for a new military science. The only concession by the military bureaucrats was that military science could not be completely disentangled from social and political factors. Yet, to quote the editors of the General Staff's journal Military Thought (Voennaia mysl'), "to include in military science questions going beyond the limits of its competence means to doom military science as a special branch of knowledge."[15] The editors went beyond the claim that military science should enjoy some autonomy from leadership direction to assert that the Party leadership may have to consider the results of the investigations by military professionals: "The missions of strategy are set by politics, but political leaders must know the potentialities of strategy in order to set tasks before it skillfully at each concrete historical stage."[16]

The balance between doktrina and military science shifted once again with Nikita Khrushchev's consolidation of power, although this time not so completely as under Stalin. In the early 1960s the first secretary sought to reassert leadership control over military science. A vehicle for this was a new doktrina. The term had fallen into disuse in the 1940s while Stalin had propounded his dogmas directly as military science. Khrushchev saw doktrina as a more indirect means to control military science; he claimed that doktrina was binding on military professionals as they developed military science. This opened a debate over the proper relationship between doktrina and military science. In the first reaction of military professionals in the early 1960s the distinction between the two was not strictly drawn.[17] Some claimed a role for military professionals in the articulation of doktrina itself. For example, writing in 1962, General N. Lomov argued that while Party and state leadership lay down "the foundations of military doctrine," military professionals play a role in the elaboration of the "unified, theoretical views" that form the basis of the state program.[18]

When in 1963 Khrushchev inaugurated another campaign to increase his control over military science, this time military professionals reacted to these pressures by trying to draw ever more precisely the distinction between doktrina and military science and to divide responsibility for each part of military thought between the two tiers. While the term military science was seldom invoked in the first edition (1962) of Marshal V. D. Sokolovskii's work on *Military strategy*, it was addressed fully in the second edition the following year.[19] The original omission is even more noteworthy because the subject matter of the book, strategy, according to the subsequent formulation, was said to be the major constituent part of military science. Defense minister Rodion Malinovskii placed his authority behind this growing refinement of the distinction, arguing much as the pioneers of post-Stalinist military science a decade earlier that the domain of military science must be preserved by narrowing.[20] Doktrina would be the exclusive prerogative of the political leadership.[21]

Under the collective leadership that came to office in 1964 relaxation of doctrinal pressure permitted military scientists to claim greater autonomy from doktrina. Marshal M. V. Zakharov, who had been removed as chief of the General Staff in March 1963 for his opposition to Khrushchev's plans, was brought back by the new leadership to oversee a reassessment of military science. Less than four months after Khrushchev's removal, in a transparent attack on the deposed first secretary, Zakharov criticized "the so-called strategic farsightedness" of "individuals who lack even a remote relationship to military strategy," and he warned that "any subjective approach to military problems, hare-brained plans, and superficiality can cause irreparable damage."[22] The renewed autonomy of the military under collective leadership elicited new pressures from military professionals to increase the influence of military science over doktrina. Major General S. N. Kozlov wrote in 1966 that doktrina should be developed jointly by political and military leaders and that military science, because it is more dynamic, leads doktrina in development. Kozlov and others argued that the state's policy would be improved the more the political leadership deferred to military science in its decisions.[23] As military professionals asserted their authority, they also began to expand the domain of military science beyond the technical issues of combat to larger concerns of preparedness of the whole country for combat.[24]

With the growth of Leonid Brezhnev's leadership in foreign policy came new doctrinal pressures on military science. Yet, the increasing institutionalization of the distinction between doktrina and military science meant that Brezhnev could not change fundamentally the relationships within military thought. Brezhnev's limited directorship brought a more precise formulation that established the leading role of doktrina but sanctioned dividing responsibilities between politicians and professionals in the articulation of military thought. By 1971, Colonel P. A. Sidorov, writing in the *Officer's Handbook (Spravochnik Ofitsera)*, presented this formulation of the relationship between doktrina and military science as follows: "Military doctrine is a state's system of views and instructions on [1] the nature of war under specific historical conditions, [2] the definition of the military tasks of the state and the armed forces and the principles of their development, as well as [3] the means and forms of solving all of these tasks, including armed combat, which stem from the war aims and the social-economic and military-technical resources of the country." Doktrina includes essential premises for all military thought, such as the identity of probable enemies and the appropriate Soviet response. Central to Sidorov's definition of doktrina was the assertion that the political leadership articulates this policy: It is "the political policy of the Party and the Soviet government in the military field." Alternatively, in this new, more precise formulation, military science is concerned with technique and does not necessarily articulate policy for the state. At the core of the seven subdisciplines that formally comprise military science is military art, or the principles of conducting warfare, that includes tactics, operational art, and strategy. Military science is the province of military professionals, and, rather than always having dogmatic or binding quality, it is legitimately the object of professional controversy. "In the system of theories known as military science there may be several different points of view, diverse scientific concepts, original hypotheses which are not selected as doctrine for practical application and thus do not acquire the character of official state views on military questions."[25] This formulation of the relationship between doktrina and military science prevailed throughout much of the 1970s.[26]

Increasing dissatisfaction with Brezhnev's doctrinal guidance led some military professionals once again to claim a greater role in military thought. Military professionals began to complain that doktrina did not adequately reflect the findings of military science.[27] The Chief of the General Staff Nikolai Ogarkov began to press for a greater role for military professionals in the articulation of doktrina itself. In the increasingly institutionalized structure of military thought, he sought to introduce a very fine distinction: He revived a distinction made by Frunze between the sociopolitical and military-technical aspects of doktrina and claimed that the latter were the province of the military high command.[28] Mounting pressures from military professionals prompted the convocation of a high-level conference of military party secretaries, at which minister of defense Dmitrii Ustinov stated the leadership's position: "it is the Party that formulates military policy and military doctrine," including its military-technical aspects.[29] The death of Brezhnev in November 1982 and of Ustinov in December 1984 relieved some of these doctrinal pressures on military science and prompted still more efforts by military professionals to expand their role. M. A. Gareev's highly influential study of Frunze published in 1985 restated the view that doktrina is divided into sociopolitical and military-technical aspects, that military professionals play a role in the adoption and articulation of doktrina, and that military science is central in the development of the military-technical aspects of *doktrina*. Military science develops through "a clash of opinions," "but at a certain stage doctrine selects the most effective views and reinforces them in official documents and manuals as guiding concepts which are obligatory for all."[30] Using the opportunity afforded by the post-Brezhnev collective leadership, the military pressed to expand its role in the articulation of military thought.

The doctrinal "turf wars" were important, for the outcome determined the relative role of first- and second-tier actors in the making of military plans. The outcome of these battles over procedures itself reflected the balance within the first tier and between tiers. The doctrinal "turf wars" produced a driving force in the development of procedural rules for articulating doctrine. In its articulation the growing institutionalization of an ever more ornate structure for military thought brought a more stable definition of the respective responsibilities of each tier.

DIALECTICS OF DOCTRINE

The institutionalist perspective on doctrinal politics places in a different light the story of doctrinal development. Much like innovation in other realms of policy, this dialectical process was intimately tied to domestic politics rooted in the constitution of Bolshevism. Three times before 1986 a directive leader intervened in the development of military science to impose a doctrinal innovation: Stalin in 1942 proclaimed the "permanently operating factors" of warfare. Khrushchev in January 1960 announced his "new look." Brezhnev in January 1977 introduced the "Tula line." The extent to which each doctrinal innovation succeeded at restructuring military science depended on the general secretary's previous success at consolidating directive rule.

After each innovation, under the next collective leadership when the new general secretary had only weakly consolidated his position, the military was able to turn back or redirect the innovations of the previous leader, to assert the dominant themes in its preferred military science, and to force a combined arms compromise. The dominance of Stalin's "permanently operating factors" (1945–1953) was followed after his death (1953–1959) by efforts of military professionals to redefine and then reject Stalinist military science. By the end of the 1950s, the General Staff had agreed on major tenets of its combined arms doctrine. The years during which Khrushchev sought to restructure military science with his "new look" (1960–1964) preceded the rejection of Khrushchev's univariant strategy and the victory of a new combined arms compromise (1965–1976). Brezhnev's attempt to impose his Tula line on military science (1977–1982) led after his death to the search for an expanded role for the conventional forces in yet another combined arms compromise, but now under the nuclear umbrella of mutual deterrence (1983–1986). That is, as a consequence of the cycling of leadership Soviet military thought went through six stages from the end of the Second World War until 1986. Yet, as a consequence of reciprocal accountability and the increasing institutionalization of roles in the articulation of military thought, these stages brought only moderate swings in the direction of policy.

Both Soviet and Western analysts have identified phases in the development of Soviet military policies and doctrines that approximate these. Organizing schemes developed by Soviet military scientists have emphasized stages in which new technologies were introduced into Soviet war plans. Without making explicit the connection to politics, these have tended to correspond to the different administrations of Soviet leaders: the period of Stalinist military thought (1945–1953) was followed under Khrushchev by the "revolution in military affairs" and its dissemination in a new military doctrine (1954–1964); under Brezhnev there was the "new stage of qualitative development" in Soviet armed forces (1965–1982); and most recently there has been the "revolutionary turn" in military affairs (1982–).[31] Western analysts Robbin F. Laird and Dale R. Herspring have identified five postwar phases in which the role of nuclear weapons has changed in Soviet policies. Although they do not draw the connection to the leadership cycle, these phases correspond to the alternation of collective and directive leadership in each administration.[32] This chapter argues that the source of these stages is in Soviet domestic politics and, ultimately, in the constitution of Bolshevism.

Recurring Themes

The dialectical development of military thought was rooted in the interaction between doktrina and military science and between leaders and military bureaucrats. Leaders and bureaucrats responded to changing international threats or opportunities and to technological possibilities; yet their responsibilities in addressing these were not identical, and their responses often diverged. Thus, doktrina and military science diverged. For example, they diverged on the issue of deterrence and war fighting, and, as Henry Trofimenko explains, this simply reflected the different missions of political leaders and military professionals: "The military in every country has one and the same mission: to do its utmost in case of war, to ensure its country the favorable outcome of every battle and of the war. . . . But if the mission of the military is to fight successfully and to win wars, then the mission of contemporary politicians is to prevent a nuclear war that can result in disaster for mankind."[33] In introducing a doctrinal innovation, the leaders often reached within the complex set of ideas in military science to extract some and elevate these ideas to priority. The leader played on divisions within the armed forces the way Khrushchev used the Strategic Rocket Forces against the Ground Forces to strengthen his hand when forcing a reform on this powerful constituency. The minister of defense might seek to counter this divide-and-rule strategy by maintaining unity in the coalition of military services. Rather than setting priorities and forcing sacrifices, the minister often tried to meet the various demands of the services in a compromise military science, as Rodion Malinovskii and Andrei Grechko did in the great combined arms logroll of the 1960s.[34] These moves by political and military leaders shaped the divergence between doktrina and military science on three larger recurring issues: the relative role of military means in ensuring national security; the balance between offense, defense, and deterrence; and the priorities in defense that could permit economies.

THE PLACE OF MILITARY FORCES IN NATIONAL SECURITY

The doctrinal innovations of general secretaries often had the effect of discounting the importance of military means and objectives while enhancing the role of political means and objectives in national security. This divergence between doktrina and military science manifested itself in two issues—the relative role of nonmilitary means in national security, and the importance of traditional military objectives in warfare.

First, doctrinal innovations tended to depreciate the role of military instruments in national security relative to political means of solving these problems. For example, Stalin's permanently operating factors placed greatest weight in defense preparation upon domestic political and social factors, particularly the "stability of the rear," while assigning secondary significance to the quantity and quality of arms. Mikhail Gorbachev's "new thinking" (discussed in chapter 9) went still further: In circumstances of mutual deterrence and with the danger that conflict might escalate to nuclear war, the relative importance of military means in contributing to national security declined, and political means increased in importance.[35] Alternatively, military science necessarily considered a much narrower range of instruments of national security, and military bureaucrats warned against undervaluing those instruments. Common were warnings that failure to take adequate military preparations would be the root of Soviet humiliations—such as those at the opening of the Second World War and in the Cuban missile crisis. Lt. General V. Serebriannikov argued that in the initial stage of World War II this was the root of disaster: "The political measures taken to avoid war were not properly linked with concern over maintaining the Armed Forces at a high state of vigilance and readiness."[36] Military science warned that no amount of diplomacy could substitute for sound military preparedness.

A second manifestation of this diverging treatment of military forces in national security was the tendency of doctrinal innovations to emphasize the political objectives of military instruments such as nuclear weapons and to question traditional military objectives in warfare. While military science continued to treat nuclear weapons as additions to firepower, doctrinal innovations increasingly treated nuclear weapons as political instruments. The emphasis upon deterrence by punishment in both the new look and Tula line highlighted political over battlefield solutions to national security. Doctrinal innovations tended to place less stock in the traditional objectives of military science—war fighting and victory. When doctrinal innovations began to question these as objectives for operational planning they brought howls of protest from military professionals, who claimed it would strip them of their raison d'être: If doktrina gave up on victory, then "the armed forces of the socialist states . . . will not be able to set for themselves the goal of defeating imperialism . . . and our military science would not even work out a strategy for the conduct of war since the latter has lost its meaning and its significance. . . . In this case, the very call to raise the combat readiness of our armed forces and improve their capability to defeat any aggressor would be senseless."[37]

DEFENSE AND DETERRENCE VS. OFFENSE

The doctrinal innovations of general secretaries were often associated with attempts to shift military science away from its emphasis on offensive operations and toward defensive postures or deterrence. Doctrinal innovations of politicians tended to depreciate the importance of the offensive and, in particular, of blitzkrieg capabilities.[38] These innovations tended to give priority to defense. Stalin's military science envisioned an active defense with initial retreat into the interior during a mobilization to prepare a massive counteroffensive. Gorbachev's concept of "defensive defense" argued for forces sufficient to repel possible aggression, but not sufficient to conduct offensive operations. Military science, conversely, tended to favor the offensive throughout this period. The Field Service Regulations of 1939 had proclaimed, "any enemy attack against the Union of Soviet Socialist Republics shall be met by a crushing blow of the entire might of our Armed forces. . . . We will conduct an offensive war, carrying it into enemy territory. The combat operations of the Red Army will be aimed at destruction, at the total annihilation of the enemy."[39] Similarly, the editors of *Military Strategy* contended in the 1960s that "offensive operations in a future war will be the basic means for solving the problems of armed conflict."[40]

The issue of deterrence proved particularly divisive when political leaders began embracing the idea that deterrence (by punishment) could be achieved without the means to wage offensive operations. Insofar as it addressed deterrence at all, military science tended to treat deterrence of imperialist aggression as the consequence of an ability to deny aggressors their objectives. Many military professionals simply dismissed deterrence as something totally outside the purview of military science. Thus, General Mikhail Milshtein is quoted as telling American specialists, "mutual assured destruction is not a military concept and should not be accepted as such by either side. It might be a political concept, or a philosophical concept, but it is not valid militarily."[41]

Doctrinal innovations by politicians accorded increasing centrality and broadening significance to the concept of deterrence—and, in particular, deterrence by punishment.[42] Stalin left an uncertain policy concerning deterrence. He had juggled contradictory dogmas: imperialism remained intrinsically aggressive; war was inevitable; and yet the Soviet Union should not resign itself to fatalism because it could deter aggression enough to avoid individual wars. Stalin's spokesmen stressed the aggressive threat posed by imperialism: In his 1950 election speech, Viacheslav Molotov proclaimed that the Soviet Union sought peaceful coexistence and economic competition, but "we are well aware of the truth that so long as imperialism exists there also exists the danger of fresh aggression;

that, given the existence of imperialism and its rapacious plans, wars are inevitable."[43] Yet, toward the end of his rule Stalin began to suggest that war might be avoided through deterrence: Even though the aggressive nature of imperialism had not changed, the threat of war for the Soviet Union was less immediate. Insofar as any concept of deterrence existed in Stalin's thought it was a curious concept of deterrence by punishment; the Soviet Union deterred capitalist aggression not so much by its ability to defeat Western forces in battle, but by its ability to call on the proletariat to rise against capitalist aggressors and destroy the capitalist system. Stalin, however, continued to emphasize that simple deterrence could not end the aggressive tendencies of imperialism. As long as Stalin lived the concept of deterrence remained an underdeveloped theme.[44]

Khrushchev made explicit the notion that the Soviet Union could deter imperialist aggression, and he dismissed the inevitability of war. Nonetheless, this shift came in steps. In his first significant speech on this issue to the 1956 Party Congress the first secretary stressed that, because the economic roots of aggression in imperialism remained, deterrence was tenuous. He went to considerable lengths to separate the motive causes of war, which were its economic roots in imperialism, and the deterrent causes, which included the correlation of forces. Concerning the former, Khrushchev argued that "the Leninist precept is still in force that so long as imperialism exists, the economic basis giving rise to wars will also be preserved." Concerning the latter, however, "the peace forces find not only the moral, but also the material means to prevent aggression." Thus war was no longer "fatalistically inevitable." At the 1959 Party Congress he reaffirmed this line.[45] In 1960, Khrushchev went still further, making nuclear deterrence of imperialist aggression a central ordering concept in his "new look" and embracing the logic of deterrence by punishment. There he claimed that "if some madman were to provoke an attack on our country or any other socialist countries, we would literally wipe the country or countries attacking us off the face of the earth."[46]

Khrushchev also began to advance arguments that would lead his successors to the recognition that deterrence was mutual. In its polemics with the Chinese in the early 1960s, the Soviet government proclaimed that "thermonuclear war would entail disastrous consequences for all peoples and the whole world." In nuclear war "all countries . . . would be thrown back in their development by decades, perhaps even by centuries."[47] The Chinese turned these statements against the Soviets by charging that the Soviet leaders "have repeatedly declared in a mass of articles, speeches, statements, and resolutions that the consequence of nuclear war will be 'universal destruction' of mankind and will be 'the end of any kind of politics.' "[48] Yet, Khrushchev did not formally articulate as doktrina the view that deterrence was a mutual constraint. It was Brezhnev in the Tula line of 1977 who committed his personal authority to the view that deterrence had become a constraint on the Soviet Union as well as the United States.

ECONOMIZING PRIORITIES IN DEFENSE

The doctrinal innovations of general secretaries were often associated with attempts to impose economies on the armed forces by setting priorities. Directive leaders were more likely than military bureaucrats to favor economizing solutions to defense problems, such as doctrines that emphasized nonmaterial elements of defense as substitutes for material claims. Directive leaders were more likely than military bureaucrats to favor setting priorities among services and weapons systems and focusing resources on decisive weapons. Directive leaders were more likely than military bureaucrats to favor setting priorities that delayed the acquisition of war-fighting capabilities at least to some future period (such as crisis mobilization) closer to the point of hostilities. Each doctrinal innovation sought to set priorities in defense—to find an economizing solution to the security problems of the Soviet Union. Stalin's permanently operating factors depreciated technological solutions to defense and justified postponing many elements of preparedness to the mobilization phase of actual hostilities. Khrushchev's "new look" argued that ground forces and conventional air forces could be cut. Brezhnev's Tula line rejected numerical superiority and introduced the standard of "sufficiency" as a structuring principle in force posture. Military professionals often resisted these efforts to set priorities. The military's preferred combined arms doctrine emphasized the vital role of all services and multimillion forces. It warned that Soviet forces should be prepared for diverse contingencies that prevented setting these sorts of economizing priorities.

Cycle 1: Dogma and Destalinization

The dialectical development of military thought began as soon as Stalin died. Stalin's autocratic rule during the postwar years permitted him to control military thought to an extent that none of his successors duplicated. Yet even Stalin's autocratic system could not guarantee the survival of his policies after his death. The period of collective leadership following Stalin's death (March 1953) brought competition within the first tier, expanded autonomy for military professionals in the second tier, and a rejection of his doctrinal guidance.

STALIN'S "PERMANENTLY OPERATING FACTORS"

Stalin's doctrine responded to a strategic paradox: The Soviet Union possessed a substantial military establishment positioned so as to determine the future of east and central Europe. Yet, it faced a strategic challenge for which this military strength was not strictly appropriate—its major competitor had become the United States. Adaptation of Soviet forces to this new challenge required a costly investment of funds; and particularly in the years of industrial reconstruction following the war these funds were not readily available. At a time when capital was needed for reconstruction, rapid development of a new surface fleet and long-range aviation made excessive demands on capital industry. Even a commitment to the more labor-intensive ground forces could be costly if it required extensive modernization of a large standing force. As Stalin replied in a 1951 *Pravda* interview, "It is not difficult to understand that such an imprudent policy would lead to the bankruptcy of the state."[49] Stalin's solution was more economical: to draw significant parts of material from existing capabilities built up during the Second World War and proceed selectively with modernization. East European states would be required to shoulder a portion of the burden in capital and manpower, despite the risks this posed to Soviet control. Modernization of Soviet forces, relying where possible upon existing production lines, proceeded by selective improvements in these forces.[50]

The military science that defined the role of these forces was Stalin's "permanently operating factors of war." As first formulated in his Order of the Day No. 55 (23 February 1942), this stated that "the outcome of the war will not be decided by a temporary [or fortuitous] factor such as surprise, but by the permanently [or constantly] operating factors— stability of the rear, morale of the army, quantity and quality of divisions, equipment of the army, [and] organizing ability of the commanding personnel of the army."[51] As elaborated after the war these principles provided an economizing-prioritizing solution to the problem of defense, focusing on the single contingency of war in Europe, emphasizing the primacy of nonmaterial elements of warfare, depreciating the role of technology, and lowering the demands of peacetime readiness. The formulation set priorities in defense policies and served as the basis for planning by military theorists.[52]

The primacy of political and nonmaterial elements of warfare was enshrined in Stalin's dogma: the keys to victory were "stability of the rear" and "morale of the army." In the words of the *Great Soviet Encyclopedia*, among the five factors Stalin placed "stability of the rear in first place." This, according to Stalin's minister of defense Voroshilov, "include[s] all that constitutes the life and activity of the whole state," but among these "the unshakable firmness of the Soviet state [is] the fundamental and decisive factor." From this view purportedly flows the wise policies and the popular support essential to victory. Even the morale of the armed forces is a consequence of these domestic political factors.[53]

In Stalin's military science, the quantity and quality of armaments received less attention. Voroshilov minimized the importance of the last three permanently operating factors—divisions, equipment, and command personnel—by commenting that their importance is "obviously irrefutable," but at root they depend upon the first two factors of stability of the rear and morale. The depreciation of technology in Stalinist military science was enforced by the claim that the search for decisive weapons such as the tank or aviation and the tendency to overlook the moral factor were hallmarks of bourgeois theorists. Indeed, it argued that bourgeois theorists in many instances must substitute technology for the moral factor because the growing class consciousness of the proletariat means that for capitalist states "victory in contemporary war cannot be won by multimillion armies but only by masses of tanks and aviation."[54]

By classifying surprise and the initial stages of warfare as having only temporary significance, Stalin's military science meant the Soviet Union need not maintain forces at full strength in peacetime, but they could rely upon mobilization during the initial stages of the war to prepare.[55] The Soviet war plan in this period appears to have expected to respond to future aggression with a retreat into the interior of the country where an active defense would wear down the advancing enemy and then, after full mobilization, launch a massive counteroffensive.[56] This plan freed the Soviet economy in peacetime to focus more of its scarce resources on industrial reconstruction.

EMERGENCE OF THE ARMED FORCES' COMBINED ARMS DOCTRINE

Collective leadership following the death of Stalin brought questioning of fundamental principles in Stalin's military science. The absence of a leader with the consolidated authority to innovate in doctrinal matters meant no common doktrina was forthcoming; indeed, competing leaders soon sought political advantage in debates over doctrine. This absence of doctrinal leadership meant the integration of doktrina and military science suffered. Military science developed with more autonomy, reflecting to a greater extent than before 1953 the professional assessments of the military. The military began to plan for offensive operations that would seize the initiative in future wars rather than defending and wearing down an enemy. The resource consequence of these professional assessments was mounting pressure for investment in a multifaceted force at a high state of readiness prepared for diverse contingencies.

Although many doctrinal innovations of significance were proposed during the post-Stalinist succession, the absence of consolidated authority made it difficult to establish any as doktrina. Apparently closely linked to Khrushchev's breakout, the debates peaked in the months before Malenkov's removal from the premiership. Two fundamental questions divided the leadership: (1) Could imperialist aggressors be deterred from war? And (2) could war with the imperialist camp be won if deterrence failed? On one side, Georgii Malenkov and his allies began to point to the costs of future war, which they described as a possible global holocaust destroying all civilization, and to the possibility of peaceful coexistence now that the Soviet Union had the capabilities to deter imperialist aggression.[57] Alternatively, Nikita Khrushchev and his conservative allies emphasized the implacable and undeterrable aggressiveness of imperialist states and the immediacy of the war danger posed by imperialism. Should imperialism initiate war, however, it would mean not global holocaust but the collapse of the world capitalist system.[58] These doctrinal debates had profound implications for force posture and defense expenditure. The reformers drew two conclusions: little military advantage was to be had in seeking superiority, and existing Soviet forces were adequate to the task of deterrence. The conservatives emphasized the peril that would face the Soviet Union if it did not further strengthen its armed forces.[59]

Following the removal of Malenkov as premier (chairman of the Council of Ministers) in February 1955, Khrushchev began to articulate a compromise position much closer to the political center—one that lowered his own previously announced expectations of warfare. Yet, the first secretary's shift at the 1956 Party Congress (February) toward the position that war was no longer fatalistically inevitable is equally noteworthy for its doctrinal modesty.[60] It left unresolved the most pressing (and contentious) issues of the time: had deterrence become a mutual constraint on the superpowers? could the Soviet Union win a thermonuclear war? would superiority in armaments bring advantage on the nuclear battlefield? and how should the Soviet Union configure forces in a nuclear age? Indeed, by restating the dogma that the economic basis for imperialist aggression remains unchanged and by stressing the need for vigilance, Khrushchev appears to have given something to all major actors, both reformers and conservatives. Not all conservatives in the leadership followed Khrushchev in this shift to a more moderate position.[61] At a time that Khrushchev had begun to expand his coalition beyond the iron triangle, but was still checked by collective leadership, from the gen-

emerged in the decade and half before 1960 was a two-stage cycle: (1) an innovation enforced on military thought by a directive leader followed by (2) mounting challenges from military professionals to that innovation under collective leadership. This pattern was rooted in the leadership cycle and would repeat itself in the late Khrushchev and early Brezhnev years, but with important differences. Both the limits on his consolidation and the growing institutionalization of the two-tier structure of military thought meant that Khrushchev's ability to shape military thought was far less than his predecessor's. In addition, his coalition began to crack toward the end of his administration, so that the challenges to his doctrinal innovation began even before his removal.

KHRUSHCHEV'S "NEW LOOK"

Khrushchev pressed a doctrinal innovation that stressed the centrality of deterrence and the priority of strategic rocket forces and permitted him to contain the growth of military expenditures.[72] The formal announcement of this doctrinal innovation came in January 1960 in an address before the Supreme Soviet: (1) In future wars nuclear weapons and missiles would constitute the principal means of combat, while traditional armed forces would rapidly become obsolete. (2) Future wars would probably be of short duration, and the initial stages would be decisive. (3) A large country such as the Soviet Union could survive a first strike by an adversary and retain sufficient forces to retaliate; thus, it could structure its forces on the ability to deter imperialist aggression. (4) Therefore, Soviet troop strength could be cut from 3.6 million to 2.4 million. From the General Staff's preferred military plans Khrushchev's doktrina had extracted and emphasized the premises that the initial stages of war would be decisive and that strategic missiles would play a primary role in war fighting. Yet the first secretary discounted the likelihood of wars of longer duration and insisted that traditional armed forces were becoming obsolete and, therefore, could be cut.[73]

Khrushchev's consolidation of directive leadership ensured that he could press his doctrinal innovation on military science. At first leading officers withheld their criticisms. Minister of Defense Rodion Malinovskii's speech to the Supreme Soviet gave overall endorsement to Khrushchev's innovation and only hinted at reservations: "The strategic rocket command of the Armed Forces unquestionably constitutes our primary object in the Forces, but we are of the opinion that it is not possible to solve all problems of war by means of one single military arm."[74] On Army Day 1960, the Commander-in-Chief of the Ground Forces Marshal A. A. Grechko defended the decision to cut troops; he argued that this did not reduce Soviet might because "defensive strength is not measured in our day by the number of soldiers but in fire power."[75] Yet, pointed criticisms came from other officers, who objected to the vision of "push-button war" and warned that "the new war would undoubtedly be fought by massive armies, involving many million troops and requiring large reserves of command personnel and vast numbers of lower ranks."[76] These criticisms brought rebukes for "dogmatism and conservatism," warnings against "fetishism of former models," and charges that "supporters of tradition . . . do not want to recognize the changed roles of the various branches and arms of the armed forces, while dogmatically expounding the well-known thesis from Soviet military thought about their harmonious development."[77] Many who objected strenuously were demoted, including Commander-in-Chief of the Warsaw Pact Forces Konev, Commander-in-Chief of the Belorussian Military District Timoshenko, and Chief of the General Staff Sokolovskii.

Yet, by the summer of 1961, against a background of mounting international tensions over Berlin, an American conventional arms buildup to support its new flexible response policy, and harsh criticism from the Chinese in the widening Sino-Soviet rift, Khrushchev's doctrinal innovation and proposed troop cut became increasingly less tenable. By June the first secretary had apparently given in to the dogma of harmonious development of all services that he had so recently denounced.[78] Khrushchev suspended the reduction in troops and announced an increase in defense expenditures, justifying these as "temporary" measures in response to U.S. actions.[79] Over the next seventeen months his silence on major doctrinal issues relaxed the pressures on the military to recast military science in terms of his January 1960 pronouncements.

Malinovskii and the General Staff used the opportunity to press a new public statement of military science—a statement that balanced among the views of military professionals and went part way toward accommodating the most important elements of Khrushchev's doctrinal innovation. In October 1961, speaking to the Party Congress, Malinovskii was far more outspoken in his qualifications to the Khrushchev plan than he had been before the Supreme Soviet just a year and a half earlier.[80] Military science could not openly reject the doctrinal innovations of Khrushchev, but instead sought to coopt these innovations with a distinctly different twist. The General Staff disseminated its new military science in a textbook on military strategy edited by Marshal Sokolovskii. Meant to be a definitive statement of the new combined arms compromise, *Military Strategy* also sought to deflect elements of the first secretary's doctrinal innovations. It accepted Khrushchev's claim that in future wars strategic nuclear strikes would be decisive, but the book went on to argue that future wars would only be won with combined arms operations by all services, including massive ground force operations to seize and hold the enemy's homeland. On the issue of the length of such a war, as Khrushchev had stated, the initial stages of war would be decisive, but a future war in Europe was also likely to be protracted. The Soviet Union must develop the capabilities and techniques to seize the initiative rapidly, go on the offensive, and consolidate its gains in a protracted war.[81]

Intervening in this development in early 1963, Khrushchev sought to reclaim his lost control over military science by reasserting the tenets of his "new look." In February 1963, the first secretary restated his position that future wars would be of short duration; thus, mass armies would be obsolete in such encounters. He made clear his continued belief that Soviet ground forces were being rendered obsolete by modern means of war fighting: "When I went out into the training field and saw the tanks attacking and how the antitank artillery hit these tanks, I became ill. After all, we are spending a lot of money to build tanks. And if—God forbid, as they say—war breaks out, these tanks will burn before they reach the line indicated by the command."[82] In April 1963 he called for further economies in defense, and in December he went on the offensive to press for budget cuts: Khrushchev's state budget for 1964 promised to cut defense expenditures by 5 percent and reduce force levels.[83] Finally, in late September 1964, the first secretary revealed a new economic plan that called for a dramatic shift away from defense industry.[84]

As the first secretary increased his pressure for doctrinal innovations after April 1963, military objections became more strident. At first the military acquiesced in the new campaign, limiting itself to reminders that because future wars might be protracted it was necessary to invest in mass multimillion-men armies.[85] Beginning in late 1963, however, military professionals grew significantly louder in their criticisms. Commander-in-Chief of Ground Forces and Civil Defense Chuikov offered a spirited defense of combined arms operations and stressed the central role of ground forces. Chuikov claimed that overreliance on so-called decisive weapons had, in fact, been a hallmark of Hitler's strategy and a source of his undoing; Chuikov contended that "to ignore the objective laws of balanced development of all types of weapons and of the different branches in the Forces and then coordinated use in warfare necessarily has catastrophic consequences."[86] During the next months senior officers highlighted the importance of preparations for a protracted war with particular stress on massive ground force operations.[87]

VICTORY OF THE MILITARY'S COMBINED ARMS COMPROMISE

Under the collective leadership that came to power in 1964, military bureaucrats had new opportunities to develop military science without the constraints of Khrushchev's doctrinal innovation. This permitted them to expand the domain of military science by asserting opinions on issues that were previously the preserve of doktrina.[88] The resulting military science was the victory of the combined arms doctrine that the military had developed toward the end of the previous decade. This provided a rationale for a multifaceted buildup of forces.

The new collective leadership did not continue Khrushchev's doctrinal pressure on the armed forces, nor did the new general secretary articulate his own doctrinal innovation.[89] Indeed, Brezhnev publicly embraced the combined arms doctrine of his military coalition partners. In stark contrast to Khrushchev's speech to the graduates of the military academies the year before, Brezhnev rejected any discussion of the obsolescence of conventional forces and emphasized that all services must play a role in the defense of the Soviet Union.[90] Supporting a buildup of forces, he warned in July 1967 that "in military matters *more than any other sector* we must not mark time."[91]

Relaxation of doctrinal pressures permitted a debate to flare among military professionals over questions left unanswered by the Party leadership. At the heart of the debate was whether deterrence could serve as a basis for Soviet policies toward the United States.[92] The debate asked several questions: could imperialist states be deterred? was victory possible in nuclear war? would superiority in arms yield military dividends?[93] With the reinforced rules against public differentiation in the first tier, this debate, unlike that among Stalin's heirs, for the most part was not a debate among Politburo members. Yet, in the absence of strong doctrinal leadership from the first tier, there was neither an authoritative answer to these debates nor the directive will to silence them.

With declining pressure from the first tier to cast military science in terms of a doctrinal innovation, military bureaucrats abandoned many priorities of Khrushchev's univariant strategy and prepared for a broader range of military operations.[94] Thus, the revisions to Marshal Sokolovskii's *Military Strategy* that appeared in the third edition (1968) emphasized the diversity of contingencies for which Soviet armed forces must be prepared.[95] This was expressed forcefully by Kozlov: "it is necessary to be ready to wage various kinds of war: global and local, swift and protracted, with nuclear weapons and without."[96] The absence of firm doctrinal guidance led to a military science dominated by logrolling and compromise. Indeed, a significant part of the writing in this period was bandwagoning by spokesmen seeking to define a mission for their various branches (such as aviation, airborne troops, or navy) within the prevailing scenario for warfare or to suggest the importance of new scenarios for which their services were uniquely qualified.[97] Although individual military professionals came to emphasize one scenario or the other, an approach that led some Western analysts to see in one or the other the true priority in Soviet military thought, more characteristic of this period is the absence of any single integrating priority among writers and, as a consequence, a diversity of views.[98] In the scenarios for superpower war, "decisive" strategic strikes were coordinated with other forces in combined arms operations.[99] A significantly expanded volume of writing addressed three primary objectives in the European theater: (1) early destruction of the nuclear and conventional forces of the North Atlantic Treaty states (particularly through nuclear strikes); (2) isolation of Europe from American support (principally through naval operations); and (3) rapid occupation of Central and Western Europe (primarily through ground operations).[100] At the same time, military professionals stressed the need to prepare for other scenarios as well—such as controlled or limited wars in Europe and power projection outside the European theater.[101]

The concomitant of this development in military science was a multifaceted and enormously expensive expansion of military capabilities. From his appointment as minister of defense in 1967 through the mid-1970s Andrei Grechko pressed for "uninterrupted modernization and development of our military strength."[102] The combined arms compromise called for the "harmonious development" of all branches of the military and placed a premium on numerical strength.[103] The emphasis on the decisive nature of the initial stages of future wars required a high state of peacetime readiness: As Marshal Sokolovskii and Major General M. Cherednichenko argued, according to these scenarios "nuclear war may be conducted only with the means existing at its beginning, since it will not be possible to count on mobilization of the economy in these conditions."[104] Moreover, military professionals began to warn in the mid-1970s that the impending technological revolution in war fighting required still more investments in developing new generations of weapons.[105]

Cycle 3: The Diverging Tula Lines

In this context in 1977 Leonid Brezhnev began to press a new doctrinal innovation. The opportunity for this innovation was his consolidation of limited personal rule in the 1970s. With less control than his predecessor, Brezhnev could only press a more modest revision of military thought. Yet, even this encountered stiff opposition from military professionals. The constraints on his doctrinal guidance from the institutionalization of the two-tier structure of military thought checked Brezhnev's ability to impose his own views on military science. The combined effects of balanced leadership and reciprocal accountability forced Brezhnev to reach a compromise within the first tier on doktrina and with the military bureaucracy on the reform of military thought.

BREZHNEV'S TULA LINE

Brezhnev's doctrinal innovation began with the issue of strategic weapons—specifically, assured destruction and deterrence by punishment as ordering principles in the Soviet relationship with the United States. Yet, in subsequent elaboration, the new line had implications far beyond this. In January 1977, he set down the broad outline of the new line before a military assemblage in Tula, but he left many of its major principles undeveloped.[106] Unlike the "permanently operating factors" and "new look," the Tula line was not offered in a single definitive statement; rather, Brezhnev developed it from 1977 to 1982.

At Tula and at the 1981 Party Congress (February–March) Brezhnev publicly endorsed deterrence by punishment as central to the Soviet relationship with the West and argued that the Soviet Union should structure its forces on the capacity to deter imperialist aggression. In the words of defense minister Ustinov: "Under contemporary conditions of available weapons systems and alertness of the strategic nuclear means of the Soviet Union, the United States will not be able to carry out a counter-force attack against the socialist countries. The aggressor will not escape an all-crushing, retaliatory strike."[107] In itself this did not constitute a major doctrinal innovation; for Brezhnev was simply restating Khrushchev's position from 1960.

More revolutionary, although not promulgated as Party doktrina, was the implication that deterrence might be a mutual constraint. Prior to the 1970s there had been timid movement in this direction. In his January 1960 Supreme Soviet speech Khrushchev had hinted that in his view deterrence was mutual. In November 1969, at the opening of the SALT talks in Helsinki the Soviet delegation reportedly read an official statement endorsing the logic of mutually assured destruction as a principle for negotiating balanced arms limitations. In the 1970s Soviet spokesmen moved beyond these statements, but Brezhnev did not present the mutuality of deterrence to a domestic audience as a binding dogma; instead, it was implied in the official endorsement of two of its corollaries.[108]

The first corollary was the rejection of victory in nuclear war as a real possibility. At the 1981 Party Congress (February–March) the leadership officially placed the weight of the Party behind the view that victory in nuclear war was unlikely. By 1973 Brezhnev had individually endorsed the view that existing nuclear weapons were "capable of blowing up the entire planet"; and in July 1974, he stated "a sufficient quantity of arms has been amassed to destroy everything alive on earth several times over." Getting the Politburo to endorse these positions was a more difficult undertaking. Indeed, a diversity of opinions characterized the leadership at this time. While some Politburo members (notably Andrei Gromyko, Andrei Kirilenko, and Aleksei Kosygin) repeated Brezhnev's position, others (including Yurii Andropov and Andrei Grechko) stopped short of the claim that a future world war would destroy all civilization and limited themselves to underscoring the unprecedented nature of the destruction that would accompany it.[109] The doctrinal position that emerged at the 1981 Party Congress was a compromise formulation. Without completely dismissing the possibility of victory, Brezhnev's advocates accepted this as highly unlikely: "to count on victory in a nuclear war is dangerous madness."[110] This compromise formulation was confirmed by the general secretary later that year; in an interview with *Pravda* correspondents the general secretary revealed that the Congress statement represented the consensus on the Politburo, but that he personally subscribed to the much stronger view that with existing nuclear stockpiles second-strike retaliation would be unavoidable, victory unattainable, and nuclear war suicidal.[111]

A second corollary of the mutuality of deterrence was escalation control. For the Soviet leadership the high probability of failure should war go nuclear meant that it would be increasingly imperative to attempt to prevent the use of nuclear weapons in future conflict. As Ustinov argued in 1982, "Understanding the impossibility of prevailing in [nuclear war] is the rationale for refusing to use nuclear weapons first." At Tula Brezhnev announced that Soviet policy would be "directed squarely at avoiding either first or second strikes and at avoiding nuclear war in general." This was followed by a campaign to secure a joint declaration from the superpowers of no-first-use. Failing to secure American cooperation, in 1982 Brezhnev unilaterally renounced the first use of nuclear weapons.[112]

The unfolding Tula line brought opportunities to slow the Soviet military buildup. Doctrinally the Tula line meant rejecting superiority as a structuring objective in Soviet force posture. At Tula Brezhnev introduced the concept of "sufficiency" as an alternative (albeit vague) structuring principle: "The defense potential of the Soviet Union must be sufficient so that no one should risk threatening our peaceful life. No aspect of our policy aims at superiority in armaments."[113] By May 1982, Ustinov was declaring, "We do not need military superiority over the West. We only need reliable security and to ensure this, it is enough to have rough balance and parity."[114] This was buttressed by the assertion that superiority in nuclear weapons would bring no military advantage. In a more practical sense, the Tula line brought a commitment to defense cuts and conversion of defense industry to civilian production.[115]

COMBINED ARMS UNDER A NUCLEAR UMBRELLA

Despite their modesty Brezhnev's innovations provoked criticism from military professionals. The compromises in the publicly articulated positions of the balanced leadership and the incremental manner in which Brezhnev unfolded the Tula line permitted military professionals considerable opportunity to debate its consequences for military science.[116] In the first half of the 1980s Brezhnev's incapacitation and death permitted military professionals the autonomy to continue this debate even after doctrinal pronouncements had been made.

Even more than in previous cases of military resistance to a doctrinal innovation, selective incorporation meant that military science adapted only incrementally. Jeremy Azrael notes that "although Ogarkov paid lip service to these innovations . . . he stripped them of all operational meaning by incorporating them within what was essentially a recapitulation and updating of the 'classical' war-fighting and war-winning credo of the Soviet high command."[117] In confronting Brezhnev's contention that nuclear weapons had brought a strategic stalemate, military bureaucrats responded by restating the need for flexible response capabilities to conduct diverse combat operations both with and without nuclear weapons.[118] The emphasis on escalation control in the Tula line found a sympathetic response among military professionals who were skeptical about the ability to control destruction once nuclear weapons had been introduced: By avoiding use of nuclear weapons the Soviet Union would also be better able to bring a future conflict to a favorable conclusion by exploiting its advantage in other arms.[119] Nonetheless, there was no abandonment of the nuclear option.[120] The chief of the General Staff was particularly outspoken on the necessity of victory as an operational objective and pressed for continued development of nuclear war-fighting capabilities. Indeed, in January 1982, in his pamphlet *Always in Readiness for Defense of the Fatherland*, Ogarkov argued that nuclear weapons should be integrated into operational planning to give theater commanders "increased ability to achieve war aims."[121] Military professionals were particularly concerned about Brezhnev's unilateral declaration of no first use.[122] In the emerging military science the central objective in warfare was to win by conventional armaments, including advanced weapons based on new physical principles, and spare the Soviet Union nuclear devastation. The Soviet Union would eschew massive nuclear strikes in the initial stages of warfare and seek to separate nuclear from conventional operations. Nuclear weapons would serve principally a deterrent role against both the initiation of hostilities and their escalation.[123]

The resource claims of these "combined arms operations under a nuclear umbrella" remained high. Military professionals concluded that the Soviet Union would need to maintain a substantial conventional capability, to invest in qualitatively new weapons associated with the revolution in war fighting, and to prepare Soviet armed forces and Soviet society to be able to conduct a protracted war.[124] Interest in new technologies "based on new principles of physics" that could revolutionize war fighting also prompted these military professionals to press the leadership for high levels of investment.[125]

Mounting objections to the military plans of the Brezhnev leadership led to a showdown at a Kremlin meeting in October 1982, in which Brezhnev attempted to sell Ogarkov and other military professionals on the spending restraints he believed his doctrine legitimated. In response the military leaders emphasized the dangers in this policy, particularly in light of the increased threat to Soviet interests posed by the American military buildup. In the last month before his death Brezhnev apparently began to retreat before this assault on his defense policies. He told the conference, "Competition in military technology has sharply intensified, often acquiring a fundamentally new character. A lag in this competition is inadmissible." As a consequence, "the times are now such that the level of combat readiness of the Army and the Navy should be even higher."[126]

The death of Brezhnev and collective leadership did not resolve these issues that divided the political leadership from military professionals. The members of the Politburo continued to repeat the formulations of the last Brezhnev years, yet from 1982 to 1984 the well-balanced leadership encountered resistance from the military. Warnings by Ogarkov of the dangers posed by international imperialism and calls for investment in "utmost military readiness" continued. In the increasingly institutionalized environment of Soviet politics both Andropov and Konstantin Chernenko were guaranteed the role of commander-in-chief (chairman of the Defense Council) and the prerogative to speak authoritatively on doktrina, yet neither had the opportunity to consolidate power sufficiently to press for a thorough redirection of military science in conformity with a new doctrinal innovation. The institutionalization of the role for military bureaucrats in the articulation of military science made this more difficult.

Into this stalemate walked Mikhail Gorbachev. Although as the commander-in-chief he began to call for "new thinking in military affairs" within a year of his appointment, as a new general secretary he had at first to be cautious. Consequently, Gorbachev initially limited his "new thinking" to the concepts of his predecessors. Central to this "new thinking in military affairs" was deterrence. Gorbachev made explicit in his report to the 1986 Party Congress (February–March) what Brezhnev had previously stated: deterrence is, indeed, mutual, and nuclear war cannot be considered a rational instrument of policy.[127] For force posture this meant seeking superiority would be futile. Thus, in his report to the Congress the general secretary endorsed the Tula line concept of "reasonable sufficiency" as the structuring principle for Soviet forces. Yet, the new general secretary at first refrained from any original doctrinal innovations and did not draw out the consequences of the "new thinking." As Dale Herspring argues, "Gorbachev was not Khrushchev," and, thus, "while he made it clear that changes were needed, [Gorbachev] left it to the marshals to design a suitable strategy and decide how to allocate funds."[128] Indeed, despite rumored warnings to the military that they would have to make due with fewer resources, the consequences of the new general secretary's initial moderation was deference to military resource demands and growth in defense spending through 1987.

DOMESTIC INSTITUTIONS AND MILITARY DOCTRINES

The history of Soviet military thought, as this shows, is not a story simply about abstract ideas or even military affairs. It is also a story of domestic politics and the relationship between political leadership and one of its most important bureaucratic constituencies. The history of doctrine is punctuated by political leaders attempting to redirect military policy through the imposition of doctrinal innovations. The short-lived success of doctrinal innovations and the increasing limits on these successes over time are among the most important manifestations of the policy dysfunction of the constitution of Bolshevism. The joint effect of balanced leadership and reciprocal accountability that were increasingly institutionalized in these years was to limit the opportunities for profound reform or redirection in military affairs between 1953 and 1986.

The institutionalist focus on domestic politics as a source of military doctrine is very different from analytic approaches usually employed by western Sovietologists. The prevailing interpretive approach has tended to treat the Soviet Union as a unified rather than complex actor. As noted in the earlier discussion of contending models of Soviet politics (chapter 3), those who employ a totalitarian model of Soviet politics have typically discounted the role of either leadership conflict or differences between leaders and bureaucrats. Many Western defense analysts who employ such a model have been led by their premises to see perfect unity between doktrina and military science. This led many to mistakenly read every statement of military science as an expression of state policy. The most important misreading in recent years came from those who saw the writings of military scientists about the methods of victory in all types of wars as the plans of the political leadership to fight and win thermonuclear war.[129] Ironically, this misreading came at precisely the time when Soviet leaders were doctrinally refuting such plans.

Such unified actor models of Soviet doctrinal development have tended to explain major changes in Soviet doctrines as responses to opportunities or threats in the international arena. Both American doctrines and the East-West correlation of forces have been cited by these theories as a major impetus in Soviet doctrinal development. For example, Roman Kolkowicz describes how Soviet military thought, lagging behind American doctrines by about five years, has developed through the "educative effect" of Western doctrines "on Soviet political and military leaders, persuading the latter to exchange their own ideas and programs for 'capitalistic' and 'bourgeois' ones."[130] Yet, a simple action-reaction model of doctrinal development would encounter the disturbing fact that Soviet doctrinal reactions were often at first asymmetrical: The immediate reaction to Dwight Eisenhower's massive retaliation after 1953 was to reassert the continuing importance of traditional war fighting. Khrushchev's reaction in 1963 to the American doctrine of flexible response was to press for his own nonflexible (later called "uni-variant") massive retaliation. The symmetrical reaction followed with considerable lag: Khrushchev's new look followed Eisenhower's by almost seven years; Brezhnev's "flexible response" followed John Kennedy's by four.[131]

The attempt to describe Soviet doctrine as the unified response to a changing correlation of forces fares little better. Khrushchev's adoption of "massive retaliation" came at a time when he did not have this capability to carry it out, when the Soviet Union lagged behind the United States in nuclear forces and lacked a comparable intercontinental delivery capability. The adoption of flexible response—purportedly in response to the stalemate at the nuclear level—anticipated by almost a half-decade the achievement of nuclear parity. Indeed, these doctrinal developments seemed to have a prospective rather than reactive quality; they served more as plans for future developments than as a codification of existing practice. In short, military doctrine developed somewhat autonomously from international pressures.

In attempting to explain these lagged, nonsynchronous, and autonomous developments, the institutionalist perspective does not deny the importance of international constraints. Yet, it points out that political actors responding to international developments acted within the constraints of domestic political institutions. As the previous discussion points up, the response of Soviet political actors to these developments was often quite diverse, conditioned by their different responsibilities within the political order. More fundamentally, leaders and bureaucrats differed in what they saw as relevant international developments: At times political leaders were more insistent on the importance of a development in the international arena, such as the emergence of mutually assured destruction, and at other times the military bureaucrats pointed, for example, to the threatening buildup of American forces. Reactions to the international arena were conditioned by the roles and relationships defined in domestic politics.

This is certainly not the first attempt to link Soviet foreign policies to Soviet domestic politics.[132] Yet, its stress on institutional structure as a constraint on policy sets it apart from most of these theories. Jack Snyder's recent analysis of the domestic politics that give rise to foreign policies of overexpansion comes closest to the analytic approach presented here. Yet these analyses diverge in important ways. These approaches parallel one another in seeing leadership coalition building among Stalinist atavisms (the iron triangle) as a source of policies more in accord with the preferences of the military. Yet these approaches differ in their analyses of the institutional environment in which this coalition building takes place and of the conditions that favor the iron triangle's preferred policies. Snyder's analysis of so-called cartelized systems presents what is in essence an interest-group theory of politics, where logrolling among interests accounts for overexpansion. Conversely, the model of the two-tier political order envisions the possibility that leaders in the first tier can rise above these interests in the second tier to organize collective action and force trade-offs among interests rather than simply logrolling within a cartel. These two views of the institutional environment have important implications for our expectations about foreign policies. Assertive foreign policies, such as overexpansion, require a strong leader in the first tier; these policies are unlikely to emerge from simple logrolling among interests in the second tier. Indeed, the three periods of overexpansion cited by Snyder closely correspond to the apex of each leader's directive rule: Stalin (1947–1950), Khrushchev (1958–1962), and Brezhnev (1975–1980). Simple logrolling among second-tier interests in a cartelized polity might lead to overexpansion of spending, as I argued in chapter 7, where this could be achieved by each bureaucracy acting on its own, but logrolling lacks the leadership necessary to carry out an assertive foreign policy. The latter appears to be associated with directive rule. But what would lead a directive leader to want to make such policy payoffs to the iron triangle when he has the power to impose sacrifices on the second tier? Overexpansion, as Snyder labels it, is apparently associated with contested directorship—a directive leader under threat of desertion from his iron triangle constituencies. This also accounts for the inconsistency observed in these periods that overexpansion came while the leader was attempting to redistribute resources at home: Particularly in the Khrushchev and Brezhnev periods, the assertive foreign policies were coupled with attempts to cut defense spending—an anomaly that cannot be explained by cartelization alone.[133] Periods of simple logrolling within a cartel without strong first-tier leadership were, instead, associated with high defense spending, but less assertive foreign policies.[134] To analyze these complexities requires moving beyond a single-tier analysis of cartels to a two-tier model of coalition formation and policymaking.

The Failure of Constitutional
Reform, 1987–1991

INSTITUTIONAL maladaptation and policy dysfunction were rooted in constitutional structures. The very same institutionalization of these structures that brought stability to the polity led to greater institutional rigidity and a political order that could not adapt to change. The development of the constitutional order brought it to the point where it faced a stark choice: On the one hand, continuation of bureaucratic reciprocal accountability was likely to bring further petrification in politics. On the other hand, the changes that might bring policy innovation and institutional adaptability struck at the very foundations of the constitutional order. Institutionalization of the rules of bureaucratic reciprocal accountability and enforcement of sanctions against violators made such reforms unlikely to succeed. Institutionalization meant that incumbents privileged by the existing order fought change by enforcing sanctions against reformers. Attempts to overwhelm the institutional defenses of the existing order elicited increasing resistance and, in the end, enough pressure brought not reform, but collapse of the constitutional order.

Constitutional reform, in the institutionalist perspective developed here, concerns changes in the fundamental rules of policymaking and accountability. This neo-institutional analysis draws attention to the ways in which institutional structures shape the objectives of the reformer, the strategy and tactics of reform, and the response of the incumbents privileged by the existing constitutional order. The objective of a constitutional reformer who seeks to attack the roots of institutional maladaptation and policy dysfunction under bureaucratic reciprocal accountability must be the structure of the selectorate and its relationship to the policymakers. Even as he attempts to reform the existing constitutional order, the reformer will be constrained by its rules, so his strategy and tactics must use the rules of the status quo against it. These constraints are enforced by the incumbents privileged by the status quo, who are likely to resist changes in the constitutional order and may threaten to stop the whole enterprise of reform. Throughout this analysis, the institutional approach focuses our attention on political institutions and the state as causal factors in this process.

The institutional development of the constitution of Bolshevism confronted Soviet leaders with a stark choice between stagnation and constitutional change. The constitutional rigidity had limited the adaptability of the political system to social change, including, paradoxically, to social changes the political system had itself engineered. By limiting membership in the selectorate and tying this to bureaucratic roles with assigned missions, the constitutional order made it difficult for the political system to respond to social changes. Institutionalization of ex officio membership in the Central Committee, routinization of appointments to key job-slots, and reinforced sanctions against expansion of the political process meant that the Soviet political system could not bring in the new social forces created by socioeconomic change. The most dynamic development of new roles had taken place outside the selectorate. As a result of the changes engineered by the bureaucracies of state building and early industrialization, the intelligentsia had rapidly grown to a significant stratum of society. Yet, the cadre of scientists, engineers, professionals, and managers could not be accommodated in the institutions of bureaucratic reciprocal accountability. This was aggravated by the stability of personnel under Leonid Brezhnev. As the waiting period to assume a job-slot stretched out to a decade or more, the excluded intelligentsia developed deep resentments against the institutional order. Yet, the problem was more fundamental than this: the institutional limits on the selectorate meant that more rapid turnover could not accommodate much of the selectorate. Turnover alone within an unchanging institutional context could not incorporate in the political process representatives of an intelligentsia that was significantly more diverse than the job-slots.

The choice to begin reform was not foreordained, and, indeed, most general secretaries in the 1980s seemed unlikely to attempt such a change; yet, the hard trade-off between greater stagnation and constitutional reform of some sort was set by the constitutional order. As both Boris Yeltsin and Yegor Ligachev have noted, the choices confronting the leaders in 1985 led in various directions—not necessarily toward constitutional reform. Powerful voices in both the Politburo and the Central Committee spoke for a very different path than constitutional reform.[1] Yeltsin and Ligachev have stressed that the leaders knew they faced such a choice; if they chose to break the institutional stagnation and policy dysfunction, then they would have to begin to reform the political order. At the February 1987 Trade Union Congress, Gorbachev framed what he saw as the stark choice confronting the country in simple terms: "So, the question today is this: either democratization or social inertia and conservatism. There is no third way, comrades."[2]

The institutionalization of the constitution of Bolshevism had ensured that the choice was the prerogative of the leadership alone. Under Leonid Brezhnev, Yurii Andropov, and Konstantin Chernenko the leadership had strengthened the barriers to entry into the political order by reinforcing departicipation. The excluded intelligentsia remained an inert social force as long as policies of departicipation deprived them of the resources essential to collective action.[3] To energize this inert social force, political actors enfranchised within the existing constitutional order had to begin changing the institutional constraints on participation. This began under Mikhail Gorbachev, who attempted to reform the constitution of Bolshevism by reaching out to the unenfranchised intelligentsia. In turning to the tasks of glasnost', perestroika, and demokratizatsiia, Gorbachev confronted the Soviet polity with issues well beyond the realm of "normal" politics. He reached outside the political system to empower the unenfranchised intelligentsia, giving them access to the resources necessary for collective action. He sought to create new rules redefining the locus and accountability of policymaking.

Although this choice was not foreordained, the agenda of reforms as well as the strategy and tactics necessary to crack the institutionalized stagnation and policy dysfunction were set by the constitutional order. So was the high likelihood that this attempt could fail. The structural constraints of the constitution of Bolshevism confronted the general secretary with an uphill battle. Gorbachev's strategy and tactics had to use the rules of the constitution of Bolshevism to change it. Yet, the very process of institutionalization had developed elaborate defenses against changes in the rules of the constitutional order. The actors privileged by those rules resisted change, and, in the end, their resistance was so intense that the order collapsed rather than change.

This is the third chapter presenting case studies of reform under the constitution of Bolshevism. It analyzes the tumultuous events in the Soviet Union under Mikhail Gorbachev—particularly, from the January 1987 Central Committee Plenum to the resignation of Gorbachev on 25 December 1991. This brief five-year period was punctuated by dramatic events to which the following discussion refers repeatedly:

January 1987	Central Committee: Democratization program begins
June 1988	19th Party Conference endorses democratization
December 1988	Parliament amends Soviet Constitution
March 1989	Elections to Congress of Peoples Deputies
Spring 1990	Republic and local elections
August 1991	Armed coup d'état fails
December 1991	USSR formally dissolved

I argue that this period cannot be understood without making constitutional reform central to our analysis. First, issues of constitutional design set the key objectives of the period—to break the constitutional basis of stagnation. Second, the constitutional structure of the old order constrained the strategy and tactics of the constitutional reformers. Third, it structured the resistance to change that blocked reform and brought down the constitutional order. Curiously, much Western analysis of this period has proceeded as though Soviet politics took place in an institution-free environment. This chapter, divided in three parts, retells this story in the new light of institutions. First, I review the constitutional changes from 1987 to 1991 that began to replace bureaucratic reciprocal accountability. Second, I examine the ways in which the existing institutional structure of bureaucratic reciprocal accountability constrained the strategy and tactics in this process of constitutional transformation. And third, I discuss how these constitutional changes began to not only remedy some policy dysfunction and institutional stagnation of the constitution of Bolshevism but also heighten resistance from the iron triangle and finally bring collapse rather than a reformed constitutional order.

ENGINEERING CONSTITUTIONAL REFORM

Constitutional reform at its most fundamental level concerns the institutions of policymaking and their accountability. To transform bureaucratic reciprocal accountability reforms must replace reciprocal accountability by hierarchy, change the bureaucratic nature of the selectorate, or both. The first change creates a sovereign power—placing either the selectors or leaders beyond accountability to the other. Under the constitution of Bolshevism, the more likely threat to reciprocal accountability came from an autocrat in the first tier who institutionalized his hierarchical control so as to pass it on to a chosen heir. With this change reciprocal accountability and its potential for oscillations between collective and directive leadership and between first- and second-tier accountability would give way to hierarchical directorship under a sovereign power. Joseph Stalin had come closest to exercising this type of power, but he was unable to institutionalize it in a way that could preserve this power beyond his death and pass it on to his chosen heir. Indeed, as early studies of the succession problem have pointed out, because any designated heir was a potential threat to the sitting autocrat, it was difficult to institutionalize the succession without jeopardizing this autocratic power.[4] The alternative hierarchical order would establish the selectorate as sovereign and deprive the leaders of control over selectors. The second threat to bureaucratic reciprocal accountability came from expansion of the selectorate beyond the bureaucracies of early state building and industrialization. Under the constitution of Bolshevism, this threat was likely to originate in the first tier and could come with either extreme fragmentation or consolidation of leadership. Fragmentation, leading to stalemate in the leadership and the breakdown of sanctions against defection, might induce individual leaders to seek to outdo one another by mobilizing new constituencies outside the selectorate. With consolidation, however, a strong leader might impose change on the composition of the selectorate.

Early in his administration Mikhail Gorbachev began to pose questions central to breaking the dead hand of stagnation—how to press reform against forces of stagnation and how to make reform both irreversible and inherent in the constitutional structure. Gorbachev began to argue that stagnation was rooted in the constitutional order and that the solution to that stagnation must be constitutional transformation. To reform the Soviet system, it was not enough to change personnel and policies; nor was it enough to tinker with individual organizations. After such changes in the past the constitutional equilibrium reasserted itself. If individual reforms were to be sustained and the Soviet system was to become adaptable to social change, a transformation of constitutional foundations was required. In his resignation speech in December 1991, Mikhail Gorbachev recounts his original assessment: "Fate ordained that when I became head of state it was already clear that things were not going well in the country. . . . The reason was evident—society was suffocating in the grip of the command-bureaucratic system. . . . All attempts at partial reforms—and there were a good many of them—failed, one after the other. The country had lost direction. It was impossible to go on living that way. Everything had to be changed fundamentally."[5] The basis of the Gorbachev agenda was constitutional reform—to transform the constitutional structure so as to make the policy processes more hospitable to reform and political institutions more adaptable to social change.

The institutional changes introduced from January 1987 to August 1991 began to assault the constitutional foundations of bureaucratic reciprocal accountability. As of the coup of August 1991 these changes in the rules of politics had begun to redefine the roles of policymakers and selectors and the relationships of accountability between them. First, they created institutions to replace reciprocal by hierarchical accountability in the relationship between selectors and policymakers and, thus, to establish a relationship of sovereignty in which selectors were principals and both policymakers and bureaucrats were their agents. Second, these changes redefined the criteria for inclusion in the selectorate—eliminating the monopoly of bureaucrats performing the tasks of early state building and industrialization. We cannot know whether these changes would have led to Western-style parliamentary or presidential democracy, for the reform was cut short by the collapse of the constitutional order. These changes, however, did break the stagnation that had gripped the constitution of Bolshevism and enabled the political system to begin to innovate in policy and to adapt to social change. In the unfolding Gorbachev agenda, three institutional changes were central: (1) the "participant" population was expanded by opening debates over policy to greater public scrutiny and by involving a broader elite; (2) the selectorate was expanded and its hierarchical control over policymakers was increasingly freed from the constraint of reciprocal accountability; and (3) control over bureaucrats was transferred to elected policymakers, while bureaucrats were deprived of their monopolistic role in the selectorate. The following sections briefly survey the laws used to shape these rules of the new political order.

Making Politics Public (Glasnost')

Beginning in 1986 the population empowered to participate in public debates—but not to select the policymakers—was expanded by opening the press, raising the veil of secrecy from around the deliberations of policymaking bodies, and lifting the limits on associational activity. Public opinion was to become a force that could constrain policymakers and bureaucrats. Gorbachev told the Party Congress on 25 February 1986, "those who have grown accustomed to doing slipshod work, who engage in hoodwinking, will indeed be uncomfortable in the light of public openness, when everything done in the state and in society is done under the people's supervision and in full sight of the people."[6] Making politics public, a critical preliminary step, did not itself change the constitutional structure through the locus or accountability of policymaking. Glasnost' permitted freer expression of opinions within official organs and the creation of an independent press and autonomous groupings outside these organs. As a first step it was a necessary precondition for institutional changes in the locus of policymaking and the accountability of policymakers to the selectorate.

To inform the citizenry of public affairs, information was made more readily available. This began in June 1986 with the abolition of prior censorship by the Main Administration of Literature and State Publishing (Glavlit) and culminated on 12 June 1990 in the law on press freedom that codified the abolition of censorship, guaranteed independence of nonparty press and freedom of citizens to establish newspapers, and obliged government officials to answer questions posed by journalists. The law established the editorial management of media outlets as juristic persons. While it provided for registration of media outlets, it permitted public dissemination by unregistered outlets with press runs under 1,000.[7]

At the same time policy debates within the leadership were increasingly being opened to larger scrutiny. At first this required breaking the convention that had suppressed appeals by Politburo members to outside constituencies. Rules requiring collective approval of major statements by its members continued to exercise significant constraint on such appeals during the first years of the Gorbachev administration, but the public solidarity of the Politburo began to break down so that at the October 1987 Central Committee Plenum Boris Yeltsin could attack his fellow Politburo member Yegor Ligachev for obstructing perestroika.[8] Subsequently conservatives pressed to punish Yeltsin for violating the norms against defection, but Gorbachev resisted this, sidestepping the issue by appointing a fact-finding commission. With Gorbachev's protection, Yeltsin continued to attack conservative leaders, and by the June 1988 Party Conference, debates among leaders were permitted to come into public view.[9]

Opening the Selectorate

The constitutional structure of bureaucratic reciprocal accountability began to change most profoundly with expansion of the selectorate and changes in the criteria for membership in it. This changed with two institutional reforms—changes in the composition of the Central Committee and transfer of Politburo decisionmaking powers to other posts accountable to alternative selectorates. These changed the incentive structures of policymakers by changing the constituencies to which they would have to appeal to gain and hold office.

The first of these changes hinged on democratizing the election procedures within the Communist party and opening recruitment into the Central Committee. Throughout these years Gorbachev pressed the Party to introduce real competition in elections to its offices. At the February 1990 Central Committee Plenum, he proposed new rules for election of delegations to the upcoming Congress, but in the face of resistance it was decided at the Plenum the following month to let each regional organization establish its own regulations to elect delegations to the Congress scheduled for July. This opened the process somewhat, for in 135 of 164 organizations elections involved competitive candidacies, but many competitive elections were still controlled by the Party secretaries.[10] The Party apparatus continued to resist, and as late as August 1991 real competitive elections throughout the Party were far from a reality.

The second of these paths to changing the selectorate entailed creation of the presidency, expansion of the legislative authority of the soviets, and devolution of central powers onto lower levels of government. The amendments to the Soviet Constitution adopted in December 1988 began this process. The office of the presidency, if left to stand, could fundamentally change the incentive structures of future leaders. Alongside the Central Committee that elected the leader in his role as general secretary, the new Congress of Peoples Deputies elected the leader in his role as president. Jerry Hough has observed about the presidency, "while the legal powers of the new president are impressive, they are not very different from the de facto powers of the old general secretary."[11] There is an important truth here, yet it misses the important shift that had taken place: This reform could dramatically change the accountability of the individual holding these powers. To win support in the Congress of People's Deputies, the leader would have to satisfy a very different set of constituencies. Initially accountability to the population was indirect, but by a further constitutional amendment adopted 13 March 1990, future candidates for the president of the USSR would stand for popular election every five years.[12] (See figure 9.1.)

Broad legislative powers previously held by the Central Committee shifted to the new Congress of Peoples Deputies and the parliament (Supreme Soviet) following the December 1988 amendments to the Soviet Constitution.[13] Already by July 1989, Nikolai Ryzhkov observed that policymaking was passing from the leading organs of the Party to those of the state.[14] The new Congress of Peoples Deputies brought together representatives of a much broader spectrum of constituencies than the Central Committee. The bureaucracies of early state building and industrialization were losing their monopolies. Citizens who were neither top political leaders nor officeholders in the upper or middle echelons of administration had held only 11.4 percent of the seats in the Central Committee elected in 1986, but they held 59.5 percent in the new Congress of Peoples Deputies.[15] As a consequence of this shift, legislation began to respond to new constituencies.

By transferring central powers to lower levels of government, policymaking was supposed to become even more responsive to the populace. Gorbachev's reports to the 1986 Party Congress and 1988 Party Conference outlined two steps to expand the accountability of local governments: First, legislative bodies (soviets or councils) would be strengthened, relative to their respective executive agencies, by elevating the status of deputies and improving their electoral control over executive and administrative officers. Second, decentralization of decisionmaking to local soviets would transfer "many powers to the local level," expand their authority over economic entities operating within their territories, and grant them some independent fiscal authority.[16]

The extent to which these organizational changes transformed the incentives of policymakers depended on the guarantees of electoral accountability. In his report to the 1988 Party Conference, Gorbachev

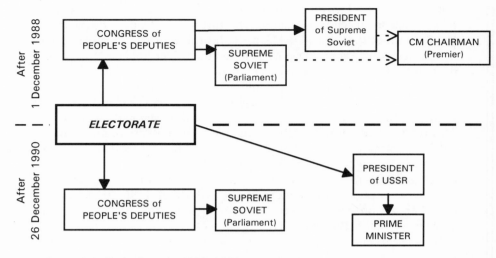

Figure 9.1. State Organs, 1988–1991

added to his list of changes improved mechanisms for nomination and election of deputies to soviets and expanded "direct democracy" to vote "much more often than is now done, especially on questions that vitally affect people and on which there is no single opinion." In June 1987, multiple candidate races in local elections had been introduced in 5 percent of the constituencies. The electoral law, adopted on 1 December 1988, applied this throughout the country.[17] The right to nominate candidates was granted to voters' meetings of 500 or more, which could nominate an unlimited number of candidates for each position. Voters would be required to pass through the booth before depositing their ballots, making it possible to defeat candidates even when only a single name appeared on the list.[18] In the 26 March 1989 elections to the Congress of Peoples Deputies, 2,895 candidates stood for election to the 1,500 seats allocated to popular constituencies.[19]

The electoral mechanism was supported by new rules to protect the organization of social interests into groups. Gorbachev called for "a mechanism for the unhindered formation and identification of the interests and will of all classes and social groups and their coordination and realization in the domestic and foreign policies of the Soviet state." For example, in the context of his discussion of the unresolved "women's question," Gorbachev argued that one "reason why this situation would last for years was the fact that women's opinions were not carefully considered. They do not have proper representation in executive bodies."[20] The third (extraordinary) convocation of the Congress of Peoples Deputies in March 1990 amended Article 7 of the Soviet Constitution to remove restrictions on social organizations outside the Communist party; a new Article 51 guaranteed the right to form alternative political parties. The Law on Public Associations signed into law on 9 October 1990 gave legal status to political parties as groups seeking representation in the soviets and seeking to form the bodies of state power and administration.[21]

Controlling the Bureaucracy

Transforming bureaucratic reciprocal accountability required improving the control of elected officials over the bureaucracy. At the January 1987 Central Committee Plenum Gorbachev claimed that bureaucrats had limited the power of Soviet deputies and Party members "in the formation of executive committees, in the selection of personnel, and in monitoring their activity," and he called for elected bodies to assert greater authority over administrators and executives.[22] To break the lock of bureaucrats over the soviets to which they were supposedly accountable, the resolution of the 1988 Party Conference "On Democratization and Political Reform" declared that soviet state bureaucrats would be prohibited from running in elections to the corresponding soviets that should exercise oversight.[23] If applied throughout the Soviet polity this would help break the bureaucracy's role in the selectorate and subject it to hierarchical control by elected politicians.

At the all-union level this meant establishing the accountability of ministers to elected officials. As a consequence of the amendments to the Soviet Constitution adopted in December 1988 and legislation adopted at the first sessions of the new Congress of Peoples Deputies, the premier (chairman of the Council of Ministers) would be nominated by the president, confirmed by the parliament (Supreme Soviet), and ratified by the larger Congress of Peoples Deputies; he could be removed upon presidential recommendation and Supreme Soviet approval.[24] (See figure 9.1.) Nominations of ministers and state committee chairmen submitted by the premier would be ratified by the parliament (Supreme Soviet). On its own initiative, the parliament (Supreme Soviet) could vote no confidence in the government (Council of Ministers) and by a two-thirds vote could remove it. Frustrated by the continued autonomy of the bureaucracy Gorbachev on 5 December 1990 proposed subordinating all executive agencies to the presidency. In the amendments to the Soviet Constitution he signed on 26 December 1990, the president gained direct control through his power of appointment over the new Cabinet of Ministers and over the prime minister who directed the cabinet's daily activities.[25]

Establishing accountability of the bureaucrats to elected state officials also required reducing independent Communist party controls over the bureaucracy and eliminating its leading role within state administrations.

At the 1988 Party Conference the resolution "On Bureaucratism" warned that "it is the duty of Party organizations and of all Communists to strive for unswerving observance of the principle that the administrative apparatus serves and is fully accountable to elected bodies, Soviet power, and the people. Any actions on its part that lead to the distortion or emasculation of laws and government decisions are unconstitutional."[26] In September 1988, to reduce the Party apparatus, the departments of the Central Committee were consolidated from twenty to nine, their staff cut by 30 percent, and the Secretariat's work was assumed by commissions; these cuts were duplicated at lower levels.[27]

Of course, the constitution of Bolshevism was not transformed simply by formal legislative enactments, but by changing the actual rules of politics. Formal rules, nonetheless, were important in codifying changes in the constitutional foundations of Soviet politics. It moved the locus of policymaking and redirected the accountability of policymakers. It redefined the criteria for inclusion in the selectorate, stripping the bureaucracies of early industrialization and state building of their previous monopoly. It began to replace reciprocal accountability with sovereign delegation in which bureaucrats were accountable to policymakers who in turn were accountable to a selectorate independent of the bureaucracy.

Whether these changes would have transformed bureaucratic reciprocal accountability was still unclear at the point the Soviet polity collapsed. The future relationship of the general secretary to the presidency was unclear, although following the August 1991 coup Gorbachev resigned the former post and began to build a presidency completely independent from the Communist party. Reassertion of Communist party discipline in state organs with Communist majorities might in the future have returned their behavior to the dependent agencies that characterized the early Soviet republic. The transformation of the Communist party apparatus into an integrated electorate machine (perhaps resembling Mexico's Partido Revolucionario Institucional) could have stripped popular elections of any real accountability control. The success of the constitutional reforms would only become clear with time as the behavior of significant political actors revealed how their mutually reinforcing expectations had changed the rules of the game.

INSTITUTIONS AND CONSTITUTIONAL TRANSFORMATION

The institutionalist perspective stresses that the task of constitutional reform that Gorbachev faced was not simply a problem of institution building, but of institutional transformation; and this shaped the strategy and tactics of reform. *Constitutional transformation* is a daunting task—

using existing institutions to create new ones. The task of the leader intent upon constitutional transformation may be more difficult than that of the classic revolutionary, for he does not step into a political vacuum or draft institutions on a tabula rasa. In constitutional transformation, existing institutions must be convinced, tricked, or forced into relinquishing responsibilities. The old constitution constrains the strategic choices of the reformer. As the constitution changes, the nature of those constraints also changes, and the task confronting the reformer is to continuously adjust strategies and tactics to accommodate these changing constraints.

Gorbachev's attempts to transform the constitutional order were constrained by the prevailing rules, which necessarily shaped his strategy and tactics and led to changes often tentative and riddled with inconsistencies. In explaining this tentativeness and inconsistency by the constraints on Gorbachev's strategy and tactics, the institutionalist analysis developed here diverges significantly from the most common approaches in Western sovietology. The latter have tended to explain the hesitation and inconsistency in Gorbachev's reform by speculating about the leader's true motives, by looking within the great man rather than at the institutions that constrained his choices.

One school of analysts has explained this hesitation and inconsistency in reform by arguing that Gorbachev was not a radical reformer in this period and certainly not a democrat; he was simply a consolidating general secretary.[28] Reviewing the first five years of the Gorbachev administration, John Gooding observes, "democratization emerges as, if not insincere, then at least highly limited in scope: it may affect life at the grassroots, but it will not be allowed to influence the major institutions of the state and its purpose is to strengthen rather than to undermine the position of the Communist party."[29] After almost six years of Gorbachev's rule, Jerry Hough argued that Westerners had erred in equating perestroika with democratization: "This image of Gorbachev involved a good deal of deception or self-deception. However democratic his pretensions, Gorbachev was engaged in a very methodical and ruthless consolidation of power."[30] The institutionalist approach developed here recognizes these assertions as important caveats. Gorbachev's constitutional revolution certainly did permit the general secretary to weaken some institutional limits on his power that had emerged under the constitution of Bolshevism. It also remains uncertain whether Gorbachev's constitutional changes were designed to build a Western-style parliamentary democracy. Yet, neither caveat denies the fact that fundamental constitutional changes introduced by Gorbachev changed normal politics, set the evolution of Soviet institutions on a radically different trajectory, and held the promise of greater institutional adaptability and policy innovation. The institutionalist approach developed here does not deny the power consolidation that accompanied Gorbachev's program. Yet, to ignore the changing institutional context in which this took place misses the most important and enduring changes.

A second school of analysts has attempted to explain the hesitation and inconsistencies in the reform effort by citing Gorbachev's pragmatism. According to this, Gorbachev began his administration with a limited reform agenda, but under political pressures he evolved into a more radical reformist. Harry Gelman argues that "Gorbachev did not have a consistent strategy or a single blueprint for reform because he lacked an integrating vision of how to coordinate advance in different spheres simultaneously. In addition, his notion of what he wanted in each arena has been continuously evolving."[31] Archie Brown argues that Gorbachev's willingness to tolerate democratization only grew with pragmatic evolution in his own position.[32] Alternatively, the institutionalist analysis developed here stresses that Gorbachev's apparent ambivalence toward or resistance to change was dictated by the strategic and tactical necessities of the existing constitutional order. Moreover, in retrospect the strategic sequencing of steps is difficult to explain by simple pragmatic adaptation. Although Gorbachev may not initially have imagined the full range of reforms in place by August 1991, he artfully orchestrated unfolding reforms that increasingly challenged the old constitutional order. Between 1987 and 1991 Mikhail Gorbachev presided over constitutional reforms that opened politics to the unenfranchised intelligentsia in a way that suggests considerable forethought and planning.

This is not to say that Gorbachev was from the very start set on a path of radical constitutional reform. Some Western sovietologists claim to see the broad outlines of a radical program even before Gorbachev's election as general secretary—for example, in his speech to Party ideological workers on 10 December 1984. He used the term glasnost' and spoke of transformation as the only way to fight "conservatism, indifference, and stagnation." Richard Sakwa describes the speech as "the manifesto of the first phase of perestroika."[33] Gorbachev has himself made such claims: In his speech to cultural leaders on 28 November 1990, Gorbachev suggested that he had resolved to transform the structural foundations of Soviet politics during his seven years service in Moscow before assuming the general secretaryship.[34] Yet, this interpretation must be viewed with some skepticism. The true initial intentions of the new general secretary cannot be ascertained with the evidence now available to us. Gorbachev's own claims about his early intentions must remain suspect. The claims of those who see his agenda in his early speeches are contradicted by many Western analysts reading the same early speeches, who at the time stressed the extent of continuity with the policies of his predecessors. His inaugural address at the March 1985 Central Committee Plenum, for example, promised to implement the "strategic line" put forth by Andropov and Chernenko, including improvement of the economic mechanism and "further perfection and development of democracy and the whole system of social self-government."[35] Nonetheless, as the following institutional analysis underscores, these speeches also cannot be taken as evidence that Gorbachev was not all along committed to constitutional transformation. If he was a revolutionary from the very start and had telegraphed his true intentions by these early speeches, then he would have probably been defeated in his bid to win and hold office and press reform. Whether the speeches mark limited intent as well as prudence cannot be ascertained.

The conundrum of constitutional transformation shaped the politics of constitutional reform. That is, at the core of constitutional transformation was the problem of nurturing the new constitution in the arms of the old—inducing political actors empowered by an existing constitutional order to change the rules of the game. Even as Gorbachev sought to transform the Soviet constitution, he was constrained by its existing roles and rules. As he implemented constitutional transformation, the locus of the first-tier shifted from Party to state, and the composition of the second tier changed; thus, his tactics had to change as he built a new constitutional order. The conundrum of constitutional transformation had three important consequences for the politics of constitutional reform: it set the *objectives* of rule change and institutionalization; it shaped the *processes* of dynamic coalition maintenance; and it constrained both the *tactics* of policy entrepreneurship and the *strategy* for sequencing and timing. The following discussion looks at each of these—objectives, processes, tactics, and strategy—in turn.

Rule Changes and Institutionalization

Constitutional transformation involved rewriting the rules of politics by using the rules of the old order to erode some and to create others. Central to this was the task of institutionalization—that is, creating new mutually reinforcing expectations among relevant political actors that would sustain the new rules. This objective severely constrained the strategy and tactics of Gorbachev.

Constitutional transformation, constrained by existing rules, had to work through these rules to subvert them. For example, between 1986 and 1990 in seeking to change the composition of the Central Committee and rules of the Party, Gorbachev was constrained by the Party statute that required (1) a two-thirds vote of the committee to remove its members and (2) Party Congress approval of rule changes.[36] By calling the June 1988 Party Conference Gorbachev sought to remedy these constraints. In preparing for the conference, Gorbachev tried to convince the June 1987 Plenum that the conference should not be limited by existing party rules: "Many conferences held at important points of our history resolved issues that went far beyond the bounds of the tactical. In a number of cases, tasks of a strategic character were raised at them; changes were made in the party rules and in the composition of central party organs."[37] Yet, by the statutes of the Party, underscored by the mandate of the Central Committee, the conference had neither the power to remove Central Committee members nor the authority to change the statutes. The 1988 Party Conference endorsed a new rule to hold Party conferences every two or three years and to give them the right to replace up to 20 percent of the membership of Party committees.[38] Nonetheless, this amendment to the statutes would have to be adopted by the next Party Congress because the conference would not violate the Party statutes and assume this power to ratify. Only at the 1990 Party Congress (July) were the statutes changed so that in the interval between congresses the Central Committee could convene conferences that could replace up to one-third of the Central Committee membership and revise the Party statutes.[39]

Institutionalization required creating expectations among major political actors that the new constitutional rules provide the most effective means to pursue their interests—that prudence dictates conformity. Institutionalization had to be built on utilitarian calculation constrained by expectations about the behavior of others: Significant actors should expect that the rules provide positive rewards to them and to other significant political actors—at least more than could be gained from nonconformity. Each political actor's expectations are reinforced by the expectation that others conform to these rules and that these others expect the actor and still others to conform. In short, Gorbachev had to create the mutually reinforcing expectation among relevant actors that by not conforming to the new expectation they would not be better off because others would conform and would expect them to conform.

Owing to these demands for institutionalization of rule changes, the process by which the new constitution was created was particularly important. First, the process had to make the focal points for mutual expectations prominent or conspicuous. Second, the task of institutionalization also demanded that significant political actors not see the rules of the new constitution as intrinsically partisan. Thus, Gorbachev had to formulate changes in rules as explicitly as possible and to elicit formal declarations of endorsement from all major actors. Gorbachev undertook the laborious process of earning endorsement of constitutional changes by the institutions of the old order—such as winning prior approval in Central Committee plenary sessions even when that body was losing its critical role—as well as gaining endorsement of the institutions of the new constitutional order such as the Congress of Peoples' Deputies. This was designed to coordinate expectations by explicit declarations of rules endorsed by all major actors.

The task of institutionalization further demanded that the tactics used to create the new constitutional order not subvert that order. Gorbachev's objective was to create new rules, but expectations that supported those rules were in part shaped by his actions to create the new constitutional order. Both right and left pressed Gorbachev for strong executive action, yet this was fundamentally at variance with the type of political order he sought to create.[40] Gorbachev argued against excessive reliance on such methods. Following his September 1988 trip to Krasnoyarsk he stressed that it is time to abandon "faith in a 'benevolent tsar,' in an omnipotent center, in someone instilling order from above and organizing restructuring."[41] In response to strong pressure from conservatives to use authoritarian methods to establish order, in November 1990 Gorbachev told a meeting of Peoples Deputies from the Armed Forces:

> I and my closest associates who are developing the concept and policies of *perestroika* proceed from the premise that in moving from undemocratic forms of life, we should resolve all questions using democratic methods, not in a way that would produce whites and red, blues and blacks, that would again lead to witch-hunts and a search for enemies, and that would all result in a civil war and confrontation, in which the main losses would be borne by our people.[42]

If the objective was to create the expectation that policy in the future would be made and implemented according to new constitutional procedures, then the means used to press reform could not subvert that expectation. ending

The process of subverting old rules and creating new ones ran three risks. First, this process could become stalled at some undesirable midpoint that was suboptimal from the perspective of all players. For example, Andrei Sakharov warned in 1988 against tactical compromises that might become permanent: "the changes in the Constitution and the electoral law will define our political life for a very long time. It will be difficult to change anything within this framework. So they must be thought out very carefully."[43] Second, the process of eroding conventions before new ones had taken their place could threaten the political order. For example, Soviet conventions against military and police intervention in politics eroded with the Party's leadership role, but new conventions of civilian state control were still weak by the time of the August 1991 coup. Where it did not create new conventions, constitutional transformation could leave simple anarchy.

Third, the leader's role in institutionalization created risks. In attempting to create new expectations about the leader's new institutionalized role, Gorbachev had to eschew personalistic or clientelistic ties to either conservatives or reformers; this meant he could not develop the loyalties that would support him to the culmination of the enterprise. Gorbachev did not cultivate strong personalistic ties to either conservatives or reformers. Gorbachev was not himself loyal to his right wing. For example, in May 1989 he conceded to the demand of the Party apparatus that he delay the elections to local and republic offices in order to permit them to regroup. Yet, in the wake of the miners' strike that summer he announced that he would permit republics to press forward with elections earlier, and he let many apparatchiki go down to defeat. Nor was he loyal to his left wing. Upon resigning, both Eduard Shevardnadze and Aleksandr Yakovlev complained that Gorbachev had not shielded them from the harsh tactics of the right. In return, neither wing was loyal to the president. Gorbachev seemed to respond with surprise to the desertion of his coalition partners. When radicals turned on him, he seemed to respond with unusual shows of a sense of betrayal. He explained the desertion of Shevardnadze and Yakovlev in the following terms: "these processes entered a phase of serious struggle. There's cross fire and the president, the general secretary is in the middle of the cross fire and not everybody can put up with it, not everybody can stand the test, the terrible strain which you have to feel and go through."[44] He was no more effective at explaining the desertion of some of his closest advisers in the August 1991 coup. This was a dilemma of constitutional transformation: Constitution building came through new institutional structures, but the process required strong loyalties to sustain the leader through its rocky moments; yet, the demands of institutionalization limited the leader's ability to form such alliances.

Dynamic Coalition-Maintenance

The enterprise of constitutional transformation was constrained by the twin imperatives of maintaining support among empowered political actors, while expanding the political process to bring in new social forces. The general secretary could not lose the support of the empowered, lest they remove him and scuttle the whole enterprise of constitutional transformation. Yet, reforming the constitutional order meant tempting exactly this because constitutional transformation reduced the weight of incumbents within the selectorate. Constitutional transformation was a delicate problem of balancing a growing coalition of empowered bureaucrats and newly enfranchised social forces.

Two ploys that helped tip the balance of organizational resources within the Gorbachev coalition were the reduction of bureaucracies and the opening of politics to public scrutiny. By cutting bureaucracies Gorbachev eroded some of their advantages in organizational resources. Gorbachev first turned his knife on the state bureaucracy. From 1986 to 1990, the number of ministers fell from fifty-five to thirty-seven and the number of state committees from twenty-three to nineteen; the staffs of the new ministries were cut by as much as one-third. He also turned on the Party bureaucracy. After the 30 September 1988 Central Committee Plenum, the number of Party departments was reduced from twenty to nine. Finally came the military and KGB; by preemptive actions permitting the overthrow of East European communist regimes, Gorbachev cut the coercive arms of the regime from significant parts of their extended bureaucracies and from some of their most important allies.

The opening of public debate through glasnost' empowered reform-minded elites to place their issues on the policy agenda. The compartmentalization of policy sectors was replaced by a more open intersectoral confrontation over scarce resources. For example, after 1987 participation in military policymaking opened. As Benjamin Lambeth notes, "by his expansion of the number of participants, the availability of selected military data, the license to hold forth on controversial issues, and the resultant diversity of inputs into the defense debate, Gorbachev has sought to bring about a fundamental change in the structure of Soviet defense decisionmaking."[45] The inclusion of *institutchiki*, in particular, provided alternative sources of information on military-technical matters in the formulation of military doctrine. In late July 1988 foreign minister Eduard Shevardnadze launched a campaign to bring the development of military policy in line with civilian foreign policy: "major innovations in defense development should be verified at the Ministry of Foreign Affairs to determine whether they correspond juridically to existing international agreements and to state political positions." He specifically endorsed use of legislative forums to bring this about.[46] By opening public discussion, glasnost' broke the monopolistic role of the bureaucracies in providing information and options.

Yet, the newly enfranchised social forces and reformers outside the bureaucracy lacked independent organizational resources equal to the task of balancing the enfranchised bureaucrats. Seven decades of forced departicipation had left civil society without strong associations and the resources necessary for political empowerment. Reformers could still be deprived of meeting halls and access to public spaces. The reformist press remained vulnerable to both editorial interventions and denial of such critical resources as paper. The inability of the new social forces to organize all-union associations that could match the organizational resources of the incumbent selectors left them at a disadvantage.

The constraints of the constitution of Bolshevism meant that to enfranchise the reformers as a counterweight to the central bureaucracies Gorbachev had to find them a bureaucratic niche. This he found in the republics. As early as June 1988 Gorbachev began pressing that "the rights of the Union republics must be rethought and brought into conformity with the radical economic reform."[47] In November 1988, Gorbachev announced that "the next major stage of political transformation will be linked to the harmonizing of relations between the USSR and its constituent republics. Questions of the status of the Union republics, of expanding their rights and possibilities in political, social, economic, and cultural life, and of consolidating our federal socialist state on this basis will be examined at this stage."[48] The political logic of this strategy was fairly straightforward. First, the republics formed the most important power base from which an alternative to the iron triangle could be created. By the terms of the Union Treaty that was drafted and redrafted in this period, the union republics would assume many responsibilities of central ministries. Second, the republics would be more effective vehicles than the central administration for incorporating previously unenfranchised intelligentsia into leading positions. Third, they would also be more effective at involving the broader population. In 1988 Gorbachev began to press republic leaders to reach out beyond the Party to mobilize larger popular constituencies.[49] Moreover, the invigoration of republic governments was an essential part of the solution to the policy dysfunction of the constitution of Bolshevism. The union republics would become the basis for a form of socialist pluralism whereby, even in the absence of private ownership or civil society, competition and markets among republics would guarantee a more innovative and dynamic policy process.

After the 1990 elections to local and republic governments the balance between bureaucrats enfranchised under the constitution of Bolshevism and the newly enfranchised members of the intelligentsia was increasingly structured by this confrontation between conservative central administrators and reformist union-republic leaders. Gorbachev attempted to institutionalize this balance in the Council (later, Cabinet) of Ministers, which included the central administrators and the Council of the Federation that brought together the union-republic leaders; president Gorbachev served as the vital pivot between them.

Dynamic Centrism and Defection

Maintaining such a coalition for constitutional transformation set the tasks of policy entrepreneurship. Coalition maintenance required compromises among coalition partners and placed a premium on the general secretary holding the center position in the coalition space.[50] Yet, these imperatives operated in a constantly changing environment: In the unfolding process of constitutional transformation compromises often served as opening wedges for further change. Constitutional transformation required dynamic centrism from the general secretary to maintain the changing central position as the coalition expanded. From this centrist position the general secretary sought to engineer rolling compromises that maintained a coalition that was itself constantly moving toward the reformist side of the political spectrum. The ever present risk in this strategy was alienating one wing of the coalition, or even both wings.

Gorbachev's coalition problem was at first structured by the task of staying atop the shifting balance between Party and state even as he managed a shifting balance within each. Later, it was complicated by the task of staying atop the changing balance between the Kremlin and the republics. In the shifting balance between Party and state and in each narrower arena of Party and state there was strength at the center position in the policy space. This centrism was expressed repeatedly in Gorbachev's actions and speeches; for example, on the October Revolution anniversary in 1987 he warned against conservatism and "avant-gardism" and argued that the reform process must steer a middle course between them.[51] Within the Communist party itself competing tendencies had emerged: reformers coalesced in January 1990 to support the democratic platform against the traditional Marxist-Leninist program of the conservative wing. Gorbachev's centrists sought to hold these two together by their own program "Toward a Human, Democratic Socialism."[52] Simultaneously, within the state organs he sought to balance between conservative economic administrators and reformist republic leaders. The grand balance was reflected in his posts as general secretary and president to oversee the transfer of more policymaking from Party to state and in his roles as head of the central government and chair of the Council of the Federation to oversee the transfer of policymaking prerogatives from the Kremlin to the republic governments.

The Gorbachev program was full of compromises in the face of conservative resistance. For example, the January 1987 Central Committee Plenum at which Gorbachev first delivered the outlines of his democratization program, according to the general secretary, was postponed three times because members would not agree to his agenda. Dusko Doder and Louise Branson report that during December and January Gorbachev met in his dacha separately with Central Committee members to convince them to support his program.[53] When it became apparent the Plenum would refuse to endorse all his proposals he called on the Central Committee to convene a Party conference that would include a broader spectrum of Party activists but lacked the plenary powers of the Central Committee.[54] In the end the resolutions of the January 1987 Central Committee Plenum diluted Gorbachev's proposals on democratizing the Party.[55] At the Party conference, called in June 1988 to win approval of his democratization program, Gorbachev had to promise that local party secretaries would generally be expected to assume chairmanship of the local soviets.[56] To win approval of more open popular elections to the new Congress of People's Deputies he had to guarantee one-third of the seats to public organizations.[57] In the March 1990 convocation of the Congress of People's Deputies Gorbachev won approval of a constitutional amendment that legalized a multiparty system, but he had to piggyback this on constitutional amendments demanded by conservatives that expanded executive power.[58]

Yet, each compromise was an opening wedge in a process of reform. After his January 1987 compromise Gorbachev continued to press for democratic elections within the Communist party. Despite his 1988 compromise, he pressed forward with elections to local soviets that led to the defeat of local party secretaries. He used the 1989 elections to empower a Congress of People's Deputies that then voted to eliminate the guaranteed seats for public organizations in future elections. As if to drive home the imperative of pragmatic compromise, in his book *Perestroika*, Gorbachev reminded us of the old saw that "politics is the art of the possible."[59] Making compromises was essential to the dynamic process.

Nonetheless, dynamic centrism was a risky enterprise, for Gorbachev's coalition was repeatedly threatened with defection from both conservatives and reformers. As a critical reformist's commentary noted, "Our leader has attempted all these years to preserve a centrist position, balancing between left and right. There have been times when such a political course has allowed us to avoid dangerous confrontations, but the end result is that the president is criticized by both sides."[60] This was the fundamental tactical problem facing a leader set on the enterprise of constitutional transformation: In nurturing a new constitutional order in the arms of the old he found himself in the end opposed by the beneficiaries of both the old order and the new. Yet, if his coalition failed to include both reformers and conservatives, the enterprise of constitutional change could be lost.

Each conservative had a different defection point as the coalition center moved.[61] As the center of the coalition and Gorbachev's policies moved in a more reformist direction, Gorbachev first forfeited the support of his most conservative colleagues like Yegor Ligachev and Viktor Chebrikov.[62] His more moderate colleagues like Nikolai Ryzhkov hung on longer by supporting Gorbachev in April 1988 in the Politburo decision to censor Ligachev over the Nina Andreeva letter. Yet, by July 1989 Ryzhkov joined Ligachev in attacks on Gorbachev for subverting the authority of the Party apparat.[63] Gorbachev sought to reduce the incentive for conservatives to turn to violent action if they did defect by protecting them from retribution by the newly enfranchised social forces. To quote George Breslauer, the president attempted to "strip the privileged corporate interests of the old regime of their political immunity, but give them enough protection against dispossession that they [did] not exit en masse and seek allies who would help them to violently reverse the democratization process."[64]

Each reformer also had a different defection point. Some, preferring to remain in opposition, never joined the coalition. Many who joined defected very soon. Gorbachev's compromises with the conservatives and his unwillingness to simply declare a partisan alliance with the radicals alienated many reformers. In 1989, for example, many academics frustrated with the slow pace of change sought to constitute themselves as an opposition. In December Georgii Arbatov tried to dissuade them from defection, calling on deputies from the Academy of Sciences to work with rather than against Gorbachev in the Congress of People's Deputies. Gorbachev himself stressed in his comments to potential defectors the necessity of compromise and the dangers of acting prematurely. At the December 1989 convocation of the Congress of Peoples Deputies, for example, he endorsed the view that the Soviet Constitution (Article 6) could be amended to eliminate the Communist party's leading role, but he warned that hasty action without the Party's consent could draw society into a debilitating conflict. At a preparatory meeting of deputies "in a remark that startled his audience Gorbachev said he was constantly being harangued by critics who asked why he is moving so slow. He wanted to go faster, Gorbachev said, but he could not."[65]

For the coalition members, defection carried risks. For conservatives, unsuccessful defection such as an abortive coup could discredit their cause and bring the very changes they most feared. For reformers defection carried the risk that the leader would turn to the conservatives for governance or that the conservatives would use the leader's vulnerability to mount an attack against reform.

Sequences and Timing

The conundrum of constitutional transformation also constrained strategic choices concerning the sequencing and timing of reforms. Samuel P. Huntington suggests that the most effective method for reformers is what he calls "the combination of a Fabian strategy with blitzkrieg tactics. To achieve his goals the reformer should separate and isolate one issue from another, but, having done this, he should, when the time is ripe, dispose of each issue as rapidly as possible, removing it from the political agenda before his opponents are able to mobilize their forces."[66] Yet, in reforming the constitution of Bolshevism, the "Fabian blitzkrieg" was only part of a more complex sequencing strategy that entailed partitioning, bundling, and interactive sequencing of reforms. That is, political reform had to be partitioned into a set of discrete steps. In the politics of compromise these steps often had to be presented as legislative bundles that satisfied both conservatives and reformers and kept them on board Gorbachev's coalition. Because reforms were often interdependent—for example, specific steps in the breakup of bureaucratic reciprocal accountability were preconditions for specific steps in economic reform and vice versa—the leader had to press forward with political and economic reform in alternating sequence.

In disposing of discrete elements of the political agenda, the Fabian blitzkrieg required that Gorbachev either mask his ultimate intentions, often denying vociferously that he would support a reform, or dissimulate so as to convince others that a reform would not have consequences they feared. Gorbachev appears to have understood that the Fabian blitzkrieg required careful timing so that critical veto groups were neutralized at the time a reform was introduced. This technique is illustrated by Gorbachev's sudden support for multipartyism in early 1990. Prior to the decision to amend Article 6 of the Soviet Constitution Gorbachev adamantly denied that democratization would undermine the Party's leading role and claimed that it would even strengthen this position.[67] At the 1988 Party Conference he defended the new independent associations "reflecting all the diversity of social interests," but he said these were taking place within the one-party system.[68] Prior to the legalization of other parties, Gorbachev forcefully denounced the "group egoism, ambition, and political careerism" found in multiparty systems.[69] As late as November 1989 Gorbachev was arguing that the Party's leading role should be maintained.[70] Yet, in January 1990, he told a crowd in Lithuania, "We should not be afraid of a multiparty system the way the devil is afraid of incense." "I don't see a tragedy in a multiparty system if it serves the people."[71] And in March he pressed for legalizing a multiparty system. According to John Gooding,

A few weeks after the crucial plenum the editor of *Pravda* I. T. Frolov, a close aide of Gorbachev, admitted that the idea of abolishing the party's monopoly had been mooted by the leadership "a very long time ago" and that the only question had been "how, in what form, and at what stage to introduce such changes." The leadership had first, however, to create the necessary preliminary conditions, among which he instanced a new body of deputies and the new Supreme Soviet. Only then, in "the concluding stages of the political reform," could it carry through what was "in the literal sense a revolution (*perevorot*), a completion and consummation of the remaking of the political system."[72]

To earn support from his coalition, this change had to be packaged with a reform demanded by the conservatives—a strong presidency to establish law and order. Gorbachev apparently had favored this reform for some time, but similar dissimulation was necessary to spring the plan at the proper moment. Robert Kaiser records,

> According to one knowledgeable informant, Yakovlev developed a proposal for a strong presidency as early as 1985. It was an obvious device to circumvent the Party, which is why many of the liberal legislators, including Sakharov, had also urged the idea on Gorbachev in 1989. . . . Until early 1990 Gorbachev had shown no interest in the idea.[73]

When the opportunity for this came in 1990, when conservatives demanded strong executive action to stop the slide into chaos, Gorbachev jumped at the opportunity and made the reform his own. The bundling of these two issues permitted Gorbachev to bring both conservative and reformist members of his coalition behind his reform. By the Fabian blitzkrieg, he was able to pick the precise moment when this bundle was likely to gain swift approval.

Key to the issues concerning sequencing and timing was a strategic choice: should they pursue political and economic reform simultaneously? If not, what sequence should they follow? Various combinations had their partisans. For example, many radical reformers argued for a simultaneous assault and claimed that Gorbachev's failures resulted from his refusal to proceed along both paths simultaneously. Alternatively, Andronik Migranian argued for sequencing: economic reform must precede political reform. The transition from totalitarian polity with command economy to democracy with market economy could only be achieved by passing through an intermediate stage of market authoritarianism. This intermediate stage could require a strong man to create a civil society based on market economics and propertied class; civil society was the necessary precondition for democracy.[74] Gorbachev's strategy was a more complex interactive sequencing. Gorbachev appears to have seen political empowerment of reformers as the wedge to force economic reform against the bureaucracy. The record of previous defeated economic reforms suggests that it could not succeed without some political preconditions. Yet, economic reforms that broke up the central economic administration also contributed to political reform. Interactive sequencing

required pressing forward with a reform in one area, following with reform in the other, and then returning to the first in a sequence where each
set the stage for the next step.

REFORM AND RESISTANCE

The changes engineered by Gorbachev brought new opportunities to end
the old order's institutionalized stagnation. Indeed, these changes elicited
a flowering of ideas and reform initiatives unprecedented under the mature constitution of Bolshevism. This may in part account for why the
iron triangle permitted the reform to go on so long. Yet reform also
brought new resistance from the iron triangle and a final refusal to change
the most fundamental constitutional principles. Bureaucratic reciprocal
accountability not only made constitutional reform an uphill battle, but
in the end it also brought down the entire enterprise.

The New "Consolidation"

Gorbachev used constitutional reform to produce a sort of "breakout"
that the institutionalized balanced leadership under the old constitutional
order had blocked. Yet, the consolidation differed from what had prevailed under the constitution of Bolshevism. Gorbachev had to search for
new institutional advantages within a changing constitutional order, for
the old advantages of the general secretary were either blocked or wither-
ing away. Following the amendments to the Soviet Constitution adopted
in December 1988, his election as president strengthened his hand against
the Central Committee, for the Central Committee could not remove him
from his government post.[75] The 1990 amendments, making the president accountable to the populace in five-year elections rather than to the
Congress of Peoples Deputies, placed his new post beyond the reach of
the sitting state bodies as well. Similarly, at the 1990 Party Congress in
July the Party rules were changed so that in his role as general secretary
Gorbachev was elected by and could only be removed by the full Party
Congress, which normally met only once in five years, rather than the
Central Committee. If the constitutional transformation was successful,
the payoff for Gorbachev would be a term in an institutionalized role
with a secure mandate to rule. Nonetheless, in the period of transition,
many of the balancing constraints of the older order continued to constrain this new leadership role.

Constitutional reform brought an opportunity to weaken some balancing constraints with which the mature constitution of Bolshevism had

checked the general secretary. In September 1988, as part of a Party reorganization, Ligachev was deprived of his control over the Secretariat; this opened the way for Gorbachev to assert more direct control over the Party apparatus.[76] Yet, Gorbachev could not duplicate the strategies of early general secretaries by simply appointing his clientele to the Party apparatus. In 1988 direction of the Party apparatus was assumed by six new party commissions, but the chairmanships and memberships of these remained balanced so that Gorbachev's protégés could not dominate all their work.[77] The Secretariat as a corporate body apparently ceased to function separately from the Politburo. Indeed, at the 1990 Party Congress, Ligachev informed delegates that after these reforms the Secretariat ceased functioning.[78] Ligachev's attempt to recapture the Secretariat by winning election to the new post of second secretary was beaten back by Gorbachev's candidate—Vladimir Ivashko. By this time, however, Gorbachev was well along in his strategy to dislodge the Secretariat and apparatus from its previous strategic position throughout Soviet society.[79]

Gorbachev acted as the leader in a new institutional role, building coalitions and championing the promotion of like-minded allies to leading positions in the iron triangle but not appointing dependent or personally loyal clients. This strategy was dictated by the institutional constraints in which Gorbachev acted, but it was also consistent with the type of constitutional transformation he sought to engineer. Constitutional transformation afforded an opportunity to bring a new generation of bureaucrats to iron triangle positions, but the change did not give Gorbachev clientelistic control.

Within the military Gorbachev worked to promote officers committed to reform, but the military retained the institutional autonomy to prevent its transformation into a dependent clientele.[80] The humiliation of the top military command following Mathias Rust's penetration of Soviet air space on 28 May 1987 provided Gorbachev an opportunity to replace Minister of Defense Sergei Sokolov by Dmitri Yazov and to sack 200 senior officers, while promoting many more reform-minded commanders. Yet the military continued to shield itself from direct control by the general secretary. As late as November 1990, when Gorbachev announced "personnel changes at the highest level of command in the armed forces," no shake-up followed. Only after the humiliation of the top military command for its involvement in the August 1991 coup was Gorbachev able to bring still more reform-minded military leaders who promised to clean the command structure.

Similarly, Gorbachev promoted reform-minded leaders atop the police, but control of the police remained balanced between more reformist and more conservative members. In the fall of 1988 Gorbachev won appointment of the reformer Vadim Bakatin to head the Ministry of Internal

Affairs, but this was balanced by appointment of the more conservative Vladimir Kriuchkov to head the KGB and Viktor Chebrikov to the Secretariat to oversee the police. In September 1989, with the growing presence of reformers in the Gorbachev coalition it became possible to retire Chebrikov, although Kriuchkov assumed his seat on the Politburo. In December 1990, as the reformers deserted Gorbachev's coalition and the balance swung back to the conservatives, Bakatin was removed from the Ministry of Internal Affairs and replaced by the conservative Boris Pugo. Finally, with the defeat of the August 1991 coup—in which Pugo and Kriuchkov played leading roles—the swing toward the reformers brought Bakatin back to lead the KGB.

The constraints of balanced leadership meant the general secretary, unlike his earlier predecessors, could not cap his consolidation by populating the Politburo with a loyal personal following. Between the January 1987 Central Committee Plenum and the 1990 Party Congress Gorbachev won removal of some conservative members, including Dinmukhamed Kunaev and Geidar Aliev in 1987, Andrei Gromyko and Mikhail Solomentsev in 1988, and Viktor Chebrikov and Vladimir Shcherbitskii in 1989. Gorbachev gained election of a couple of close associates, including Aleksandr Yakovlev in 1987 and Vadim Medvedev in 1988. Yet, the new appointments were balanced by election of representatives of the iron triangle, including Nikolai Sliunkov and Viktor Nikonov in 1987 (the latter removed in 1989), and Vladimir Ivashko, Vladimir Kriuchkov, and Yurii Masliukov in 1989. These changes did not bring Gorbachev a personally loyal majority in the Politburo, and in the end Gorbachev continued to press for marginalizing the Politburo. At the 1990 Party Congress, Gorbachev won approval of a reform that expanded the Politburo into a twenty-four-member body by including the republic first secretaries. By limiting this body to Party matters Gorbachev was able to speed the transfer of its policymaking prerogatives to the state bodies.[81]

Policy Innovation

The constitutional transformation began to break the policy dysfunction of the old order. Growing empowerment of new social forces began to break the monopoly of the enfranchised bureaucrats and created a constituency for more reformist policies. Thus, policy began to shift as soon as the constitutional reform was underway. Nonetheless, the continuing constraint of the iron triangle limited the leader's opportunities to shift policy priorities. In spending, for example, the resulting compromises produced disastrous fiscal consequences—perhaps, far worse than earlier periods of logrolling. In military planning, military science began to accommodate the general secretary's doctrinal innovations in a way that gave them an operational meaning that was very different from the general secretary's initiative.

In contrast to the conservative priorities of the collective leadership of the mid-1980s, official projections of spending showed a dramatic reformist shift in late 1988. In presenting the next year's plan to the October 1988 meeting of the parliament (Supreme Soviet), the State Planning Committee (Gosplan) chair noted that it featured "a major shift to priority growth for Group B industry [consumer goods production]. . . . This country has never before known such priority growth for Group B." Investment was to decrease and consumption increase. Retail trade was projected to grow at a rate 150 percent more than from 1986 to 1987. The proportionate share in national income for consumption and social-cultural investment in 1989 would rise to 81.6 percent, against the 78.5 percent projected in the five-year plan.[82] Similarly, a year later in presenting the budget for 1990 the minister of finance noted that social-cultural measures would show the highest growth rates of any category in order to bring about "a major redistribution of resources for urgent social needs." While he projected that budgetary spending on the national economy would decrease by 6 percent, including a 42.4 percent cut in centralized capital investment, spending on social-cultural measures would rise 10.7 percent.[83] The first vice-premier, summarizing the priorities of the plan, observed that "this social reorientation of the plan permeates all its sections." "It is envisioned that in 1990 the growth in Group B will be thirteen times that for Group A. In its essence, this is an extraordinary change of proportions in industry."[84]

A similar shift in priorities became evident in military planning as Gorbachev began to introduce a doctrinal innovation that would bring a reorientation of Soviet national security. Unlike his first two years in office, he began to draw out the economizing consequences of his doctrinal innovations and urge this innovation on military science. Using his powers as commander-in-chief, he began to press "defensive defense" and "reasonable sufficiency" as structuring principles for Soviet armed forces. At their May 1987 meeting in Berlin the Warsaw Pact leaders supported his initiative for "reduction of armed forces and conventional armaments in Europe to a level where neither side, while making sure of its own defenses, would have the means for a surprise attack on the other side or for mounting offensive operations in general."[85] In his December 1988 speech to the United Nations General Assembly Gorbachev announced unilateral reductions in Soviet forces by 500,000 men, 5,000 tanks, and substantial artillery and aircraft.[86] By mid-1989 he began to push the West for negotiations to reduce nuclear weapons to levels appropriate to minimum deterrence.[87]

Some of the most important spending cuts in the period came in defense. In late 1988 Gorbachev announced unilateral military cuts, and in succeeding years the military budget was slashed. In the 1990 budget alone defense spending was projected to fall 8.3 percent from 1989 levels. By 1991 the total budgetary allocation was projected to fall 14.2 percent from its 1989 level, including a 19.5 percent reduction in weapons procurement and 15 percent in research and development.[88] According to the chief of the General Staff, purchases of tanks were actually reduced by 40 percent from 1988 to 1990, infantry vehicles and armored personnel carriers by 30 percent, military aircraft by 30 percent, and munitions by 27 percent.[89]

The continuing constraints of balancing left from the constitution of Bolshevism meant that it was easier to begin reform initiatives than to set priorities and force sacrifices on the iron triangle. A consequence was a growing fiscal crisis. Without sacrifices from the iron triangle commensurate with the new spending on social programs, budget deficits skyrocketed. The fiscal planners became increasingly alarmed. In his presentation of the 1989 plan, the State Planning Committee chair warned of state expenditures continuing to grow faster than revenues. He noted that cash incomes would jump 6.2 percent in 1988—well above the 3.6 percent projected in the five-year plan.[90] That year the minister of finance warned that "the growth in the population's income exceeded the possibilities for satisfying public demand, which led to the economically unwarranted issuance of new money and to inflationary processes." The minister noted that previous wishful thinking had proved unwarranted: "in the course of fulfilling the budget it was expected that about 25 billion rubles would be mobilized through increased efficiency of economic management, but we will be getting only 10 billion rubles." Nonetheless, he presented a budget with a 7.3 percent shortfall in revenues.[91]

By late 1989 and 1990 this deficit had become a central concern in the plan and budget. In presenting the 1990 budget the minister of finance reported, "monetary circulation remains in an extremely grave condition. . . . The emission of money will total . . . 50 percent more than last year. It will be accompanied by a decline in the purchasing power of the ruble and increasing shortages of more and more goods and services." He warned that to stabilize the fiscal crisis, even with increasing revenues, expenditures would have to fall by 1.3 percent.[92] In presenting the 1990 Plan, the first vice-premier sounded even more ominous: "It is perfectly clear that even the most resolute efforts to increase the total amount of available goods will certainly not be able to keep up with the uncontrolled growth of cash incomes." He outlined actions to fill the gap, including increased imports and substantial wishful thinking that higher revenues would result from greater profitability and expanded retail trade.[93]

That the availability of products did not keep up with incomes was seen in the jump in savings accounts. The annual growth rate in savings nearly doubled from the fiscally irresponsible first half of the decade to the reckless latter half—from 6.6 percent (1980–1984) to 11.2 percent (1985–1989).[94] Even more than in previous periods of logrolling constrained by balancing, the inability to force sacrifices on the iron triangle equal to the new spending commitments led to soaring expenditures, deficits, shortages, inflation, and galloping savings.

Similar resistance and logrolling was evident in the response to Gorbachev's efforts at doctrinal innovation in military planning. Military professionals raised serious questions about the general secretary's initiatives. Defense Minister Yazov, questioning the shift to "defensive defense," noted that "it is impossible to achieve the crushing defeat of an aggressor by defense alone."[95] As before, the military gave the doctrinal innovations a new twist: For example, in actual military planning, special attention was still given to offensive operations that reportedly used military hardware exactly as before—but now under the label "counteroffensive." General V. Varennikov warned against the unrealistically low estimates of defense requirements implied by "reasonable sufficiency" and minimum deterrence: "We remember that imperialism is a treacherous and ruthless enemy. If it senses weakness, it will stop at nothing. It is necessary, therefore, today as never before to maintain the Army and Navy at the highest level of combat readiness."[96] Others took up Nikolai Ogarkov's theme that sufficiency would require more, not less, investment in technology based on new principles of physics; sometimes they extended this line of reasoning to argue that these new technologies would necessitate keeping troops at even higher states of readiness than before. In a 1988 interview, the head of the Air Defense Forces General I. Tretiak criticized economists who planned to shift resources from defense to the domestic economy and reminded his listeners that a similar cut by Khrushchev "dealt a colossal blow at our defense potential."[97] In 1989 Gorbachev reported that senior commanders had found "radical reconstruction" of the armed forces difficult: "It was so painful that I began to receive information that the Defense Council and its chairman were moving too sharply, and the Marshals requested me to bear this comment in mind."[98]

The Double Defection, 1990–1991

The enterprise of constitutional reform reached a critical stage before the transformation of bureaucratic reciprocal accountability was complete. At this intermediate stage, the threat of a double defection reached a climax. With the empowerment of new social forces, the threat to incumbent selectors rose at the same time they saw their ability to stop this deterioration begin to decline. Some in the iron triangle foresaw the approach of the last clear chance to turn back from calamity. The threat that conservatives might turn against the reform process by decisive action against the president was matched by the growing threat of defection by reformers. As they saw their power grow, many reformers became increasingly impatient with the compromises that participation in Gorbachev's coalition had entailed. In 1991 the double defection of both factions brought down the Gorbachev coalition and his attempt to reform the constitution of Bolshevism.

As the balance between conservatives and reformers became structured by the balance between central administrations and republic governments, this shaped the crises that were likely to provoke a defection by either or both sides. The crises came to focus on the issue of decentralization. This institutional context also structured the ultimate threat that each could pose to the enterprise of constitutional transformation: For the central administration it was a coup d'état; for the republics, secession. The conservatives became strident in their criticism and more overt in their threats of armed action following their dismal failure in the 1990 republic and local elections and as Gorbachev inched the Soviet Union toward a new union treaty that would give these republic governments many of the central administrations' policymaking powers.

This institutional balance also structured their respective institutional strategies. The reformers pressed for decentralization and institutional changes to strengthen reformist leaders within the republics in their confrontation with the center. In many republics this meant creating republic presidents who could exercise strong executive powers in the confrontation with the iron triangle. The conservatives responded by resisting these initiatives and attempting to strengthen the central economic administrations and the Party apparatus against the republic governments. For example, in Russia, after losing badly in the republic elections of 4 March 1990, many conservatives came together in the movement to create a new Communist party organization for the Russian Republic. Grass-roots pressure from "initiative committees" within the Communist party organizations of the Russian Republic forced Gorbachev to accede to a republic congress and a separate Russian union-republic Party organization.[99] The conservatives used this as a counterweight to both the Russian republic government led by Yeltsin's reformers and the central Party organs where Gorbachev's reformers had a strong presence. After the same republic elections Russia's reformers held a strong position in the republic legislature; in May 1990 the legislature elected Boris Yeltsin as the republic's chief of state (chairman of the Presidium of the Supreme Soviet). To strengthen him still more against the Russian Communist party and against the central Soviet government, the reformers pressed for creation of a popularly elected president of the Russian republic, and in June 1991 Yeltsin won this with 57 percent of the popular vote.[100]

The precarious balance that Gorbachev maintained in his coalition meant that prior to 1990 almost every time he had left Moscow, conservatives found opportunities to threaten the process of change or even turn back the clock. Gorbachev's vacations on the Black Sea each August and his travels abroad seemed to become regular occasions for such attempts. During his 1986 August vacation, KGB officials detained the American correspondent Nicholas Daniloff, charged him with espionage, and imprisoned him in Lefortovo prison—an apparent provocation by the KGB to undermine the general secretary's policies. During Gorbachev's 1987 and 1988 summer vacations and his 1988 visit to Yugoslavia, Ligachev and Chebrikov used the opportunity of the general secretary's absence to launch propaganda campaigns attacking reform.[101] In April 1989, during Gorbachev's visit to Cuba and Britain, Ligachev chaired the emergency meeting that sent troops against demonstrators in Tblisi, killing nineteen.[102]

As empowerment of new social forces proceeded, warnings from the iron triangle, including threats of armed action, became more overt. At the inaugural Congress of the Russian Communist party in June 1990, General Albert Makashov ominously warned that "the army and the navy will yet stand the Union and Russia in good stead."[103] In September unusual military maneuvers around Moscow gave rise to rumors of a coup by the military and KGB and led Boris Yeltsin to warn deputies in the Russian Parliament that paratroopers were actually headed toward Moscow. The subsequent flurry of articles in the press included ominous warnings from conservatives of an impending left-wing coup and explanations that the maneuvers were designed to head off a seizure of power by the democrats.[104]

The threat of double defection came to the brink twice in debates over decentralization in late 1990 and mid-1991. The first of these crises came over the Shatalin Plan in the latter half of 1990. In August 1990 Gorbachev had appointed Stanislav Shatalin to chair the commission to draft an economic reform. The resulting plan assaulted the policy priorities and prerogatives of the iron triangle. Not only did the plan call for sharp cutbacks in spending on the military and police, but it also suggested selling off many of the state enterprises run by the central ministries, transfering economic and fiscal planning to the republics, and limiting the central government's economic role to issuance of currency and control of monetary policy. On 11 September 1990 Gorbachev announced his support for the Shatalin Plan over more conservative programs. The conservatives, however, apparently drew the line at this point and refused to compromise: within the next two weeks military maneuvers around Moscow supported a threat of a coup d'état if Gorbachev did not pull back from the so-called "500-day plan" for radical decentralization. Gorbachev adjusted by moving back toward a more centrist position between conservatives and reformers: On October 16 he presented a new economic plan that combined elements of the Shatalin Plan with the proposals of his premier Nikolai Ryzhkov. By this time many reformers, equally unwilling to compromise and inclined to desert Gorbachev's coalition, promptly announced they had gone into opposition. Shatalin lambasted the president in an open letter in *Komsomolskaia Pravda*: "Why do you not want to take the right course? You are able to, but you don't. Why not?" Shatalin's answer: "You are afraid of losing power."[105] In the logic of the coalition politics of constitutional transformation, Gorbachev feared losing something more fundamental—by pressing too fast he could prompt the defection of the conservatives and a coup that would topple the whole enterprise.

The consequences of the desertion by the reformist wing of his coalition were enormous for Gorbachev's strategy. The extremely vulnerable leader of the coalition, suddenly stripped of his reform wing, moved quickly to find the center of what remained of his coalition, and he began to concede more to the conservatives. In December 1990 and January 1991 Gorbachev brought in Pugo as minister of internal affairs, replaced Bakatin by Kriuchkov atop the KGB, replaced Ryzhkov by Valentin Pavlov as prime minister, and accepted Gennadii Yanaev as his vice-president. In part the problem for Gorbachev was to satisfy the conservatives to such an extent that they would not take advantage of his vulnerability to thoroughly scuttle the reform project. Archie Brown speculates that part of Gorbachev's strategy had been to bring inside his coalition those prominent conservatives that might otherwise be focal points for a conservative cabal against his reform program.[106]

The second crisis over decentralization came the following year over the union treaty. Gorbachev sought to restart the process of constitutional transformation in early 1991, by pressing forward on a new union treaty that would shift power to the union-republics. A grand accord among the leaders of nine republics was reached in negotiations on 23 April 1991. The conservatives responded with another coup attempt, but this time by legislative means with a proposal on 17 June 1991 to strip away most of the president's executive powers and place these in the hands of the iron triangle in the Cabinet of Ministers.[107] The iron triangle sought to block the shift of power toward the republics by an institutional maneuver that would transfer leadership of the Soviet Union to the committees in which they predominated—the cabinet of heads of chief bureaucracies of economic administration, military, and police, headed by a prime minister (Pavlov) who reflected their priorities. Gorbachev beat back this attempt in the Congress of People's Deputies and on 23 July 1991 won approval of his program (the union treaty) to shift this power from the central administration to the republics. With a formal signing by republic leaders scheduled for 20 August 1991, the treaty would create a new Union of Sovereign States in which the central power of the iron triangle would decisively and perhaps irreversibly shift to the republic capitals.

On the day before the union treaty was scheduled for signing, the iron triangle finally staged its armed coup d'état. The eight-man State Committee for the State of Emergency in the USSR brought together the leaders of the iron triangle, including the KGB head Kriuchkov, Minister of Internal Affairs Pugo, Minister of Defense Yazov, and head of economic administration Pavlov. The leaders of the iron triangle had resolved that their last chance to block a constitutional reform from which there probably would be no return to the former bureaucratic reciprocal accountability was now armed resistance. The chairman of the parliament promptly announced that, before its signing at some indefinite date in the future, the Union Treaty would have to be revised to reflect the need for stronger central organs of power.[108]

The defection of the conservatives, the failure of their coup d'état, and the arrest of their leaders transformed the task of coalition building for Gorbachev. Having lost the close cooperation of both reformist and conservative wings, the president stood alone without a coalition to govern. The reformers in the republics, particularly Boris Yeltsin, pressed for still more radical decentralization. The interim national government established on 5 September 1991 reflected this shift: the central institutions of executive power were to be replaced by bodies composed of delegations from each republic, including a new State Council of republic leaders under Gorbachev's chairmanship to replace the Council of Federation and an Inter-Republic Economic Council to replace the Cabinet of Ministers.[109] Within a month of the failed coup, the State Council had recognized the independence of the three Baltic republics (September 6), and nine of the remaining twelve republics had declared their own independence. In November disagreements between republic leaders favoring a federation with strong central government and those pressing for a confederation with weak center reached a deadlock over yet another draft union treaty. The Russian government used this stalemate to begin a slow motion coup d'état within Moscow as it seized assets of the central government such as the mint, foreign ministry, and academy of sciences, and then sought to starve the central government into submission by refusing to forward the taxes collected on its territory for the support of the central government.

With the sudden collapse of the conservative wing of the coalition, the role of the leader who was formerly central to the coalition seemed superfluous. Gorbachev attempted to recreate a balance between the leadership of the Western republics, who tended to favor more radical decentralization, and the leaders of the Central Asian republics, who favored continuation of a stronger central government. In this balance Gorbachev sought to create a strategic advantage for the Soviet president in dealing with individual republic leaders (particularly with the Russian president): The Soviet president would balance among the dozen republic leaders, constraining each by the larger coalition. To avoid becoming bound by such institutional constraints on his newly won prerogatives, Boris Yeltsin walked out of the 25 November 1991 meeting of the Council of State called to sign the latest draft of the union treaty. On 8 December 1991 Yeltsin confronted Gorbachev and the Central Asian leaders with an alternative coalition on his own terms—a Commonwealth of Independent States among the three Slavic republics of Russia, Ukraine, and Belarus.[110] In this the Russian president, freed from the constraints of the Soviet president and larger coalition, could play the critical role of hegemon. Five days later the Central Asian leaders relented and accepted Yeltsin's terms for a new commonwealth; and Gorbachev acquiesced. On 21 December representatives of eleven former republics met in Alma Ata to sign the treaties creating the new Commonwealth.[111] On 25 December 1991 Mikhail Gorbachev resigned as the last general secretary and only president of the USSR. The Soviet polity had collapsed and with it Gorbachev's bold attempt to provide its constitutional order with innovative and adaptable institutions.

The Soviet constitutional order founded on a vanguard party seeking to carry Russia and its neighbors through early industrialization simply collapsed. It left behind many institutional vestiges that would play critical roles in each of the fifteen successor states. Yet, the constitutional order that integrated these institutions had ceased to exist. Mikhail Gorbachev's attempt to transform that order so that it could reach beyond the tasks of early state building and industrialization had encountered the resistance of the iron triangle. The political order created by the constitution of Bolshevism in the end was not reformed and died in the attempt.

INSTITUTIONS AND THE COLLAPSE

This chapter has examined Gorbachev's attempt to transform the constitutional foundations of Soviet politics by stressing the institutional constraints under which he labored. These constraints set the objectives of constitutional transformation—rulemaking and institutionalization. These constraints also shaped the process of coalition balancing, the tactics of dynamic centrism, and the strategic sequencing of changes. This focus on institutions draws our attention to the remarkable complexities of constitutional transformation and the equally remarkable successes achieved by Gorbachev as he began to nurture a new constitutional order in the arms of the old.

This analytic focus on institutions stands apart from the biographical approach that is so common in the histories of this period. Certainly the vision and foibles of Mikhail Gorbachev as well as the clash of titanic egos in Moscow are very much a part of the rich drama of the last days of Soviet politics. Yet, this study has attempted to see beyond these. Institutional analysis alerts us to much in this "great man" approach that is simply ad hoc or that requires nonexistent intimate knowledge of inner thoughts and motivations. Moreover, institutional analysis leaves us with a significantly stronger conceptual framework for comparisons of these dramatic events with other instances of constitutional transformation at other times and in other authoritarian polities.

The institutional approach to these events from 1987 to 1991 also draws out the intimate link between this last half-decade of Soviet power and the political developments of the preceding seven decades. Of course, much was not predetermined by these preceding developments, such as the actual choice to begin reform. Yet, the nature of the choice between stagnation and transformation that faced the Soviet leadership at the beginning of this experiment and the nature of the daunting tasks of constitutional transformation were foreordained by previous constitutional developments. In the end, the collapse of the Soviet Union underscored not only the daunting nature of constitutional transformation but also the remarkable strength of Soviet institutions developed over seven decades. In this strength with perverse consequences is the answer to a puzzle with which this book began—how such a stable polity could simply fall like a house of cards.

CHAPTER TEN

Can Authoritarian Institutions Survive?

THIS BOOK began with simple questions and puzzles concerning the collapse of the Soviet Union. How could a political system that was so dynamic become gripped by stagnation from which it seemed unable to escape? How could a political system that had been so stable suddenly collapse? This book also began with three promissory notes to the reader concerning the analytic approach employed throughout this work—the new institutionalism of authoritarianism. I promised to unravel the puzzles with which this book began by examining the constitutional structure created by the Bolsheviks; that is, I promised an institutionalist analysis to explain the development and failure of Soviet politics. I promised that the application of the new institutionalism to a case study would reveal and explain many dynamics of authoritarian politics. Moreover, I promised that this analysis would provide an example of how the new institutionalism might develop a distinctly political rather than political economic focus for comparative analysis of authoritarianism.

This conclusion presents an admittedly prejudiced assessment of this project's success measured against these objectives. I turn to three issues: What does the new institutionalist analysis say about the failure of the Soviet polity? Is there a future for these types of authoritarian institutions—particularly in the Soviet successor republics? Is there a future for the new institutionalism in the study of authoritarianism?

WHY DID THE SOVIET POLITY FAIL?

The Soviet polity failed when its inability to innovate and adapt produced a crisis of stagnation. This rigidity was rooted in the vanguard regime created by the Bolsheviks after taking power in 1917. They sought to create a regime that was able to complete the tasks of state building and early industrialization as quickly as possible. In a sense they succeeded too well at this, and their regime continued to press forward with these tasks but could not move beyond them. The analytic approach of new institutionalism sees these outcomes as a consequence of political processes shaped by the institutional structure.

As is common to modern bureaucratic reciprocal accountability, three structural features were at the heart of the constitutional order: a two-tiered structure linked by reciprocal accountability; initial indeterminacy of leadership in the first tier; and a restrictive, bureaucratic selectorate in the second tier. First, like so many other modern authoritarian regimes, the Soviet polity was structured by reciprocal accountability. To maintain their continuing domination over society the leadership in the first tier came to depend upon an elaborate bureaucracy in the second tier. In this context individual leaders began to seek high office and to extend their control over other leaders by building alliances with these bureaucracies. Leaders came to depend on, and to be held accountable by, a selectorate of these bureaucracies, yet these bureaucracies were in turn controlled by the leaders. Thus, accountability became reciprocal. Under the constitution of Bolshevism this was increasingly institutionalized in the relationship between Politburo and Central Committee.

Second, like so many new authoritarian regimes, the founders of the constitution of Bolshevism imagined that leadership in the first tier would be exercised by a collectivity—in the Soviet Union called the Politburo rather than junta or revolutionary command council. The assignment of policymaking powers to specific roles within the collective leadership was at first indeterminate: The extent of the powers held by office holders, the term of office, and the mechanisms for transfer of power were poorly defined. As is common in new authoritarian regimes two central ambiguities were left in the assignment of these prerogatives: the relationship of the chair of the collectivity to its other members, and the relationship of the prime organ of collective leadership to centers of policymaking in the state such as the cabinet. This gave rise to the opportunity for vacillations, between collective and directive leadership within the Politburo, and between policymaking concentrated in the Politburo and that dispersed among several organs. With time the development of rules and sanctions to preserve collective leadership led to balanced leadership with the institutionalization of the roles of general secretary and the Politburo.

Third, like other regimes structured by bureaucratic reciprocal accountability, the selectorate in the second tier that chose the leadership was a restrictive body drawn from the bureaucracies that reflected the purposes of its founders—in the Soviet Union the iron triangle bureaucracies of early industrialization and state building. This special role was enforced by stripping the majority of the adult population of the resources necessary for autonomous political activity. Not only did civil society cease to exist, but the society ceased to be an independent actor in politics and was relegated to the place of elemental constraint like nature. The privileged position of the iron triangle within the selectorate became institutionalized in rules of "job-slot" cooptation into the Central Committee.

These structural features constrained the coalition politics by which political actors sought office and made policy. In the first tier there was conflict over consolidation of policy leadership, and in the second tier there was conflict among bureaucrats over resources and policies. Between tiers there was conflict over control and autonomy. Yet, leaders in the first tier also needed to form coalitions among themselves to succeed in their pursuit of leadership; leaders and bureaucrats needed to form coalitions across tiers to retain office and fulfill their policy objectives. This coalition process limited the ability of the Soviet polity to innovate, for within the selectorate those bureaucracies that mirrored the founders' original purposes held a privileged position. The nature of this limitation on innovation fluctuated with vacillations between collective and directive rule, but the longer-term development of the polity reinforced these limitations and made policy innovation more difficult still.

The institutionalization of bureaucratic reciprocal accountability produced an equilibrium within the political system from which it was difficult to move. Bureaucratic reciprocal accountability could be transformed either by replacing reciprocal with hierarchical accountability or by changing the restrictive, bureaucratic nature of the selectorate. The former creates a sovereign power in either the leadership or selectorate; the latter brings entirely different constituencies into the selectorate. Yet attempts to make either type of change under the constitution of Bolshevism encountered sanctions from actors empowered and privileged by the existing order. The institutionalization of "early warning systems" and sanctions made it difficult for leaders to upset the institutional order of reciprocal accountability, balanced leadership, or the privileged place of the iron triangle in the selectorate. Yet this equilibrium also produced a perverse consequence: political institutions found it harder to accommodate change in their environment. The cruel paradox of this bureaucratic reciprocal accountability was that, although created to lead in the transformation of society, it could neither sustain this transformation nor even adapt to the transformations it initially engineered. This equilibrium institutionalized stagnation.

The model of bureaucratic reciprocal accountability developed in this book brings together in a new synthesis the major earlier attempts to develop models of Soviet politics. It also provides "higher-order" propositions to explain when the attributes identified by each of these earlier models—autocratic control, leadership conflict, and bureaucratic influence—should be most important. Unlike these earlier models, it also provides conceptual foundations for examining not only the recurring dynamics of politics, but also long-term political change. Most important, it provides a conceptual framework for comparative analysis of Soviet authoritarianism with other regimes.

IS THERE A FUTURE FOR AUTHORITARIAN INSTITUTIONS?

The Soviet polity was among the most stable modern authoritarian regimes of the twentieth century. Indeed, it lasted almost three-quarters of the century. It was, in a sense, the "hard case" for studying the institutional sources of authoritarian failure because its institutions were among the most successful. Yet, the failure of even these institutions begs the question: If Soviet authoritarianism could not last, then can *any* modern authoritarian regime last? Certainly some modern regimes, structured on bureaucratic reciprocal accountability, appear durable; Egypt's, for example, is more than four decades old at this point. Yet, to the extent that the institutions of these regimes ultimately suffer the petrification found in the Soviet case there is reason to hope they cannot last.

Some modern authoritarian regimes may yet develop more enduring institutions. Bureaucratic authoritarianism has been created when either a bureaucracy seizes power, turning itself into a governing party, or a party seizes power, turning itself into a governing bureaucracy. The former pattern, which most often begins with a military coup d'état and creation of a military junta, seems inherently less durable. The limited bureaucratic selectorate of these regimes seems to produce policy dysfunction and institutional stagnation far earlier. The latter pattern, pioneered by the Bolsheviks in the Soviet Union, was a distinct step forward toward a more complex, durable constitutional structure. In the future, authoritarian leaders may improve on the latter pattern's more diverse bureaucratic selectorate to purchase still greater longevity.

Does the collapse of the Soviet Union mean that the institutions of bureaucratic reciprocal accountability are at an end in the former Soviet Union? Will the leaders of the successor republics pause after this failure before creating new authoritarian institutions? Sadly, the temptations of power—and even of vanguardism—seem very much alive on the soil of the former Soviet Union.

At present a least three different strands of vanguardism seek to use the immense power of the state to transform the societies of the Soviet Union's successor republics—socialist, capitalist, and revivalist. In some republics the old ruling coalition of Leninism managed to hold on to power after December 1991 and maintained its commitment to the socialist vision of the future. Even in those republics where these leaders have been displaced, the stalwarts of this transformational vision remain very strong. In a paradoxical twist, even many who claim to oppose the socialist vision and subscribe to the liberal values of the marketplace have urged using the autocratic powers of the state to force society to be free. Although they are reticent to acknowledge this publicly, the examples of

Augusto Pinochet's Chile or the military's Brazil are paradigms for this abuse of power in the name of freedom. In all republics there are also many who reject either of these modern Western visions and seek an indigenous cultural revival, whether behind the banner of religion such as Islam or folk such as Slavophilism, and some of these seek to use the levers of the state to produce this revival of purportedly lost cultural values. The model of Iran's republic of virtue is particularly appealing to many in the Islamic republics, but this model could as easily be used for other cultural orthodoxies as well. Vanguardism is a temptation in the modern period at least as old as Savanarola and John Calvin, and its modern socialist, capitalist, and revivalist variants appear much alive in the contemporary republics of the former Soviet Union.

The discrediting of the institutions of the Soviet period means that many who would create new authoritarian regimes will have to turn to institutions other than the Communist party for foundations. Nationalist one-party or no-party regimes—perhaps on the model so common in postindependence Africa and Asia—may be attractive to the newly independent states. In less modernized countries, such as some Central Asian republics, the new leaders may seek to build an authoritarian regime based on the power of clan or tribal leaders. In all republics, regardless of level of social modernization, the legacy of the Soviet institutions may make the bureaucratic survivors a potent base for new bureaucratic authoritarianism, although the exact balance of bureaucracies in each republic is likely to differ from the constitution of Bolshevism. In more modernized republics, where popular participation has grown to a powerful force, authoritarian leaders may seek to harness these democratic pressures through integrated electoral machines that deliver votes and deny real choice to voters. All three of these models for authoritarian institutions appear to have powerful devotees in the successor republics.

The prospects for authoritarianism—and specifically of vanguardism and bureaucratic reciprocal accountability—appear very strong within the former Soviet Union. For those of us who lament this fact, the heartening message of this study is that these are not likely to be durable, and new chances to develop democracy should present themselves in the future. Until authoritarian institutions have disappeared, their dynamics will remain an issue that demands further analysis.

IS THERE A FUTURE FOR A NEW INSTITUTIONALISM OF AUTHORITARIANISM?

The approach to the constitution of Bolshevism developed in this book suggests a mode of analysis that could be employed in comparative study of authoritarian institutions—in the successor republics and around the globe. The new institutionalist analysis of authoritarianism seeks to fill a curious gap in comparative politics. The institutional dynamics *within* the democratic state are well established and the institutions characteristic of relations *between* society and the authoritarian state are well defined, yet the institutional dynamics *within* the authoritarian state are less well understood.[1] The prevailing approaches to the authoritarian polity stress the institutions and dynamics linking the state and society. For example, in his splendid survey of the treatment of authoritarianism by political science, Juan Linz defines the objective of social science's study of authoritarianism as answering questions about the relationship among polity, society, economy, and the cultural-religious realm.[2] Similarly, Carl Friedrich's now classic treatment of totalitarianism stresses the relationship of politics to society and gives surprisingly little attention to the dynamics of the autocratic polity.[3] The new institutionalism brings our attention back to the institutions of the state.

This exercise, bringing together an analytic approach and an empirical subject that have previously largely ignored one another, does raise important suggestions for the research strategies of both the new institutionalism and the study of authoritarian politics. First, the analysis of authoritarian institutions forces us to be aware when institutions do not conform to formal structures. Perhaps inevitably the new institutionalism began by studying the familiar, such as democratic institutions. This strategy has brought the new institutionalism quick returns of remarkable insight and explanatory success. Yet as the school begins to mature it is time to reach beyond. This manuscript has argued for extending this analysis to the less familiar authoritarian institutions. As the new institutionalism reaches out in this way to explore the possibilities as well as the possible limitations of its explanatory powers, we look increasingly beyond formal organizations.

Second, the study of authoritarian institutions forces us to pay special attention to the place of individual institutions in larger structures. Perhaps inevitably the new institutionalism also began by focusing on parts of political orders, such as legislatures and electoral systems, rather than on wholes. This manuscript, arguing for expanding the vision of the new institutionalism to encompass wholes, began with a concept of constitutions as the foundations of such a holistic approach. It began with a concept of constitutions not as formal documents, but as the roles and rules that define a political system. It stressed that in the analysis of authoritarianism, no less than democracy, we must give special attention to the locus of policymaking and the structure of accountability. In future work, the study of authoritarian regimes must develop concepts that capture basic institutional differences as successfully as the distinction between presidentialism and parliamentarism characterizes democratic institutions.

Third, the new institutionalism in turn invites us to rethink some of our more traditional approaches to authoritarian institutions. Certainly this new development in political science is not the first to point up the centrality of institutions in politics and political development. Indeed, the reader would be correct in suspecting that this study owes much to the work of Samuel P. Huntington, even as it argued that his first insights could be improved upon. Yet, the new institutionalism leads to a concept of institutions that permits us to analyze the regularities in political environments with weak or fluid formal structures.[4] In particular, the definition of institutions as roles and rules and the concept of institutionalization as reinforcement of mutual expectations has two important consequences: (1) it leads us to a more careful separation of institutions from their consequences, and (2) it leads us to drop some normative baggage that the concept institutionalization has often carried. Huntington had originally defined institutionalization as a process by which institutions become complex, autonomous, coherent, and adaptable; yet we have encountered in the Soviet Union a process of institutionalization that led to the first three consequences, but lacked adaptability.[5] Huntington had tended to impute to institutionalization positive normative shadings, yet we have encountered in the Soviet Union institutionalization that led to the most perverse dysfunction and maladaptation.

Fourth, the new institutionalist approach to authoritarian institutions stresses the importance of distinguishing state and society and in particular recognizing that the dynamics of the state are not simply derivative of the developments in society. In particular, it underscores the importance of distinguishing political development from social modernization. The former is not simply derivative of the latter. Political institutions create political processes of strategic behavior that can give politics a developmental logic of its own—a natural history. Moreover, political stability can be achieved for an extended period of time even though the institutionalization of the political order does not reflect the changing social modernization of society. Perhaps few polities will enjoy the freedom from social constraints that characterized the Soviet polity after forced departicipation of society. Yet, this case makes us aware of the need to investigate the natural history of political development alongside social modernization.

As is so common in projects, we conclude with more lines for further investigation than those with which we began. Although the new institutionalism answers the initial questions about the failure of Soviet politics, it is a tribute to the fruitfulness of this approach that it suggests broad agendas for further research. The comparison of the adaptability and survivability of alternative forms of vanguardism and authoritarianism—a point raised in the previous section—is, indeed, one area for study; the processes by which different forms of authoritarian institutions are created is another. The diverging political dynamics and developmental patterns of these different types of authoritarian institutions form yet a third, and the interplay of the natural history of authoritarian institutions with different patterns of social modernization offers a forth. All these suggest an important role for a new institutionalism of authoritarianism.

Notes

Chapter One
Why Did Soviet Bolshevism Fail?

1. Robert C. Tucker, "A Choice of Lenins?" in *Stalinism: Its Impact on Russia and the World*, ed. G. R. Urban (Cambridge: Harvard University Press, 1986), 170.

2. Daniel Chirot describes the Soviet Union as "the world's most advanced late nineteenth-century economy" in "What Happened in Eastern Europe in 1989?" in *The Crisis of Leninism and the Decline of the Left* (Seattle: University of Washington Press, 1991), 5–9.

3. Roger A. Clarke and Dubravko J. I. Matko, *Soviet Economic Facts, 1917–81* (London: Macmillan Press, 1983), 34, 49–50.

4. Albert O. Hirschman, *Journeys toward Progress* (New York: Twentieth-Century Fund, 1963), 267. Although the term *reform* has been widely used in the field of Soviet studies, there is no consensus on its meaning; see, for example, the very different use of this term in Thane Gustafson, *Reform in Soviet Politics: Lessons of Recent Policies on Land and Water* (Cambridge: Cambridge University Press, 1981), x.

5. Aristotle, *The Politics*, trans. T. A. Sinclair (Baltimore: Penguin Books, 1962), 6.1.151.

6. This point is made in a number of works on economic policy in Western democracies, such as G. John Ikenberry, David A. Lake, and Michael Mastanduno, eds., *The State and American Foreign Economic Policy* (Ithaca: Cornell University Press, 1988).

7. This study drew its original insight into the relationship among power, process, and policy from the classic study by Zbigniew K. Brzezinski and Samuel P. Huntington, *Political Power: USA/USSR* (New York: Viking Press, 1965), 191–232. It also draws from the analysis of the consequences of domestic process for policy outcomes in the still earlier work of Huntington in *The Common Defense* (New York: Columbia University Press, 1961) and of Warner Schilling, Paul Y. Hammond, and Glenn Snyder in *Strategy, Politics, and Defense Budgets* (New York: Columbia University Press, 1962).

8. The issue of path dependence in institutional development is raised in Douglass C. North, *Institutions, Institutional Change, and Economic Performance* (Cambridge: Cambridge University Press, 1990), 92–104.

9. Terry M. Moe, "The New Economics of Organization," *American Journal of Political Science* 28 (November 1984): 739–77; Terry M. Moe, "The Politics of Structural Choice: Toward a Theory of Public Bureaucracy" (Stanford: Stanford University, n.d., manuscript), 22; Douglass C. North and Barry R. Weingast, "Constitutions and Commitment: The Evolution of Institutions Governing Public Choice in Seventeenth-Century England," *The Journal of Economic History* 49 (December 1989): 803–32; Gary W. Cox, *The Efficient Secret: The Cabinet and*

the Development of Political Parties in Victorian England (Cambridge: Cambridge University Press, 1987).

10. Douglass C. North, *Institutions, Institutional Change, and Economic Performance* (Cambridge: Cambridge University Press, 1990), 3; Robert O. Keohane, "International Institutions: Two Approaches," *International Studies Quarterly* 32 (December 1988): 383–94; Oran Young, "International Regimes: Toward a New Theory of Institutions," *World Politics* 39 (October 1986): 107.

11. Contrast the behavioral approach that emphasizes the parochial perceptions of incumbents in James G. March and Johan P. Olsen, *Rediscovering Institutions* (New York: Free Press, 1989).

12. David K. Lewis, *Convention* (Cambridge: Harvard University Press, 1969), 78.

13. Harry Eckstein, "Constitutional Engineering and the Problem of Viable Representative Government," in *Comparative Politics: A Reader*, ed. Harry Eckstein and David E. Apter (New York: Free Press, 1963), 97–99. The term "rules in use" is found in Elinor Ostrom, *Crafting Institutions for Self-Governing Irrigation Systems* (San Francisco: ICS Press, 1992), 19–20.

14. Armen A. Alchian, "Uncertainty, Evolution, and Economic Theory," *Journal of Political Economy* 58 (June 1950): 211–21.

15. George Tsebelis, *Nested Games: Rational Choice in Comparative Politics* (Berkeley: University of California Press, 1990), 32–34.

16. David R. Mayhew, *Congress: The Electoral Connection* (New Haven: Yale University Press, 1974), 13, 16.

17. Barry Ames, *Political Survival: Politicians and Public Policy in Latin America* (Berkeley: University of California Press, 1987), 1.

18. The assumption that Soviet leaders were concerned with power has been criticized because it purportedly treats them as unique and, therefore, treats Soviet politics as sui generis. Yet, just the opposite is true: The strategic behavior of Soviet politicians can be compared with that of their Western counterparts by the methods of institutional analysis as long as we can begin with the premise that members of the Politburo were no *more* principled and no *less* concerned with holding on to office than, say, United States congressmen. This analogy with the "electoral connection" that has led to such powerful analysis in studying other polities, permits comparative analyses and integration of the study of Soviet politics in the broader field of political science.

19. Douglass C. North, *Structure and Change in Economic History* (New York: W. W. Norton & Company, 1981), 20–32.

20. Margaret Levi, *Of Rule and Revenue* (Berkeley: University of California Press, 1988), 3.

21. Douglas W. Rae, *The Political Consequences of Electoral Laws* (New Haven: Yale University Press, 1967); Matthew Soberg Shugart and John M. Carey, *Presidents and Assemblies: Constitutional Design and Electoral Dynamics* (Cambridge: Cambridge University Press, 1992).

22. George F. Kennan, "Introduction," in Boris I. Nicolaevsky, *Power and the Soviet Elite* (New York: Frederick A. Praeger, Publishers, 1965), xiii–xxi.

23. Jerome Gilison, "New Factors of Stability in Soviet Collective Leadership," *World Politics* 19 (June 1967): 568–69; Myron Rush, "Succession and Institutions in the Soviet Union," *Journal of International Affairs* 18, no. 1

(1964): 69; Myron Rush, "The Khrushchev Succession Problem," *World Politics* 14 (January 1962): 259–63.

24. T. H. Rigby, "Khrushchev and the Rules of the Soviet Political Game," in *Khrushchev and the Communist World*, ed. R. F. Miller and F. Feher (Totowan: Barnes and Noble, 1984), 39.

25. Thane Gustafson and Dawn Mann, "Gorbachev's First Year: Building Power and Authority," *Problems of Communism* 35 (May–June 1986): 1. Also see George W. Breslauer, "Evaluating Gorbachev as Leader," *Soviet Economy* 5 (October–December 1989): 308.

26. Graeme Gill, "Institutionalisation and Revolution: Rules and the Soviet Political System," *Soviet Studies* 37 (April 1985): 212–26.

27. Juan J. Linz, "Totalitarian and Authoritarian Regimes," in *Macropolitical Theory*, ed. Fred I. Greenstein and Nelson W. Polsby (Reading: Addison-Wesley Publishing Company, 1975), 175, 179–80. Also see the institutional analysis of state-society relations in Amos Perlmutter, *Modern Authoritarianism: A Comparative Institutional Analysis* (New Haven: Yale University Press, 1981).

28. These categories are not exclusive, so that a two-by-two classification would yield four distinct analytic approaches.

29. Brian Barry, *Sociologists, Economists, and Democracy* (London: Macmillan Company, 1970), 3–7.

30. Eric A. Nordlinger, "Taking the State Seriously," in *Understanding Political Development*, ed. Myron Weiner and Samuel P. Huntington (Boston: Little, Brown and Company, 1987), 353–90; Theda Skocpol, "Bringing the State Back," in *Bringing the State Back In*, ed. Peter B. Evans, Dietrich Rueschemeyer, and Theda Skocpol (Cambridge: Cambridge University Press, 1985), 3–37; Stephen D. Krasner, "Approaches to the State: Alternative Conceptions and Historical Dynamics," *Comparative Politics* 16 (January 1984): 223–46.

31. Hans J. Morgenthau and Kenneth W. Thompson, *Politics Among Nations*, 6th ed. (New York: Alfred A. Knopf, 1985), 13, 16.

32. Stephen F. Cohen, *Rethinking the Soviet Experience* (New York: Oxford University Press, 1985), 146.

33. Carl J. Friedrich and Zbigniew K. Brzezinski, *Totalitarian Dictatorship and Autocracy* (New York: Frederick A. Praeger, 1961), 70, 84.

34. Merle Fainsod, *How Russia is Ruled*, rev. ed. (Cambridge: Harvard University Press, 1967), 596; also see 580–81.

35. Friedrich and Brzezinski, *Totalitarian Dictatorship*, 298. Also see Zbigniew K. Brzezinski, *Ideology and Power in Soviet Politics* (New York: Frederick A. Praeger, 1962), 82–91.

36. Carl A. Linden, *The Soviet Party-State: The Politics of Ideocratic Despotism* (New York: Praeger Publishers, 1983), 157.

37. Gail W. Lapidus, "Gorbachev and the Reform of the Social System," *Daedelus* 116 (Spring 1987): 8–9.

38. Chirot, "What Happened in Eastern Europe," 18, 20.

39. George W. Breslauer, "Soviet Economic Reforms Since Stalin: Ideology, Politics, and Learning," *Soviet Economy* 6 (July–September 1990): 255, 268.

40. James Clay Moltz, "Divergent Learning and the Failed Politics of Soviet Economic Reform," *World Politics* 45 (January 1993): 301–25.

41. Cited in Alfred G. Meyer, "Theories of Convergence," in *Change in Communist Systems*, ed. Chalmers Johnson (Stanford: Stanford University Press, 1970), 320.

42. Geoffrey Hosking, *The Awakening of the Soviet Union*, enlarged ed. (Cambridge: Harvard University Press, 1991), 5.

43. Moshe Lewin, *The Gorbachev Phenomenon: A Historical Interpretation* (Berkeley: University of California Press, 1988), 130.

44. Ibid., 54.

45. Robert V. Daniels, *Is Russia Reformable? Change and Resistance from Stalin to Gorbachev* (Boulder: Westview Press, 1988), 80.

46. Timothy J. Colton, *The Dilemma of Reform in the Soviet Union*, rev. ed. (New York: Council on Foreign Relations, 1986), 106, 109–10. Generational change need not be society-centered. Jerry F. Hough develops a state-centered generational analysis that focuses on changing political selection mechanisms: Each period of Soviet history selected, trained, and promoted different types of individuals, who brought distinctive values into high political positions. Hough stresses that the Soviet system was not so much petrified in the Brezhnev period as lagging in its normal development because the generation that had come to power prematurely after the Purge held power for an abnormally long time. Jerry F. Hough, *Soviet Leadership in Transition* (Washington, D.C.: Brookings Institution, 1980), 9–15, 29–35.

47. Jack Snyder makes a similar critique of "holistic" analyses in the study of Soviet foreign policy; see "Science and Sovietology: Bridging the Methods Gap in Soviet Foreign Policy Studies," *World Politics* 40 (January 1988): 177.

48. Seweryn Bialer, *Stalin's Successors: Leadership, Stability, and Change in the Soviet Union* (Cambridge: Cambridge University Press, 1980), 103. Also see Robert Conquest, "Stalin's Successors," *Foreign Affairs* 48 (April 1970): 514.

49. Robert Conquest, *Power and Policy in the U.S.S.R.: The Study of Soviet Dynastics* (New York: Harper & Row, 1967), 26–27; Alexander Dallin, "Soviet Foreign Policy and Domestic Politics: A Framework for Analysis," *Journal of International Affairs* 23 (Fall–Winter 1969): 250–65; Carl A. Linden, *Khrushchev and the Soviet Leadership, 1957–1964* (Baltimore: Johns Hopkins University Press, 1966), 18–19; Thomas H. Rigby, "The Limits and Extent of Authority," *Problems of Communism* 12 (September–October 1963): 36–41.

50. Mark R. Beissinger, "In Search of Generations in Soviet Politics," *World Politics* 38 (January 1986): 304–12; George W. Breslauer, "Is There a Generation Gap in the Soviet Political Establishment?: Demand Articulation by RSFSR Provincial Party First Secretaries," *Soviet Studies* 36 (January 1984): 1–25.

51. Breslauer, "Is there a Generation Gap?" 12. Beissinger's study of articles by ninety-eight officials (first or second secretaries of Party oblast committees and chairmen of oblast soviet executive committees) in thirty-eight provinces shows that "younger officials in general do not display economic concerns that are significantly different from those of their elders." Only on three of thirteen issues that he examined did Beissinger find support for "the hypothesis that the regional apparatus is divided on economic issues along generational lines." Beissinger, "In Search of Generations," 288, 303.

52. Cohen, *Rethinking the Soviet Experience*, 146.

Chapter Two
The Authoritarian Constitution

1. A parallel study of Chinese politics is Susan Shirk, *The Political Logic of Economic Reform in China* (Berkeley: University of California Press, 1993).

2. This metaphor, obviously, draws on Thomas S. Kuhn's distinction between "normal" science that proceeds within the rules of a given paradigm and scientific revolutions that seek to change those paradigms; *The Structure of Scientific Revolutions*, 2d ed. (Chicago: University of Chicago Press, 1970).

3. Graham Maddox, "A Note on the Meaning of 'Constitution,' " *American Political Science Review* 76 (December 1982): 806.

4. S. E. Finer, *Comparative Government* (New York: Basic Books, 1971), 145. Also see K. C. Wheare, *Modern Constitutions* (New York: Oxford University Press, 1966), 1.

5. Juan J. Linz, "Totalitarian and Authoritarian Regimes," in *Macropolitical Theory*, ed. Fred I. Greenstein and Nelson W. Polsby (Reading: Addison-Wesley Publishing Company, 1975), 176, 182–83. There are some important exceptions to this, such as the studies of the dynamics of one-party regimes in Samuel P. Huntington and Clement H. Moore, eds., *Authoritarian Politics in Modern Society: Dynamics of Established One-Party Systems* (New York: Basic Books, 1970).

6. Aristotle, *The Politics*, trans. T. A. Sinclair (Baltimore: Penguin Books, 1962), 3.7.115–16. That Aristotle intends this to be distinct from the issue of accountability becomes clear when he discusses elective kingship with fixed terms of office as a form of rule by one (see 3.14.178–82).

7. For example, see Mancur Olson, Jr., *The Logic of Collective Action: Public Goods and the Theory of Groups* (Cambridge: Harvard University Press, 1965), chaps. 1–2.

8. Ellen Comisso, "Introduction: State Structures, Political Processes, and Collective Choice in CMEA States," in *Power, Purpose, and Collective Choice: Economic Strategies in Socialist States*, ed. Ellen Comisso and Laura D'Andrea Tyson (Ithaca: Cornell University Press, 1986), 37–59.

9. Montesquieu, *The Spirit of the Laws*, trans. Thomas Nugent (New York: Hafner Publishing Company, 1949), Book 2, 2.

10. Robert A. Dahl, *Polyarchy: Participation and Opposition* (New Haven: Yale University Press, 1971), 4.

11. Kenneth J. Arrow, "The Economics of Agency," in *Principals and Agents: The Structure of Business*, ed. John W. Pratt and Richard J. Zeckhauser (Boston: Harvard Business School Press, 1985), 37.

12. Terry M. Moe, "The New Economics of Organization," *American Journal of Political Science* 28 (November 1984): 765.

13. Terry M. Moe, "Political Control and Professional Autonomy: The Institutional Politics of the NLRB" (Paper prepared for delivery at the Annual Meeting of the American Political Science Association, Washington, D.C., 27–31 August 1986).

14. David R. Mayhew, *Congress: The Electoral Connection* (New Haven: Yale University Press, 1974).

15. Francis X. Murphy, "Vatican Politics: Structure and Function," *World*

Politics 26 (July 1974): 542–59; John F. Avedon, *In Exile from the Land of Snows* (New York: Knopf, 1984).

16. Guillermo A. O'Donnell, *Modernization and Bureaucratic-Authoritarianism: Studies in South American Politics* (Berkeley: Institute of International Studies, University of California, 1973).

17. J. V. Stalin, *Foundations of Leninism* in *Works* (Moscow: Foreign Languages Publishing House, 1953), 6:177–78.

18. Raymond William Baker, *Egypt's Uncertain Revolution under Nasser and Sadat* (Cambridge: Harvard University Press, 1978), 159, 161; see also 48–51.

19. Amos Perlmutter, *Egypt: The Praetorian State* (New Brunswick: Transaction Books, 1974), 135.

20. One mechanism to convert democratic-appearing institutions into authoritarianism through reciprocal accountability is the integrated electoral machine. This machine that reaches from the pinnacle of the political system down into each electoral district delivers votes either through pork or manipulation. See the description of the electoral machines in Robert H. Bates and Paul Collier, "The Politics of Economic Reform in Zambia" (ms., January 1991); Chan Heng Chee, *The Dynamics of One-Party Dominance: The PAP at the Grass-roots* (Singapore: Singapore University Press, 1976); Dilip Hiro, *Iran Under the Ayatollahs* (London: Routledge & Kegan Paul, 1985).

21. Jean-Jacques Rousseau, *The Government of Poland*, trans. Willmoore Kendall (Indianapolis: Bobbs-Merrill, 1972).

22. The parallel most frequently drawn with Western practices in order to capture the essence of this reciprocity in the Soviet Union and other institutionalized authoritarianism regimes is patron-clientage. Yet this is a misleading parallel because the structure of rights in a reciprocal relationship differs from those in Western patron-clientage. In the economic model of patron-clientage both actors have definitive rights: the patron to land, the client to his labor. (Ammar Siamwalla, "An Economic Theory of Patron-Client Relationships: With Some Examples from Thailand" [Paper delivered to the Thai-European Seminar on Social Change in Contemporary Thailand, 28–30 May 1980].) Insofar as there is delegation it is a unilateral transfer of some control over the landlord's property—a hierarchical principal-agent relationship. In the political model of patron-clientage the client has a definitive right to vote, but the patron's right to public office is contingent. This hierarchical relationship has one dependent actor, the patron. In reciprocal relationships the rights of both actors are contingent, and both actors are dependent on each other for the continued exercise of those rights.

23. Perlmutter, *Egypt*, 135–38.

24. Eugene F. Fama, "Agency Problems and the Theory of the Firm," *Journal of Political Economy* 88 (April 1980): 290–92.

25. Baker, *Egypt's Uncertain Future*, 52, 160.

26. Alfred Stepan, *The Military in Politics: Changing Patterns in Brazil* (Princeton: Princeton University Press, 1971), 222.

27. For an illustration of these institutional problems, see the discussion of the Numeiri regime in Peter Woodward, *Sudan, 1898–1989: The Unstable State* (Boulder: Lynne Reiner Publishers, 1990), 137–64.

28. Karen L. Remmer, *Military Rule in Latin America* (Boston: Unwin Hyman, 1989), 129.

29. Myron Rush, *How Communist States Change Their Rulers* (Ithaca: Cornell University Press, 1974), 17–19.

30. Fernando Henrique Cardoso, "On the Characterization of Authoritarian Regimes in Latin America," in *The New Authoritarianism in Latin America*, ed. David Collier (Princeton: Princeton University Press, 1979), 42.

31. Barry Ames, *Political Survival: Politicians and Public Policy in Latin America* (Berkeley: University of California Press, 1987), 1, 44–45, 47–73.

32. Karen L. Remmer, *Party Competition in Argentina and Chile: Political Recruitment and Public Policy, 1890–1930* (Lincoln: University of Nebraska Press, 1984), 218–19.

33. Carl J. Friedrich, "Public Policy and the Nature of Administrative Responsibility," *Public Policy* (Cambridge: Harvard University Press, 1940), 1:3–24; Randall L. Calvert, Mark J. Moran, and Barry R. Weingast, "Congressional Influence Over Policy Making: The Case of the FTC," in *Congress: Structure and Policy*, ed. Mathew D. McCubbins and Terry Sullivan (Cambridge: Cambridge University Press, 1987), 498.

34. Thomas E. Skidmore, "Politics and Economic Policy Making in Authoritarian Brazil, 1937–71," in *Authoritarian Brazil: Origins, Policies, and Future*, ed. Alfred Stepan (New Haven: Yale University Press, 1973), 17.

35. George Tsebelis, *Nested Games: Rational Choice in Comparative Politics* (Berkeley: University of California Press, 1990), 8. Tsebelis cites the example of parties that feel disadvantaged in legislative elections and then seek to change the rule for apportioning legislative seats or governing reelection. See the discussion of "punctuated equilibrium," which gives the relationship between the two games a temporal relationship, in Stephen D. Krasner, "Approaches to the State: Alternative Conceptions and Historical Dynamics," *Comparative Politics* 16 (January 1984): 240–44.

36. Fernando Henrique Cardoso, "On the Characterization of Authoritarian Regimes in Latin America," in *The New Authoritarianism in Latin America*, ed. David Collier (Princeton: Princeton University Press, 1979), 41.

37. Arturo Valenzuela, "The Military in Power: The Consolidation of One-Man Rule in Chile," in *The Struggle for Democracy in Chile, 1982–1990*, ed. Paul Drake and Ivan Jaksic (Lincoln: University of Nebraska Press, 1991), 34.

38. Chilton Williamson, *American Suffrage from Property to Democracy, 1760–1860* (Princeton: Princeton University Press, 1960), 158.

39. Samuel P. Huntington, *Political Order in Changing Societies* (New Haven: Yale University Press, 1968), 443; Stein Rokkan, *Citizens, Elections, Parties: Approaches to the Comparative Study of the Processes of Development* (Oslo: Universitetsforlaget, 1970), 31–33.

40. Stepan, *The Military in Politics*, 265.

41. Alfred Stepan, *Rethinking Military Politics: Brazil and the Southern Cone* (Princeton: Princeton University Press, 1988), 36, 40–41.

42. Alfred Stepan, *The State and Society: Peru in Comparative Perspective* (Princeton: Princeton University Press, 1978), 292–93.

43. E. E. Schattschneider, *The Semisovereign People: A Realist's View of Democracy in America* (Hinsdale: Dryden Press, 1960), 4, 16, 99–100.

44. Huntington, *Political Order in Changing Societies*, 448–61. Also see Wil-

liam R. Keech, *The Impact of Negro Voting: The Role of the Vote in the Quest for Equality* (Chicago: Rand McNally & Co., 1968), 93.

45. O'Donnell, *Modernization and Bureaucratic-Authoritarianism*, 53, 91–92.

46. Thomas E. Skidmore, "Politics and Economic Policy Making in Authoritarian Brazil, 1937–71," in *Authoritarian Brazil: Origins, Policies, and Future*, ed. Alfred Stepan (New Haven: Yale University Press, 1973), 26–28.

47. Robert H. Bates, *Markets and States in Tropical Africa: The Political Bases of Agricultural Policies* (Berkeley: University of California Press, 1981), 106.

48. Where the participant population is limited as well, politicians may also seek to expand the political arena by only expanding the unenfranchised participants.

49. Kenneth A. Oye, "Explaining Cooperation Under Anarchy: Hypotheses and Strategies," in *Cooperation Under Anarchy*, ed. Kenneth A. Oye (Princeton: Princeton University Press, 1986), 7; Robert Axelrod, *The Evolution of Cooperation* (New York: Basic Books, 1984).

50. Huntington, *Political Order in Changing Societies*, 460.

51. These strategies are illustrated by the relationship between Gosplan and producers in the Soviet command economy.

52. Thomas C. Schelling, *The Strategy of Conflict* (New York: Oxford University Press, 1963), 86. Also see David Lewis's discussion of conventions in his *Convention* (Cambridge: Harvard University Press, 1969), 78; Russell Hardin, *Collective Action* (Baltimore: Johns Hopkins University Press, 1982), 158–61.

53. Ibid., 59.

54. Carl A. Linden, *Khrushchev and the Soviet Leadership, 1957–1964* (Baltimore: Johns Hopkins University Press, 1966), 5, 7; also 12–15.

55. Moe describes the institutionalization of the appointments structure on the National Labor Relations Board in the following way: "Participants speak of the 'traditional' way in which appointments are made. They know their own roles, they know everyone else's roles, and a new vacancy on the Board prompts them to do what they have 'always' done—evoking what is roughly a programmed response by the system, with all roles meshing well with one another." Moe, "Political Control and Professional Autonomy," 16.

56. Huntington, *Political Order in Changing Societies*, 12–24.

57. On the nature of models in social science, see Karl W. Deutsch, *The Nerves of Government* (New York: The Free Press, 1966), 3–21. Also see Mark Monmonier, *How to Lie with Maps* (Chicago: University of Chicago Press, 1991).

Chapter Three
Creating the Constitution of Bolshevism, 1917–1953

1. V. I. Lenin, *Chto delat'?* in *Polnoe sobranie sochinenii*, 5th ed. (Moscow: Izdatel'stvo Politicheskoi Literatury, 1979), 6:1–192. See also Kenneth Jowitt, "Inclusion and Mobilization in European Leninist Regimes," *World Politics* 28 (October 1975): 70, 81; T. H. Rigby, *The Changing Soviet System: Mono-organizational Socialism from Its Origin to Gorbachev's Restructuring* (Brookfield: Edward Elgar, 1990), 1–19.

2. Merle Fainsod, *How Russia is Ruled*, rev. ed. (Cambridge: Harvard University Press, 1967), 426, 428, 430.

3. Alexander Dallin and George W. Breslauer, *Political Terror in Communist Systems* (Stanford: Stanford University Press, 1970), 7, 32, 34.

4. Peter Kenez, *The Birth of the Propaganda State* (Cambridge: Cambridge University Press, 1985).

5. Samuel P. Huntington and Joan Nelson, *No Easy Choice* (Cambridge: Harvard University Press, 1976), 85. Also see Leonard Schapiro, *The Origins of the Communist Autocracy* (London: Macmillan, 1977); Philip Selznick, *The Organizational Weapon* (Santa Monica: Rand Corporation, 1952).

6. Leonard Schapiro, *The Origins of the Communist Autocracy: Political Opposition in the Soviet State* (Cambridge: Harvard University Press, 1977), 111–209.

7. V. I. Lenin, "O prodovol'stvennom naloge," in *Polnoe sobranie sochinenii*, 5th ed. (Moscow: Izdatel'stvo Politicheskoi Literatury, 1977), 43:241. See Oliver Henry Radkey, *The Sickle under the Hammer: The Russian Socialist Revolutionaries in the Early Months of Soviet Rule* (New York: Columbia University Press, 1963); Vladimir N. Brovkin, *The Mensheviks after October: Socialist Opposition and the Rise of the Bolshevik Dictatorship* (Ithaca: Cornell University Press, 1987).

8. Kenez, *Birth of the Propaganda State*, 44, 100–101.

9. "Rezoliutsii i postanovleniia VIII s"ezda RKP(b): 'Po organizatsionnomu voprosu,' " in Institut Marksizma-Leninizma pri Ts. K. KPSS, *Vos'moi s"ezd RKP(b): Protokoly* (Moscow: Izdatel'stvo Politicheskoi Literatury, 1959), 428.

10. Lenin, *Chto delat'?* 1–192; "Pis'mo k tovarishchu o nashikh organizatsionnykh zadachakh," in *Polnoe sobranie sochinenii*, 5th ed. (Moscow: Izdatel'stvo Politicheskoi Literatury, 1979), 7:1–32.

11. Julian Towster, *Political Power in the U.S.S.R., 1917–1947* (New York: Oxford University Press, 1948), 187–295; Edward Hallett Carr, *The Bolshevik Revolution, 1917–1923* (New York: Macmillan Company, 1951), 124–50.

12. Leonard Schapiro, *The Communist Party of the Soviet Union*, 2d ed. (New York: Vintage Books, 1971), 242–45; Robert Service, *The Bolshevik Party in Revolution: A Study in Organisational Change, 1917–1923* (London: Macmillan Press, 1979), 123–33.

13. T. H. Rigby, *Lenin's Government: Sovnarkom, 1917–1922* (Cambridge: Cambridge University Press, 1979), 72, 129, 183.

14. "Po organizatsionnomu voprosu," in *Kommunisticheskaia Partiia Sovetskogo Soiuza v rezoliutsiiakh i resheniiakh s"ezdov, konferentsii i plenumov TsK* (Moscow: Gosudarstvennoe Izdatel'stvo Politicheskoi Literatury, 1954), 1:443.

15. "Otchet o rabote Ts. K. za period ot 9 do 10 partiinogo s"ezda," *Izvestiia Tsentral'nogo Komiteta Rossiiskoi Kommunisticheskoi Partii (bol'shevikov)*, no. 29 (7 March 1921), 7; "O material'nom polozhenii aktivnykh partrabotnikov," in *Kommunisticheskaia Partiia Sovetskogo Soiuza v rezoliutsiiakh i resheniiakh s"ezdov, konferentsii i plenumov TsK* (Moscow: Gosudarstvennoe Izdatel'stvo Politicheskoi Literatury, 1954), 1:677.

16. V. I. Lenin, "Ocherednye zadachi Sovetskoi vlasti," in *Polnoe sobranie*

sochinenii, 5th ed. (Moscow: Izdatel'stvo Politicheskoi Literatury, 1981), 36:165–208.

17. V. I. Lenin, "Doklad Tsentral'nogo Komiteta, 29 marta 1920 g.," in *Polnoe sobranie sochinenii*, 5th ed. (Moscow: Izdatel'stvo Politicheskoi Literatury, 1981), 40:237–57.

18. "Otchet uchetno-raspredelitel'nogo otdela," *Izvestiia Tsentral'nogo Komiteta Rossiiskoi Kommunisticheskoi Partii (bol'shevikov)*, no. 29 (5 March 1921): 13.

19. J. V. Stalin, "The Organizational Report of the Central Committee to the R.C.P.(b)," in *Works* (Moscow: Foreign Languages Publishing House, 1953), 5:199–226.

20. Graeme Gill, *The Origins of the Stalinist Political System* (Cambridge: Cambridge University Press, 1990), 164–65; T. H. Rigby, "The Origins of the Nomenklatura System," *Soviet Studies* 40 (October 1988): 523–37.

21. "Otchet uchetno-raspredelitel'nogo otdela," *Izvestiia Tsentral'nogo Komiteta Rossiiskoi Kommunisticheskoi Partii (b)*, no. 3 [51] [March 1923]: 28–31.

22. Ibid., 51–52.

23. Terry M. Moe, "The New Economics of Organization," *American Journal of Political Science* 28 (November 1984): 754–55.

24. Amos Perlmutter and William M. LeoGrande, "The Party in Uniform: Toward a Theory of Civil-Military Relations in Communist Political Systems," *American Political Science Review* 76 (December 1982): 779.

25. T. D. Ionkina, *Vse rossiiskie s"ezdy sovetov v pervye gody proletarskoi diktatury* (Moscow: Nauka, 1974), 118, 225.

26. These nine commissariats include Internal Affairs, Health, Agriculture, Foreign Affairs, Navy, Justice, Nationalities, Cheka (Police), and the National Economic Council.

27. These eight commissariats include State Control, Army, Food Supplies, Transport, Social Security, Trade and Industry, Labor, and Finance.

28. M. P. Iroshnikov, *Predsedatel' Soveta Narodnykh Komissarov: Vl. Ul'ianov (Lenin)* (Leningrad: Nauka, 1974), 366–69, 390–93, 404–6.

29. Ia. M. Bineman and S. Kheiman, *Kadry gosudarstvennogo i kooperativnogo apparata SSSR* (Moscow: Gosudarstvennoe Planovo-Khoziaistvennoe Izdatel'stvo, 1930), 202–7.

30. Mathew D. McCubbins and Thomas Schwartz, "Congressional Oversight Overlooked: Police Patrols versus Fire Alarms," *American Journal of Political Science* 28 (February 1984): 165–79.

31. E. A. Rees, *State Control in Russia: The Rise and Fall of the Workers' and Peasants' Inspectorate, 1920–34* (London: Macmillan Press, 1987), 6–7, 12–24; Fainsod, *How Russia Is Ruled*, 386–420.

32. V. I. Lenin, "Politicheskii otchet Tsentral'nogo Komiteta RKP(b), 27 marta," in *Polnoe sobranie sochinenii*, 5th ed. (Moscow: Izdatel'stvo Politicheskoi Literatury, 1982), 45:114.

33. Quoted in Jeremy Azrael, *Managerial Power and Soviet Politics* (Cambridge: Harvard University Press, 1966), 65. See also Kendall E. Bailes, *Technology and Society under Lenin and Stalin: Origins of the Soviet Technical In-*

telligentsia, 1917–1941 (Princeton: Princeton University Press, 1978), 44–66.

34. Bineman and Kheiman, *Kadry gosudarstvennogo i kooperativnogo apparata*, 202–7.

35. "O edinstve partii," in *Kommunisticheskaia Partiia Sovetskogo Soiuza v rezoliutsiiakh i resheniiakh s"ezdov, konferentsii i plenumov TsK* (Moscow: Gosudarstvennoe Izdatel'stvo Politicheskoi Literatury, 1954), 1:529.

36. "Ustav Rossiiskoi Kommunisticheskoi Partii (Bol'shevikov)," in *Kommunisticheskaia Partiia Sovetskogo Soiuza v rezoliutsiiakh i resheniiakh s"ezdov, konferentsii i plenumov TsK* (Moscow: Gosudarstvennoe Izdatel'stvo Politicheskoi Literatury, 1954), 1:467.

37. "O edinstve partii," 529. Also see Schapiro, *Origins of the Communist Autocracy*, 211–361.

38. "Ustav Rossiiskoi Kommunisticheskoi Partii (Bol'shevikov)," 467.

39. Robert V. Daniels, *Conscience of the Revolution: Communist Opposition in Soviet Russia* (Cambridge: Harvard University Press, 1961), 103, 168.

40. Isaac Deutscher, *The Prophet Unarmed, Trotsky: 1921–1929* (London: Oxford University Press, 1959), 123.

41. J. V. Stalin, "Report on the Immediate Tasks in Party Affairs, 17 January," *Works* (Moscow: Foreign Languages Publishing House, 1953), 6:5–26.

42. Borys Levytsky, *The Soviet Political Elite* (Stanford: Hoover Institution Press, 1969).

43. Ibid.; Roy D. Laird, *The Politburo: Demographic Trends, Gorbachev, and the Future* (Boulder: Westview Press, 1986); John Lowenhardt, James R. Ozinga, and Erik van Ree, *The Rise and Fall of the Soviet Politburo* (New York: St. Martin's Press, 1992), 161–228.

44. Gill, *Origins of the Stalinist Political System*, 149.

45. Nikita S. Khrushchev, *Khrushchev Remembers* (Boston: Little, Brown and Co., 1970), 133, 174, 281–82.

46. Robert Conquest, *Power and Policy in the USSR* (New York: Harper & Row, 1967), 31–32.

47. Khrushchev, *Khrushchev Remembers*, 614–15.

48. Robert V. Daniels, "Office Holding and Elite Status: The Central Committee of the CPSU," in *The Dynamics of Soviet Politics*, ed. Paul Cocks, Robert V. Daniels, and Nancy Whittier-Heer (Cambridge: Harvard University Press, 1976), 78.

49. Azrael, *Managerial Power and Soviet Politics*, 77–90.

50. Robert V. Daniels, "Soviet Politics Since Khrushchev," in *The Soviet Union under Brezhnev and Kosygin*, ed. John W. Strong (New York: van Nostrand-Reinhold Co., 1971), 20.

51. T. H. Rigby, "Early Provincial Cliques and the Rise of Stalin," *Soviet Studies* 33 (January 1981): 3–28.

52. Fainsod, *How Russia is Ruled*, 151.

53. Computed from Gill, *Origins of the Stalinist Political System*, 145.

54. Institut Marksizma-Leninizma pri Ts. K. KPSS, *Spravochnyi tom k vos'momu izdaniiu "KPSS v rezoliutsiiakh i resheniiakh s"ezdov, konferentsii i plenumov TsK"*, 2d ed. (Moscow: Izdatel'stvo Politicheskoi Literatury, 1984), 11.

55. Roy A. Medvedev, *Let History Judge* (New York: Alfred A. Knopf, 1972), 155–57. Also see J. Arch Getty, *Origins of the Great Purges: The Soviet Communist Party Reconsidered, 1933–1938* (Cambridge: Cambridge University Press, 1985), 10–37.

56. At some risk of belaboring a point: In a hierarchical constitutional order, leaders make appeals to, but cannot remove and appoint, selectors. Reciprocity complicates the former, by the latter.

57. T. H. Rigby, *Communist Party Membership in the U.S.S.R., 1917–1967* (Princeton: Princeton University Press, 1968), 119, 131.

58. Daniels, "Soviet Politics Since Khrushchev," 20; Robert V. Daniels, "The Evolution of Leadership Selection in the Central Committee, 1917–1927," in *Russian Officialdom: The Bureaucratization of Russian Society from the Seventeenth to the Twentieth Century*, ed. Walter McKenzie Pinter and Don Karl Rowney (Chapel Hill: University of North Carolina Press, 1980), 357–60; Gill, *Origins of the Stalinist Political System*, 140–41, 150.

59. *XIV s"ezd Vsesoiuznoi Kommunisticheskoi Partii (b)—Stenograficheskii otchet* (Moscow: Gosudarstvennoe Izdatel'stvo, 1926), 321; Krupskaia's comments appear on p. 165.

60. Edward Hallett Carr, *The Interregnum, 1923–1924* (London: Macmillan and Company, 1954), 257–346; Isaac Deutscher, *Stalin: A Political Biography* (New York: Oxford University Press, 1949), 228–93.

61. *XIV s"ezd Vsesoiuznoi Kommunisticheskoi Partii (b)*, 194.

62. Graeme Gill, *The Rules of the Communist Party of the Soviet Union* (London: Macmillan Press, 1988), 147.

63. "Po delu Lashevicha i dr. i o edinstve partii," "O narushenii partiinoi distsipliny Zinov'evym i Trotskim," "Ob iskliuchenii Zinov'eva i Trotskogo iz TsK VKP(b)," in *Kommunisticheskaia Partiia Sovetskogo Soiuza v rezoliutsiiakh i resheniiakh s"ezdov, konferentsii i plenumov TsK* (Moscow: Gosudarstvennoe Izdatel'stvo Politicheskoi Literatury, 1954), 2:280–86, 387–94, 488–90.

64. Malcolm Mackintosh, *Juggernaut: A History of the Soviet Armed Forces* (New York: Macmillan Company, 1967), 52–58; Mark von Hagen, *Soldiers in the Proletarian Dictatorship* (Ithaca: Cornell University Press, 1990), 195–205, 210–20.

65. Amy W. Knight, *The KGB: Police and Politics in the Soviet Union* (Boston: Unwin Hyman, 1988), 21–22.

66. Boris Nicolaevsky, *Power and the Soviet Elite* (New York: Frederick A. Praeger, Publishers, 1965), 105–20.

67. Khrushchev, *Khrushchev Remembers*, 81.

68. This underscores that in reciprocal accountability the constituencies are not simply autonomous principals exercising hierarchical control over leaders.

69. Carl J. Friedrich and Zbigniew K. Brzezinski, *Totalitarian Dictatorship and Autocracy*, 2d ed. (Cambridge: Harvard University Press, 1965); Zbigniew K. Brzezinski, *Ideology and Power in Soviet Politics* (New York: Frederick A. Praeger, 1962).

70. Zbigniew K. Brzezinski and Samuel P. Huntington, *Political Power: USA/USSR* (New York: Viking Press, 1964), chap. 4.

71. Carl A. Linden, *Khrushchev and the Soviet Leadership, 1957–1964* (Bal-

timore: Johns Hopkins University Press, 1966), 2–15. Also see Conquest, *Power and Policy in the USSR*, 3–75; Sidney Ploss, *Conflict and Decision-making in Soviet Russia* (Princeton: Princeton University Press, 1965), 1–24.

72. H. Gordon Skilling, "Groups in Soviet Politics: Some Hypotheses," in *Interest Groups in Soviet Politics*, ed. H. Gordon Skilling and Franklyn Griffiths (Princeton: Princeton University Press, 1967), 20. Also see Darrell P. Hammer, *U.S.S.R.: The Politics of Oligarchy* (New York: Praeger Publishers, 1974), 223–54; Susan Gross Solomon, ed., *Pluralism in the Soviet Union* (London: Macmillan Press, 1983).

Chapter Four
Reciprocal Accountability, 1953–1986

1. Roy A. Medvedev and Zhores A. Medvedev, *Khrushchev: The Years in Power* (New York: W. W. Norton and Co., 1978), 2–3; Myron Rush, *The Rise of Khrushchev* (Washington, D.C.: Public Affairs Press, 1958), 40; Edward Crankshaw, *Khrushchev: A Career* (New York: Viking Press, 1966), 188. Although the Politburo was renamed Presidium of the Central Committee in October 1952 and continued to bear this name until 1965, the former name will be used to avoid confusion with the Presidium of the Council of Ministers.

2. Medvedev and Medvedev, *Khrushchev: The Years in Power*, 5; Roy Medvedev, *Khrushchev* (Garden City: Anchor Press, 1983), 64–65.

3. Nikita S. Khrushchev, *Khrushchev Remembers* (Boston: Little, Brown and Co., 1970), 336.

4. Medvedev, *Khrushchev*, 57; Robert Conquest, *Power and Policy in the USSR* (New York: Harper & Row, 1967), 197.

5. Rush, *The Rise of Khrushchev*, 78–79; also see T. H. Rigby, "How Strong is the Leader?" *Problems of Communism* 11 (September–October 1962): 3; Giuseppe Boffa, *Inside the Kremlin* (New York: Marzani and Munsell, 1959), 26; Roger Pethybridge, *A Key to Soviet Politics: The Crisis of the Anti-Party Group* (New York: Frederick A. Praeger, 1962), 106.

6. R. Lynev, "Ot ottepeli do zastoia: Beseda s personal'nym pensionernom, byvshim chlenom Politbiuro TsK KPSS," *Izvestiia*, 18 November 1988.

7. Medvedev and Medvedev, *Khrushchev: The Years in Power*, 172; William Hyland and Richard W. Shryock, *The Fall of Khrushchev* (New York: Funk and Wagnalls, 1968), 188–89; Sergei Khrushchev, *Khrushchev on Khrushchev* (Boston: Little, Brown and Co., 1990), 159–60. The elaborate consultation with Central Committee members is confirmed in accounts offered by Khrushchev's son Sergei (ibid., 70, 77) and Khrushchev's son-in-law Aleksei Adzhubei. Michel Tatu, "La Chute de Khrouchtchev racontee par son gendre: Un entretien avec Alexei Adjobei," *Le Monde*, 19–20 February 1989.

8. Donald R. Kelley, *Soviet Politics from Brezhnev to Gorbachev* (New York: Praeger Publishers, 1987), 45–49; Baruch A. Hazan, *From Brezhnev to Gorbachev: Infighting in the Kremlin* (Boulder: Westview Press, 1987), 44–45, 97–104, 142–48; Christian Schmidt-Hauer, *Gorbachev: The Path to Power* (Topsfield: Salem House, 1986), 112–13.

9. Zhores A. Medvedev, *Andropov* (New York: Penguin Books, 1984), 21–22.

10. E. K. Ligachev, "XIX Vsesoiuznaia Konferentsiia KPSS—Vystuplenie tovarishcha Ligacheva E. K.," *Pravda*, 2 July 1988.

11. Boris Yeltsin, *Against the Grain: An Autobiography* (New York: Summit Books, 1990), 138–39.

12. Yegor Ligachev, *Inside Gorbachev's Kremlin: The Memoirs of Yegor Ligachev* (New York: Pantheon Books, 1993), 66–82, 126–27.

13. Pethybridge, *A Key to Soviet Politics*, 102.

14. Ibid., 193.

15. Khrushchev, *Khrushchev Remembers*, 335–36. Also see Medvedev, *Khrushchev*, 62; Medvedev and Medvedev, *Khrushchev: The Years in Power*, 10, 39–42.

16. Hyland and Shryock, *The Fall of Khrushchev*, 187; Michel Tatu, *Power in the Kremlin* (New York: Viking Press, 1970), 419–20.

17. "Kak smeshchali N. S. Khrushcheva," *Argumenty i fakty*, no. 20 (20–26 May 1989), 5–6; Amy W. Knight, *The KGB: Police and Politics in the Soviet Union* (Boston: Unwin Hyman, 1988), 65; Hyland and Shryock, *The Fall of Khrushchev*, 195.

18. Khrushchev, *Khrushchev on Khrushchev*, 136.

19. Hazan, *From Brezhnev to Khrushchev*, 49; Ilya Zemtsov, *Chernenko: The Last Bolshevik* (New Brunswick: Transaction Publishers, 1989), 185.

20. For a case study of coalition-formation in Soviet politics, see Barbara Ann Chotiner, *Khrushchev's Party Reform: Coalition Building and Institutional Innovation* (Westport: Greenwood Press, 1984).

21. Carl A. Linden, *Khrushchev and the Soviet Leadership, 1957–1964* (Baltimore: Johns Hopkins University Press, 1966), 3, 12, 14; Conquest, *Power and Policy in the USSR*, 11.

22. Anthony D'Agostino, *Soviet Succession Struggles: Kremlinology and the Russian Question from Lenin to Gorbachev* (Boston: Allen & Unwin, 1988).

23. Myron Rush, *Political Succession in the USSR*, 2d ed. (New York: Columbia University Press, 1968), 25–30, 58–71; Crankshaw, *Khrushchev*, 191; Conquest, *Power and Policy in the USSR*, 27.

24. Pethybridge, *A Key to Soviet Politics*, 118–19; Howard R. Swearer, *The Politics of Succession in the U.S.S.R.* (Boston: Little, Brown and Co., 1964), 17.

25. George W. Breslauer, *Khrushchev and Brezhnev as Leaders* (London: George Allen and Unwin, 1982). Also see George W. Breslauer, "Politics, Ideology, and Learning in Soviet Economic Reform since Stalin," in *Political Control of the Soviet Economy*, ed. Peter Hauslohner and David Cameron (forthcoming): "Power consolidation entails building one's power base through the allocation of patronage and the recruitment into positions of influence of old or new, but presumably loyal, associates." "Authority-building . . . is the process by which leaders seek to foster an image for themselves as effective problem-solvers and political constitution-builders."

26. Theodore H. Friedgut, "Interests and Groups in Soviet Policy-Making: The MTS Reform," *Soviet Studies* 28 (October 1976): 524–47; Charles E. Ziegler, "Issue Creation and Interest Groups in Soviet Environmental Policy,"

Comparative Politics (January 1986): 171–92. Compare Donald R. Kelley, "Environmental Policy-Making in the USSR: The Role of Industrial and Environmental Interest Groups," *Soviet Studies* 28 (October 1976): 570–89.

27. Heather Campbell, *Controversy in Soviet R&D: The Airship Controversy* [R-1001-PR] (Santa Monica: Rand Corporation, 1972), 1.

28. Jeremy R. Azrael, "Decision-Making in the U.S.S.R.," in *The Soviet Political System*, ed. Richard Cornell (Englewood Cliffs: Prentice-Hall, 1970), 211; Archie Brown, "Policymaking in the Soviet Union," *Soviet Studies* 23 (July 1971): 140. Wolfgang Leonhard in 1961 identified these as the "five pillars of Soviet society"—Party machine, economic managers and planners, state or governmental apparatus of ministers and state committees, army, and state police. These are the core of Myron Rush's slightly broader list of the chief bases of political power—"the institutions of dictatorship" that included Party apparatus, military, police, and public organizations such as trade unions; "territorial bases of power" in the union-republic Party-state organizations; and "professional groups" like enterprise managers. Wolfgang Leonhard, *The Kremlin Since Stalin* (New York: Praeger, 1962), 11–15; Rush, *Political Succession in the USSR*, 84–86.

29. Ellen Jones, "Committee Decision-Making in the Soviet Union," *World Politics* 36 (January 1984): 167, 170.

30. The remaining 6 percent (non-office-holders) included pensioners, laborers, and enterprise managers.

31. Robert V. Daniels, "Political Processes and Generational Change," in *Political Leadership in the Soviet Union*, ed. Archie Brown (Bloomington: Indiana University Press, 1989), 102.

32. Khrushchev, *Khrushchev Remembers*, 328–30; Zbigniew K. Brzezinski, *The Permanent Purge* (Cambridge: Harvard University Press, 1956), 158–60; Rush, *The Rise of Khrushchev*, 24; Leonard Schapiro, "Keynote—Compromise," *Problems of Communism* 20 (July–August 1971): 4.

33. Harry Gelman, *The Brezhnev Politburo and the Decline of Detente* (Ithaca: Cornell University Press, 1984), 71, 73–74; Darrell P. Hammer, *USSR: The Politics of Oligarchy* (Hinsdale: Dryden Press, 1974), 321; Paul J. Murphy, *Brezhnev: Soviet Politician* (Jefferson: McFarland & Co., 1981), 252–53.

34. Zemtsov, *Chernenko*, 149; Marc D. Zlotnik, "Chernenko Succeeds," *Problems of Communism* 33 (March–April 1984): 22.

35. This counts the number of appointments, divided by the years. It dates the beginning of Khrushchev's chairmanship from his victory over the Anti-Party Group rather than the removal of Bulganin.

36. The major services are the Ground Forces, Strategic Rocket Forces, Navy, Air Defense Forces, and Air Force. Averages can be calculated only out to nine years.

37. The uses of clientelism are explored extensively in John P. Willerton, *Patronage and Politics in the USSR* (Cambridge: Cambridge University Press, 1992); Michael E. Urban, *An Algebra of Soviet Power: Elite Circulation in the Belorussian Republic, 1966–86* (Cambridge: Cambridge University Press, 1989).

38. Sidney Ploss, *Conflict and Decision-Making in Soviet Russia* (Princeton: Princeton University Press, 1965), 59–112.

39. Richard F. Fenno, Jr., *The President's Cabinet* (Cambridge: Harvard University Press, 1959), chap. 6.

40. The breakout attempts are discussed more fully in the next chapters. In Figure 4.3, the first full year of each breakout attempt or consolidation of foreign policy leadership is 1953, 1958, 1966, 1973, and 1986.

41. Compare Michael Leiserson, "Factions and Coalitions in One-Party Japan: An Interpretation Based on the Theory of Games," *American Political Science Review* 62 (September 1968): 770.

42. William H. Riker, *The Theory of Political Coalitions* (New Haven: Yale University Press, 1962), 32–33.

43. Robert Axelrod, *Conflict of Interest: A Theory of Divergent Goals with Applications to Politics* (Chicago: Markham Publishing Company, 1970), 170.

44. Michael Leiserson, "Coalition Government in Japan," in *The Study of Coalition Behavior*, ed. Sven Groennings, E. W. Kelley, and Michael Leiserson (New York: Holt, Rinehart, and Winston, 1970), 90.

45. Lawrence C. Dodd, *Coalitions in Parliamentary Government* (Princeton: Princeton University Press, 1976), 44–46.

46. Leiserson, "Coalition Government in Japan," 87.

47. Ibid.

48. "Kak smeshchali N. S. Khrushcheva."

49. Ronald J. Hill and Alexander Rahr, "The General Secretary, the Central Party Secretariat, and the Apparat," in *Elites and Political Power in the USSR*, ed. David Lane (Brookfield: Edward Elgar, 1988), 49–73.

50. Axelrod, *Conflict of Interest*, 169.

51. Requests for investments in economic infrastructure (energy and fuels production, water resources, and transportation), heavy industry, and minerals industry constituted 58 percent of the requests for capital allocation, with infrastructure alone constituting 41.2 percent. Agriculture trailed at 23.2 percent, but this was still significantly ahead of requests for investment in light industry or housing and services (9.8 percent). Requests for investment in labor and training constituted the balance of requests (9.0 percent). Howard L. Biddulph, "Local Interest Articulation at CPSU Congresses," *World Politics* 36 (October 1983): 40.

52. Terry M. Moe, "The New Economics of Organization," *American Journal of Political Science* 28 (November 1984): 755–58.

53. Condoleeza Rice, "The Party, the Military, and Decision Authority in the Soviet Union," *World Politics* 40 (October 1987): 55.

54. Alec Nove, *The Soviet Economic System*, 3d ed. (Boston: Allen & Unwin, 1986), 104. Also see Jerry F. Hough, "The Brezhnev Era: The Man and the System," *Problems of Communism* 25 (March–April 1976): 14.

55. Azrael, "Decision-Making in the U.S.S.R.," 208.

56. Alexander Dallin, "Domestic Factors Influencing Soviet Foreign Policy," in *The U.S.S.R. and the Middle East*, ed. Michael Confino and Shimon Shamir (New York: John Wiley, 1971), 34; Graeme Gill, *The Origins of the Stalinist Political System* (New York: Cambridge University Press, 1990), 105; Leonhard, *The Kremlin Since Stalin*, 16.

57. Fritz W. Ermath, "Contrasts in American and Soviet Strategic Thought,"

International Security 3 (Fall 1978): 143; David Holloway, "Military Power and Political Purpose in Soviet Policy," *Daedelus* 109 (Fall 1980): 26; Dennis Ross, "Rethinking Soviet Strategic Policy: Inputs and Implications," *Journal of Strategic Studies* 1 (May 1978): 14; Dmitri Simes, "The Soviet Invasion of Czechoslovakia and the Limits of Kremlinology," *Studies in Comparative Communism* 8 (Spring–Summer 1975): 180.

58. Holloway, "Military Power and Political Purpose," 26.

59. Moe, "The New Economics of Organization," 769–70. The importance of expertise is illustrated in studies of the development of government tort liability legislation: Donald D. Barry, "The Specialist in Soviet Policy-Making: The Adoption of a Law," *Soviet Studies* 16 (October 1964): 152–165; and Peter H. Solomon, *Soviet Criminologists and Criminal Policy* (New York: Columbia University Press, 1978), 131–132.

60. Charles Lindblom, *The Policy-Making Process* (Englewood Cliffs: Prentice-Hall, 1968), 65–67. On second-tier political activity, see H. Gordon Skilling, "Interest Groups and Communist Politics Revisited," *World Politics* 36 (October 1983): 1–27; Hammer, *USSR: The Politics of Oligarchy*, 229–30; Jerry F. Hough and Merle Fainsod, *How the Soviet Union is Governed* (Cambridge: Harvard University Press, 1979), 531–34.

61. Loren R. Graham, "Reorganization of the U.S.S.R. Academy of Sciences," in *Soviet Policy-Making: Studies in Communism in Transition*, ed. Peter H. Juviler and Henry W. Morton (New York: Frederick A. Praeger, Publishers, 1967), 139.

62. Roman Kolkowicz, *The Soviet Military and the Communist Party* (Princeton: Princeton University Press, 1967), 117–19.

63. Joseph S. Berliner, *Factory and Manager in the U.S.S.R.* (Cambridge: Harvard University Press, 1957), 75–113.

64. Marshall I. Goldman, *The Spoils of Progress: Environmental Pollution in the Soviet Union* (Cambridge: MIT Press, 1972), 178–209.

65. Berliner, *Factory and Manager in the U.S.S.R.*, 114–81.

66. Hyland and Shryock, *The Fall of Khrushchev*, 170; Frederick C. Barghoorn, "The Security Police," in *Interest Groups in Soviet Politics*, ed. H. Gordon Skilling and Franklyn Griffiths (Princeton: Princeton University Press, 1971), 114–15. Also see Kolkowicz, *The Soviet Military and the Communist Party*, 165–66.

67. D. Roderick Kiewiet and Mathew D. McCubbins, *The Logic of Delegation: Congressional Parties and the Appropriations Process* (Chicago: University of Chicago Press, 1991), 27–34.

68. John N. Hazard, Isaac Shapiro, and Peter B. Maggs, *The Soviet Legal System*, rev. ed. (New York: Oceana Publications, 1969); Nove, *The Soviet Economic System*, 103.

69. Holloway, "Military Power and Political Purpose," 26.

70. Nove, *The Soviet Economic System*, 69–74.

71. Bohdan Harasymiw, "Nomenklatura: The Soviet Communist Party's Leadership Recruitment System," *Canadian Journal of Political Science* 2 (November 1969): 493–512; Rolf H. W. Theen, "Party and Bureaucracy," in *Public Policy and Administration in the Soviet Union*, ed. Gordon B. Smith (New York:

Praeger Publishers, 1980), 41–44; John H. Miller, "The Communist Party: Trends and Problems," in *Soviet Policy for the 1980s*, ed. Archie Brown and Michael Kaser (Bloomington: Indiana University Press, 1982), 21.

72. Robert E. Blackwell, Jr., "Cadres Policy in the Brezhnev Era," *Problems of Communism* 28 (March–April 1979): 29–30, 36. Also see T. H. Rigby, "The Soviet Government: Towards a Self-Stabilizing Oligarchy?" *Soviet Studies* 22 (October 1970): 167–91.

73. Nove, *The Soviet Economic System*, 87–94.

74. For examples of monitoring within the armed forces, see Kolkowicz, *The Soviet Military and the Communist Party*, 87; Merle Fainsod, *How Russia is Ruled*, rev. ed. (Cambridge: Harvard University Press, 1967), 491; Michael J. Deane, *Political Control of the Soviet Armed Forces* (New York: Crane, Russak and Co., 1977); Jeffrey T. Richelson, *Sword and Shield: Soviet Intelligence and Security Apparatus* (Cambridge: Ballinger Publishing Co., 1986), 231–36.

75. Jean Tirole, "Hierarchies and Bureaucracies: On the Role of Collusion in Organizations," *Journal of Law, Economics, and Organization* 2 (Fall 1986): 184; Berliner, *Factory and Manager in the U.S.S.R.*, 243–47; Jerry F. Hough, "The Party *Apparatchiki*," in *Interest Groups in Soviet Politics*, ed. H. Gordon Skilling and Franklyn Griffiths (Princeton: Princeton University Press, 1971), 61. Also see Timothy J. Colton, *Commissars, Commanders, and Civilian Authority: The Structure of Soviet Military Politics* (Cambridge: Harvard University Press, 1979), 85–112.

76. Frederick C. Barghoorn and Thomas F. Remington, *Politics: USSR*, 3d ed. (Boston: Little, Brown, and Company, 1986), 216.

77. William E. Odom, "The Party-Military Connection: A Critique," in *Civil-Military Relations in Communist Systems*, ed. Dale R. Herspring and Ivan Volgyes (Boulder: Westview Press, 1978), 37.

78. John A. Armstrong, *Ideology, Politics, and Government in the Soviet Union*, 4th ed. (New York: Praeger Publishers, 1978), 92. Also see Hammer, *U.S.S.R.: The Politics of Oligarchy*, 191–92; Gordon B. Smith, *Soviet Politics: Struggling with Change*, 2d ed. (New York: St. Martin's Press, 1992), 113.

79. Roman Kolkowicz, "The Military," in *Interest Groups in Soviet Politics*, ed. H. Gordon Skilling and Franklyn Griffiths (Princeton: Princeton University Press, 1971), 135.

80. Ken Booth, "Soviet Defense Policy," in *Contemporary Strategy—The Nuclear Powers*, ed. John Baylis et al. (New York: Holmes and Meier, 1987), 76.

81. Hough and Fainsod, *How the Soviet Union is Governed*, 362, 544.

Chapter Five
Balanced Leadership, 1953–1986

1. Myron Rush, "Brezhnev and the Succession Issue," *Problems of Communism* 20 (July–August 1971): 9–10; Myron Rush, *Political Succession in the USSR*, 2d ed. (New York: Columbia University Press, 1968), 73, 204.

2. Philip E. Mosely, "Soviet Myths and Realities," *Foreign Affairs* 39 (April 1961): 342–43.

3. The importance of the indeterminacy of the general secretary's power to

political dynamics is made in Teresa Rakowska-Harmstone, "Toward a Theory of Soviet Leadership Maintenance," in *The Dynamics of Soviet Politics*, ed. Paul Cocks, Robert V. Daniels, and Nancy Whittier-Heer (Cambridge: Harvard University Press, 1976), 51–76; Howard R. Swearer, *The Politics of Succession in the U.S.S.R.* (Boston: Little, Brown and Co., 1964), 14. Coalition-building strategies are discussed in Edward Crankshaw, *Khrushchev, A Career* (New York: Viking Press, 1966), 197. The succession-consolidation cycle is discussed in Myron Rush, *The Rise of Khrushchev* (Washington, D.C.: Public Affairs Press, 1958), 2; George Breslauer, *Khrushchev and Brezhnev as Leaders* (London: George Allen and Unwin, 1982).

4. Avery Goldstein, *From Bandwagoning to Balance-of-Power Politics: Structural Constraints and Politics in China, 1949–1978* (Stanford: Stanford University Press, 1991), 38, 42, 49.

5. Harry Gelman, *The Brezhnev Politburo and the Decline of Detente* (Ithaca: Cornell University Press, 1984), 53; Robert Conquest, *Power and Policy in the USSR* (New York: Harper & Row, 1967), 47; Jeremy R. Azrael, "Decision-Making in the U.S.S.R.," in *The Soviet Political System*, ed. Richard Cornell (Englewood Cliffs: Prentice-Hall, 1970), 211.

6. Joel J. Schwartz and William R. Keech, "Group Influence and the Policy Process in the Soviet Union," *American Political Science Review* 62 (September 1968): 849; Philip D. Stewart, Margaret G. Hermann, and Charles F. Hermann, "Modeling the 1973 Soviet Decision to Support Egypt," *American Political Science Review* 83 (March 1989): 38–41. Also see Bruce Parrott, "Political Change and Civil-Military Relations," in *Soldiers and the Soviet State*, ed. Timothy J. Colton and Thane Gustafson (Princeton: Princeton University Press, 1990), 51, 59; Rush, *The Rise of Khrushchev*, 78–81, 84, 86–87.

7. Marc D. Zlotnik, "Chernenko Succeeds," *Problems of Communism* 33 (March–April 1984): 20–21.

8. George W. Breslauer, "On the Adaptability of Soviet Welfare-State Authoritarianism," in *Soviet Society and the Communist Party*, ed. Karl W. Ryavec (Amherst: University of Massachusetts Press, 1978), 7. Also see Grey Hodnett, "The Pattern of Leadership Politics," in *The Domestic Context of Soviet Foreign Policy*, ed. Seweryn Bialer (Boulder: Westview Press, 1981), 99.

9. Rush, "Brezhnev and the Succession Issue," 14; Robert G. Wesson, "The USSR: Oligarchy or Dictatorship?" *Slavic Review* 31 (June 1972): 316.

10. Richard Lowenthal, "Crisis in Moscow," *Problems of Communism* 4 (May–June 1955): 3.

11. L. Slepov, "Kollektivnost'—vysshii printsip partiinogo rukovodstva," *Pravda*, 16 April 1953.

12. Conquest, *Power and Policy in the USSR*, 231; Wolfgang Leonhard, *The Kremlin Since Stalin* (New York: Frederick A. Praeger, 1962), 90.

13. *Economist*, 14 March 1953; reprinted as "Changes in the Kremlin," *Problems of Communism* 2 (May–August 1953): 5. Also see Roy Medvedev, *Khrushchev* (Garden City: Anchor Press, 1983), 57; Roy A. Medvedev and Zhores A. Medvedev, *Khrushchev: The Years in Power* (New York: W. W. Norton and Co., 1978), 2–7; Nikita S. Khrushchev, *Khrushchev Remembers* (Boston: Little, Brown and Co., 1970), 324.

14. "Postanovlenie sovmestnogo zasedaniia Plenuma Tsentral'nogo Komiteta Kommunisticheskoi Partii Sovetskogo Soiuza, Soveta Ministrov Soiuza SSR, Prezidiuma Verkhovnogo Soveta SSSR," *Pravda*, 7 March 1953.

15. Rush, *The Rise of Khrushchev*, 10.

16. Richard Lowenthal, "The Revolution Withers Away," *Problems of Communism* 14 (January–February 1965): 12.

17. Akademiia obshchestvennykh nauk pri TsK KPSS, Kafedra istorii KPSS, *Lektsii po Istorii KPSS (prochitany aspirantam Akademii obshchestvennykh nauk pri TsK KPSS v 1961/62 g.)* (Moscow: Izdatel'stvo VPSh i AON pri TsK KPSS, 1963), 349.

18. Martin Ebon, "Malenkov's Power Balance," *Problems of Communism* 2 (March–June 1953): 8; Bertram D. Wolfe, "The Struggle for the Soviet Succession," *Foreign Affairs* 31 (July 1953): 558–59.

19. Khrushchev, *Khrushchev Remembers*, 319, 330–35.

20. Merle Fainsod, "The Soviet Union since Stalin," *Problems of Communism* 3 (March–April 1954): 3.

21. This reform is discussed more fully in chapter 7.

22. Jerome M. Gilison offers a functional interpretation of the apex role in "New Factors of Stability in Soviet Collective Leadership," *World Politics* 19 (July 1967): 570. Also see T. H. Rigby, "How Strong Is the Leader?" *Problems of Communism* 11 (September–October 1962): 7.

23. Appointments included two in 1955 (Nikolai Beliaev and Dmitrii Shepilov), two in 1956 (Leonid Brezhnev and Ekaterina Furtseva), and four in 1957 (Nikolai Ignatov, Otto Kuusinen, Aleksei Kirichenko, and Nurutdin Mukhitdinov).

24. The removals were Averkii Aristov, Leonid Brezhnev, Ekaterina Furtseva, Nikolai Ignatov, Aleksei Kirichenko, and Petr Pospelov.

25. These four included Anastas Mikoian, Frol Kozlov, Dmitri Ustinov, and Aleksandr Zasiadko.

26. Rigby, "How Strong is the Leader?" 6; Richard Lowenthal, "The Nature of Khrushchev's Power," *Problems of Communism* 9 (July–August 1960): 3.

27. Merle Fainsod, "The Party in the Post-Stalin Era," *Problems of Communism* 7 (January–February 1958): 9.

28. "Rezoliutsiia XXII s"ezda Kommunisticheskoi Partii Sovetskogo Soiuza po Otchetu Tsentral'nogo Komitetu KPSS," *Pravda*, 1 November 1961.

29. Roger Pethybridge, *A Key to Soviet Politics: The Crisis of the Anti-Party Group* (New York: Frederick A. Praeger, 1962), 42.

30. "Sily kollektivnogo rukovodstva," *Krasnaia zvezda*, 24 October 1964.

31. T. H. Rigby, "The Soviet Government: Towards a Self-Stabilizing Oligarchy?" *Soviet Studies* 22 (October 1970): 173, 175. Also see Darrell P. Hammer, *USSR: The Politics of Oligarchy* (Hinsdale: Dryden Press, 1974), 319–20; Rigby, "The Soviet Government: Towards a Self-Stabilizing Oligarchy?" 173–75; Archie Brown, "Political Developments: Some Conclusions and an Interpretation," in *The Soviet Union since the Fall of Khrushchev*, ed. Archie Brown and Michael Kaser (New York: Free Press, 1975), 219.

32. Brown, "Political Developments," 219; Rigby, "The Soviet Government: Towards a Self-Stabilizing Oligarchy?" 175.

33. T. H. Rigby, "The Soviet Regional Leadership: The Brezhnev Generation," *Slavic Review* 37 (March 1978): 4.

34. "XXIII s"ezd Kommunisticheskoi Partii Sovetskogo Soiuza—Rech' tovarishcha G. S. Zolotukhina," *Pravda*, 7 April 1966.

35. Data concerning turnover of obkom secretaries were provided by John P. Willerton (University of Arizona). As part of his research with William Reissinger the data were reported in "Troubleshooters, Political Machines, and Moscow's Regional Control," *Slavic Review* 50 (Summer 1991): 347–58.

36. Robert E. Blackwell, Jr., "Cadres Policy in the Brezhnev Era," *Problems of Communism* (March–April 1979): 29.

37. Roman Kolkowicz, *The Soviet Military and the Communist Party* (Princeton: Princeton University Press, 1967), 345.

38. Robert E. Blackwell, Jr., "Career Development in the Soviet Obkom Elite: A Conservative Trend," *Soviet Studies* 24 (July 1972): 38–39; Jerry F. Hough, "The Party *Apparatchiki*," in *Interest Groups in Soviet Politics*, ed. H. Gordon Skilling and Franklyn Griffiths (Princeton: Princeton University Press, 1971), 53–57; Rigby, "The Soviet Regional Leadership: The Brezhnev Generation," 13.

39. Gelman, *The Brezhnev Politburo and the Decline of Detente*, 52, 54. Richard Anderson stresses the strategic importance of "going public" in "Competitive Politics and Soviet Foreign Policy: Authority Building and Bargaining in the Brezhnev Politburo" (Ph.D. diss., University of California, Berkeley, 1989).

40. Rush, "Brezhnev and the Succession Issue," 10, 14.

41. John Dornberg, *Brezhnev: The Masks of Power* (New York: Basic Books, 1974), 243.

42. Gelman, *The Brezhnev Politburo and the Decline of Detente*, 129; Christian Deuvel, "Marginal Notes on a Soviet Leadership Crisis," *Radio Liberty Research* CRD 272/70 (23 July 1970). Contrast Paul J. Murphy, *Brezhnev: Soviet Politician* (Jefferson: McFarland and Co., 1981), 300.

43. Dornberg, *Brezhnev: The Masks of Power*, 262–64.

44. Jerome Gilison, "New Factors of Stability in Soviet Collective Leadership," *World Politics* 19 (July 1967): 578.

45. "Postanovleniia Plenuma Ts. K. KPSS priniatoe 6 dekabria 1965 goda: 'O preobrazovanii organov partiino-gosudarstvennogo kontrolia," *Pravda*, 7 December 1965; L. I. Brezhnev, "Rech' Pervogo sekretaria Ts. K. KPSS tovarishcha L. I. Brezhneva," *Pravda*, 7 December 1965; Gelman, *The Brezhnev Politburo and the Decline of Detente*, 76, 77; Fedor Burlatsky, *Khrushchev and the First Russian Spring* (New York: Charles Scribner's Sons, 1988), 217. The "center" may also have faced opposition from a "Suslov faction" during and after the Czechoslovakian crisis of 1968; see Rigby, "The Soviet Government: Towards a Self-Stabilizing Oligarchy?" 188–90.

46. Frol Kozlov was relieved of his posts in the Politburo and Secretariat at the November 1964 CC Plenum, apparently for genuine reasons of ill health. In April 1966 Anastas Mikoian and Nikolai Shvernik retired. Two appointments were made at the time of establishing the new collective leadership in November 1964 (Petr Shelest and Aleksandr Shelepin), and two subsequently (Kirill Mazurov in March 1965 and Arvid Pel'she in April 1966).

47. The terminations were Gennadii Voronov, Petr Shelest, Aleksandr

Shelepin, Dmitrii Polianskii, Nikolai Podgornyi. The appointments were Viktor Grishin, Vladimir Shcherbitskii, Dinmukhamed Kunaev, Fedor Kulakov, Andrei Gromyko, Andrei Grechko, Yurii Andropov, Dmitrii Ustinov, and Grigorii Romanov.

48. Thomas W. Wolfe, *The SALT Experience* (Cambridge: Ballinger Publishers, 1979), 51–52; Grey Hodnett, "The Pattern of Leadership Politics," in *The Domestic Context of Soviet Foreign Policy*, ed. Seweryn Bialer (Boulder: Westview Press, 1981), 102–3.

49. Murphy, *Brezhnev: Soviet Politician*, 249–50, 308.

50. Baruch A. Hazan, *From Brezhnev to Gorbachev: Infighting in the Kremlin* (Boulder: Westview Press, 1987), 57–59, 73–74, 106.

51. D. F. Ustinov, "Bessmertnyi podvig," *Pravda*, 9 May 1983; "Chernenko Named Defense Council Chairman," Beijing *Xinhua* (in English), 26 February 1984, in Foreign Broadcast Information Service, *Daily Report (USSR)*, 27 February 1984; "Gorbachev Defense Council Head," Hamburg DPA 1 August 1985 in Foreign Broadcast Information Service, *Daily Report (USSR)*, 1 August 1985.

52. "Gorbachev Speech Reported," TASS (in English), 11 April 1984, in Foreign Broadcast Information Service, *Daily Report (USSR)*, 11 April 1984.

53. "Gorbachev Nomination Speech," TASS (in English), 2 July 1985, in Foreign Broadcast Information Service, *Daily Report (USSR)*, 2 July 1985.

54. Boris Meissner, "Transition in the Kremlin," *Problems of Communism* 32 (January–February 1983): 11, 14. Compare Archie Brown, "Andropov: Discipline and Reform?" *Problems of Communism* 32 (January–February 1983): 27–28.

55. Michel Tatu and Daniel Vernet, "Un entretien avec le numéro deux sovietique," *Le Monde*, 4 December 1987.

56. Indeed, continued resistance from the cadre department to Gorbachev's mandate led the general secretary at the June 1987 CC Plenum to criticize CC departments for their failure to press lower level party bodies into compliance. M. S. Gorbachev, "O zadachakh partii po korennoi perestroike upravleniia ekonomikoi," *Pravda*, 25 June 1987.

57. Thane Gustafson and Dawn Mann, "Gorbachev's Next Gamble," *Problems of Communism* 36 (July–August 1987): 7.

58. Ilya Zemtsov, *Chernenko: The Last Bolshevik* (New Brunswick: Transaction Publishers, 1989), 142; Zhores A. Medvedev, *Gorbachev* (New York: W. W. Norton & Co., 1986), 133.

59. M. S. Gorbachev, "O sozyve ocherednogo XXVII s"ezda KPSS i zadachakh sviazannykh s ego podgotovkoi i provedeniem," *Pravda*, 24 April 1985.

60. Hazan, *From Brezhnev to Gorbachev*, 196.

61. Myron Rush, *The Fate of the Party Apparatus under Gorbachev* [R-4001-A] (Santa Monica: Rand Corporation, 1990), 6.

62. Gustafson and Mann, "Gorbachev's Next Gamble," 12–13.

63. Hazan, *From Brezhnev to Gorbachev*, 206; Gustafson and Mann, "Gorbachev's Next Gamble," 2.

64. Dale R. Herspring, *The Soviet High Command, 1967–1989* (Princeton: Princeton University Press, 1990), 222.

65. Zemtsov, *Chernenko*, 260.

66. Herspring, *The Soviet High Command*, 223, 308.

67. Medvedev, *Gorbachev*, 168.

68. "Plenum Ts. K. KPSS, oktiabr' 1987 goda—Stenograficheskii otchet," *Izvestiia TsK KPSS* (February 1989), 243.

69. Compare the discussion of Brezhnev's patron network with that of the Gorbachev coalition in John P. Willerton, *Patronage and Politics in the USSR* (Cambridge: Cambridge University Press, 1992), 54–63, 136–47. Although Willerton stresses many similarities, he describes two very different levels of patronage.

70. Jerry F. Hough, "Gorbachev Consolidating Power," *Problems of Communism* 36 (July–August 1987): 30–31; Jeffrey Surovell, "Ligachev and Soviet Politics," *Soviet Studies* 43, no. 2 (1991): 366.

71. Jerry F. Hough, "Gorbachev's Endgame," *World Policy Journal* 7 (Fall 1990): 639–72; Jerry F. Hough, "Understanding Gorbachev," *Soviet Economy* 7 (April–June 1991): 97.

Chapter Six
Institutionalized Stagnation

1. Albert O. Hirschman, *Journeys toward Progress* (New York: Twentieth Century Fund, 1963), 251.

2. Terry M. Moe, "An Assessment of the Positive Theory of 'Congressional Dominance,' " *Legislative Studies Quarterly* 12 (November 1987): 475; Margaret Weit and Theda Skocpol, "State Structures and the Possibilities for 'Keynesian' Responses to the Great Depression in Sweden, Britain, and the United States," in *Bringing the State Back In*, ed. Peter Evans, Dietrich Rueschemeyer, and Theda Skocpol (New York: Cambridge University Press, 1985), 118–19.

3. Norman Frohlich and Joe A. Oppenheimer, *Modern Political Economy* (Englewood Cliffs: Prentice-Hall, 1978), 67–71.

4. Abram DeSwaan develops this as the central assumption in his policy distance theory; see DeSwaan, *Coalition Theories and Cabinet Formations: A Study of Formal Theories of Coalition Formation Applied to Nine European Parliaments after 1918* (Amsterdam: Elsevier Scientific Publishing Company, 1973), 88.

5. "Sila partii v edinstve ee riadov, v kollektivnosti ee rukovodstva," *Kommunist*, no. 10 (July 1957): 5. The political motivation behind reform proposals is illustrated in the subsequent reforms to strengthen the State Economic Commission (*Gosekonomkomissiia*) and create the Councils of the National Economy (*sovnarkhozy*); Alec Nove, *An Economic History of the U.S.S.R.* (Baltimore: Penguin Books, 1969), 344–46.

6. Harry Gelman, *The Brezhnev Politburo and the Decline of Detente* (Ithaca: Cornell University Press, 1984), 94.

7. The exceptions to this are the limiting and perhaps only hypothetical cases (1) when a single second-tier institution is the sole support of the leadership, (2) when a single first-tier actor has so consolidated power as to enforce his personal success indicators upon all institutions, or (3) when external constraints such as total war coordinate success indicators of first- and second-tier actors.

8. Stated differently, leaders were often torn between the demands of two

competing forms of centrist advantage—being at the center of the policy space of one's own coalition and being at the center of the entire participant population.

9. This is not to say that the leader's preferences change, for these can remain constant even as his public pronouncements shift.

10. Helmut Sonnenfeldt, "Russia, America, and Detente," *Foreign Affairs* 56 (January 1978): 277–78. For a historical description of coalition and centrist strategies, see Anthony D'Agostino, *Soviet Succession Struggles* (Boston: Allen & Unwin, 1988).

11. Henry W. Morton, "The Structure of Decision-Making in the U.S.S.R.," in *Soviet Policy-Making: Studies of Communism in Transition*, ed. Peter H. Juviler and Henry W. Morton (New York: Frederick A. Praeger, 1967), 21.

12. George W. Breslauer, "Politics, Ideology, and Learning in Soviet Economic Reforms Since Stalin," in *Political Control of the Soviet Economy*, ed. Peter Hauslohner and David Cameron (forthcoming), 9. Also see Richard D. Anderson, "Competitive Politics and Soviet Foreign Policy: Authority and Bargaining in the Brezhnev Politburo," (Ph.D. diss., University of California, Berkeley, 1989), 42–51.

13. Warner R. Schilling, Paul Y. Hammond, and Glenn H. Snyder, *Strategy, Politics, and Defense Budgets* (New York: Columbia University Press, 1962), 23. As Samuel Huntington has argued, the effectiveness of a committee usually "depends upon the ability of its participants to produce not just majority opinion but unanimous opinion"; Samuel P. Huntington, *The Common Defense* (New York: Columbia University Press, 1961), 155.

14. The technique of using "expert coders" is discussed in Barry Ames, *Political Survival* (Berkeley: University of California Press, 1987), 41–42.

15. Philip G. Roeder, "Soviet Policies and Kremlin Politics," *International Studies Quarterly* 28 (June 1984): 172; and Philip G. Roeder, "Do New Soviet Leaders Really Make a Difference? Rethinking the 'Succession Connection,' " *American Political Science Review* 79 (December 1985): 963. Philip Stewart, Margaret Hermann, and Charles Hermann define political regimes as "a given structure of power and a set of more or less accepted decision norms" in Philip D. Stewart, Margaret G. Hermann, and Charles F. Hermann, "Modeling the 1973 Soviet Decision to Support Egypt," *American Political Science Review* 83 (March 1989): 38. Also see the use of this concept in Michael J. Sodaro, *Moscow, Germany, and the West from Khrushchev to Gorbachev* (Ithaca: Cornell University Press, 1990), 21–29.

16. In reality no regime perfectly corresponds to the polar extremes of each axis, which could be treated as ideal-types.

17. Ilya Zemtsov, *Chernenko: The Last Bolshevik* (New Brunswick: Transaction Publishers, 1989), 236; Myron Rush, *Political Succession in the USSR*, 2d ed. (New York: Columbia University Press, 1968), 1, 74.

18. The rankings of regimes are drawn from the following descriptive studies: Seweryn Bialer, "The Soviet Political Elite and Internal Developments in the USSR," in *The Soviet Empire*, ed. William E. Griffiths (Lexington: Lexington Books, 1976), 31; George W. Breslauer, *Khrushchev and Brezhnev as Leaders* (London: George Allen and Unwin, 1982), 17, 115–33; Archie Brown, "Political Developments: Some Conclusions and an Interpretation," in *The Soviet Union*

40. K. U. Chernenko, "Narod i partiia ediny—Rech' tovarishcha K. U. Chernenko," *Pravda*, 3 March 1984.

41. K. U. Chernenko, "Rech' tovarishcha K. U. Chernenko na Plenume TsK KPSS, 10 aprelia 1984 goda," *Pravda*, 11 April 1984.

42. It is useful to examine assessments made at the time. For example, commenting on his policies after his first three months, analysts at the Soviet biographical service noted that "in fact, the continuity in the economic, agricultural, and foreign policies of Brezhnev, Andropov, Chernenko, and Gorbachev should be stressed, and one should not go too far . . . expecting radical changes from the new General Secretary." *Soviet Biographical Services* 1 (June 1985): 57. Zhores Medvedev observed that at the end of one year, "the changes in domestic policy were merely cosmetic"; see Zhores A. Medvedev, *Gorbachev* (W. W. Norton & Co., 1986), 208. Baruch Hazan noted that "the remedies he proposed could have been taken from any of his predecessors' speeches"; see his *From Brezhnev to Gorbachev* (Boulder: Westview Press, 1987), 202.

43. M. S. Gorbachev, "Rech' General'nogo sekretaria TsK KPSS tovarishcha M. S. Gorbacheva," *Pravda*, 12 March 1985.

44. M. S. Gorbachev, "Korennoi vopros ekonomicheskoi politiki partii," *Pravda*, 12 June 1985.

45. Hazan, *From Brezhnev to Gorbachev*, 202.

46. Alexander Dallin, "Domestic Factors Influencing Soviet Foreign Policy," in *The U.S.S.R. and the Middle East*, ed. Michael Confino and Shimon Shamir (New York: John Wiley, 1973), 34.

47. Huntington, *The Common Defense*, 166–74; Schilling, Hammond, and Snyder, *Strategy, Politics, and Defense Budgets*, 24; T. H. Rigby, "The Soviet Leadership: Toward a Self-Stabilizing Oligarchy?" *Soviet Studies* 22 (October 1970): 190; Bialer, "The Soviet Political Elite and Internal Developments in the USSR," 32; Hazan, *From Brezhnev to Gorbachev*, 87.

48. Schilling, Hammond, and Snyder, *Strategy, Politics, and Defense Budgets*, 24; Huntington, *The Common Defense*, 167. Although consistency may be a virtue, with extremely high levels of consistency, policy is simply inertial; it perpetuates policies well beyond their usefulness. Although coherence in policy is essential to achieving a state's objectives, extreme coherence may simply reflect a state's inability to pursue a flexible or differentiated policy.

49. Huntington, *The Common Defense*, 164.

50. Joel J. Schwartz and William R. Keech, "Group Influence and the Policy Process in the Soviet Union," *American Political Science Review* 62 (September 1968): 849; Stewart, Hermann, and Hermann, "Modeling the 1973 Soviet Decision to Support Egypt," 38–41.

51. Roman Kolkowicz, *The Soviet Military and the Communist Party* (Princeton: Princeton University Press, 1967), 108, 115; Wolfgang Leonhard, *The Kremlin since Stalin* (New York: Frederick A. Praeger, 1962), 95–96.

52. Daniels, "Soviet Politics Since Khrushchev," 22; Linden, *Khrushchev, and the Soviet Leadership, 1957–1964*, 119–28, 147–49, 157–61, 207.

53. V. I. Lenin, "Karl Marks," in *Polnoe sobranie sochinenii*, 5th ed. (Moscow: Izdatel'stvo Politicheskoi Literatury, 1961), 26:53–55. Compare Archie Brown, "Leadership Succession and Policy Innovation," in *Soviet Policy for the*

1980s, ed. Archie Brown and Michael Kaser (Bloomington: Indiana University Press, 1982), 228.

54. Richard Lowenthal, "The Revolution Withers Away," *Problems of Communism* 14 (January–February 1965): 12–13.

55. Breslauer, *Khrushchev and Brezhnev as Leaders*, 193–94.

56. Philip G. Roeder, "Modernization and Participation in the Leninist Developmental Strategy," *American Political Science Review* 83 (September 1989): 859–84.

57. Jerry F. Hough, *Soviet Leadership in Transition* (Washington, D.C.: Brookings Institution, 1980), 70.

58. Specifically, the percentage of previous Central Committee members reelected was 82.3 (1966), 76.9 (1971), 83.4 (1976), and 80.1 (1981). Also see Robert E. Blackwell, Jr., "Cadres Policy in the Brezhnev Era," *Problems of Communism* (March–April 1970): 31–33.

59. Thane Gustafson and Dawn Mann, "Gorbachev's Next Gamble," *Problems of Communism* 36 (July–August 1987): 12–13.

60. Robert V. Daniels, "Office Holding and Elite Status: The Central Committee of the CPSU," in *The Dynamics of Soviet Politics*, ed. Paul Cocks, Robert V. Daniels, and Nancy Whittier-Heer (Cambridge: Harvard University Press, 1976), 94.

61. Valerie Bunce, *Do New Leaders Make a Difference? Executive Succession and Public Policy under Capitalism and Socialism* (Princeton: Princeton University Press, 1981).

62. Breslauer, *Khrushchev and Brezhnev as Leaders*, 273–75.

63. Jack Snyder, *Myths of Empire: Domestic Politics and International Ambition* (Ithaca: Cornell University Press, 1991).

64. Bunce, *Do New Leaders Make a Difference?* 36.

65. Breslauer, *Khrushchev and Brezhnev as Leaders*, 286–88.

66. Snyder, *Myths of Empire*, 246–51. Bunce introduces the element of institutionalization when sketching her theory, but she does not develop this in other than an ad hoc manner.

Chapter Seven
The Domestic Policy Spiral

1. Arthur W. Wright, "Soviet Economic Planning and Performance," in *The Soviet Union Since Stalin*, ed. Stephen F. Cohen, Alexander Rabinowitch, and Robert Sharlet (Bloomington: Indiana University Press, 1980), 114.

2. I. V. Stalin, "Ob oshibkakh t. Iaroshenko L. D.," in *Sochineniia* (Stanford: Hoover Institution Press, 1967), 3:269; emphasis added.

3. Alexander Dallin, "Soviet Foreign Policy and Domestic Politics: A Framework for Analysis," *Journal of International Affairs* 23 (Fall–Winter 1969): 260.

4. Data from: Ministerstvo Finansov SSSR, Biudzhetnoe upravlenie, *Gosudarstvennyi biudzhet SSSR i biudzhety soiuznykh respublik, 1976–1980 gg.: statisticheskii sbornik* (Moscow: Finansy i statistika, 1982), 22–23; N. K. Baibakov, "O Gosudarstvennom plane ekonomicheskogo i sotsial'nogo razvitiia SSSR na 1980 god i o khode vypolneniia Gosudarstvennogo plana ekonomicheskogo i sotsial'nogo razvitiia v 1979 godu," *Pravda*, 29 November 1979; V. F. Garbuzov,

"O Gosudarstvennom biudzhete SSSR na 1980 goda i ob ispolnenii Gosudarstvennogo biudzheta SSSR za 1978 goda," *Pravda*, 29 November 1979; N. K. Baibakov, "O Gosudarstvennom plane ekonomicheskogo i sotsial'nogo razvitiia SSSR na 1981 god i o khode vypolneniia Gosudarstvennogo plana ekonomicheskogo i sotsial'nogo razvitiia v 1980 godu," *Pravda*, 23 October 1980; V. F. Garbuzov, "O Gosudarstvennom biudzhete SSSR na 1981 goda i ob ispolnenii Gosudarstvennogo biudzheta SSSR za 1979 goda," *Pravda*, 23 October 1980; U.S. Congress, Joint Economic Committee, *Allocation of Resources in the Soviet Union and China—1981*, Pt. 7, 97th Cong., 1st sess., 8 July 1981 and 15 October 1981, 281; U.S. Arms Control and Disarmament Agency, *World Military Expenditures and Arms Transfers, 1985* (Washington, D.C.: GPO, 1985), 81.

5. Martin McCauley, "Leadership and the Succession Struggle," in *Soviet Union after Brezhnev*, ed. Martin McCauley (New York: Holmes & Meier, 1983), 23.

6. A. G. Zverev, "O Gosudarstvennom biudzhete SSSR na 1954 goda," *Pravda*, 22 April 1954; Wolfgang Leonhard, *The Kremlin Since Stalin* (New York: Frederick A. Praeger, 1962), 88; Lazar Volin, "The Malenkov-Khrushchev New Economic Policy," *Problems of Communism* 3 (September–October 1954): 19.

7. Zverev, "O Gosudarstvennom biudzhete SSSR na 1954 goda."

8. Leon Herman, "The Pattern of Soviet Industrial Expansion," *Problems of Communism* 2 (November–December 1953): 21. Indeed, given the minuscule sum invested in consumer-goods production, major relative increases would be made with marginal sums; see Philip E. Mosely, "How 'New' is the Kremlin's New Line?" *Foreign Affairs* 33 (April 1955): 384.

9. Tsentral'noe Statisticheskoe Upravlenie, *Narodnoe khoziaistvo SSSR v 1959 godu* (Moscow: Gosstatizdat, 1960), 141.

10. Colin D. Campbell and Rosemary G. Campbell, "Soviet Price Reductions for Consumer Goods, 1948–1954," *American Economic Review* 45 (September 1955): 614.

11. Leon M. Herman, "Soviet Economic Policy Since Stalin," *Problems of Communism* 5 (January–February 1956): 10.

12. Volin, "The Malenkov-Khrushchev New Economic Policy," 21.

13. Zverev, "O Gosudarstvennom biudzhete SSSR na 1954 goda."

14. G. M. Malenkov, "Preniia po dokladu o Gosudarstvennom biudzhete SSSR na 1954 god," *Pravda*, 27 April 1954.

15. I. S. Khokhlov, "O Gosudarstvennom biudzhete SSSR na 1953 godu i ob ispolnenii Gosudarstvennogo biudzheta SSSR za 1951 i 1952 gody," *Pravda*, 7 August 1953.

16. A. M. Safronov, "Zakliuchitel'noe slovo Predsedatelia Biudzhetnoi komissii Soveta Natsional'nostei deputata A. M. Safronova," *Pravda*, 28 April 1954.

17. One stopgap measure without forcing trade-offs among sectors was to tear down reserves. Goods from government emergency stockpiles and other commodities were disgorged into the economy. Gold reserves were sold abroad to finance imports of meat, butter, eggs, and textiles from Europe and South America. But this could meet only a small fraction of the promised

increase in consumer goods and could not be sustained beyond a few months. Herman, "Soviet Economic Policy Since Stalin," 10; Richard Lowenthal, "Crisis in Moscow," *Problems of Communism* 4 (May–June 1955): 6; Merle Fainsod, "The Soviet Union Since Stalin," *Problems of Communism* 3 (March–April 1954): 6.

18. Naum Jasny, "The New Economic Course in the U.S.S.R." *Problems of Communism* 3 (January–February 1954): 7.

19. A. I. Mikoian, "Rech' tovarishcha A. I. Mikoiana na sobranii izbiratelei Erevanskogo-Stalinskogo izbiratel'nogo okruga, 11 marta 1954 goda," *Kommunist* (Erevan), 12 March 1954.

20. Data for savings from Raymond Hutchings, *The Soviet Budget* (Albany: State University of New York Press, 1983), 160. In the Soviet command economy, personal savings were not a source of investment funds, but remained essentially idle.

21. "Beseda tov. N. S. Khrushcheva s angliiskim uchenym i obshchestvennym deiatelem Dzhonom Bernalom," *Pravda*, 24 December 1954.

22. Zverev, "O Gosudarstvennom biudzhete na 1955 goda."

23. Ibid.; Tsentral'noe statisticheskoe upravlenie, *Narodnoe khoziaistvo SSSR v 1961 godu* (Moscow: Gosstatizdat, 1962), 169.

24. K. Ostrovitianov, "Protiv vul'garizatorskogo ponimaniia osnovnogo ekonomicheskogo zakona sotsializma," *Pravda*, 27 March 1955.

25. Herman, "Soviet Economic Policy Since Stalin," 11.

26. Harry Gelman, *The Brezhnev Politburo and the Decline of Detente* (Ithaca: Cornell University Press, 1984), 84.

27. V. F. Garbuzov, "O Gosudarstvennom biudzhete SSSR na 1965 god i ob ispolnenii Gosudarstvennogo biudzheta SSSR za 1963 goda," *Pravda*, 8 December 1965.

28. Tsentral'noe Statisticheskoe Upravlenie, *Narodnoe khoziaistvo SSSR* (annual editions, 1961–69) (Moscow: Statistika, 1962–70).

29. William Hyland, "Brezhnev and Beyond," *Foreign Affairs* 58 (Fall 1979): 51–54; Sidney Ploss, "Soviet Politics on the Eve of the 24th Party Congress," *World Politics* 23 (October 1970): 62.

30. L. I. Brezhnev, "Velikaia pobeda sovetskogo naroda," *Pravda*, 9 May 1965; L. I. Brezhnev, " 'Zolotaia zvezda' na znameni Leningrada," *Pravda*, 11 July 1965; L. I. Brezhnev, "Narod i Armiia Ediny," *Pravda*, 4 July 1965; L. I. Brezhnev, "Pust' krepnet i razvivaetsia Sovetsko-Rumynskaia Druzhba—Rech' tovarishcha L. I. Brezhneva," *Pravda*, 11 September 1965; L. I. Brezhnev, "Na znameni Kieva—zvezda geroia," *Pravda*, 24 October 1965.

31. Garbuzov, "O Gosudarstvennom biudzhete SSSR na 1965 god i ob ispolnenii Gosudarstvennogo biudzheta SSSR za 1963 goda."

32. V. F. Garbuzov, "O Gosudarstvennom biudzhete SSSR na 1968 god i ob ispolnenii Gosudarstvennogo biudzheta SSSR za 1966 goda," *Pravda*, 11 October 1967.

33. These figures are consistent with Western estimates, discussed later in this chapter.

34. Boris Meissner, "Transition in the Kremlin," *Problems of Communism* 32 (January–February 1983): 13.

35. Iu. V. Andropov, "Rech' Iu. V. Andropova," *Pravda*, 13 November 1982;

Iu. V. Andropov, "Rech' General'nogo sekretaria TsK KPSS Iu. V. Andropova na plenume TsK KPSS, 22 noiabria 1982 goda," *Pravda*, 23 November 1982.

36. "V Tsentral'nom Komitete KPSS i Sovete Ministrov SSSR," *Pravda*, 7 May 1983. Also see Jerry F. Hough, "Andropov's First Year," *Problems of Communism* 32 (November–December 1983): 49.

37. K. U. Chernenko, "Dostoino zavershit' piatiletku, uskorit' intensifikatsiiu ekonomiki," *Pravda*, 16 November 1984.

38. The redefinition of economic categories in the budget with the introduction of the agro-industrial complex makes it difficult to compare spending proposals in other categories with earlier budgets and plans.

39. "Kompleksnaia programma razvitiia proizvodstva tovarov narodnogo potrebleniia i sfery uslug na 1986–2000 gody," *Pravda*, 9 October 1985. Also see Zhores A. Medvedev, *Gorbachev* (New York: W.W. Norton, 1986), 197.

40. L. I. Brezhnev, "Politicheskii doklad Tsentral'nogo Komiteta KPSS XXVII s"ezdu Kommunisticheskoi Partii Sovetskogo Soiuza," *Pravda*, 26 February 1986; N. I. Ryzhkov, "Ob osnovnykh napravleniiakh ekonomicheskogo i sotsial'nogo razvitiia SSSR na 1986–1990 gody i na period do 2000 goda," *Pravda*, 4 March 1986.

41. M. S. Gorbachev, "O sozyve ocherednogo XXVII s"ezda KPSS i zadachakh, sviazannykh s ego podgotovkoi i provedeniem," *Pravda*, 24 April 1985.

42. *Financial Times* (London), 10 November 1989.

43. U.S. Congress, Joint Economic Committee, *Allocation of Resources in the Soviet Union and China—1987*, Pt. 13, 100th Cong., 2nd sess., 13, 21 April 1988, 23; Leonard Vid, "Guns into Butter, Soviet Style," *Bulletin of Atomic Scientists* 46 (January–February 1990): 17–19.

44. Imogene Erro, "And What of the Consumer?" *Problems of Communism* 12 (November–December 1963): 34.

45. A. G. Zverev, "O Gosudarstvennom biudzhete SSSR na 1956 god i ob ispolnenii Gosudarstvennogo biudzheta SSSR za 1954 goda," *Pravda*, 27 December 1955.

46. Merle Fainsod, "The CPSU Takes Stock of Itself," *Problems of Communism* 5 (May–June 1956): 8.

47. Zverev, "O Gosudarstvennom biudzhete SSSR na 1956 god."

48. Roy A. Medvedev and Zhores A. Medvedev, *Khrushchev: The Years in Power* (New York: W. W. Norton, 1978), 75.

49. "Kontrol'nye tsifry razvitiia narodnogo khoziaistva SSSR na 1959–1965 gody," *Pravda*, 8 February 1959. Also see Leon M. Herman, "The Seven-Year Haul," *Problems of Communism* 8 (March–April 1959): 9–14.

50. "V Tsentral'nom Komitete KPSS i Sovete Ministrov SSSR: 'O merakh po uvelicheniiu proizvodstva, rasshireniiu assortimenta i uluchsheniiu kachestva tovarov kul'turno-bytovogo naznacheniia i khoziaistvennogo obikhoda,' " *Pravda*, 16 October 1959.

51. A. N. Kosygin, "O plane razvitiia narodnogo khoziaistva SSSR na 1960 god," *Pravda*, 28 October 1959; see discussion in Marshall I. Goldman, "Living Standards and Consumer Goods," *Problems of Communism* 9 (September–October 1960): 32–46.

52. N. S. Khrushchev, "Ob otmene nalogov s rabochikh i sluzhashchikh

i drugikh meropriiatiiakh, napravlennykh na povyshenie blagosostoianiia sovetskogo naroda," *Pravda*, 6 May 1960.

53. N. S. Khrushchev, "Za novye pobedy mirogo kommunisticheskogo dvizheniia," *Pravda*, 25 January 1961. Budgets in these years do not, however, tell us either what was to be or what was actually spent on these sectors.

54. F. R. Kozlov, "43-ia godovshchina Velikoi Oktiabr'skoi sotsialisticheskoi revoliutsii," *Pravda*, 7 November 1960.

55. N. S. Khrushchev, "Povyshenie blagosostoianiia naroda i zadachi dal'neishego uvelicheniia proizvodstva sel'skokhoziaistvennykh produktov," *Pravda*, 21 January 1961.

56. V. F. Garbuzov, "O Gosudarstvennom biudzhete SSSR na 1961 god i ob ispolnenii Gosudarstvennogo biudzheta SSSR za 1959 goda," *Pravda*, 21 December 1960; V. F. Garbuzov, "O Gosudarstvennom biudzhete SSSR na 1962 god i ob ispolnenii Gosudarstvennogo biudzheta SSSR za 1960 goda," *Pravda*, 7 December 1961; V. F. Garbuzov, "O Gosudarstvennom biudzhete SSSR na 1963 god i ob ispolnenii Gosudarstvennogo biudzheta SSSR za 1961 goda," *Pravda*, 11 December 1962.

57. "Rezoliutsiia XXII s"ezda Kommunisticheskoi Partii Sovetskogo Soiuza po Otchetu Tsentral'nogo Komiteta KPSS," *Pravda*, 1 November 1961.

58. William Hyland and Richard W. Shryock, *The Fall of Khrushchev* (New York: Funk and Wagnalls, 1968), 67.

59. N. S. Khrushchev, "Rech' tovarishcha N. S. Khrushcheva na sobranii izbiratelei Kalininskogo izbiratel'nogo okruga gor. Moskvy, 27 fevralia 1963 goda," *Pravda*, 28 February 1963.

60. V. F. Garbuzov, "O Gosudarstvennom biudzhete SSSR na 1964–65 gody i ob ispolnenii Gosudarstvennogo biudzheta SSSR za 1962 goda," *Pravda*, 17 December 1963.

61. "Ob osnovnykh napravleniiakh v razrabotke plana razvitiia narodnogo khoziaistva na blizhaishii period," *Pravda*, 2 October 1964.

62. V. F. Garbuzov, "O Gosudarstvennom biudzhete SSSR na 1969 god i ob ispolnenii Gosudarstvennogo biudzheta SSSR za 1967 goda," *Pravda*, 11 December 1968; V. F. Garbuzov, "O Gosudarstvennom biudzhete SSSR na 1970 god i ob ispolnenii Gosudarstvennogo biudzheta SSSR za 1968 goda," *Pravda*, 17 December 1969.

63. L. I. Brezhnev, "Tvorcheski reshat' novye zadachi kommunisticheskogo stroitel'stva," *Pravda*, 13 June 1970.

64. The external shocks are not sufficient explanation for the shift, however, for a far more direct threat to Soviet control two years earlier, when the balance of power in the leadership was different, led to a very different response in spending priorities.

65. "Proekt Ts. K. KPSS—Direktivy XXIV s"ezda KPSS po piatiletnomy planu razvitiia narodnogo khoziaistva SSSR na 1971–1975 gody," *Pravda*, 14 February 1971.

66. L. I. Brezhnev, "Otchetnyi doklad Tsentral'nogo Komiteta KPSS XXIV s"ezdu Kommunisticheskoi Partii Sovetskogo Soiuza," *Pravda*, 31 March 1971.

67. "Proekt TsK KPSS k XXV s"ezdu: 'Osnovnye napravleniia razvitiia narodnogo khoziaistva SSSR na 1976–1980 gody,' " *Pravda*, 14 December 1975;

A. N. Kosygin, "Osnovnye napravleniia razvitiia narodnogo khoziaistva SSSR na 1976–1980 gody," *Pravda*, 2 March 1976; "Osnovnye napravleniia razvitiia narodnogo khoziaistva SSSR na 1976–1980 gody," *Pravda*, 7 March 1976.

68. U.S. Congress, Joint Economic Committee, *Allocation of Resources in the Soviet Union and China—1984*, Pt. 10, 98th Cong., 2nd sess., 21 November 1984 and 15 January 1985, 53, 54.

69. "Proekt TsK KPSS k XXVI s"ezdu partii: 'Osnovnye napravleniia ekonomicheskogo i sotsial'nogo razvitiia SSSR na 1981–1985 gody i na period do 1990 goda,' " *Pravda*, 2 December 1980; N. A. Tikhonov, "Osnovnye napravleniia ekonomicheskogo i sotsial'nogo razvitiia SSSR na 1981–1985 gody i na period do 1990 goda," *Pravda*, 27 February 1981; "Osnovnye napravleniia ekonomicheskogo i sotsial'nogo razvitiia SSSR na 1981–1985 gody i na period do 1990 goda," *Pravda*, 5 March 1981.

70. The figures for industrial spending must rely on annual projections of spending because breakdowns for actual spending on industry are missing for most years in this period.

71. Bruce Parrott, "Political Change and Civil-Military Relations," in *Soldiers and the Soviet State*, ed. Timothy J. Colton and Thane Gustafson (Princeton: Princeton University Press, 1990), 63.

72. John W. Parker, *Kremlin in Transition: From Brezhnev to Chernenko, 1978 to 1985* (Boston: Unwin Hyman, 1991), 27–40, 47–50; Gelman, *The Brezhnev Politburo and the Decline of Detente*, 177.

73. The most controversial of these data sets is, of course, the data on military spending. For example, see the discussions in Franklyn D. Holzman, *Financial Checks on Soviet Defense Expenditure* (Lexington: Lexington Books, 1975); William T. Lee, *The Estimation of Soviet Defense Expenditures, 1955–75: An Unconventional Approach* (New York: Praeger Publishers, 1977); R. T. Maddock, *The Political Economy of Soviet Defense Spending* (London: Macmillan Press, 1988); Steven Rosefielde, *False Science: Underestimating the Soviet Arms Buildup* (New Brunswick: Transaction Books, 1982).

74. Source of data: Central Intelligence Agency, Directorate of Intelligence, *Soviet Statistics on Capital Formation* (Washington, D.C.: CIA, August 1982), 5.

75. Source of data: Tsentral'noe Statisticheskoe Upravlenie, *Narodnoe khoziaistvo SSSR* (annual editions, 1959–) (Moscow: Statistika, 1960–). The ratio of Social-Cultural Measures to Defense is used in lieu of the ratio of SCM to the total budget because the latter includes many elements (such as consumer-goods industry) that should covary positively with directive leadership and SCM.

76. Central Intelligence Agency estimates are reported in the annual editions of U.S. Arms Control and Disarmament Agency, *World Military Expenditures and Arms Transfers* (Washington, D.C.: GPO, 1969–). Stockholm International Peace Research Institute estimates are reported in its *SIPRI Yearbook of World Armaments and Disarmament* (New York: Humanities Press, 1970–). Because no single series covers the entire period, I have used several different, overlapping series from each source and included a dummy variable to adjust the different base years for each series.

77. The data divide the antilog of the residual by the antilog of the predicted value from equations that fit the logarithm of spending to a trend line.

78. Quoted in Robert Conquest, *Power and Policy in the U.S.S.R.* (New York:

Harper & Row, 1967), 158. For a slightly different description of the configuration of the membership in the Bureau of the Presidium, see Fedor Burlatsky, *Khrushchev and the First Russian Spring* (New York: Charles Scribner's Sons, 1988), 77–78.

79. "Postanovlenie sovmestnogo zasedaniia Plenuma Tsentral'nogo Komiteta Kommunisticheskoi Partii Sovetskogo Soiuza, Soveta Ministrov Soiuza SSR, Prezidium Verkhovnogo Soveta SSSR," *Pravda*, 7 March 1953.

80. Alec Nove, "The Soviet Industrial Reorganization," *Problems of Communism* 6 (November–December 1957): 20.

81. Edward Crankshaw, *Khrushchev: A Career* (New York: Viking Press, 1966), 246. Also see Medvedev and Medvedev, *Khrushchev: The Years in Power*, 105; Leonhard, *The Kremlin Since Stalin*, 237.

82. "Zakon: 'O dal'neishem sovershenstvovanii organizatsii upravleniia promyshlennost'iu i stroitel'stvom,' " *Pravda*, 11 May 1957; "Zakon: 'O vnesenii izmenenii i dopolnenii v tekst Konstitutsii (Osnovnogo Zakona) SSSR," *Pravda*, 11 May 1957; Leonhard, *The Kremlin Since Stalin*, 265.

83. Nove, "The Soviet Industrial Reorganization," 21.

84. Crankshaw, *Khrushchev: A Career*, 248.

85. Jerry F. Hough, "A Harebrained Scheme in Retrospect," *Problems of Communism* 14 (July–August 1965): 27–29; Boris Meissner, "Party and Government Reforms: A Provisional Balance Sheet," *Survey*, no. 56 (July 1965): 31–45.

86. Ye. Bugaev, "Eto samaia dlia nas interesnaia politika," *Pravda*, 26 December 1962.

87. F. Petrenko, "Proizvodstvo—glavnaia sfera partiinogo rukovodstva," *Partiinaia zhizn'*, no. 2 (January 1963): 16.

88. Robert Conquest, "The Struggle Goes On," *Problems of Communism* 9 (July–August 1960): 7.

89. "O razvitii ekonomiki SSSR i perestroike partiinogo rukovodstva narodnym khoziaistvom—Postanovlenie Plenuma TsK KPSS po dokladu tovarishcha N. S. Khrushcheva," *Pravda*, 24 November 1962.

90. Sidney I. Ploss, "Politics in the Kremlin," *Problems of Communism* 19 (May–June 1970): 2.

91. "Ustav Kommunisticheskoi Partii Sovetskogo Soiuza," *Pravda*, 3 November 1961.

92. Barbara Ann Chotiner, *Khrushchev's Party Reform: Coalition Building and Institutional Innovation* (Westport: Greenwood Press, 1984), 183–87.

93. John A. Armstrong, "Party Bifurcation and Elite Interests," *Soviet Studies* 17 (April 1966): 421; Grey Hodnett, "The Obkom First Secretaries," *Slavic Review* 14 (December 1965): 638.

94. Alec Nove, "Revamping the Economy," *Problems of Communism* 12 (January–February 1963): 14.

95. Armstrong, "Party Bifurcation and Elite Interests," 422.

96. Tsentral'noe Statisticheskoe Upravlenie, *Narodnoe khoziaistvo SSSR v 1963 godu* (Moscow: Statistika, 1965), 33.

97. "Postanovlenie plenuma: 'Ob ob"edinenii promyshlennykh i sel'skikh oblastnykh, kraevykh partiinykh organizatsii,' " in Institut Marksizma-Leninizma pri TsK KPSS, *Kommunisticheskaia Partiia Sovetskogo Soiuza v rezoliu-*

tsiiakh i resheniiakh s"ezdov, konferentsii, i plenumov TsK (Moscow: Izdatel' stvo Politicheskoi Literatury, 1986), 10:419–20.

98. Armstrong, "Party Bifurcation and Elite Interests," 426–27.

99. Jerry Hough, *The Soviet Prefects* (Cambridge: Harvard University Press, 1969), 75.

100. "Zasedanie Verkhovnogo Soveta SSSR—Rech' deputata G. I. Popova," *Izvestiia*, 11 December 1964.

101. "Piataia sessiia Verkhovnogo Soveta SSSR—Rech' deputata G. I. Popova," *Leningradskaia Pravda*, 11 December 1964.

102. A. N. Kosygin, "Ob uluchshenii upravleniia promyshlennost'iu, sovershenstvovanii planirovaniia i usilenii ekonomicheskogo stimulirovaniia promyshlennogo proizvodstva," *Pravda*, 28 September 1965.

103. Eugene Zaleski, *Planning Reforms in the Soviet Union, 1962–1966* (Chapel Hill: University of North Carolina Press, 1967), 141–83.

104. "V Tsentral'nom Komitete KPSS i Sovete Ministrov SSSR," *Pravda*, 3 April 1973.

105. L. I. Brezhnev, "Otchet Tsentral'nogo Komiteta KPSS i ocherednye zadachi partii v oblasti vnutrenei i vneshnei politiki," *Pravda*, 25 February 1976.

106. Karl W. Ryavec, *Implementation of Soviet Economic Reforms: Political, Organizational, and Social Processes* (New York: Praeger Publishers, 1975), 125.

107. Alec Nove, *The Soviet Economic System*, 3d ed. (Boston: Allen and Unwin, 1986), 69–70.

108. George R. Feiwel, *The Soviet Quest for Economic Efficiency: Issues, Controversies, and Reforms*, exp. ed. (New York: Praeger Publishers, 1972), 341–44; Alice Gorlin, "The Soviet Economic Associations," *Soviet Studies* 26 (January 1874): 3; Nove, *The Soviet Economic System*, 71–72.

109. Ryavec, *Implementation of Soviet Economic Reforms*, 128.

110. Joseph S. Berliner, "Planning and Management," in *The Soviet Economy: Toward the Year 2000*, ed. Abram Bergson and Herbert S. Levine (London: George Allen and Unwin, 1983), 358.

111. See the debate in Valerie Bunce, "The Succession Connection: Policy Cycles and Political Change in the Soviet Union and Eastern Europe," *American Political Science Review* 74 (December 1980): 966–77; Philip G. Roeder, "Do New Leaders Really Make a Difference?" *American Political Science Review* 79 (December 1985): 958–76; Valerie Bunce and Philip G. Roeder, "The Effects of Leadership Succession in the Soviet Union," *American Political Science Review* 80 (March 1986): 215–24.

Chapter Eight
The Dialectics of Military Planning

1. Barry Posen, *The Sources of Military Doctrine* (Ithaca: Cornell University Press, 1984), 14; John J. Dziak, *Soviet Perceptions of Military Power: The Interaction of Theory and Practice* (New York: Crane, Russak & Co., 1981), 61.

2. H. S. Dinerstein, *War and the Soviet Union*, rev. ed. (New York: Frederick A. Praeger, 1962), 93, 163; Raymond L. Garthoff, "Mutual Deterrence and

Strategic Arms Limitation in Soviet Policy," *International Security* 3 (Summer 1978): 114–15. Also see George G. Weickhardt, "Ustinov versus Ogarkov," *Problems of Communism* 34 (January–February 1985): 78; Alfred L. Monks, *Soviet Military Doctrine: 1960 to the Present* (New York: Irvington Publishers, 1984), 273.

3. David Holloway, "Military Power and Political Purpose in Soviet Policy," *Daedelus* 109 (Fall 1980): 25–26; Condoleeza Rice, "The Party, the Military, and Decision Authority in the Soviet Union," *World Politics* 40 (October 1987): 64–67.

4. V. I. Lenin, "Karl Marks," in *Polnoe sobranie sochinenii*, 5th ed. (Moscow: Izdatel'stvo Politicheskoi literatury, 1961), 26:53–55.

5. A. M. Plekhov, comp., *Slovar' voennykh terminov* (Moscow: Voennoe Izdatel'stvo, 1988), 50. On the structure of military thought, also see T. Hasegawa, "Soviets on Nuclear-War-Fighting," *Problems of Communism* 35 (July–August 1986): 69.

6. S. Kozlov, *Spravochnik ofitsera* (Moscow: Voennoe Izdatel'stvo, 1971), translated as *The Officer's Handbook—A Soviet View* (Washington, D.C.: GPO, 1977), 62.

7. Kozlov, *The Officer's Handbook*, 53.

8. "Voennaia nauka," in *Voennaia entsiklopedicheskii slovar'*, ed. N. V. Ogarkov et al. (Moscow: Voennoe Izdatel'stvo, 1983), 137; Kozlov, *The Officer's Handbook*, 65. See the relationship between military science and *doktrina* in A. Epishev, "Voennaia politika KPSS," in *Sovetskaia voennaia entsiklopediia*, ed. N. V. Ogarkov et al. (Moscow: Voennoe Izdatel'stvo, 1977), 2:193.

9. M. V. Frunze, "Edinaia voennaia doktrina i Krasnaia Armiia," in *Izbrannye proizvedeniia* (Moscow: Voennoe Izdatel'stvo, 1977), 31.

10. M. A. Gareev, *M. V. Frunze—Voennyi teoretik* (Moscow: Voennoe Izdatel'stvo, 1985); translated as *M. V. Frunze—Military Theorist* (Washington, D.C.: Pergamon-Brassey's, 1988), 98–101; P. Tsiffer, "Voennaia doktrina," in *Bol'shaia sovetskaia entsiklopediia*, 1st ed. (Moscow: Sovetskaia Entsiklopediia, 1928), 12:163–65.

11. "Voennye nauki," in *Bol'shaia sovetskaia entsiklopediia*, 1st ed. (Moscow: Sovetskaia Entsiklopediia, 1928), 12:326–27.

12. V. V. Kurasov, "On the Characteristic Features of Stalin's Military Art," *Voennaia mysl'*, no. 1 (January 1950); this was excerpted in Harriet Fast Scott and William F. Scott, *The Soviet Art of War: Doctrine, Strategy, and Tactics* (Boulder: Westview Press, 1982), 85. Also see Raymond L. Garthoff, *Soviet Military Policy: A Historical Analysis* (New York: Frederick A. Praeger, Publishers, 1966), 44.

13. N. Talenskii, "K voprosu o kharaktere zakonov voennoi nauki," *Voennaia mysl'*, no. 9 (September 1953): 30.

14. This effort to create an autonomous military science provoked a reaction from those who sought to stress the subordination of military science to political objectives; see A. Pshenichkin, S. Pekarskii, M. Marienko, R. Zverev, and R. Gusakov, "K voprosu o kharaktere zakonov voennoi nauki," *Voennaia mysl'*, no. 11 (November 1954): 33–34; R. Gusakov, "Odnostoronnii podkhod k izu-

cheniiu zakonov vooruzhennoi bor'by," *Voennaia mysl'*, no. 9 (September 1954): 34; A. Vasilevskii, "Na strazhe bezopasnosti Sovetskoi Rodiny," *Krasnaia zvezda*, 23 February 1954.

15. Editorial, "K itogami diskussii o kharaktere zakonov voennoi nauki," *Voennaia mysl'*, no. 4 (April 1955): 17. Also see P. Rotmistrov, "Za tvorcheskuiu razrabotku voprosov sovetskoi voennoi nauki," *Krasnaia zvezda*, 24 March 1955.

16. Editorial, "O nekotorykh voprosakh sovetskoi voennoi nauki," *Voennaia mysl'*, no. 3 (March 1955): 6.

17. P. Zhilin, "Diskussiia o edinoi voennoi doktrine," *Voenno-istoricheskii zhurnal*, no. 5 (May 1961): 61–74.

18. N. Lomov, "O sovetskoi voennoi doktrine," *Kommunist vooruzhennykh sil*, no. 10 (May 1962): 11ff.

19. V. D. Sokolovskii et al., *Voennaia strategiia*, 1st–3d ed. (Moscow: Voennoi Izdatel'stvo, 1962, 1963, 1968); translated as *Soviet Military Strategy* (New York: Crane, Russak and Co., 1975), 237–38.

20. R. Kolkowicz, *The Communist Party and the Soviet Military* (Princeton: Princeton University Press, 1967), 273.

21. L. Belousov, "Konferentsiia o sovetskoi voennoi doktrine," *Voenno-istoricheskii zhurnal*, no. 10 (October 1963): 122.

22. M. V. Zakharov, "Vlastnoe trebovanie vremeni," *Krasnaia zvezda*, 4 February 1965.

23. S. N. Kozlov, "Military Doctrine and Military Science," in *Metodologicheskie problemy voennoi teorii i praktiki*, ed. N. Sushko et al. (Moscow: Voenizdat, 1966); translated as *Methodological Problems of Military Theory and Practice* (JPRS 41,452; 20 June 1967), 71–72, 77, 79. Also see A. A. Strokov, *Istoriia voennogo iskusstva* (Moscow: Voenizdat, 1966), 599.

24. Marshall V. D. Sokolovskii and General Major M. Cherednichenko, "Military Strategy and its Problems," *Voennaia mysl'*, no. 10 (October 1968); translated in *Selected Translations from Voyennaya Mysl'* FPD 0084/69 (29 August 1969): 35.

25. Kozlov, *The Officer's Handbook*, 47, 62, 63, 64.

26. A. A. Grechko, "Voennaia nauka," in *Sovetskaia voennaia entsiklopediia*, ed. N. V. Ogarkov et al. (Moscow: Sovetskaia entsiklopediia, 1977), 2:183, 188; "Doktrina voennaia," in *Sovetskaia voennaia entsiklopediia*, ed. N. V. Ogarkov et al. (Moscow: Sovetskaia entsiklopediia, 1977), 3:228–29; N. V. Ogarkov, "Strategiia voennaia," in *Sovetskaia voennaia entsiklopediia*, ed. N. V. Ogarkov et al. (Moscow: Sovetskaia entsiklopediia, 1979), 7:556.

27. L. Korzun, "Rol' voennoi strategii v podgotovke strany k voine," *Voenno-istoricheskii zhurnal*, no. 7 (July 1982): 46.

28. N. V. Ogarkov, *Vsegda v gotovnosti k zashchite otechestva* (Moscow: Voennoe Izdatel'stvo, 1982), 21.

29. "Vernost' partii, vernost' narodu," *Pravda*, 12 May 1982.

30. Gareev, *M. V. Frunze*, 379.

31. S. Kozlov, "The Development of Soviet Military Science After World War II," *Voennaia mysl'*, no. 2 (February 1964); translated in *Selected Translations from Voyennaya Mysl'* FDD 934 (20 July 1965): 29; V. G. Kulikov, ed.,

Akademiia General'nogo Shtaba (Moscow: Voenizdat, 1976), 11–14, 178–83; Notra Trulock, "Weapons of Mass Destruction in Soviet Strategy" (Paper presented at Conference on Soviet Military Strategy in Europe, Royal United Services Institute, Oxfordshire, England, 24–25 September 1984), 7–10.

32. Robbin F. Laird and Dale R. Herspring, *The Soviet Union and Strategic Arms* (Boulder: Westview Press, 1984), 9.

33. Henry Trofimenko, "Changing Attitudes Toward Deterrence," in *National Security and International Stability*, ed. Bernard Brodie, Michael D. Intrilligator, and Roman Kolkowicz (Cambridge: Oelgeshlager, Gunn, and Hain, 1983), 81–82.

34. Malinovskii sought to maintain a compromise not only among the views of the various services but also between the views of the first secretary and the first secretary's most severe critics in the military; in the early 1960s Malinovskii continued to balance professional pressures for a multifaceted force with recognition of the revolutionary nature of new weapons and the need to keep defense expenditures within limits. See Thomas W. Wolfe, *Soviet Strategy at the Crossroads* (Cambridge: Harvard University Press, 1965), 33; Kolkowicz, *The Communist Party and the Soviet Military*, 162–63, 266. Sokolovskii's textbook was instrumental in cementing this compromise; see Edward L. Warner, *The Military in Contemporary Soviet Politics: An Institutional Analysis* (New York: Praeger Publishers, 1977), 145; Herspring, *The Soviet High Command*, 38.

35. M. S. Gorbachev, "Politicheskii Doklad Tsentral'nogo Komiteta XXVII s"ezdu Kommunisticheskoi Partii Sovetskogo Soiuza," *Pravda*, 25 February 1986.

36. V. Serebriannikov, "Sootnoshenie politicheskikh i voennykh sredstv v zashchite sotsializma," *Kommunist vooruzhennykh sil*, no. 18 (September 1987): 12.

37. K. Bochkarev, "The Question of the Sociological Aspects of the Struggle Against the Forces of Aggression and War," *Voennaia mysl'*, no. 9 (September 1968); translated in *Selected Translations from Voyennaya Mysl'* FPD 0115/69 (16 December 1969): 14.

38. John Mearsheimer, *Conventional Deterrence* (Ithaca: Cornell University Press, 1983), 29.

39. Quoted in Sokolovskii, *Soviet Military Strategy*, 133.

40. Ibid., 292.

41. Harriet Fast Scott and William F. Scott, *Soviet Military Doctrine: Continuity, Formulation, and Dissemination* (Boulder: Westview Press, 1988), 70.

42. An important survey of the development of Soviet thinking about deterrence is Raymond L. Garthoff, *Deterrence and the Revolution in Soviet Military Doctrine* (Washington, D.C.: Brookings Institution, 1990).

43. V. M. Molotov, "Rech' tov. V. M. Molotova na sobranii izbiratelei Molotovskogo izbiratel'nogo okruga g. Moskvy 10 marta 1950 goda," *Pravda*, 11 March 1950.

44. I. V. Stalin, "Beseda s korrespondentom 'Pravdy,' " in *Sochineniia* (Stanford: Hoover Institution Press, 1967), 3[XVI]:179–80.

45. N. S. Khrushchev, "Otchetnyi Doklad Tsentral'nogo Komiteta Kom-

munisticheskoi Partii Sovetskogo Soiuza XX s"ezdu partii," *Pravda*, 15 February 1956.

46. N. S. Khrushchev, "Razoruzhenie—put' k uprocheniiu mira i obespecheniiu druzhby mezhdu narodami," *Pravda*, 15 January 1960.

47. *Soviet Government Statement*, 21 September 1963; translated in William E. Griffith, *The Sino-Soviet Rift* (Cambridge: MIT Press, 1964), 444.

48. Liu Chih Ch'ao, "Examination of the Question of War Must Not Run Counter to Marxist-Leninist Viewpoint of Class Struggle," *Hung Ch'i* (Red Flag), 15 August 1963, cited in Garthoff, *Soviet Military Policy*, 196.

49. Thomas W. Wolfe, *Soviet Power and Europe* [RM-5838-PR] (Santa Monica: Rand Corporation, 1968), 45–52; I. Stalin, "Beseda s korrespondentom 'Pravdy,' " 174.

50. A provocative assessment of Soviet force posture under Stalin is Matthew A. Evangelista, "Stalin's Postwar Army Reappraised," *International Security* 7 (Winter 1982–83): 110–38.

51. I. V. Stalin, "Prikaz Narodnogo Komissara Oborony, 23 fevralia 1942, no. 55, Moskva," in *O velikoi Otechestvennoi voine Sovetskogo Soiuza*, 4th ed. (Moscow: OGIZ, 1944), 40–41.

52. Dinerstein, *War and the Soviet Union*, 6; Trulock, "Weapons of Mass Destruction in Soviet Strategy," 17.

53. "Voennaia nauka," in *Bol'shaia sovetskaia entsiklopediia*, 2d ed. (Moscow: Bol'shaia Sovetskaia Entsiklopediia, 1951), 8:409; I. Stalin, "Rech' na predvybornom sobranii izbiratelei Stalinskogo izbiratel'nogo okruga goroda Moskvy, 9 fevralia 1946 g.," in *Sochineniia* (Stanford: Hoover Institution Press, 1967), 3 (XVI), 6–20; K. Voroshilov, *Stalin i vooruzhennye sily SSSR* (Moscow: n.p., 1951), 105–20; N. A. Bulganin, "Tridtsat' let Sovetskikh Vooruzhennykh Sil," *Pravda*, 24 February 1948.

54. "Voennaia nauka," in *Bol'shaia Sovetskaia Entsiklopediia*, 2d ed., 8:407–8; "Voennoe iskusstvo," in *Bol'shaia Sovetskaia Entsiklopediia*, 2d ed. (Moscow: Bol'shaia Sovetskaia Entsiklopediia, 1951), 8:438.

55. Voroshilov, *Stalin i vooruzhennye sily SSSR*, 118.

56. Malcolm Mackintosh, *Contemporary Soviet Military Doctrine* (Oxford: St. Anthony's College, 1959), 2.

57. G. M. Malenkov, "Rech' tovarishcha G. M. Malenkova na sobranii izbiratelei Leningradskogo izbiratel'nogo okruga g. Moskvy, 12 marta 1954 goda," *Pravda*, 13 March 1954; A. I. Mikoian, "Rech' tovarishcha A. I. Mikoiana na sobranii izbiratelei Erevanskogo-Stalinskogo izbiratel'nogo okruga, 11 marta 1954 goda," *Kommunist* [Erevan] 12 March 1954. Allies on this issue included Mikhail Pervukhin, Petr Pospelov, and Maksim Saburov.

58. N. S. Khrushchev, "Rech' tovarishcha N. S. Khrushcheva na sobranii izbiratelei Kalininskogo izbiratel'nogo okruga g. Moskvy, 6 marta 1954 goda," *Pravda*, 7 March 1954. Also see Editorial, "Sud'by mira i tsivilizatsii reshaiut narody," *Kommunist*, no. 4 (March 1955): 16; K. E. Voroshilov, "Rech' tovarishcha K. E. Voroshilova na sobranii izbiratelei Kirovskogo izbiratel'nogo okruga g. Leningrada, 10 marta 1954 goda," *Pravda*, 11 March 1954; L. M. Kaganovich, "Rech' tovarishcha L. M. Kaganovicha na sobranii izbiratelei

Tashkent-Leninskogo izbiratel'nogo okruga, 11 marta 1954 goda," *Pravda*, 13 March 1954; V. M. Molotov, "Rech' tovarishcha V. M. Molotova na sobranii izbiratelei Molotovskogo izbiratel'nogo okruga g. Moskvy, 11 marta 1954 goda," *Pravda*, 12 March 1954.

59. N. A. Bulganin, "Rech' tovarishcha N. A. Bulganina na sobranii izbiratelei Moskovskogo gorodskogo izbiratel'nogo okruga, 10 marta 1954 goda," *Izvestiia*, 11 March 1954; Garthoff, *Soviet Military Policy*, 48.

60. Khrushchev, "Otchetnyi Doklad Tsentral'nogo Komiteta Kommunisticheskoi Partii Sovetskogo Soiuza XX s"ezdu partii."

61. "Rech' tov. Molotova V. M." and "Rech' tov. Kaganovicha L. M.," in *XX S"ezd Kommunisticheskoi Partii Sovetskogo Soiuza—stenograficheskii otchet* (Moscow: Izdatel'stvo Politicheskoi Literatury, 1956), 1:457, 459, 512.

62. M. Gus, "General'naia liniia Sovetskoi vneshnei politiki," *Zvezda*, no. 11 (November 1953): 109; G. Fedorov, "Marksizm-Leninizm o voine i armii," *Krasnaia zvezda*, 6 January 1954.

63. Kulikov, *Akademiia General'nogo Shtaba*, 156–59.

64. Kozlov, "The Development of Soviet Military Science After World War II," 39–40; G. Pokrovskii, "Vooruzhenie v sovremennoi voine," in *Marksizm-Leninizm o voine, armii, i voennoi nauke: sbornik statei*, ed. B. S. Lialikov and P. A. Sidorov (Moscow: Voennoe Izdatel'stvo, 1955), 168.

65. K. Moskalenko, "Uchit'sia pobezhdat' sil'nogo i tekhnicheski osnashchennogo protivnika," *Krasnaia zvezda*, 25 September 1954.

66. N. A. Lomov was replaced by A. I. Gastilovich. Kulikov, "The Development of Soviet Military Science After World War II," 157.

67. "Otvety N. S. Khrushcheva na voprosy glavnogo diplomaticheskogo korrespondenta amerikanskogo gazety 'N'iu-Iork taims' Dzh. Restona," *Pravda*, 11 October 1957; N. S. Khrushchev, "Za novuiu pobedu nerushimogo bloka kommunistov i bespartiinykh—Rech' tovarishcha N. S. Khrushcheva," *Pravda*, 15 March 1958.

68. Kulikov, "The Development of Soviet Military Science After World War II," 152–53; Mackintosh, *Contemporary Soviet Military Doctrine*, 14; Oleg Penkovsky, *The Penkovsky Papers* (New York: Avon, 1966), 254–55.

69. P. Kurochkin, "Pobeda sovetskogo voennogo iskusstva v velikoi Otechestvennoi voine," *Voennaia mysl'*, no. 5 (May 1955): 18.

70. A. Vasilevskii, "Velikaia pobeda Sovetskogo naroda," *Izvestiia*, 8 May 1955; S. Shatilov, "Bol'shaia blagorodnaia tema," *Literaturnaia gazeta*, 28 May 1955; V. Kurasov, "K voprosu ob uprezhdaiushchem udare," *Krasnaia zvezda*, 27 April 1958; N. Pukhovskii, "Tvorcheskii kharakter sovetskoi voennoi nauki," in *Marksizm-Leninizm o voine, armii, i voennoi nauke: sbornik statei*, ed. B. S. Lialikov and P. A. Sidorov (Moscow: Voennoe Izdatel'stvo, 1955), 100.

71. P. Rotmistrov, "O roli vnezapnosti v sovremennoi voine," *Voennaia mysl'*, no. 2 (February 1955): 14–26.

72. Dale R. Herspring, *The Soviet High Command, 1967–1989* (Princeton: Princeton University Press, 1990), 34.

73. Khrushchev, "Razoruzhenie—put' k uprocheniiu mira i obespecheniiu druzhby mezhdu narodami." Also see Roy Medvedev, *Khrushchev* (Garden City: Anchor Press, 1983), 136–37.

74. R. Ia. Malinovskii, "Rech' Ministra oborony SSSR Marshala Sovetskogo Soiuza tov. R. Ia. Malinovskogo," *Krasnaia zvezda*, 15 January 1960.

75. A. A. Grechko, "Nashi doblestnye vooruzhennye sily," *Krasnaia zvezda*, 23 February 1960.

76. S. Krasil'nikov, "O kharaktere sovremennoi voiny," *Krasnaia zvezda*, 18 November 1960. Also see V. Kurasov, "Voprosy sovetskoi voennoi nauki v proizvedeniiakh V. I. Lenina," *Voenno-istoricheskii zhurnal*, no. 3 (March 1961): 3–14.

77. S. Kozlov, "Tvorcheskii kharakter sovetskoi voennoi nauki," *Kommunist vooruzhennykh sil*, no. 11 (June 1961): 52–53.

78. N. S. Khrushchev, "Bessmertnyi podvig sovetskogo naroda—Rech' tovarishcha N. S. Khrushcheva," *Pravda*, 22 June 1961.

79. N. S. Khrushchev, "Rech' tovarishcha N. S. Khrushcheva," *Pravda*, 9 July 1961; N. S. Khrushchev, "Vystuplenie N. S. Khrushcheva po radio i televideniiu 7 avgusta 1961 goda," *Izvestiia*, 9 August 1961.

80. R. Ia. Malinovskii, "Rech' tovarishcha R. Ia. Malinovskogo," *Pravda*, 25 October 1961; R. Ia. Malinovskii, "Programma KPSS i voprosy ukrepleniia vooruzhennykh sil SSSR," *Kommunist*, no. 7 (May 1962): 11–22.

81. Sokolovskii, *Soviet Military Strategy*, 210. Also see P. Rotmistrov, "Prichiny sovremennykh voin i ikh osobennosti," *Kommunist vooruzhennykh sil*, no. 2 (January 1963): 30–31; S. M. Shtemenko, "Sukhoputnye voiska v sovremennoi voine i ikh boevaia podgotovka," *Krasnaia zvezda*, 3 January 1963; V. Kruchinin, "Pochemu sushchestvuiut massovye armii," *Krasnaia zvezda*, 11 January 1963.

82. N. S. Khrushchev, "Rech' tovarishcha N. S. Khrushcheva na sobranii izbiratelei Kalininskogo izbiratel'nogo okruga gor. Moskvy 27 fevralia 1963 goda," *Pravda*, 28 February 1963.

83. N. S. Khrushchev, "Vse rezervy promyshlennosti i stroitel'stva—na sluzhbu kommunizmu," *Pravda*, 26 April 1963; N. S. Khrushchev, "Vse sily partii i naroda na vypolnenie planov kommunisticheskogo stroitel'stva," *Izvestiia*, 15 December 1963; "Uskorennoe razvitie khimicheskogo promyshlennosti—vazhnogo pod"ema sel'skokhoziaistvennogo proizvodstva i rosta blagosostoianiia naroda," *Pravda*, 16 December 1963.

84. N. S. Khrushchev, "Vyshe znamia bor'by! Tverzhe shag, tesnee riady!" *Pravda*, 22 September 1964; "Ob osnovnykh napravleniiakh v razrabotke plana razvitiia narodnogo khoziaistva na blizhaishii period," *Pravda*, 2 October 1964; Garthoff, *Soviet Military Policy*, 60.

85. S. Baranov and E. Nikitin, "Rukovodstvo KPSS—osnova osnov sovetskogo voennogo stroitel'stva," *Kommunist vooruzhennykh sil*, no. 8 (April 1963): 17–25; D. Kazakov, "Teoreticheskaia i metodologicheskaia osnova sovetskoi voennoi nauka," *Kommunist vooruzhennykh sil*, no. 10 (May 1963): 7–15; I. Korotkov, "O razvitii sovetskoi voennoi teorii v poslevoennye gody," *Voenno-istoricheskii zhurnal*, no. 4 (April 1964): 39–50.

86. V. Chuikov, "Sovremennye sukhoputnye voiska," *Izvestiia*, 22 December 1963.

87. N. Lomov, "Osnovnye polozheniia sovetskoi voennoi doktriny," *Krasnaia zvezda*, 10 January 1964; P. A. Rotmistrov, "Voennaia nauka i

akademii," *Krasnaia zvezda*, 26 April 1964; P. Rotmistrov, "Metodicheskie eksperimenty ili pogonia za sensatsiei?" *Krasnaia zvezda*, 20 May 1964.

88. Trulock, "Weapons of Mass Destruction in Soviet Strategy," 44–46; Samuel B. Payne, Jr., *The Soviet Union and SALT* (Cambridge: MIT Press, 1980), 15; Robert C. Powers, "Flexible Response and External Force: A Contrast of U.S. and Soviet Strategies," *Strategic Review* 9 (Winter 1981): 37.

89. Harry Gelman, *The Brezhnev Politburo and the Decline of Detente* (Ithaca: Cornell University Press, 1984), 80–82.

90. L. I. Brezhnev, "Narod i armiia ediny," *Pravda*, 4 July 1965; c.f. N. S. Khrushchev, "Na strazhe mira," *Pravda*, 9 July 1964.

91. L. I. Brezhnev, "Vooruzhennym silam—dostoinoe popolnenie," *Pravda*, 6 July 1967; emphasis added.

92. Payne, *The Soviet Union and SALT*, 22, 29–48.

93. N. Talenskii, "Razdum'ia o minuvshei voine," *Mezhdunarodnaia zhizn'*, no. 5 (May 1965): 23; N. I. Krylov, "Pouchitel'nye uroki istorii," *Sovetskaia Rossiia*, 30 August 1969; A. A. Grechko, "Velikii podvig sovetskogo naroda," *Pravda*, 9 May 1970; A. Milovidov, "Filosofskie analiz voennoi mysli," *Krasnaia zvezda*, 17 May 1973; V. V. Sheliag, "Dva mirozzreniia—dva vzgliada na voinu," *Krasnaia zvezda*, 7 February 1974; A. Dmitriev, "Marksistsko-leninskoe uchenie o voine i armii—vazhnyi element nauchnogo mirozzreniia voennykh kadrov," *Kommunist vooruzhennykh sil*, no. 13 (July 1975): 9–17; S. Tiushkevich, "Razvitie ucheniia o voine i armii na opyte velikoi otechestvennoi voine," *Kommunist vooruzhennykh sil*, no. 22 (November 1975): 9–16; I. Grudinin, "K voprosu o sushchnosti voiny," *Krasnaia zvezda*, 21 July 1966; Roman Kolkowicz, *The Red "Hawks" on the Rationality of Nuclear War* [RM-4899-PR] (Santa Monica: Rand Corporation, 1966).

94. S. A. Tiushkevich et al., *Sovetskie vooruzhennye sily: istoriia stroitel'stva* (Moscow: Voenizdat, 1978), 476.

95. Sokolovskii, *Soviet Military Strategy*, 279–80.

96. Kozlov, "Soviet Military Doctrine and Military Science," 73–76.

97. S. A. Krasovskii, "Trends in the Use of Aircraft in a Nuclear War," *Voennaia mysl'*, no. 3 (March 1967); translated in *Selected Translations from Voyennaya Mysl'* FPD 1224/67 (26 December 1967): 25–32. I. I. Andrukhov and V. Bulatnikov, "The Growing Role of Airborne Troops in Modern Military Operations," *Voennaia mysl'*, no. 7 (July 1969); translated in *Selected Translations from Voyennaya Mysl'* FDD 0475/67 (17 May 1967): 26–35. S. G. Gorshkov, "Razvitie Sovetskogo Voenno-Morskogo iskusstva," *Morskoi sbornik*, no. 2 (February 1967): 9–21. Also see George Hudson, "Soviet Naval Doctrine and Soviet Politics, 1953–1975," *World Politics* 29 (October 1976): 104–8.

98. G. Wardak, comp., *The Voroshilov Lectures* (Washington, D.C.: National Defense University Press, 1989), 68–78.

99. V. Reznichenko, "Tactics—A Component Part of the Art of Warfare," *Voennaia mysl'*, no. 12 (December 1973); translated in *Selected Translations from Voyennaya Mysl'* FPD 0048 (20 August 1974): 31–45.

100. A. Sidorenko, *Nastuplenie* (Moscow, 1970); translated as *The Offensive* (Washington, D.C.: GPO, 1974); V. V. Voznenko, "Modern Means of Conducting Military Operations and Military Strategy," in *Nauchno-tekhnicheskii pro-*

gress i revoliutsiia v voennom dele, ed. N. A. Lomov et al. (Moscow: Voenizdat, 1973); translated as *Scientific-Technical Progress and the Revolution in Military Affairs (A Soviet View)* (Washington, D.C.: GPO, 1974), 134–41.

101. Trulock, "Weapons of Mass Destruction in Soviet Strategy," 49–65; V. Bondarenko, "Sovremennaia revoliutsiia v voennom dele i boevaia gotovnost' vooruzhennykh sil," *Kommunist vooruzhennykh sil*, no. 24 (December 1968): 22–29; D. Samorukov, "Combat Operations Involving Conventional Means of Destruction," *Voennaia mysl'*, no. 8 (August 1967); translated in *Selected Translations from Voyennaya Mysl'* FPD 0125/68 (26 August 1968): 29–41. S. Shtrik, "The Encirclement and Destruction of the Enemy During Combat Operations Not Involving the Use of Nuclear Weapons," *Voennaia mysl'*, no. 1 (January 1968); translated in *Selected Translations from Voyennaya Mysl'* FPD 0093/68 (22 May 1968): 53–61. On the external function, see A. A. Grechko, "Rukovodiashchaia rol' KPSS v stroitel'stve armii razvitogo sotsialisticheskogo obshchestva," *Voprosy istorii KPSS*, no. 5 (May 1974): 30–47.

102. A. A. Grechko, "Na strazhe mira i sotsializma," *Kommunist*, no. 3 (February 1970): 51–64. Also see A. A. Grechko, "V. I. Lenin i stroitel'stvo sovetskikh vooruzhennykh sil," *Kommunist*, no. 3 (February 1969): 15–26; A. A. Grechko, "Vernost' leninskim zavetam o zashchite rodiny," *Kommunist vooruzhennykh sil*, no. 7 (April 1970): 19–26; A. A. Grechko, "Rech' tovarishcha A. A. Grechko," *Pravda*, 3 April 1971; A. A. Grechko, "Nesokrushimyi shchit rodiny," *Pravda*, 23 February 1971.

103. A. A. Grechko, "O proekte zakona o vseobshchei voinskoi obiazannosti," *Pravda*, 13 October 1967; A. A. Grechko, "Piat'desiat let na strazhe zavoevanii velikogo oktiabria," *Pravda*, 24 February 1968; "Voenno-tekhnicheskoe prevoskhodstvo," in *Sovetskaia voennaia entsiklopediia* (Moscow: Voenizdat, 1976), 2:253.

104. V. Sokolovskii and M. Cherednichenko, "Military Strategy and Its Problems," *Voennaia mysl'*, no. 10 (October 1968); translated in *Selected Translations from Voyennaya Mysl'* FPD 0084/69 (4 September 1969): 39.

105. Jeremy R. Azrael, *The Soviet Civilian Leadership and the Military High Command, 1976–1986* [R-3521-AF] (Santa Monica: Rand Corporation, 1987), v.

106. L. I. Brezhnev, "Vydaiushchiisia podvig zashchitnikov Tuly," *Pravda*, 19 January 1977; L. I. Brezhnev, "Otvet tovarishcha L. I. Brezhneva na voprosy ezhenedel'nika sotsial-demokraticheskoi partii Germanii 'Forverts,' " *Izvestiia*, 4 May 1978. Also see Garthoff, "Mutual Deterrence and Strategic Arms Limitation in Soviet Policy," 114–16, 119–20; Hans Heymann, Jr., "Modernization and the Military-Civil Competition for Resources: Gorbachev's Dilemma," in *Soviet National Security Policy under Perestroika*, ed. George E. Hudson (Boston: Unwin Hyman, 1990), 95; Robert L. Arnett, "Arms Control in Soviet National Security under Gorbachev," in *Soviet National Security Policy under Perestroika*, ed. George E. Hudson (Boston: Unwin Hyman, 1990), 279–80.

107. D. F. Ustinov, "Otvesti ugrozu iadernoi voiny," *Pravda*, 12 July 1982.

108. Erik Beukel, "Analyzing Views of Soviet Leaders on Nuclear Weapons," *Cooperation and Conflict* 15 (1980): 74–75.

109. Robert L. Arnett, "Soviet Attitudes Towards Nuclear War: Do They Really Think They Can Win?" *Journal of Strategic Studies* 2 (September 1979): 177–78; Thomas N. Bjorkman and Thomas J. Zamostny, "Soviet Politics and Strategy Toward the West: Three Cases," *World Politics* 36 (January 1984): 199–202.

110. L. I. Brezhnev, "Otchet Tsentral'nogo Komiteta KPSS XXVI s"ezdu Kommunisticheskoi Partii Sovetskogo Soiuza i ocherednye zadachi partii v oblasti vnutrennei i vneshnei politiki," *Pravda*, 24 February 1981.

111. L. I. Brezhnev, "Otvet L. I. Brezhneva na vopros korrespondenta 'Pravdy,' " *Pravda*, 21 October 1981.

112. D. F. Ustinov, "Otvesti ugrozu iadernoi voiny"; L. I. Brezhnev, "Vtoroi spetsial'noi sessii General'noi Assamblei OON," *Pravda*, 16 June 1982; D. F. Ustinov, *Sluzhim Rodine, delu kommunizma* (Moscow, 1982); translated as *Serving the Country and the Communist Cause* (New York: Pergamon, 1983), 41.

113. Brezhnev, "Vydaiushchiisia podvig zashchitnikov Tuly."

114. Ustinov, *Serving the Country and the Communist Cause*, 42.

115. D. F. Ustinov, "Otstoiat' mir," *Pravda*, 22 June 1981; Brezhnev, "Otchet Tsentral'nogo Komiteta KPSS XXVI s"ezdu Kommunisticheskoi Partii Sovetskogo Soiuza"; Azrael, *The Soviet Civilian Leadership and the Military High Command*, 19.

116. For an excellent analysis of the debate between politicians and professionals, see Bruce Parrott, "Political Change and Civil-Military Relations," in *Soldiers and the Soviet State*, ed. Timothy J. Colton and Thane Gustafson (Princeton: Princeton University Press, 1990), 62–75. Also see Herspring, *The Soviet High Command*, 5.

117. Azrael, *The Soviet Civilian Leadership and the Military High Command*, 13.

118. M. M. Kir'ian et al., *Voenno-tekhnicheskii progress i Vooruzhennye Sily SSSR* (Moscow: Voennoe Izdatel'stvo, 1982), 326. Also see Laird and Herspring, *The Soviet Union and Strategic Arms*, 24–25; P. Konoplya and A. Malyshev, "Sovremennyi nastupatel'nyi boi," *Voennyi vestnik*, no. 1 (January 1984): 26–30.

119. V. G. Kulikov, "Obusdat' gonku vooruzhennii," *Krasnaia zvezda*, 21 February 1984; M. A. Gareev, "Boevaia gotovnost' Sovetskikh Vooruzhennykh Sil i oboronnaia moshch' strany," in *Marksistsko-leninskoe uchenie o voine i armii*, ed. D. A. Volkogonov (Moscow: Voenizdat, 1984), 289–305; N. V. Ogarkov, "Zashchita sotsializma: opyt istorii i sovremennost,' " *Krasnaia zvezda*, 9 May 1984; L. I. Ol'shtynskii, *Vzaimodeistvie armii i flota* (Moscow: Voenizdat, 1983), 7; Gareev, *M. V. Frunze*, 216.

120. Dan L. Strode and Rebecca V. Strode, "Diplomacy and Defense in Soviet National Security Policy," *International Security* 8 (Fall 1983): 95; Mary C. Fitzgerald, "Gorbachev's Concept of Reasonable Sufficiency in National Defense," in *Soviet National Security Policy under Perestroika*, ed. George E. Hudson (Boston: Unwin Hyman, 1990), 178.

121. Ogarkov, *Vsegda v gotovnosti k zashchite otechestva*, 32–34, 50.

122. Ustinov, "Otvesti ugrozu iadernoi voiny."

123. Michael MccGwire, *Military Objectives in Soviet Foreign Policy* (Washington, D.C.: Brookings Institution, 1987).

124. A. Plekhov, "Edinstvo nauchnoi teorii i revoliutsionnoi praktiki," *Krasnaia zvezda*, 11 January 1980; N. Ogarkov, "Uroki istorii," *Krasnaia zvezda*, 9 May 1981; N. Ogarkov, "Tvorcheskaia mysl' polkovodstva," *Pravda*, 2 October 1982.

125. N. Ogarkov, "Pobeda i sovremennost,' " *Izvestiia*, 9 May 1983; N. Ogarkov, "Zashchita sotsializma—opyt istorii i sovremennost,' " *Krasnaia zvezda*, 9 May 1984; Ogarkov, *Vsegda v gotovnosti k zashchite otechestva*, 36; N. N. Azovtsev, *V. I. Lenin i Sovetskaia voennaia nauka*, 2d ed. (Moscow: Nauka, 1981), 299.

126. L. I. Brezhnev, "Soveshchanie voenachal'nikov v Kremle," *Pravda*, 28 October 1982.

127. Gorbachev, "Politicheskii Doklad Tsentral'nogo Komiteta XXVII s"ezdu Kommunisticheskoi Partii Sovetskogo Soiuza."

128. Herspring, *The Soviet High Command*, 258.

129. Richard Pipes, "Why the Soviet Union Thinks It Could Fight and Win a Nuclear War," *Commentary* 64 (July 1977): 21–34. See the discussions of the structure of military thought in Scott and Scott, *Soviet Military Doctrine*.

130. Roman Kolkowicz, Matthew Gallagher, and Benjamin S. Lambeth, *The Soviet Union and Arms Control: A Superpower Dilemma?* (Baltimore: Johns Hopkins University Press, 1970), 37.

131. See Notra Trulock's attempt to tie Khrushchev's doctrinal innovation to the Eisenhower doctrine and to link Brezhnev's doctrinal innovations to American initiatives that actually followed it in time; Trulock, "Weapons of Mass Destruction in Soviet Strategy," 40, 81. To explain the seeming asymmetry of Soviet responses to Western doctrine, James M. McConnell has argued that the Soviet Union did not duplicate Western developments but sought to exploit Western vulnerabilities by asymmetrical responses. Yet this leaves us unable to explain the subsequent symmetry. James M. McConnell, "Shifts in Soviet Views on the Proper Focus of Military Development," *World Politics* 37 (April 1985): 317–18.

132. See, for example, the collection of essays in Jiri Valenta and William Potter, ed., *Soviet Decisionmaking for National Security* (London: George Allen and Unwin, 1984), or a slightly older work such as Edward L. Warner, *The Military in Contemporary Soviet Politics: An Institutional Analysis* (New York: Praeger Publishers, 1977).

133. Philip G. Roeder, "Soviet Policies and Kremlin Politics," *International Studies Quarterly* 28 (June 1984): 171–94.

134. Jack Snyder, *Myths of Empire: Domestic Politics and International Ambition* (Ithaca: Cornell University Press, 1991), 17–19, 31–49, 212–54.

Chapter Nine
The Failure of Constitutional Reform, 1987–1991

1. E. Ligachev, "Vystuplenie tovarishcha Ligacheva E. K.," *Pravda*, 2 July 1988; Boris Yeltsin, *Against the Grain: An Autobiography* (New York: Summit Books, 1990), 138–39.

2. M. S. Gorbachev, "Perestroika—krovnoe delo Naroda," *Pravda*, 26 February 1987.

3. See Vladimir Shlapentokh, *Soviet Intellectuals and Political Power: The Post-Stalin Era* (Princeton: Princeton University Press, 1990).

4. Myron Rush, *Political Succession in the USSR*, 2d ed. (New York: Columbia University Press, 1968), 74–78.

5. "The President of the USSR Resigns," *Rossiiskaia gazeta*, 26 December 1991; translated in *The Current Digest of the Soviet Press* 43 (29 January 1992): 1.

6. M. S. Gorbachev, "Politicheskii Doklad Tsentral'nogo Komiteta KPSS XXVII s"ezdu Kommunisticheskoi Partii Sovetskogo Soiuza," *Pravda*, 26 February 1986. Also see T. H. Rigby, *The Changing Soviet System: Mono-organizational Socialism from its Origins to Gorbachev's Restructuring* (Brookfield: Edward Elgar, 1990), 213.

7. "Zakon SSSR: 'O pechati i drugikh sredstvakh massovoi informatsii,' " *Izvestiia*, 20 June 1990.

8. Robert G. Kaiser, *Why Gorbachev Happened* (New York: Simon and Schuster, 1991), 186.

9. Harry Gelman, *Gorbachev's First Five Years in the Soviet Leadership* [R-3951-A] (Santa Monica: Rand Corporation, 1990), 46–47. The 19th Party Conference also committed the Party to inform citizens of the activities of its leading organs—a decision implemented in early 1989 with the publication of *Izvestiia Tsentral'nogo Komiteta*; "Rezoliutsii XIX Vsesoiuznoi Konferentsii: 'O glasnosti,' " *Pravda*, 5 July 1988.

10. M. S. Gorbachev, "Doklad M. S. Gorbacheva na plenume TsK KPSS," *Pravda*, 12 March 1990.

11. Jerry F. Hough, "Gorbachev's Endgame," *World Policy Journal* 7 (Fall 1990): 659.

12. "Zakon SSSR: 'Ob uchrezhdenii posta Prezidenta SSSR i vnesenii izmenenii i dopolnenii v Konstitutsiiu (Osnovnoi Zakon) SSSR,' " *Pravda*, 16 March 1990. Fedor Burlatsky suggests that Khrushchev had also considered creating a Presidency that could be used to force reform; see Fedor Burlatsky, *Khrushchev and the First Russian Spring* (New York: Charles Scribner's Sons, 1988), 200.

13. For a descriptive overview of this process, see Michael E. Urban, *More Power to the Soviets: The Democratic Revolution in the USSR* (Brookfield: Edward Elgar, 1990). Descriptions of the formal institutions created by these amendments can be found in Robert T. Huber and Donald R. Kelley, eds., *Perestroika-era Politics: The New Soviet Legislature and Gorbachev's Political Reforms* (Armonk: M. E. Sharpe, 1991); Eugene Huskey, ed., *Executive Power and Soviet Politics: The Rise and Decline of the Soviet State* (Armonk: M. E. Sharpe, 1992).

14. N. I. Ryzhkov, "Po novomu osmyslit' funktsii i rol' partii v obshchestve," *Pravda*, 21 July 1989.

15. A. Nazimov and V. Sheinis, "Vybor sdelan," *Izvestiia*, 6 May 1989.

16. Gorbachev, "Politicheskii Doklad Tsentral'nogo Komiteta KPSS XXVII s"ezdu Kommunisticheskoi Partii Sovetskogo Soiuza"; M. S. Gorbachev, "O khode realizatsii reshenii XXVII s"ezda KPSS i zadachakh po uglubleniiu perestroiki," *Pravda*, 29 June 1988.

17. "Zakon SSSR: 'O vyborakh narodnykh deputatov SSSR,' " *Pravda*, 4 December 1988.

18. "Postanovlenie Verkhovnogo Soveta SSSR: 'O dal'neishykh shagakh po osushchestvleniiu politicheskoi reformy v oblasti gosudarstvennogo stroitel'-stva,' " *Pravda*, 2 December 1988.

19. V. Voronetskii, "Vybory: uroki i tendentsii," *Argumenty i fakty*, 13–19 May 1989; I. Karpenko, "Nachalis' vybory narodnykh deputatov," *Izvestiia*, 11 March 1989.

20. Gorbachev, "O khode realizatsii reshenii XXVII s"ezda KPSS i zadachakh po uglubleniiu perestroiki."

21. "Zakon SSSR: 'Ob obshchestvennykh ob"edineniiakh,' " *Pravda*, 16 October 1990.

22. Gorbachev, "O perestroike i kadrovoi politike partii," *Pravda*, 28 January 1987.

23. "Rezoliutsii XIX Vsesoiuznoi konferentsii: 'O demokratizatsii sovetskogo obshchestva i reforme politicheskoi sistemy," *Pravda*, 5 July 1988.

24. "Zakon SSSR: 'Ob izmeneniiakh i dopolneniiakh Konstitutsii (Osnovnogo Zakona) SSSR,' " *Pravda*, 3 December 1988.

25. "Zakon SSSR: ' Ob izmeneniiakh i dopolneniiakh Konstitutsii (Osnovnogo Zakona) SSSR v sviazi s sovershenstvovaniem sistemy gosudarstvennogo upravleniia," *Pravda*, 27 December 1991.

26. "Rezoliutsii XIX Vsesoiuznoi konferentsii: 'O borbe biurokratizmom,' " *Pravda*, 5 July 1988.

27. "Postanovlenie Politbiuro TsK KPSS: 'K Voprosu o reorganizatsii partiinogo apparata'—Zapiska t. Gorbacheva M. S. ot 24 avgusta 1988 g.," *Izvestiia Tsentral'nogo Komiteta* (January 1989): 81–98.

28. R. Judson Mitchell, *Getting to the Top in the USSR* (Stanford: Hoover Institution Press, 1990).

29. John Gooding, "Gorbachev and Democracy," *Soviet Studies* 42 (April 1990): 195.

30. Hough, "Gorbachev's Endgame," 639.

31. Gelman, *Gorbachev's First Five Years in the Soviet Leadership*, 109–10.

32. Archie Brown, "Power and Policy in a Time of Leadership Transition, 1982–1988," in *Political Leadership in the Soviet Union*, ed. Archie Brown (Bloomington: Indiana University Press, 1989), 185–212.

33. Richard Sakwa, *Gorbachev and His Reforms, 1985–1990* (New York: Prentice-Hall, 1990), 7. Also see Stephen White, *Gorbachev in Power* (Cambridge: Cambridge University Press, 1990), 17; Rigby, *The Changing Soviet System*, 211.

34. M. S. Gorbachev, "Vystuplenie M. S. Gorbacheva," *Pravda*, 1 December 1990. See Eduard Shevardnadze's discussion of his conversations on the Black Sea with Gorbachev prior to 1985 in *The Future Belongs to Freedom* (New York: Free Press, 1991), 23, 26.

35. M. S. Gorbachev, "Rech' General'nogo sekretaria TsK KPSS tovarishcha M. S. Gorbacheva na plenume TsK KPSS 11 marta 1985 goda," *Pravda*, 12 March 1985.

36. "Ustav KPSS," Article 25, *Pravda*, 18 July 1990; also see Article 11.

37. M. S. Gorbachev, "O zadachakh partii po korennoi perestroike upravleniia ekonomiki," *Pravda*, 26 June 1987.

38. "Rezoliutsii XIX Vsesoiuznoi konferentsii: 'O demokratizatsii sovetskogo obshchestva i reforme politicheskoi sistemy."

39. "Ustav KPSS," Article 26.

40. A. Migranian, "Dolgii put' k evropeiskomu domu," *Novyi mir* 7 (July 1989): 166–84.

41. M. S. Gorbachev, "Na novom etape perestroiki," *Pravda*, 25 September 1988. Also see M. S. Gorbachev, "Vystuplenie tovarishcha Gorbacheva M. S.," *Pravda*, 1 July 1988.

42. M. S. Gorbachev, "Sud'ba naroda—sud'ba armii," *Pravda*, 16 November 1990.

43. Vitalii A. Korotich et al., " Supporters and Opponents of *Perestroyka*: The Second Joint *Soviet Economy* Roundtable," *Soviet Economy* 4 (October–December 1988): 294.

44. Interview with Peter Jennings, "ABC World News Tonight" (29 July 1991) [unpublished transcript], 4.

45. Benjamin S. Lambeth, *Is Soviet Defense Policy Becoming Civilianized?* [R-3939-USDP] (Santa Monica: Rand Corporation, 1990), vii.

46. Cited in Harry Gelman, *The Soviet Turn Toward Conventional Force Reduction* [R-3876-AF] (Santa Monica: Rand Corporation, 1989), 10.

47. Gorbachev, "O khode realizatsii reshenii XXVII s"ezda KPSS."

48. M. S. Gorbachev, "K polnovlastiiu sovetov i sozdaniiu sotsialisticheskogo pravogo gosudarstva," *Pravda*, 30 November 1988.

49. See, for example: "Za realizm mysli i otvetstvennost' deistvii—Vstrecha A. N. Iakovleva s predstaviteliami tvorcheskoi intelligentsii," *Sovetskaia Latviia*, 12 August 1988.

50. On policy entrepreneurship, see Norman Frohlich and Joe A. Oppenheimer, *Modern Political Economy* (Englewood Cliffs: Prentice-Hall, 1978), 67–71; on centrism, see Abram DeSwaan, *Coalition Theories and Cabinet Formation* (Amsterdam: Elsevier, 1973), 88.

51. M. S. Gorbachev, "Oktiabr' i perestroika: Revoliutsiia prodolzhaetsia," *Pravda*, 3 November 1987.

52. Ronald J. Hill, "The CPSU: From Monolith to Pluralist?" *Soviet Studies* 43, no. 2 (1991): 224–26.

53. Dusko Doder and Louise Brandon, *Gorbachev: Heretic in the Kremlin* (New York: Penguin Books, 1990), 177.

54. M. S. Gorbachev, "O perestroike i kadrovoi politike partii," *Pravda*, 28 January 1987; M. S. Gorbachev, "Zakliuchitel'noe slovo General'nogo sekretaria TsK KPSS na plenume TsK KPSS 28 oktiabria 1987 goda," *Pravda*, 30 January 1987.

55. Thane Gustafson and Dawn Mann, "Gorbachev's Next Gamble," *Problems of Communism* 36 (July–August 1987): 3.

56. Gelman, *Gorbachev's First Five Years in the Soviet Leadership*, 41.

57. Aryeh L. Unger, "The Travails of Intra-Party Democracy in the Soviet Union: The Elections to the 19th Conference of the CPSU," *Soviet Studies* 43, no. 2 (1991): 350.

58. "Zakon SSSR: 'Ob uchrezhdenii posta Prezidenta SSSR.' "

59. Mikhail S. Gorbachev, *Perestroika* (New York: Harper & Row, 1988), 65.

60. L. Shevtsova, "Krizis vlasti: Pochemu on voznik i kak iz nego vyiti," *Izvestiia*, 17 September 1990.

61. Tipping phenomena are discussed in Thomas C. Schelling, *Micromotives and Macrobehavior* (New York: W. W. Norton, 1978), 101–2.

62. Gelman, *Gorbachev's First Five Years in the Soviet Leadership*, 32.

63. Ryzhkov, "Po novomu osmyslit' funktsii i rol' partii v obshchestve."

64. George W. Breslauer, "Evaluating Gorbachev as Leader," *Soviet Economy* 5 (October–December 1989): 323. Also see Archie Brown, "Gorbachev's Leadership: Another View," *Soviet Economy* 6 (April–June 1990): 145.

65. Kaiser, *Why Gorbachev Happened*, 310.

66. Samuel P. Huntington, *Political Order in Changing Societies* (New Haven: Yale University Press, 1968), 346.

67. M. S. Gorbachev, "Prakticheskimi delami uglubliat' perestroiku," *Pravda*, 15 July 1987.

68. Gorbachev, "O khode realizatsii reshenii XXVII s"ezda KPSS."

69. M. S. Gorbachev, "Narashchivat' intellektual'nyi potentsial perestroiki," *Pravda*, 8 January 1989.

70. M. S. Gorbachev, "Sotsialisticheskaia ideia i revoliutsionnaia perestroika," *Pravda*, 26 November 1989.

71. Esther Fein, "Gorbachev Hints He Would Accept Multiparty Rule," *New York Times*, 14 January 1990.

72. John Gooding, "The XXVIII Congress of the CPSU in Perspective," *Soviet Studies* 43, no. 2 (1991): 240.

73. Kaiser, *Why Gorbachev Happened*, 323.

74. Migranian, "Dolgii put' k evropeiskomu domu," 166–84.

75. Jerry F. Hough, "Understanding Gorbachev: The Importance of Politics," *Soviet Economy* 7 (April–June 1991): 97.

76. Gelman, *Gorbachev's First Five Years in the Soviet Leadership*, 44.

77. John P. Willerton, *Patronage and Politics in the USSR* (Cambridge: Cambridge University Press, 1992), 149–50.

78. E. K. Ligachev, "XXVII s"ezd Kommunisticheskoi Partii Sovetskogo Soiuza, Otchety chlenov i kandidaty v chleny Politbiuro, sekretarei TsK KPSS," *Pravda*, 5 July 1990.

79. "Khronika s"ezda, den' odinadtsatyi," *Pravda*, 13 July 1990.

80. For description of the larger changes taking place within the Soviet military, see Stephen M. Meyer, "How the Threat (and the Coup) Collapsed: The Politicization of the Soviet Military," *International Security* 16 (Winter 1991–1992): 5–38. As in previous attempts to establish control over the armed forces, Gorbachev had to play on divisions within the armed forces; see Eugene B. Rumer, "The End of a Monolith: The Politics of Military Reform in the Soviet Armed Forces" [R-3993-USDP] (Santa Monica: Rand Corporation, 1990).

81. Theodore Karasik and Brenda Horrigan, *Gorbachev's Presidential Council* [P-7665] (Santa Monica: Rand Corporation, August 1990).

82. Iu. D. Masliukov, "O Gosudarstvennom plane ekonomicheskogo i

sotsial'nogo razvitiia SSSR na 1990 god i o khode vypolneniia plana v 1988 godu," *Pravda*, 28 October 1988.

83. V. S. Pavlov, "O Gosudarstvennom biudzhete SSSR na 1990 god i ob ispolnenii biudzheta za 1988 god," *Izvestiia*, 26 September 1989.

84. L. A. Voronin, "O Gosudarstvennom plane ekonomicheskogo i sotsial'nogo razvitiia SSSR na 1990 god," *Pravda*, 26 September 1989.

85. "Kommunike soveshchaniia Politicheskogo konsul'tativnogo komiteta gosudarstv-uchastnikov Varshavskogo Dogovora," *Pravda*, 30 May 1987.

86. Bill Keller, "Gorbachev Pledges Major Troop Cutback, Then Ends Trip, Citing Vast Soviet Quake," *New York Times*, 8 December 1988.

87. M. S. Gorbachev, "Obshcheevropeiskii protsess idet vpered," *Pravda*, 7 July 1989. For overviews of the doctrinal developments in this period, see Raymond L. Garthoff, *Deterrence and the Revolution in Soviet Military Doctrine* (Washington, D.C.: Brookings Institution, 1990), 94–185; Michael MccGwire, *Perestroika and Soviet National Security* (Washington, D.C.: Brookings Institution, 1991), 297–344.

88. "Vstrecha M. S. Gorbacheva s predstaviteliami 'Trekhstoronnei komissii,' " *Pravda*, 19 January 1989; Pavlov, "O Gosudarstvennom biudzhete SSSR na 1990 god."

89. M. Moiseev, "Dialogi v shtab—kvartire NATO," *Krasnaia zvezda*, 6 November 1990.

90. Masliukov, "O Gosudarstvennom plane ekonomicheskogo i sotsial'nogo razvitiia SSSR na 1990 god."

91. B. I. Gostev, "O Gosudarstvennom biudzhete SSSR na 1989 god i ob ispolnenii Gosudarstvennogo biudzheta SSSR za 1987 goda," *Pravda*, 28 October 1988.

92. Pavlov, "O Gosudarstvennom biudzhete SSSR na 1990 god."

93. Voronin, "O Gosudarstvennom plane ekonomicheskogo i sotsial'nogo razvitiia SSSR na 1990 god."

94. Tsentral'noe Statisticheskoe Upravlenie, *Narodnoe khoziaistvo SSSR v 1985 g.* (Moscow: Finansy i statistika, 1986), 448; Gosudarstvennyi Komitet SSSR po Statistike, *Narodnoe khoziaistvo SSSR v 1989 g.* (Moscow: Finansy i Statistika, 1990), 92.

95. D. Iazov, *Na strazhe sotsializma i mira* (Moscow: Voennoe Izdatel'stvo, 1987), 33. Also see G. G. Lukava, "Voenno-teoreticheskie vzgliady V. I. Lenina i sovetskaia voennaia nauka," in *Voenno-teoreticheskoe nasledie V. I. Lenina i problemy sovremennoi voiny*, ed. A. S. Milovidov (Moscow: Voenizdat, 1987), 251–52.

96. V. Varennikov, "Na strazhe mira i bezopasnosti narodov," *Partiinaia zhizn'*, no. 5 (March 1987): 12.

97. "Moscow News Interviews General Tretyak," *Moscow News*, no. 8 (21 February 1988): 12; translated in Foreign Broadcast Information Service, *Daily Report (Soviet Union)*, 24 February 1988, 73.

98. Paul Quinn-Judge, "Censored Words—Gorbachev Hints at Troubles in Military," *Christian Science Monitor*, 12 July 1989.

99. Gooding, "The XXVIII Congress of the CPSU in Perspective," 242–45.

100. "Soobshchenie Tsentral'noi izbiratel'noi komissii po vyboram Prezidenta RSFSR," *Pravda*, 20 June 1991.

101. "Velikii primer sluzheniia revoliutsionnym ideiam," *Pravda*, 11 September 1987; "Za dela—bez raskachki," *Pravda*, 8 August 1988; Michel Tatu, "19th Party Conference," *Problems of Communism* 37 (May–August 1988): 4.

102. Shevardnadze, *The Future Belongs to Freedom*, 192–93.

103. "Makashov Addresses 19 June Russian Conference," Russian Television, 19 June 1990; translated in Foreign Broadcast Information Service, *Daily Report (Soviet Union)*, 21 June 1990, 93.

104. See, e.g., A. Pankratov, "A marshal otvetil—ucheniia net," *Komsomolskaia pravda*, 4 October 1990.

105. S. Shatalin, "Nel'zia borot'sia so zlom pri pomoshchi zla," *Komsomolskaia pravda*, 22 January 1991. Also see M. Berger, "Soiuz liderov—nadezhda na soglasie," *Izvestiia*, 2 August 1990; S. Shatalin et al., "Chelovek, svoboda, rynok," *Izvestiia*, 4 September 1990; "Obrashchenie Prezidenta SSSR," *Izvestiia*, 11 September 1990; "Osnovnye napravleniia stabilizatsii narodnogo khoziaistva i perekhoda k rynochnoi ekonomike," *Izvestiia*, 27 October 1990. For an interpretation that discounts the constraints imposed on Gorbachev from the conservatives, see Anders Aslund, *Gorbachev's Struggle for Economic Reform*, rev. ed. (Ithaca: Cornell University Press, 1991), 203–24.

106. Archie Brown, "Gorbachev's Leadership: Another View," *Soviet Economy* 6 (April–June 1990): 145.

107. "Sovmestnoe zaiavlenie o bezotlagatel'nykh merakh po stabilizatsii obstanovki v strane i preodoleniiu krizisa," *Izvestiia*, 24 April 1991; "Prem'er-Ministr prosit novykh polnomochii," *Izvestiia*, 17 July 1991; "Postanovlenie Kabineta Ministrov SSSR: 'Ob organizatsionnykh merakh po razrabotke proizvodstvennykh programm i prognozov sotsial'no-ekonomicheskogo razvitiia predpriiatii, regionov, respublik, i Soiuza SSSR na 1992 god v usloviiakh formirovaniia rynochnykh otnoshenii,' " *Izvestiia*, 17 July 1991.

108. See the official statements translated in "Hard-Liners Launch Coup, Yeltsin Resists," *The Current Digest of the Soviet Press* 43 (18 September 1991): 1–6.

109. "Zakon SSSR: 'Ob organakh gosudarstvennoi vlasti i upravleniia Soiuza SSR v perekhodnoi period,' " *Izvestiia*, 6 September 1991.

110. "Zaiavlenie glav gosudarstv respubliki Belarus', RSFSR, Ukrainy," *Izvestiia*, 9 December 1991.

111. "V Alma-Ate rodilos' sodruzhestvo 11 nezavisimykh gosudarstv," *Izvestiia*, 23 December 1991.

Chapter Ten
Can Authoritarian Institutions Survive?

1. See, for example, the work of Arend Lijphart, *Democracies: Patterns of Majoritarian and Consensus Government in Twenty-One Countries* (New Haven: Yale University Press, 1984); Matthew Soberg Shugart and John M. Carey, *Presidents and Assemblies: Constitutional Design and Electoral Dynamics* (Cambridge: Cambridge University Press, 1992).

2. Juan J. Linz, "Totalitarian and Authoritarian Regimes," in *Macropolitical Theory*, ed. Fred I. Greenstein and Nelson W. Polsby (Reading: Addison-Wesley Publishing Company, 1975), 175, 179–80, 182. Also see Amos Perlmutter, *Mod-*

ern Authoritarianism: A Comparative Institutional Analysis (New Haven: Yale University Press, 1981).

3. Carl J. Friedrich and Zbigniew K. Brzezinski, *Totalitarian Dictatorship and Autocracy* (Cambridge: Harvard University Press, 1956).

4. I have borrowed from the literature on international institutions because it forces us to think about institutions with fewer formal structures; others thinking about these patterns across a spectrum of environments might produce some fruitful integration of insights across fields. See Robert O. Keohane, *After Hegemony: Cooperation and Discord in the World Political Economy* (Princeton: Princeton University Press, 1984); Stephen D. Krasner, ed., *International Regimes* (Ithaca: Cornell University Press, 1983), 93–114.

5. Samuel P. Huntington, *Political Order in Changing Societies* (New Haven: Yale University Press, 1968), 12–20.

Select Bibliography

THE FOLLOWING list of works suggests further reading in the literature relevant to the new institutionalism or about the development of Soviet politics. The list is very selective, including only works in English of interest to a broad readership. Specialized studies of interest to area specialists, listed in the notes to chapters, are not repeated here.

Theoretical and Comparative Perspectives

Ames, Barry. *Political Survival: Politicians and Public Policy in Latin America.* Berkeley: University of California Press, 1987.

Axelrod, Robert. *Conflict of Interest: A Theory of Divergent Goals with Applications to Politics.* Chicago: Markham Publishing Company, 1970.

Bates, Robert H. *Markets and States in Tropical Africa: The Political Bases of Agricultural Policies.* Berkeley: University of California Press, 1981.

Cox, Gary W. *The Efficient Secret: The Cabinet and the Development of Political Parties in Victorian England.* Cambridge: Cambridge University Press, 1987.

DeSwaan, Abram. *Coalition Theories and Cabinet Formations: A Study of Formal Theories of Coalition Formation Applied to Nine European Parliaments after 1918.* Amsterdam: Elsevier Publishing Company, 1973.

Dodd, Lawrence C. *Coalitions in Parliamentary Government.* Princeton: Princeton University Press, 1976.

Goldstein, Avery. *From Bandwagoning to Balance-of-Power Politics: Structural Constraints and Politics in China, 1949–1978.* Stanford: Stanford University Press, 1991.

Groennings, Sven, E. W. Kelley, and Michael Leiserson, eds. *The Study of Coalition Behavior.* New York: Holt, Rinehart, and Winston, 1970.

Huntington, Samuel P. *Political Order in Changing Societies.* New Haven: Yale University Press, 1968.

Kiewiet, D. Roderick, and Mathew D. McCubbins. *The Logic of Delegation: Congressional Parties and the Appropriations Process.* Chicago: University of Chicago Press, 1991.

Levi, Margaret. *Of Rule and Revenue.* Berkeley: University of California Press, 1988.

Linz, Juan J. "Totalitarian and Authoritarian Regimes." In *Macropolitical Theory,* ed. Fred I. Greenstein and Nelson W. Polsby, pp. 175–411. Reading: Addison-Wesley Publishing Company, 1975.

Mayhew, David R. *Congress: The Electoral Connection.* New Haven: Yale University Press, 1974.

Moe, Terry M. "The New Economics of Organization," *American Journal of Political Science* 28 (November 1984): 739–77.

North, Douglass C. *Institutions, Institutional Change, and Economic Performance.* Cambridge: Cambridge University Press, 1990.

North, Douglass C. *Structure and Change in Economic History*. New York: W. W. Norton & Company, 1981.

North, Douglass C., and Barry R. Weingast. "Constitutions and Commitment: The Evolution of Institutions Governing Public Choice in Seventeenth Century England." *The Journal of Economic History* 49 (December 1989): 803–32.

O'Donnell, Guillermo A. *Modernization and Bureaucratic-Authoritarianism: Studies in South American Politics*. Berkeley: Institute of International Studies, University of California, 1973.

Olson, Mancur. *The Logic of Collective Action: Public Goods and the Theory of Groups*. Cambridge: Harvard University Press, 1965.

Riker, William H. *The Theory of Political Coalitions*. New Haven: Yale University Press, 1962.

Schelling, Thomas C. *The Strategy of Conflict*. New York: Oxford University Press, 1963.

Shirk, Susan. *The Political Logic of Economic Reform in China*. Berkeley: University of California Press, 1993.

Snyder, Jack. *Myths of Empire: Domestic Politics and International Ambition*. Ithaca: Cornell University Press, 1991.

Stepan, Alfred. *The Military in Politics: Changing Patterns in Brazil*. Princeton: Princeton University Press, 1971.

Tsebelis, George. *Nested Games: Rational Choice in Comparative Politics*. Berkeley: University of California Press, 1990.

Development of Soviet Political Institutions

Berliner, Joseph S. *Factory and Manager in the U.S.S.R.* Cambridge: Harvard University Press, 1957.

Bialer, Seweryn. *Stalin's Successors: Leadership, Stability, and Change in the Soviet Union*. Cambridge: Cambridge University Press, 1980.

Boffa, Giuseppe. *Inside the Kremlin*. New York: Marzani and Munsell, 1959.

Breslauer, George W. *Khrushchev and Brezhnev as Leaders*. London: George Allen and Unwin, 1982.

Brown, Archie, ed. *Political Leadership in the Soviet Union*. Bloomington: Indiana University Press, 1989.

Brzezinski, Zbigniew K., and Samuel P. Huntington. *Political Power: USA/USSR*. New York: Viking Press, 1965.

Bunce, Valerie. *Do New Leaders Make a Difference? Executive Succession and Public Policy under Capitalism and Socialism*. Princeton: Princeton University Press, 1981.

Carr, Edward Hallett. *The Bolshevik Revolution, 1917–1923*. New York: Macmillan Company, 1951.

Cocks, Paul, Robert V. Daniels, and Nancy Whittier Heer, eds. *The Dynamics of Soviet Politics*. Cambridge: Harvard University Press, 1976.

Colton, Timothy J. *Commissars, Commanders, and Civilian Authority: The Structure of Soviet Military Policies*. Cambridge: Harvard University Press, 1979.

———. *The Dilemma of Reform in the Soviet Union*. Rev. ed. New York: Council on Foreign Relations, 1986.

Colton, Timothy J., and Thane Gustafson. *Soldiers and the Soviet State.* Princeton: Princeton University Press, 1990.

Conquest, Robert. *Power and Policy in the U.S.S.R.: The Study of Soviet Dynastics.* New York: Harper & Row, 1967.

D'Agostino, Anthony. *Soviet Succession Struggles.* Boston: Allen & Unwin, 1988.

Dinerstein, H. S. *War and the Soviet Union.* Rev. ed. New York: Frederick A. Praeger, 1962.

Fainsod, Merle. *How Russia is Ruled.* Rev. ed. Cambridge: Harvard University Press, 1967.

Friedrich, Carl J., and Zbigniew K. Brzezinski. *Totalitarian Dictatorship and Autocracy.* New York: Frederick A. Praeger, 1961.

Garthoff, Raymond L. *Soviet Military Policy: A Historical Analysis.* New York: Frederick A. Praeger, 1966.

Gelman, Harry. *The Brezhnev Politburo and the Decline of Detente.* Ithaca: Cornell University Press, 1984.

Gill, Graeme. *The Origins of the Stalinist Political System.* Cambridge: Cambridge University Press, 1990.

———. *The Rules of the Communist Party of the Soviet Union.* London: Macmillan Press, 1988.

Hazan, Baruch A. *From Brezhnev to Gorbachev: Infighting in the Kremlin.* Boulder: Westview Press, 1987.

Herspring, Dale R. *The Soviet High Command, 1967–1989.* Princeton: Princeton University Press, 1990.

Hough, Jerry F. *Soviet Leadership in Transition.* Washington, D.C.: Brookings Institution, 1980.

———. *The Soviet Prefects.* Cambridge: Harvard University Press, 1969.

Hough, Jerry F., and Merle Fainsod. *How the Soviet Union is Governed.* Cambridge: Harvard University Press, 1979.

Hudson, George E., ed. *Soviet National Security Policy under Perestroika.* Boston: Unwin Hyman, 1990.

Hyland, William, and Richard W. Shryock. *The Fall of Khrushchev.* New York: Funk and Wagnalls, 1968.

Juviler, Peter H., and Henry W. Morton, eds. *Soviet Policy-Making: Studies of Communism in Transition.* New York: Frederick A. Praeger, 1967.

Kaiser, Robert G. *Why Gorbachev Happened.* New York: Simon and Schuster, 1991.

Khrushchev, Nikita S. *Khrushchev Remembers.* Boston: Little, Brown and Company, 1970.

Khrushchev, Sergei. *Khrushchev on Khrushchev.* Boston: Little, Brown and Co., 1990.

Kolkowicz, Roman. *The Soviet Military and the Communist Party.* Princeton: Princeton University Press, 1967.

Leonhard, Wolfgang. *The Kremlin Since Stalin.* New York: Frederick A. Praeger, 1962.

Linden, Carl A. *Khrushchev and the Soviet Leadership, 1957–1964.* Baltimore: Johns Hopkins University Press, 1966.

Medvedev, Roy A. *Khrushchev.* Garden City: Anchor Press, 1983.

Medvedev, Roy A., and Zhores Medvedev. *Khrushchev: The Years in Power.* New York: W. W. Norton and Co., 1978.

Medvedev, Zhores A. *Andropov.* New York: Penguin Books, 1984.

Nicolaevsky, Boris I. *Power and the Soviet Elite.* New York: Frederick A. Praeger, 1965.

Nove, Alec. *The Soviet Economic System.* 3d ed. Boston: Allen & Unwin, 1986.

Parker, John W. *Kremlin in Transition: From Brezhnev to Chernenko, 1978 to 1985.* Boston: Unwin Hyman, 1991.

Pethybridge, Roger. *A Key to Soviet Politics: The Crisis of the Anti-Party Group.* New York: Frederick A. Praeger, 1962.

Rigby, T. H. *The Changing Soviet System: Mono-organizational Socialism from Its Origins to Gorbachev's Restructuring.* Brookfield: Edward Elgar, 1990.

———. *Communist Party Membership in the U.S.S.R., 1917–1967.* Princeton: Princeton University Press, 1968.

———. *Lenin's Government: Sovnarkom, 1917–1922.* Cambridge: Cambridge University Press, 1979.

Rush, Myron. *Political Succession in the USSR.* 2d ed. New York: Columbia University Press, 1968.

———. *The Rise of Khrushchev.* Washington, D.C.: Public Affairs Press, 1958.

Schapiro, Leonard. *The Communist Party of the Soviet Union.* 2d ed. New York: Vintage Books, 1971.

———. *The Origins of the Communist Autocracy.* London: Macmillan, 1977.

Skilling, H. Gordon, and Franklyn Griffiths, eds. *Interest Groups in Soviet Politics.* Princeton: Princeton University Press, 1967.

Solomon, Susan Gross, ed. *Pluralism in the Soviet Union.* London: Macmillan Press, 1983.

Tatu, Michel. *Power in the Kremlin: From Khrushchev to Kosygin.* New York: Viking Press, 1968.

Towster, Julian. *Political Power in the U.S.S.R., 1917–1947.* New York: Oxford University Press, 1948.

Urban, Michael E. *More Power to the Soviets: The Democratic Revolution in the USSR.* Brookfield: Edward Elgar, 1990.

Warner, Edward L. *The Military in Contemporary Soviet Politics: An Institutional Analysis.* New York: Praeger Publishers, 1977.

White, Stephen. *Gorbachev in Power.* Cambridge: Cambridge University Press, 1990.

Willerton, John P. *Patronage and Politics in the USSR.* Cambridge: Cambridge University Press, 1992.

Wolfe, Thomas W. *Soviet Strategy at the Crossroads.* Cambridge: Harvard University Press, 1965.

Yeltsin, Boris. *Against the Grain: An Autobiography.* New York: Summit Books, 1990.

Zemtsov, Ilya. *Chernenko: The Last Brezhnev.* New Brunswick: Transaction Publishers, 1989.